Austrian Cinema

Austrian Cinema
A History

ROBERT VON DASSANOWSKY

McFarland & Company, Inc., Publishers
Jefferson, North Carolina, and London

The present work is a reprint of the illustrated case bound edition of Austrian Cinema: A History, *first published in 2005 by McFarland.*

This book has been made possible in part by a grant from the Austrian Federal Ministry of Education, Science and Culture.

All of the photographs used in this book were provided by the Film Archive Austria (Vienna).

LIBRARY OF CONGRESS CATALOGUING-IN-PUBLICATION DATA

Dassanowsky, Robert.
Austrian cinema : a history / Robert von Dassanowsky.
p.   cm.
Includes bibliographical references and index.

ISBN-13: 978-0-7864-3733-7
softcover : 50# alkaline paper) ∞

1. Motion pictures — Austria — History.
I. Title
PN1993.5.A83D37   2008   791.43'09436 — dc22   2005011456

British Library cataloguing data are available

Cover photograph: Robert Wiene's *Der Rosenkavalier*, 1926

Manufactured in the United States of America

*McFarland & Company, Inc., Publishers
Box 611, Jefferson, North Carolina 28640
www.mcfarlandpub.com*

Table of Contents

For the Austrian film artists

Preface

In suggesting Austria's role among nations, nineteenth-century Austrian politician Karl von Vogelsang focused on the empire's very theatrical quality: "The events of the world are rehearsed on the stages of Austria." Certainly, this sprawling multicultural, polyglot state at the center of Europe was the setting for a great many sociopolitical, artistic and scientific beginnings. Frederic Morton's literary docudrama on the beginning of the end of Old Europe, *Thunder at Twilight*, places such diverse figures as Freud, Trotsky, Lenin, Hitler, Stalin, Tito, and Archduke Francis Ferdinand within mere city blocks of each other in Vienna during the years of 1913 and 1914.[1]

The historically parturient traits of the Austrian capital may certainly be attributed to its status as the crossroad of the continent and to the many centuries of Habsburg colonization and absorption of Eastern and Southeastern Europe and its peoples. These polyglot subjects in turn helped create the empire's unique intellectual and creative blend, which was then sent back into the world. Herein also lies the simplest reason behind Austria's identity crisis in the twentieth century. When the empire was replaced by a small nation-state arbitrarily carved out along indistinct German linguistic lines by the victorious Allies of 1918, Austria was expected (and expected itself) to behave like its more homogeneous European neighbors. In its provincial form with cosmopolitan Vienna at its head, it became a true melting pot of the Germanic, Slavic, and Latin ethnicities that had constituted the Danube monarchy. For Austrians abroad, a reverse, disintegrative process was evident. Imperial and postimperial Austrian immigrants in the United States and elsewhere failed to form a diasporic culture; instead, they cleaved into their Hungarian, Czech, Slovak, Polish, or other heritage ethnic groups, or allowed themselves to meld into the German immigrant mass. But an Austrian among Germans is still an Austrian, although pan–German and later National Socialist forces in Germany and Austria hoped to remove that difference as they ultimately removed the country from the map in 1938. The assertion of a distinct Austrian nation, as opposed to historical association with various incarnations of the German nation, provided the framework for a re-visioning of national identity after the reestablishment of an independent Austria in 1945. But questions regarding recent history were not resolved, and the nation transformed itself into the neutral "Alpine Republic," which was selective with the past and determined to function as a bridge between Cold War blocs. With its membership in the European Union, the collapse of Soviet Europe, and two decades of controversial political developments behind it, Austria is now a crucial element in a reborn notion of *central* Europe, and has begun to more extensively examine and deal with its many legacies.

Just as late nineteenth- and early twentieth-century Austria gave influential modernism to the world in the fields of medicine, urban planning, architecture, design, literature, music, and theater, so the Austrian film industry created a significant national cinema that seeded talents and concepts internationally, yet it remains among the most neglected subjects in film scholarship. Austria's creation, dissolution, and recreation as a nation-state in the twentieth century, its ethno-cultural mix, and reductive images abroad may explain such elusiveness. Yet the very nature of the Austrian suggests a sympathy and sensitivity for the medium. Successful acculturation in a multicultural empire and its multivalent republican successor state implies an astute understanding of mimicry and individuality, role playing and storytelling, as well as an adaptability for sociopolitical and national definition — Austria having taken on four different political forms in the twentieth century alone. Add to this Austria's particular affinity for the Baroque, which, like Italy and, to a certain extent, France, translates the theatrical *Schein und Sein* (appearance and being) philosophy of the epoch into dramatic architecture, grand opera, and finally, the ultimate realization of an imagined world — motion pictures. Film historian Frieda Grafe posits that "authentic" Viennese film was created "extraterritorially — somewhere else" (several Austrian filmmakers worked in Berlin during the 1920s and 1930s, and some of the independent co-productions between 1934 and 1937 were shot abroad). Grafe considers Austrian film history a "phantasm," as it was not bound to a specific location. Austrian film was international from its very inception, and international cinema profited from the free-floating Austrian talent and the "reservoir of dreams" Vienna and its clichés represented.[2] The reflection of this phenomenon in the larger international-national American cinema also suggests why Austrians and Austro-Hungarians were attracted to, and became such a considerable part of, Golden Age Hollywood.

This first comprehensive survey of Austrian film in English is an attempt to place Austrian cinema back into the Anglo-American understanding of an international film canon. As Peter Bondanella has done in his redoubtable *Italian Cinema*, a text that has long inspired my writings on film, this work will also "attempt to rescue" the study of *Austrian* cinema "from the monolingual bias of most English and American critics,"[3] and provide a basis for more specific future study. Unlike the linguistically unique Italian film, however, Austrian cinema has seldom been understood as *Austrian* in the English language world, when it has been discussed at all. And when it has been a subject of discourse, whether in casual review or detailed analysis, it has too often been labeled as or folded into German cinema. This mislabeling may be due to a lack of recognition caused by the underrepresentation of the cinema abroad between the 1960s and 1990s, or because of the complex relationship between Austrian and German cinema, or because it has been categorized as German-*language* film, which is too easily misunderstood as German rather than Germanophone. The relationship between these two national cinemas and their German-speaking talent is strong and has been variously beneficial and detrimental to the Austrian film industry at different times in history. But for all their similarities and reflections, they are as different in genre development, style, and cultural imprint as French and Belgian, or even British, Canadian and American film. Austria's important bond with American film is also underappreciated due to a lack of accessible English-language scholarship on the early careers of Austro-Hollywood artists and on influential developments in Austrian film history. While the roots of film noir have been traced to the German expressionistic cinema and to the dark experiences of Central European filmmakers fleeing Nazism, an examination of the more basic influences from Austrian social critical film is missing. Similarly, screwball comedy's debt to Viennese cabaret and Austrian comedy genres in film has yet to be recognized.

Beyond Nazi German infiltration and manipulation of the pre–Anschluss Viennese film industry and its eventual incorporation into the cinema of the Third Reich, Austrian film has naturally overlapped with German film for several reasons. Shared language made work in Germany's larger industry attractive for Austrian actors and filmmakers as it has for Germans in Austria at certain historical junctures. Financial factors also influence this mix. In the postwar era, West German distributors traditionally dominated the German-language film market. Moreover, the governments of Second Republic Austria (from 1955 to the present) had long neglected the film industry, and although a federal film promotion fund was finally created in 1980, support still pales in comparison with other European countries and with regards to Austria's funding of the other arts. Since the international reemergence of Austrian film in the 1990s, co-production with German or other European companies has become one possible development option, which also includes co-production with the national television network ORF, support from Vienna's Film Fund, regional contribution, private investment, or a combination of various models.

National cinema study has developed rapidly in Austria in recent years. The studies of Walter Fritz, which held authority for many decades, were joined in the 1980s and 1990s by several government- and archive-sponsored publications, film conference compilations, and studies on avant-garde cinema and New Austrian Film issued by Vienna's Wespennest publishing firm. The Film Archive Austria has more recently published a variety of outstanding texts analyzing the work of specific directors, actors and genres linked to premiere videos of restored classic films, and a highly detailed two-volume study by Elisabeth Büttner and Christian Dewald examines the history of Austrian film by cinematic theme and stylistic vocabulary.

In order to make this introduction of more than a century of Austrian cinema comprehensive but also comprehensible to the English-language reader, I have structured it chronologically, following the development of the industry through the nation's various transformations. I have attempted to highlight important movements, genres, and films with sociopolitical, cultural or aesthetic details and analysis, and to give an accurate picture of the economic trends that have so influenced Austrian film. While directors and actors are central to popular film reception and the examination of a star system–based industry, the inclusion of producers, writers, cinematographers, editors, art directors, composers, and other film artists is essential to the discussion of the qualities of any national cinema, particularly one as multicultural as that of Austria. Overall, I have striven to create a readable narrative that avoids theoretical jargon, includes a sampling of creative and critical voices, and draws attention to recognizable films and artists, as well as those unknown outside the Germanophone world, as fresh sources for cinematic enjoyment and study. The limitations of this book in dealing with such an immense subject will hopefully not detract from stimulating interest not only in this national cinema, but also in its long obscured value to European and American film.

This survey defines an Austrian film as a production created by a majority of Austrian talent, inside or outside the country (including certain German-language films not for export to Germany that were produced or co-produced by Hungarian, Czech, Swedish and Dutch companies between 1934 and 1937). Among television films, only those receiving theatrical release or those that are particularly significant to artistic or industry development are included.

English translations of the German-language film titles in this text are separated from the German with a slash mark (/). Many of the English versions of German-language titles are literal translations specifically made for this book. Non-literal English "translations" are the official English-language release titles. Translations of other German phrases, including titles of non-film works, are enclosed in parentheses.

The writing of this type of text is always a shadow collaborative effort, and I am indebted to three good friends for their early inspiration and input. Gertraud Steiner-Daviau's *Film Book Austria*, her seminal research on the *Heimatfilm*, and her many projects at the Austrian Federal Press Office provided the very stimulus for this work. Together with Thomas Bauer, professor of media and communication at the University of Vienna, who has been so generous with his encouragement and knowledge, our creation of the Austrian American Film Association (AAFA) has exposed me to more dialogue on Austrian cinema than I could have hoped for. Donald G. Daviau, professor emeritus of German at the University of California, Riverside, has been an influence on my research since my days in graduate school. His long editorship of *Modern Austrian Literature* has provided a significant path for Austrian cultural studies in the United States, and it allowed my initial attempts at Austrian film discussion to see print.

I am thankful to Ernst Kieninger, director of the Film Archive Austria for securing texts and videos, and to Peter Spiegel of the Archive's Film Documentation Center, for his generous time and effort in the selection and processing of photographic material; to the Austrian Ministry of Education, Science, and Culture for the grant to process the archival stills; to director Martin Schweighofer, Charlotte Rühm, and Karin Schiefer of the Austrian Film Commission for their publications and their readiness to assist in my research; to Hellmuth Bauer, former studio chief of Filmstadt Wien, for his always open door; to the Margaret Herrick Library at the Academy of Motion Picture Arts and Sciences and its staff; to Matthias Greuling, editor of *Celluloid*, Bernhard Grundner, editor of *Blimp Film Magazine*, and Willi Goetschel, editor of *The Germanic Review*, for their advice and publication of my various essays that ultimately became the genesis of this book; to Thomas Elsaesser for his kind encouragement early on, when encouragement was most needed; and to the Modern Austrian Literature and Culture Association (MALCA) for superb conferences that have fostered presentations and discussions on Austrian film culture. I would also like to express my thanks to Alexander and Ingrid Drei-hann-Holenia, Heinrich and Elisabeth Schuschnigg, Friedbert Aspetsberger, Ernst Aichinger, Peter Launsky-Tieffenthal, Günther Berger, Elisabeth Littell Frech, Russell Moore, Kenneth Marchand, Teresa Meadows-Sohlich and Wolfgang Sohlich.

I am grateful to Andrea Widy, who class-tested a portion of my manuscript in her spring 2004 course on Austrian Film History 1945–2003 at the University of Glasgow. I could not have completed this book and many other related projects without the editing suggestions and indexing skills of Dana L. Booth, and I am very lucky to have her support and dear friendship. I am, of course, most indebted to the many directors, producers, writers, actors and technical artisans in Austrian film with whom I have had the pleasure to communicate over several years. I hope this book will be a small indication of my appreciation for the experiences and visions they have shared with me.

— Robert von Dassanowsky
Colorado Springs, Los Angeles and Vienna

1

Schein und Sein: 1895–1928

The First Cinephiles; A Female Pioneer;
End of Empire; World-Class Silent Film

The exact beginnings of Austrian film are difficult to trace. The sprawling nature of the multinational Austro-Hungarian monarchy makes the overlapping of early Austrian film with that of Hungarian, Czech, Slovakian, and other Central European national cinemas an inescapable fact. During the silent era, the criterion of language, in this case German, can obviously not be applied; nor can one consider Austrian only those films made within the German-speaking territory of the empire. Although Austrian filmmakers started somewhat later than the French and the Germans, the Austro-Hungarian public was certainly among the first enthusiastic film audiences in the world. An Edison Kinetoscope for the viewing of the inventor's *A Barroom Scene* (USA 1894) was unveiled in Vienna's entertainment park, the Prater, in the summer of 1895 and the Deutsch-Österreichische Edison Kinetoskop Gesellschaft (German-Austrian Edison Kinetoscope Society) had been founded that spring to promote Edison's films in the German empire and Austria-Hungary.[1] By early 1896, the Prater had installed fifteen such machines in a special viewing hall. A scant three months after the first Lumière film presentation in Paris in 1896, motion pictures were shown in Vienna on the famed first district boulevard, the Kärntnerstrasse, producing what the Viennese are always said to crave — a sensation. The new art form was presented by Eugene Dupont, employed by the Brothers Lumière, and ultimately approved of by Emperor Franz Joseph, a monarch not known for his appreciation of progress for its own sake. The aging symbol of Habsburg Central Europe even attended a presentation of these new motion pictures. Gabor Steiner, who had created a "Venice in Vienna" show at the Prater in 1895 (the famous Ferris wheel was later built on the site), understood the benefits of adding film to his fantasy set piece and presented the new French equipment as an "Edisonoscope" in August 1896. Shortly thereafter, the Zoological Theater (which featured everything from ethnographic displays to circus animal performances) at the Prater installed its own "Kinematograph" machines in its Ashanti Village.[2] But it was Louis Veltée who receives credit for developing the first

7

true Viennese cinema house that year. The Veltée family, which had gained notability in nineteenth-century Austria as pyrotechnicians, had originally immigrated
to Vienna from Lyon, the city that was home to the Brothers Lumière. In 1896,
Louis Veltée began showing films in his Stadt-Panoptikum wax museum on the
first district's fashionable Kohlmarkt street near the imperial Hofburg palace, and
he swiftly became known as the father of the Austrian movie theater. His daughter, Louise (a.k.a. Luise), worked as a cashier at her father's business and learned
about the nascent art from one of its earliest public sources. She was soon to become
one of the first significant female filmmakers in the world.

The Louis Veltée soon had competitors in the race to develop the finest permanent
cinema theater in Vienna. By 1898, the Urania, a majestic new building in Vienna's
first district (the historical and governmental core of the imperial capital) devoted
to popular education, and housing a telescope, began showing Kinematographs.
In 1900, Josefine Kirbes and her son Josef Stiller opened the first actual cinema house
in the Prater, the Kino Stiller, which remained functional until 1927. The creation
of additional *Kinos* (cinemas) followed: Gustav Münstedt's ornately baroque Palast
Kino (1902–1945); the Kern family's 450-seat Kino Kern, created from a former
carousel structure (1903–1945); Therese Klein's Kino Klein, later renamed the Krys-
tall Palast, with its dual onion-shaped domes, long one of the most impressive
buildings at the Prater (1905–1945); and the Schaaf family's variously named cinema houses (1912–1924).[3] Sadly, the majority of these historic theaters were
destroyed in the fire that ravaged the Prater during the final days of World War II.

The Erika Cinema was established in the seventh district of Vienna in 1900
or 1909 (there are conflicting records) and remained the oldest permanent cinema
in the world until its closure in 1999. The Admiral Cinema — operative since 1912
in the seventh district — has now succeeded it in longevity. By the second year of
World War I, Vienna hosted no less than 150 cinemas. Soon ranked among the
largest, most sumptuous and technologically advanced in the world, Viennese houses
such as the Schäffer-Haushofer cinema, established in 1906, featured an orchestra
pit, formal boxes and a gallery for 500 patrons. As provincial capitals also moved
from tent cinemas to theaters, the Edison Cinema in Graz managed to outdo its
Viennese rivals by adding an additional seventy seats and boasting one of the largest
screens in Europe.

Several inventors who helped international development of the film camera
were Austrian. Astronomer Simon Stampfer (1790–1864) created a "Strobescope"
in 1833, which was produced under the name Zauberscheiben (magic windows).
Franz von Uchatius (1811–81) attempted to combine the Zauberscheiben with the
popular Laterna Magica in an effort to show the movement of pictorial figures. His
result was first presented in Vienna's Josefstädter Theater by magician Ludwig
Döbler (1801–64). In 1891, Victor von Reitzner (1844–1916), an instructor at the
Imperial Military Academy, registered his "photographic continuous series projection
machine" for a patent. The short-lived innovation was renamed the Kinetograph
in 1896. Theodor Reich (1861–1949) patented his "series photographic camera" in
London in 1896, apparently too late to be considered among the international claims

for the invention of the motion picture camera. Finally, August Musger (1868–1929), a physics and mathematics instructor, registered a film camera in 1904, the concept of which became the basis for an instrument created by the Ernemann company in Dresden in 1914, with no credit to Musger.[4]

Among the first films in Austria were the short clips of the satisfied viewer-turned-cinema-icon Emperor Franz Joseph, who had allowed some filming of his official appearances for the audiences of his imperial and royal (the dual crowns of Austria and Hungary) world. While the French, Germans, Americans, Italians, Spanish, Swedish and English had all created their first motion pictures by the end of the nineteenth century, Austria supposedly lagged behind in actual film production. Given the breadth of the sprawling empire, this is again a matter of interpretation. The Czech and Slovak film industries can be traced back to the late nineteenth century, but until 1918 these talents were also Austro-Hungarian. Certainly, creations in the other arts from non–German speaking areas of the empire have been considered "Austrian," if for nothing else but the shared culture and regional identity. The sprawling concept of a Central European homeland has made Austria's film beginnings in the other linguistic regions of the empire equally disputed. But the lack of a Vienna-based production company in those early years helped contribute to the audience's appreciation of various internal cultural influences as well as the style of foreign films via Viennese cinemas and the *Wanderkinos* (wandering cinemas) of Josef Stiller (1896), Karl Juhasz (1899), Louis Geni (1903), Emerich Frank (1905) and Franz Schober (1907), which crisscrossed the empire.

Traditionally, Count Alexander "Sascha" von Kolowrat-Krakowsky (1896–1927) has been labeled the father of the Austrian film industry, but the first Austrians to actually produce feature films was the team of Louise Veltée (1873–1950), her husband, photographer Anton Kolm (1865–1922), and their cameraman Jakob Julius Fleck (1881–1953). Moreover, early Austrian erotic films were rediscovered in the late 1990s, which appear to predate even the Veltée-Kolm productions, but it was the Kolm-Fleck efforts beginning in 1906 that mark the mainstream beginning of an actual Austrian film industry. Their first reels consisted of simple live-action scenes, such as horse races and candid documentation of life and events at Vienna's Prater amusement park.[5] Although they aimed at features, their primitive equipment and lack of financial support allowed them only the short documentary form.[6]

The impetus toward a first feature film was created during the meeting of the trio with twenty-five-year-old stage actor Heinz Hanus (1882–1972) at the popular Viennese theater-haunt the Café Dobner. Having performed throughout the empire and fascinated by the new medium he had experienced in the *Wanderkinos*, Hanus wanted to try his hand at film direction and enthusiastically joined up as the dramatic arm of the Veltée/Kolm/Fleck production team.[7] The result of this new collaboration was a six-minute drama (120 meters), produced in the film quartet's first studio, which was located in the attic of an office building in Vienna's first district.[8] This long-awaited birth of Vienna's film industry, however, coincided with a general crisis in early international film during 1907 and 1908. The short, non-narrative form had lost public fascination and even the ten-minute narratives had started to lose audiences. New ideas regarding feature-length film attempted to transform the medium, and the Kolm-Fleck group adapted to trends with relative ease. Soon, the Kolm couple and Jakob Fleck would produce more than half of the nearly one hundred lengthier Austrian films that attempted to bring literature and stage work to film. Heinz Hanus had maintained that he had, in fact, directed the first feature film in Austrian cinema history, *Von Stufe zu Stufe*/From Step to Step in 1908, but the film, apparently produced by Anton Kolm, is lost and has been an ongoing subject of controversy among Austrian film scholars. The redoubtable Walter Fritz recorded his interviews with Heinz Hanus in many publications and notes that the film was supposedly shot in the Kolm studio, at the Prater amusement park and at Burg (Castle) Liechtenstein. The script was co-written by Hanus and Louise Kolm and was shot by Jakob Fleck. The actors of this approximately thirty-five-minute film were Hanus, Rudolf Stiassny and Louise Kolm's brother, Claudius Veltée. Its subject was a pure Viennese literary/operetta convention framed by the era's class consciousness: a young girl meets a count at the Prater, is rejected by his social circle and returns to her father's home. A contrived happy ending saves the film from becoming the German-language theatre genre known as the bourgeois tragedy.[9] Hanus claimed that the film premiered in Vienna in December 1908, but it is missing from film publications of the time, although several films were produced with this title in France, the United States and in Germany. Hanus also claimed the film was shown abroad.[10] The Filmarchiv Austria (Film Archive Austria), which is today central to the collection, research and restoration of Austria's film legacy, has failed to locate any supporting documentation and considers the film to have been an incomplete project.[11]

Two other "first" Austrian productions surround the Hanus project. In 1906, photographer Johann Schwarzer (1880–1914) created his Saturn-Film company and produced *Pikante Szenen für Herrenabende*/Piquant Scenes for Gentlemen's Evenings, a series of short and internationally popular erotic films. His work was subsequently censored in 1911, and his film career ended with service in World War I when he became an early casualty in 1914.[12] Additionally, one scene from the performance of a new operetta by Oscar Straus, *Ein Walzertraum*/A Waltz Dream, which premiered in Vienna in March 1907, had been committed to film, and it has long been erroneously regarded as the first Austrian feature.[13] In 1909, Austria's first long documentary film appeared, *Der Kaisermanöver in Mähren*/The Imperial Maneuvers in Moravia, which featured Emperor Franz Joseph and the German monarch, Wilhelm II. The film was produced by the short-lived Photobrom firm. Although successfully received by public and critics, Photobrom did not continue and the production of Austrian documentaries passed to the Kolm/Fleck partnership, which gave audiences such events as *Denkmalenthüllung in Ischl*/Monument Unveiling in Ischl (1910), *Österreichische Alpenbahn, eine Fahrt nach Maria-Zell*/Austrian Alpine Train, a Journey to Maria-Zell (1910), *Der Hut im Kino*/The Hat in the Cinema (a film instructing women on the new etiquette regarding the wearing

of large hats in theaters; 1910), *Brandkatastrophe Wien — Nordbahnhof*/Fire Catastrophe in Vienna — North Train Station (1911), and *Das Gänsehäufel* (a film about
an outlying resort area of Vienna; 1912).

In January 1910, the first official Austrian film production company was formed
by Louise and Anton Kolm with Jakob Fleck, and suitably named the Erste österreichische Kinofilms-Industrie (First Austrian Cinema Film Company), which that
same year was changed to embrace the entire empire as the Österreichisch-
Ungarische Kino-Filmindustrie G.m.b.H (Austrian-Hungarian Cinema Film Company Ltd.). Louise Kolm's father, Louis Veltée, who had made a financial success
of his early cinema house, financially supported their efforts. The new company
relocated to a spacious and prominent building at Währingerstrasse 15. It was clear
by the display of film actors' photographs and the pompous elegance of the office
that the Kolm/Fleck undertaking not only had faith in the nascent art form as a
potential international industry but that it also would gain a credibility and respect
on par with Austrian theater and opera. Advertisements were placed in Austria's
new film publication *Österreichischer Komet* (Austrian Comet), seeking financial
investment in the company to help them compete with the larger and more established foreign firms, which were screening films throughout the empire. At the same
time, the young and wealthy Count Sascha Kolowrat established the first film laboratory with Oskar Berka in his castle at Gross-Meierhofen and proceeded to create short nature films with Karl Freund and Emanuel Kabath. By 1912, Kolowrat's
laboratory had developed into a full-fledged studio in the outlying twentieth district of Vienna. There is also speculation, although no surviving proof, that
Kolowrat, who was obsessed with feminine beauty,[14] had also produced a few erotic
films. Ultimately, the Kolm/Fleck and Kolowrat companies dominated Austrian
film until the eve of the World War I.

The first film to emerge from the new Kolm/Fleck company was, like Kolo-
wrat's, a documentary, *Der Faschingszug in Ober St. Veit*/The Carnival Parade in
Ober St. Veit, completed on February 6, 1910, and premiered two days later in
Vienna. By March of that year, they had produced their second film, the histori-
cally valuable record of *Der Trauerzug Sr. Exzellenz des Bürgermeisters Dr. Karl
Lueger*/The Funeral Parade of His Excellence the Mayor Dr. Karl Lueger. The
Kolm/Fleck firm was able to secure the rights to film the funeral of the once
immensely popular and still controversial Viennese mayor, beating out the French
competitor, Pathé Frères, which had nearly dominated the filming of major Austro-
Hungarian events. The film proved popular and brought Austrian film to a wider
European audience for the first time. Although the French companies had long
held the rights to film at the imperial court, Kolm and Fleck managed to secure
the privilege of filming Emperor Franz Joseph during his visit to a flying field, and
thus secured their reputation as Austria's primary film company. But the Kolm/Fleck
films still lagged behind international feature productions and the French *film d'art*
trend (1908–12), which encouraged literary and theatrical subject matter. The first
short feature in Austrian film was also Jakob Fleck's debut as film director. *Die
Ahnfrau*/The Medium (1910), was based on Austrian neoclassicist playwright Franz

Grillparzer's (1791–1872) tragedy about a family's self-destruction. The film may have lacked true cinematic realization, being a truncated stage production presented on film, but it signaled the vast possibilities of filming Austrian literature. The film was remade by Jakob Fleck and Louise Kolm as a full-length feature (over 2,000 meters) in 1919. With its cutting-edge lighting and editing effects, the second *Ahnfrau* suggests the expressionist direction of German film, rather than the socially critical melodrama, which the Kolm/Fleck group would be instrumental in developing. Long believed lost, a nearly complete nitrate copy of the film was discovered in Brazil, and following the Film Archive Austria's painstaking restoration of the disintegrating film, it received its second premiere in Vienna in 1991.

The 1910 Kolm/Fleck production of Theodor Gleisner's *Der Müller und sein Kind*/The Miller and His Child, based on the play by Silesian author Ernst Raupach (1784–1852), is today considered the first true Austrian feature film. This peasant melodrama was also the first to utilize and thus establish the concept of a cinema prop company. A major draw in Vienna and the provinces, the film was remade the following year in a vastly improved version. The continued success and growing visibility of the Kolm/Fleck productions enabled the studio to expand its undertakings, and the film company subsequently opened a distribution office and began publishing a weekly newsletter. Kolm and Fleck would distribute their own works but also films by German, French, British, American and Italian firms throughout the empire.[15] The company desired a wider European reputation and by 1911, Kolm and Fleck were able to more than double the four feature films they had produced in the previous year. Despite the *film d'art* trend, not all of the fifteen feature films produced by Austrian companies between 1910 and 1911 were literary-based tragedy or drama. Several short comedies were also produced, including Heinz Hanus's *Das Bartwuchsmittel*/The Beard Growth Elixer (1910), and two featuring German comic actor Oskar Sabo —*Die böse Schwiegermutter*/The Mean Mother-in-Law (1910) and *Volkssänger*/Folk Singers (1911). This new concept of the "star" performance was later expanded in 1912 with *Karl Blasel als Zahnarzt*/Karl Blasel as the Dentist, which presented one of Vienna's most famous comic theater actors of the nineteenth century in a unique visual record of one of his skits. It made Blasel accessible to the regional audiences that might never have seen him perform and also increased his already legendary status. Also of interest are *Martha mit dem Hosenrock*/Martha and the Trouser-Dress and *Ein misslungener Trick*/A Failed Jest, both from 1911.[16] The former pokes fun at the foibles of women's fashion, taking on the subject of the new pant-dress, which evolved from the hobble skirt of the time. The latter emulates American slapstick in its saga of a disastrous wedding trip. But these creations were not as popular as melodramas and moralist tales, and so three films satisfying those particular audience interests were produced in 1911: the social critical dramas *Nur ein armer Knecht, Mutter*/Only a Poor Servant, Mother, *Der Dorftrottel*/The Town Fool, and *Die Glückspuppe*/The Doll of Happiness. These films also signaled an increasing length of the Kolm/Fleck productions, which ranged from 300 to over 600 meters.[17]

Austrian film began to display a more sophisticated style of film writing, acting and music composition by this time. The aforementioned *Glückspuppe*, which was written and directed by the team of Louise Kolm, Anton Kolm, Jakob Fleck and Claudius Veltée, featured original music created by noted Viennese composer Erich Hiller.[18] He also helped Louise Kolm bring Jacques Offenbach's fantastic opera about the stories of Romantic era writer E. T. A. Hoffmann, *Hoffmanns Erzählungen*/The Tales of Hoffmann (1911), to the screen. The original libretto had to be shortened and altered somewhat to suit the aria-less performance, but the 317-meter film succeeded in remaining loyal to the spirit of the opera. Star publicity also emerged with this film: the Kolm/Fleck company newsletter considered the names of Hoffmann, Offenbach, Hiller and the actors to be a major draw for the film, and they were proven correct.[19] *Die Glückspuppe* is above all noteworthy as the first feature in Austria to be partially credited to a woman, Louise Kolm, who had been one of the first women in international cinema history to found a film studio, and with this film she was then the second female director in the world. While Alice Guy's (1876–1968) role as the first film director (male or female) has been discounted in film history texts or qualified by her gender as the first *female* film director, Louise Kolm is almost completely missing from cinema scholarship. Although she is known to historians in Austria and Germany as an early filmmaker who was partnered with her two husbands and above all for her socially critical work, the notion of her pioneering stature seems to have been quietly ignored by a century of film critics and historians.[20]

There is scant primary documentation on Louise Kolm as an individual or on her thoughts and concepts as filmmaker. The best source regarding this aspect of research has been her son, Austrian film director Walter Kolm-Veltée (1910–99), who describes his mother in simple terms as "energetic and full of humor. She loved fantasy but also desired to comment on the problems of society and the relationships between men and women."[21] Unfortunately, much of her prolific work in silent film is now lost. The resurgent interest in Austrian cinema brought on by New Austrian Film has, however, returned a few of her creations to the screens of Viennese art houses.

Given imperial Vienna's reputation for high art, architectural bombast, and music, one might wrongly assume that the most dominant subject matter in early Austrian cinema would be the operetta text or even that mainstay of Italian silent film, the epic historical costume drama. But it was socially critical melodrama, with topics ranging from rural tragedy and the abuse of women to the plight of the urban working class, that dominates early Austrian cinema. However, this filmic response to an empire chafing under its old elitist class structure was not paralleled with images regarding the sociopolitical stress rising from growing nationalist movements. Austrian author and film writer Alexander Lernet-Holenia (1897–1976) suggested a particular reason for this social focus in the arts and culture of Austria-Hungary:

> That strangely heterogeneous organism, which was nevertheless internally homo-
> geneous enough to allow a Count Görz incomparably easier communication with

a district commissioner from Czernowic, than a court councilor from the third
Vienna city district with his housemaid from the fifteenth. The reason is that the
Austrian monarchy, consisting of so many nations and classes, was layered only
socially, not nationally. In fact, national elements were even consciously
negated.[22]

But the subject matter of Austria's early features also shows the progressive, even
revolutionary, nature present among the intellectuals and artists of the Danubian
Empire. Viennese mayor Karl Lueger, whose state funeral was the subject of the
aforementioned 1910 Kolm/Fleck documentary and who is today remembered more
for his "pragmatic anti–Semitism" than for his civic development schemes, was popular among the middle- and lower-class Viennese for his policies aimed at creating
a better quality of urban life. But whether it was Lueger's Catholic-Social politics
or those of Austromarxist Victor Adler, the psychological studies of Sigmund Freud
or the psychological fictions of Arthur Schnitzler, the poems of Hugo von Hofmannsthal and Rainer Maria Rilke, secessionist paintings by Gustav Klimt, Egon
Schiele and Oskar Kokoschka, modernist architecture of Otto Wagner and Adolf
Loos, or post–Wagnerian compositions by Gustav Mahler, Hugo Wolf, Arnold
Schönberg, Anton von Webern, and Alban Berg, progressive social and cultural
thought was Vienna's forte in the decade prior to the Great War, despite the reactionary atmosphere of the "official" city.

The premiere of the second version of Kolm/Fleck's *Der Müller und sein Kind*
on October 21, 1911, signals the first true stride of feature film production in Austria. The film was not considered a great work of literature transferred to the screen,
but rather promoted the specific trend of the Austrian socially critical melodrama,
which would come to rival the French *film d'art* concept. The original play by Raupach, which depicts the conflict between rich and poor, young and old, and cli-
maxes in a doomed love story involving opposite ends of the social spectrum, was
perfect material for the Austrian tastes of the time. With the addition of the horror elements of ghostly occurrences, a Gothic cemetery, and an overly dramatic
death scene, the film promised entertainment value far beyond the intellectual value
of the original play. The director of the 1911 film was Walter Friedmann, head of
Vienna's Volksoper (People's Opera — a more popular and operetta-based house
than the Court Opera), who immediately understood the nature of the medium. This
was not to be a filmed play but a drama created by film: "The theater director generally works in width, the film director in depth.... The actor in the theater must
find harmony between word and gesture; in cinema, he must ultimately make himself understood through attitude and gesture.... Every gesture must have meaning
and have a logical connection with the previous one."[23] The scenic/technical director and cameraman was Joseph Delmont, who previously photographed and directed
westerns for Vitagraph in the United States. The 600-meter film was shot in studio and exterior settings and used the technique of tinting, often combining coloration with different tones to simulate night scenes or various interior lighting
qualities. Color values were particularly important in the era's Austrian and German

symbolist and pre–expressionist theater, where Max Dauthendey (1867–1918), the son of an early photographer, experimented with mood enhancement of colored lighting and the integration of color symbols as major elements of progressive stage presentation. Not only was this trend an attempt to bridge the visual values of art nouveau and early abstraction but it also combined the science of photography and early cinema with performance. The coloration of Kolm/Fleck productions continues this movement into film, but instead of adding symbolic value to live performance for more abstract and philosophical artistic expression, it was used in film to achieve the opposite — the suggestion of reality.

Two more films were made by Kolm/Fleck's Österreichisch-Ungarische Kino-Filmindustrie company in 1911 and 1912 before it ended its work: *Das goldene Wiener Herz*/The Golden Viennese Heart (1911) and *Trilby* (1912). The latter, based on the immensely popular novel by George du Maurier, and co-written and directed by Anton and Louise Kolm, Jakob Fleck and Claudius Veltée, told the story of a Hungarian musician who commands hypnotic control of his singing protégée. But even this sensationalistic melodrama is not as distant from the popular socially critical topics of the time as it would appear. Class conflict and female oppression, as well as the new science of psychology are strongly represented in the novel. The Kolm/Fleck team may have competed with many important theater treatments of the novel, but it led world cinema in bringing the work to the screen twice, remaking it in 1914 as *Svengali*. Both versions are now lost. That same year, Felix Dörmann's *Die Zirkusgräfin*/The Circus Countess (1912) also dealt frankly with class and gender roles, as it followed the corruption of an innocent circus dancer (Eugenie Bernay) into her transformation as a high-society mistress, to the heartbreak of the clown who loves her (Heinrich Eisenbach).

At odds with the major financial investor in their film company who wanted to determine the subject matter of production, Louise and Anton Kolm departed the association along with Jakob Fleck and Claudius Veltée in early 1912 and formed a new company named Wiener Kunstfilm (Viennese Art Film). They upgraded their technical prowess with new facilities and soundstages in Vienna's seventh district. Although the establishment received initial admiration from all of Austria's film publications, the filmmakers desperately needed to score a major success to support the new undertaking. Given the international interest in literary adaptations, the Kolm/Fleck partnership sought out one of Vienna's most heralded authors, Arthur Schnitzler (1862–1931), who agreed in principle to provide material for a possible film. Unfortunately, the project was stalled and ultimately abandoned due to the atmosphere of an ongoing rivalry between the theater and film worlds, which suggested to Schnitzler that his reputation as a great writer might be hurt with cinema involvement — at least in his own country. The intended material, Schnitzler's famous play *Liebelei*, subsequently received its first cinematic treatment outside of Austria in a 1913 Copenhagen-based Nordisk-Film production. The Kolms and Fleck would eventually create their cinematic version of *Liebelei*, but not until the end of the silent era in 1927. Another popular writer of the day, Oskar Bendiener, recipient of the prestigious Raimund Prize, was chosen to replace Schnitzler, and his theater drama *Der Unbekannte*/The Unknown Man was the first feature from the new Kunstfilm company. Unlike Schnitzler's *Liebelei*, which would have fit the theme of Kolm/Fleck's previous work with its critical look at class-consciousness in romantic relationships, Bendiener's criminal drama was far more sensationalist and less socially critical than anything the Kolm/Fleck team had created. The pre-production of the film built anticipation and interest in a manner that has become a standard aspect of international filmmaking. Famous stage actors were selected for the roles and the casting was advertised in newspapers. It was also announced that beloved Viennese operetta composer Franz Lehár (1870–1948) would score the film, although this failed to materialize. Nevertheless, the film emerged as the first all-star feature in Austrian cinema history: Eugenie Bernay, Viktor Kutschera, Hans Lackner, and Karl Blasel were among the large cast of what became Austrian cinema's longest feature film (1,070 meters cut from 10,000 meters of negative) to that date. It was also the first film wholly directed by Louise Kolm.

Kunstfilm spared no expense in surpassing the expectations of European standards of the time, since their project aimed at an international market. Establishing norms for cinema publicity, the film's aristocratic female lead, Claire Wolff-Metternich-Wallentin, appeared in film and fashion magazines modeling the creations of the Austrian Theatre Costume and Decoration Studio Company. The limited press screening (the start of another industry convention) proved to be such a successful word-of-mouth tactic that the film was a hit before it was widely shown in Austria-Hungary and Germany. Although the *film d'art* aspect of the work was met by the reputation of the author rather than by the material, the directorial and artistic/technical aspects of the film were impressive.

Despite the success of the film, Louise Kolm preferred co-direction, and would return to shared creation with Anton Kolm, and her second husband, Jakob Fleck, in future projects. There is no statement from her or her husbands regarding their working relationships, but her son indicates that it was a truly collaborative effort, rather than a process of specific tasks. Apparently, Louise Kolm and her husbands worked as a "committee" on the set although Louise had the more dominant voice in actual acting direction, particularly in her work with second husband Jakob Fleck.[24]

The firm's goals of artistic reputation and financial stability required more than one sensation, and larger event films were planned. Unfortunately, the following productions did not find the same level of success as *Der Unbekannte*, and this was exploited by the film journal *Österreichischer Komet* (Austrian Comet), which had taken up an anti–Kolm attitude, partially influenced by Elias Tropp, a disgruntled member of the new Kolm/Fleck company. His subsequent and malicious "exposé" of the company and Kolm's work bordered on slander and was intended to ruin the new studio and the reputations of its artists. But Louise Kolm and her partners survived the smear and managed to produce thirty-seven films between 1913 and 1914.[25]

Most of the films during this prolific phase of the Kolm/Fleck partnership were progressive social dramas and include the important 1913 production *Der*

An early feature from the Louise and Anton Kolm film company: *Das goldene Wiener Herz*, 1911.

Psychiater/The Psychiatrist, also known as *Das Proletarierherz*/The Heart of the Proletarian. An attempt in melding documentary, operetta and feature film on a subject that became one of the more popular "Austrian" themes in international film history, *Johann Strauss an der schönen blauen Donau*/Johann Strauss on the Beautiful Blue Danube was a misfire in 1913, despite its lavish conception and its premiere, which coincided with the unveiling of the Johann Strauss Jr. Memorial in Vienna's City Park. Imperial Court Theater star Carl von Zeska, who directed the 2,000-meter film, which was saturated with performances and cameos by prominent names from Viennese theater, opera, and operetta, portrayed the "Waltz King." Also appearing in the film was Walter Kolm-Veltée, the young son of Louise and Anton, who would later become one of the important film writers and directors in post–World War II Austrian cinema and the founder of the Vienna Film Academy. Unfortunately, the silent operetta and fictionalized Strauss biography failed due to the too recent presence of Strauss in Viennese cultural life: at the time he had only been dead for ten years. The film's disappointing reception once again underscored the Austro-Hungarian public's desire for serious social drama rather than frothy Viennese cliché. Its failure also exacerbated the ongoing rivalry between theater and film institutions. Stage loyalists condemned film as a dangerous threat to Austrian theater and called for a boycott of film by all theater actors. Cineastes pointed to the growing popular success of cinema and railed against the publicity tactics of what was considered a reactionary elite. But the Kolm/Fleck company had a well-designed response at the ready. They boldly announced that although the dictatorial director of Imperial Court Protocol and Affairs, Prince Montenuevo, had forbidden all members of the Imperial Court Theater from appearing in cinema, he had in fact issued an official decree allowing Carl von Zeska to play the role of Johann Strauss Jr. in their film.[26] This decision essentially removed any doubts about the correctness of cinema performance. The age of the film actor had begun, and the division between film and theater, which was to quickly disappear by the onset of the Great War, had only helped delineate and foster the new acting in theory and practice. Von Zeska subsequently announced that there could be harmony between the two arts and claimed that only a well-trained theater actor could become a good film actor, a notion that has lingered in Austria to the present day.[27]

Despite the Strauss debacle, Kolm/Fleck productions had notable successes on the eve of World War I, including *Die Hochzeit von Valeni*/The Wedding of Valeni (1914) and *Der Pfarrer von Kirchfeld*/The Priest from Kirchfeld (1914). The *Valeni* film was based on the turn-of-the-century theater piece on Romanian gypsy life penned by Marco Brociner and Ludwig Ganghofer. Unlike previous theater-based films, which had cut the dramatic elements to skeletal plot structure, the Kolms and Fleck sought to extend the film narrative to include more character background and motivation, and again laid the groundwork for future film treatments of theatrical and literary properties. *Der Pfarrer von Kirchfeld*, based on the work by Austrian naturalist playwright Ludwig Anzengruber (1839–89), followed and brought together various elements that would ensure lasting success: a realistic social drama with moving and strongly emotional aspects, famous actors, nature photography, stunning crowd scenes, and the overall reputation of Viennese literary quality.[28] Anzengruber's play became so synonymous with the film style and reputation of Louise Kolm and Jakob Fleck that the couple remade the work twice, in 1926 and 1937.

Since 1912, Count Sascha Kolowrat had been the only true rival to the Kolm/ Fleck team. A scion of old and wealthy Bohemian nobility, Kolowrat was born in Glenridge, New York, for reasons that remain unclear. It has been suggested that Sascha Kolowrat's father, Count Leopold Philipp (1852–1910), was in American exile as punishment for acting dishonorably in the face of a perceived insult. Whatever the imperial court's directive may have been to such errant aristocratic behavior, Sascha's father met and married Baroness Nadine Huppmann-Valbella, the daughter of a successful cigarette manufacturer from St. Petersburg, while in the United States and they had Sascha in 1886. Socially and financially secure with the inheritance of impressive estates and the wealth of both parents, Sascha Kolowrat became an extrovert and an active participant in all that life had to offer. He was fascinated with technical advancements, particularly dealing with vehicular movement, and participated in motorcycle and automobile races; he also obtained one of the first private pilot licenses in Austria. The Austro-Hungarian film director, Mihály Kertész (1888–1962) later Hollywood's Michael Curtiz, once commented upon visiting Kolowrat's headquarters that it was not clear if he was "in the office of a film magnate or in the workroom of an automobile industrialist."[29] Kolowrat's passion turned to film in 1910, after his trip to Paris and the studios of Pathé. The first film of the Sascha Filmfabrik (Sascha Film Factory), which he had founded in Bohemia after inheriting the Kolowrat estates upon his father's death in 1910 and later moved to Vienna, was *Die Gewinnung des Eisens am steirischen Erzberg im Eisenerz*/The Extraction of Iron at the Styrian Erz Mountain at Eisenerz (1912). It clearly melded his interests in film and industry. That same year, his first attempt at creating a short comic film with actor Max Pallenberg as the grotesque character Pampulik was ruined by poor artificial lighting. Having solved the problem with new mercury film lights from Berlin, Kolowrat created Austrian cinema's first comedy team, "Cocl und Seff" (Rudolf Walter and Josef Haloub), which he featured in a long series of shorts. His first dramatic feature was the 1912 *Kaiser Joseph II*/Emperor Joseph II, directed by J. H. Gross, but it was the following film that secured Kolowrat's reputation as a rival to the Kolm/Fleck partnership and as a major player in early Austrian film production. Convincing the popular theater and operetta star Alexander Girardi to perform in the new medium was no easy feat, but Kolowrat succeeded and the resulting film, *Der Millionenonkel*/The Millionaire Uncle (1913), directed by Kolowrat with Hubert Marischka (1882–1959), and written by Girardi, Hubert Marischka and his brother Ernst (1893–1963), was not only a triumph for Girardi but was also Kolowrat's first true artistic and commercial success. The narrative catered to Girardi's famous characterizations and presented him in no less than thirty roles through a montage effect that was revolutionary for the era.[30] Cinematography was by Eduard Hoesch and the famous "Silver Age"[31] operetta composer Robert Stolz (1880–1975) scored the film. Hailed as one of his most brilliant works, Stolz conducted it at the film's premiere at Vienna's Beethoven Hall. His comments on the film suggest the complexity of the project: "This was no easy task for a composer because it wasn't to be a collection or potpourris of Girardi's best moments [from operetta], but a thoroughly new and complete composition which interweaves a mosaic of Girardi's unforgettable operetta roles."[32] The film quickly became a sensation outside of the empire as well. Girardi, who keenly appreciated the possibilities of the new medium, was also the first cinema figure to be the subject of what is known today as the product tie-in. His many fans happily purchased Girardi portraits, engravings, photographs, busts, candies, ties, scarves, buttons and the most popular of the souvenir items, the Girardi Hat, modeled after his trademark wide-rimmed straw boater. The Kolm/Fleck team followed up on Kolowrat's success with their vehicle for Girardi by teaming him with Hansi Niese in *Frau Gertraud Namenlos*/Mrs. Gertraud Nameless (1913).

Austria-Hungary took a major step in institutionalizing and expanding its film industry in 1913 with the creation of the Reichsverband der Lichtspieltheater (Imperial Association of Cinemas), which instituted the first systematic conditions for film distribution within the empire. Mirroring the growth of Austrian film, this organization grew enormously within the following two years. The achievement of Kolowrat's Girardi film encouraged the producer to found a new company, Sascha-Film, in

The star vehicle: Alexander Girardi in Hubert Marischka's *Der Millionenonkel*, 1913.

1914. It was to become Austria's largest film firm after the Great War, and its dominance was ended only by the forced incorporation of the company into the state-run Wien-Film after Austria's Anschluss by Nazi Germany in 1938. But despite Kolowrat's growing reputation and aristocratic rank, his plan to gain something akin to official acknowledgment of his importance from the emperor was dashed. While Franz Joseph did not mind being captured on film at certain events, he flatly rejected Kolowrat's request to film him and members of the imperial family for a "patriotic film" that might be viewed as commercial and political exploitation of the monarchy.[33]

Kolowrat was determined to continue his leadership within the film industry even at the outbreak of war in 1914. Volunteering as an officer of the automobile corps, he utilized his military and court connections to seek official permission to film war footage. Approval was given and Kolowrat immediately began producing the newsreel *Kino-Wochenbericht vom nördlichen und südlichen Kriegschauplatz/* Weekly Cinema Report from the Northern and Southern Theaters of War. Despite its successes, the early Sascha-Film remained among the smallest of the European distributors in Austria. But Kolowrat used the war to turn an otherwise impossible profit: by 1915 the count had managed to gain an appointment as head of the film department in the Imperial and Royal War Press Office. He continued to produce features, but now they had a distinct martial theme, as in *Wien im Krieg*/Vienna at War (1916). The film, however, is most notable for its radical visual style: in a street scene viewed through the eyes of a drunken man, one can locate the beginnings of expressionist cinematography, which would later be developed by Austrian director Robert Wiene in his landmark *Das Kabinett des Dr. Caligari*/The Cabinet of Dr. Caligari (Germany 1919).[34]

By 1916, Sascha Kolowrat held a monopoly in newsreel creation with his *Sascha-Kriegswochenbericht*/Sascha Weekly War Report. Often sweetening these documentaries with studio effects and fictional scenes, the power of such sensationalized images taught Kolowrat a lesson regarding the medium's attraction and also gave him a recipe for its exploitation — "nothing appears as real as an illusion."[35] Film historians Elisabeth Büttner and Christian Dewald argue that Sergei Eisenstein had a similar philosophy about the dynamics of film, which led him to sacrifice historical fact for visual effect in recreating the 1917 Russian revolution in *Oktober* (USSR 1927).[36] Kolowrat scholar Günter Krenn points out that these reportages were masterpieces of narrative cinema in their own right. Kolowrat became so skilled in choreographing war footage in newsreels that his postwar feature film *Der Junge Medardus*/The Young Medardus (1923) was considered to then have the "largest and most beautiful war tapestry cinematography" by film theoretician Bela Balász.[37] 1916 also marked the physical expansion of the Sascha firm, as Kolowrat completed the construction of his studio in Sievering, a district of Vienna. The original building, an airplane hangar imported from Düsseldorf, was redesigned as Austria's first standalone soundstage. It would become the core of one of Austria's major studio complexes until it ultimately shared the fate of demolition with so many others around the globe in the post-studio era of the 1970s and 1980s. This was followed by Kolowrat's two-year partnership with the German film mogul Oskar Messter, which, through the new Sascha-Messter-Film company, dominated both Austrian and German film production. Among their most important productions was the documentary on the funeral of Emperor Franz Joseph (*Die Trauerfeierlichkeiten für Weiland Sr. Majestät Kaiser Franz Joseph*/The Funeral Ceremonies for His Late Majesty Emperor Franz Joseph), who died in 1916. The film was completed and distributed with 255 copies in three days.[38] It was followed almost immediately by a film that celebrated the opposite emotion with no less baroque ritual, the documentary depicting new Austrian Emperor Karl I and Empress Zita being crowned King and Queen of Hungary on December 30, 1916.[39]

The near-monolithic power of this Austrian/German film company between 1917 and early 1918 is analogous to the tightening of the military alliance between Austria-Hungary and Germany in the wake of the revelations that Emperor Karl and Empress Zita had attempted to negotiate a separate peace with the Allied powers in an effort to pull Austria-Hungary out of the war.[40] Unlike Franz Joseph, Emperor Karl encouraged the filming of his appearances for patriotic documentaries and the Kolowrat/Messter partnership was happy to oblige. The partnership also produced such war films as *Die wirtschaftliche Erschliessung Montenegros*/The Economic Embargo of Montenegro (1917), *Der Zusammenbruch der italienischen*

Front/The Collapse of the Italian Front (1917), and *Die Befreiung Bukowina*/The Liberation of Bukovina (1917), which underscored the use of the new medium (albeit heavily controlled by the censors) for propaganda purposes. Even features had become bluntly political: Kolowrat's *Der Nörgler*/The Complainer, directed by Fritz Freisler in 1916, attacked defeatism and encouraged the public to buy war bonds. The successes of Kolowrat's Austrian war films inspired the Germans to do similar work, and in 1917, the German Universum-Film firm, better known as UFA, was founded in Berlin for the specific purpose of creating filmed war propaganda.[41] It subsequently bought up all available German and Austrian production companies, theaters and studios, including Messter's film company, which gave UFA financial interest in Sascha-Film, along with the Austrian Creditanstalt Bank when Kolowrat's firm was turned into a limited company in 1918. The Sascha-Messter partnership was now at an end, but Kolowrat made up for the loss by merging the Vienna distribution firm of Philipp und Pressburger into the new Sascha-Filmindustrie in September 1918. The UFA seat on the board of directors also signaled the beginning of the problematic involvement of Germany in the Austrian interwar film industry.

The Kolm/Fleck Kunstfilm was also significant in bringing the Great War into the cinema theaters. While Kolowrat promoted his war reportage, Kolm/Fleck abandoned their reputation for social and literary drama and offered Austria-Hungary's most successful pro–Habsburg patriotic feature films with music by famed maestros of the operetta. These films melded heroic notions with sentimental drama and rousing scores. Following *Der Traum eines österreichischen Reservisten*/The Dream of an Austrian Reserve Officer (1915), based on the tone poem by operetta and waltz composer Carl Michael Ziehrer (1843–1922), Louise Kolm and Jakob Fleck wrote and directed *Mit Herz und Hand fürs Vaterland*/With Heart and Hand for the Fatherland (1915) with war songs by Franz Lehár, *Mit Gott für Kaiser und Reich*/With God for Emperor and Empire (1916) with music by Ziehrer, and produced the 1918 drama *Freier Dienst*/Voluntary Service. These films inspired similar undertakings by short-lived small companies such as Filmmag, A-Zet, Astoria, Leyka and the Robert Müller firm, which produced the 1915 drama written by Alfred Deutsch-German and directed by Emil Leyde, *Das Kriegspatenkind*/The Godchild of the War, with music by a new operetta composer named Edmund Eysler (1874–1949). A-Zet-Film presented *Das Kind meines Nächsten*/The Child of My Neighbor with music by Eysler in 1918, and Filmag produced *Konrad Hartls Lebensschicksal*/Konrad Hartl's Fate, written by Karl Tema. The timely genre did not escape criticism from literary and cultural critic Karl Kraus (1874–1936), who detested the use of film for the sake of propaganda and as a form of "emotional war" on the audiences. He particularly rejected the manipulated documentaries and reportage of Sascha-Film, the War Press Office, and Kolowrat's associate, Hubert Marischka. But even with this scathing attack on the use of film, one scene of Kraus's 1919 play *Die letzten Tage der Menschheit*/The Final Days of Mankind is set in a cinema theater. After a concerted effort by filmmakers to bring literature into the cinema, cinema had now finally become part of literature.

But not all film production was dedicated to war propaganda. The Kolm/Fleck Kunstfilm team filmed Austrian folk-dramatist Ferdinand Raimund's (1790–1836) magical tale, *Der Verschwender*/The Spendthrift in 1917 to build up the star career of actress Liane Haid. The Raimund film was so successful that several other artistic feature films were made by Kunstfilm in 1918, including *Don Cäsar, Graf von Irun*/Don Cesar, Count of Irun, based on the work by Dumanoir and d'Emery; *Die Jüdin*/The Jewess, by Eugene Scribe; Victor Hugo's *Der König amüsiert sich (Rigoletto)*/The King Amuses Himself; and *Tiefland*/Lowands, after the play by Angel Guimera and the opera by Eugene d'Albert.[42] Although these were considered large-scale costume dramas for the time, every attempt was made to reduce costs while giving impressive production values. The Gothic "sets" of *Der König amusiert sich*, for example, were not constructed in a studio but were on-location sites of neo–Gothic architecture found in Vienna, including the Rathaus (City Hall) on the Ringstrasse.[43]

Although studios had issued newsletters and several professional publications devoted to cinema art and technology, daily film criticism was not published in the Austrian newspapers until 1916. That same year, the first government regulations pertaining to the protection of children and young people attending cinemas were published and enforced in Austria-Hungary. Tastes soon changed after the first years of the war and during the expansion of film from shorts to feature-length works. Grotesque and slapstick comedies had faded from the scene and were replaced by more sophisticated fare based on stage plays. Parody and farce first appeared on the screens during this period. But literary-based social dramas continued to dominate. Anzengruber's rural images were particularly desired and often filmed: *Der Meineidbauer*/The Perjured Peasant (1915), *Im Banne der Pflicht*/In the Line of Duty (1917), and *Der Schandfleck*/The Stain of Shame (1917). There were also social dramas based on works by Rudolf Hawel (*Mutter Sorge*/Mother's Worry, 1915), Louis Taufstein (*Armer Teufel*/Poor Devil, 1916), Eugène Brieux (*Der Geisel der Menschheit*/The Hostage of Mankind, 1918), and Henrik Ibsen (*Gespenster*/Ghosts, 1918). Among the most interesting films of this period are those melding the social drama with occult or mystical subject matter, a style brought on by heroic war and death propaganda, as well as by popular Orientalia and the mythological atmosphere of symbolist art and monistic philosophy. Sascha-Film's 1918 *Am Tor des Lebens* (a.k.a. *Am Tor des Todes*/At the Gate of Life/Death), ostensibly the first Austrian film to deal with reincarnation, was one of the most successful of this hybrid genre. It was written and directed by the brothers Conrad and Robert Wiene. The following year, Robert Wiene (1873–1938) gained international attention for bringing the expressionism of German painting to the screen in a film written by Austrians Carl Mayer and Hans Janowitz, *Das Kabinett des Dr. Caligari*/The Cabinet of Dr. Caligari (Germany 1919). The roots of German expressionist film and its nightmarish drama can be located in the Austrian social/mystical film, and this genre gave Austria-Hungary a brief new stylistic identity in European cinema.[44] As the war progressed, the escapism of Viennese operetta also gained a foothold in Austrian film production. Carl Michael Ziehrer's 1899 *Die Landstreicher*/The Vagabonds was produced

Liane Haid in Louise Kolm's patriotic drama *Mit Herz und Hand fürs Vaterland*, 1915.

by Kunstfilm in 1916 and Hubert Marischka, whose name would become synonymous with elegant musicals and entertainment films, scored a cinematic coup when he managed to produce Franz Lehár's *Wo die Lerche Singt*/Where the Lark Sings in 1918, the same year as its operetta premiere in Budapest and Vienna.

An important aspect of the propaganda value of motion pictures during the war years was the cultivation of the first film stars. Early silent features had, of course, relied on the attraction of name performers to sell a production and generate box office. But these were for the most part appearances by known personalities from the stage or operetta. The Great War had convinced even the most ardent antifilm circles that the medium was a powerful propaganda machine and this had swept away any residual snobbishness against the medium. Conscious cultivation of the film star also made cinema a more potently influential force in mass culture. A woman had been among the first pioneers behind the camera in Austria, and the first recognizable film stars in front of the camera were women as well. Born in Vienna, Liane Haid (1897–2000) had already performed as a neoclassical dancer using the apt pseudonym Hypolita d'Hellas on stage in Vienna and Budapest when Kunstfilm offered her a role in *Mit Herz und Hand fürs Vaterland* in 1915. Her success led to an exclusive contract with the company, where she specialized in playing the type of sympathetic ingenue Lillian Gish was famous for in American film.

By 1918, she had become Austria's greatest film star and commanded the highest salary of any cinema performer in Vienna. Following her star turn in *Eva, die Sünde*/Eva, The Sin (1920), in which she portrays a femme fatale who attempts to seduce a monk, Haid sued Kunstfilm for having exploited her physically (by exposing her to dangerous situations) and financially (she had to arrange her own makeup and costuming). After her break with Kunstfilm, Haid's husband, industrialist Fritz von Haymerle, built her a studio in the neighborhood of Vienna's Schönbrunn Palace, and established Micco-Film to promote her career. In contrast to Haid's "Viennese maiden" persona, Kolowrat launched Magda Sonja (1895–?), Austrian cinema's vamp, whose impressive talents and demonic roles in the occult genre of the Sascha-Messter films made her a star of nearly equal fame. Haid continued as a silent actress in Austrian and German film throughout the 1920s, most notably in the 1921 *Frau in weiß*/Woman in White, based on the popular 1860 mystery novel by Wilkie Collins, and in the 1926 operetta film *Im weißen Rössl*/At the White Horse Inn. She even attempted a belated comeback in sound with *Die fünf Karnickel*/The Five Rabbits in 1953. Following these two stars there were, of course, imitations: Dora Kaiser and Thea Rosenquist became Haid's successors at Kunstfilm, and the Danish actress Eva Roth impersonated Sonja's sultry image. The most important male star was director/producer Hubert Marischka, who embodied the elegant Viennese gentleman, followed by future sound stars Raoul Aslan, Georg Reimers, Otto Tressler and theater actor Willy Thaller. Following his return from military service, Max Neufeld gained attention as leading man and Karl Götz was well known as a character actor specializing in grotesque roles. One of Götz's memorable appearances was in Sascha-Film's mystical *Mandarin* (1918), a quasi-expressionist film pre-suggesting *Dr. Caligari*–esque horror. Rudolf Schildkraut (1862–1930) and his son, Josef Schildkraut (1895–1964) were briefly popular and then emigrated to the United States in 1920, where both became respected stage and film character actors. Finally, just prior to the collapse of the monarchy, Fritz Kortner (1892–1970) attained star status for his portrayal of Beethoven in the Sascha-Messter film *Märtyrer seines Herzens*/Martyr of His Heart (1918). It paid tribute to the German musical genius and his creative zenith in Vienna, and thereby also suggested the natural and successful concept of the German-Austrian wartime alliance.

The Central Powers' loss of the Great War and the subsequent collapse of the Austro-Hungarian monarchy radically transformed the Austrian film industry. Germany had become a republic but, despite loss of some territory, remained intact. Austria-Hungary, however, exploded into several Central European republics. The remnant core of Austria, a German-speaking territory carved inaccurately from the tatters of the empire by the Allies and the 1919 Treaty of Saint Germain, was established as a small, impoverished republic with no clear identity. Many German-speaking Austrians were now citizens of other countries or their property outside of the new republic had been nationalized. As he had done during the war, Sascha Kolowrat succeeded in manipulating the tragedy into a beneficial situation for his company. Due to the location of his landholdings, he had become a Czechoslovakian citizen and, unlike his vanquished Austrian colleagues, he could therefore maintain healthy contacts with film and government sources in Paris and London. The studio network he had built throughout the empire was replaced by a commonwealth of production branches bearing different names to appear "home grown," but which were wholly run by Sascha-Film: Raius-Film in Budapest, Slavia-Film in Prague, Bosna-Film in Belgrade, Dorian-Film in Bucharest, and Peter-Film in Warsaw. Additionally, he created an American branch known as the Herz Film Corporation and assumed the Austrian representation of Paramount Pictures.[45] Kolowrat had long admired American films and their easy exportability, and his intention to create an Austrian cinema international in theme and groundbreaking in presentation was something that he had planned throughout the war years. Between 1920 and 1925, Kolowrat would attempt to fulfill that desire. It would shape his greatest phase as a producer and contribute impressively to the international development of silent film. In a genre reminiscent of both the American biblical film and the Italian historical epic, Kolowrat's new work combined the monumental silent and the Viennese social drama to create an entirely new Austrian national cinema style. It was as if the lost empire and its role as a leading world power would now be continued in the expanse and grandeur of the republic's cinematic illusions. In 1919, Kolowrat signed Mihály Kertész, who had come to Vienna following a brief stint with the cultural committee of the short-lived communist dictatorship in Budapest. When his "bourgeois" film was condemned by the regime, Kertész joined the exodus of other Hungarian filmmakers emigrating to Vienna, Berlin, London, or Hollywood. Kertész had wanted to produce historical epics in Hungary but understood the problems of selling Central European history on the international film market. Kertész and his colleague, Sandor (Alexander) Korda (1893–1956), welcomed Kolowrat's intention to create and export monumental historical films with great enthusiasm. These were to be modeled after D. W. Griffith's 1916 *Intolerance*, which, coincidentally, had employed Austrian expatriate and future Hollywood director Erich von Stroheim (1885–1957) as an assistant.

The first two Kolowrat films in this nascent style were not yet monumental, but they offered themes that would be geared toward international audiences such as Korda's *Prinz und Bettelknabe*/The Prince and the Pauper (1920), based on the story by Mark Twain and featuring an "Old London" set erected by designer Artur Berger within the shadows of Vienna's Prater. Kolowrat's recipe for Austrian film success was to make the films less specifically "Austrian." This was done by adding rather than subtracting. To the mélange of the multicultural Viennese film essence, he contributed two elements: Hollywood epic sensibility and a fresh creativity from Budapest. Although the vision was still Austrian given its influences from "baroque theater, the representation of the Habsburgs, literary–Romantic scripts, art nouveau and expressionist stage writing, a mixture that could only have come about in Vienna,"[46] it was now transformed and universalized by Kertész and Korda.

The first monumental film of the new Kertész/Kolowrat concept is considered a high point in the history of Austrian silent film. *Sodom und Gomorrah* (1922) was immediately understood by critics to be a condemnation of the new forces of capitalism in the impoverished fledgling republic. The filmmakers had succeeded in adapting the subtexts of D. W. Griffith's *Birth of a Nation* (USA 1915), *Intolerance* (USA 1916), and even Henry Otto's *Dante's Inferno* (USA 1924), which offered biblical subtexts as moral commentary on sin in America. In Hollywood or Vienna, the Bible was a safe way to introduce sex into the cinema without fear of censorship. Eroticism would be served even as it is condemned. That it was served at all was one of the aspects of this genre's popularity, along with the visual pleasure of the enormous sets, exotic costumes, and the ubiquitous "cast of thousands." Following the promise of its subtitle, *Die Legende von Sünde und Strafe* (The Legend of Sin and Punishment, a.k.a. The Queen of Sin), *Sodom und Gomorrah* was the longest, most spectacular film created in Austria to that date. Shown in two parts and running three hours at a length of 3,900 meters, the picture took two years to film and was shot at various studio and open-air locations in and around Vienna. Like its American counterpart, the Austrian biblical epic consisted of a dream sequence framed by a contemporary story of desire: Mary Conway, the young daughter of a banker's mistress, is forced to marry a wealthy widower who has ruined many lives. Developing into a femme fatale, she nearly causes her husband's suicide and seduces his innocent son. The biblical dream, which underscores the sin of her vampish nature and Jazz Age irresponsibility, rehabilitates her and she returns to her similarly repentant husband. The wife of director Kertész, Lucy Doraine (Ilonka Kovács, 1898–1989) portrays both the central contemporary (Mary) and biblical (Lot's Wife) female roles in the film. The banker's offspring was the first film role for Austrian and American star Walter Slezak (1902–83), son of opera singer Leo Slezak. Head cameraman was future film director Gustav Ucicky (1898–1961), son of Austrian *Jugendstil* artist Gustav Klimt. Although there remains no actual record, the number of extras is believed to have ranged from three to fourteen thousand, among them a few important names from Austrian and German cinema to come: director Willi Forst, actors Paula Wessely and Hans Thimig, and film writer/theoretician Bela Balász.

The film not only demanded a sizeable mass of atmosphere actors but, it also employed a small army behind the cameras. Unlike the select practices of the wealthy Hollywood industry, the employment of so many people in a monumental silent shot in Vienna was made feasible by the inflation and unemployment of the First Republic. Kolowrat gave thousands of craftspeople work as set builders, technicians, carpenters, metalworkers, prop creators, and pyrotechnicians. He built workshops that employed hundreds of women and men for the creation of costumes, wigs, beards, sandals, jewelry, flags, banners, and equipage. Thousands of the unemployed and their children were paid daily for their work on the film. Kolowrat also managed to utilize much of Vienna's available film crew talent as cameramen, hairstylists, makeup artists, tailors, wardrobe personnel, and their assistants. In a 1970 interview, Walter Slezak commented: "Have you any idea what 14,000 extras requires? It means approximately 1,200 … make-up artists, then circa 2,000 costumers; the people had to all be fitted for wigs, that was an unbelievable expense. It was one of the most expensive films ever made in Austria, or in the world. It cost almost 5½ times as much as was originally planned."[47] Immense wood and cardboard constructions of Sodom and Gomorrah and Assyria were built in an abandoned brick foundry. The masterwork of the film's architectural edifices, which betrayed a strong influence from Viennese *Jugendstil* and the Secessionist architecture of Josef Hoffmann, was the temple of Sodom, created by three set designers under the direction of Julius von Borsody (1892–1963), the brother of cameraman and director Eduard von Borsody. The temple was to be destroyed in the closing moments of the film, necessitating the dynamiting of the structure. The outcome was a spectacular scene that resulted in several deaths and injuries. The director was not implicated in the accident, but the head technician was fined 500,000 Kronen and sentenced to ten days' imprisonment. Kolowrat had hoped to build a new palace of film for the premiere but this remained unrealized. The film's successful premiere in Berlin was accompanied by a sprawling musical pastiche by Guiseppe Becce made up of themes from Bizet, Tchaikovsky, Verdi, Massnet, Sibelius, and Marschner.

Until 1987, only twenty-five minutes of this landmark film, a gift from the Soviet Film Archives in the 1950s, were known to exist in Austria. Walter Fritz, the former director of the Austrian Film Archives, eventually located additional sequences in Hungary, East Germany, Italy and the Soviet Union, and the film was reconstructed in three separate phases from 1987 to 1997. Film historian Gyöngyi Balogh finds misogynistic correlations between the director's work in this film and in his later *Casablanca* (USA 1942). Just as the frivolously lascivious acts of a woman set in motion the destruction of her family, and in the biblical parallel, that of the world, so in *Casablanca* the rejection of female love during the fight against Nazism might help save the world.[48] It is precisely this strict either/or attitude toward morality and passion that eventually allowed *Sodom und Gomorrah* to be eclipsed in world cinematic memory by Griffith's *Intolerance*, which was comparably less moralistic.[49]

Alexander Korda, who was also employed with Vita-Film, the renamed Kolm/Fleck Kunstfilm, decided to create a monumental biblical epic as well and did so for 12 million Kronen with *Samson und Delila* (1922). Echoing Kertész's casting of his wife as lead, Korda's wife, Maria Corda, played Delilah to Italian-Hungarian actor Alfredo Gal's Samson. The film, which finds its duality less in the aspects of morality and immorality and more in the opposition between innocence and decadence, was also constructed with a contemporary frame, this time with special effects rivaling those of the biblical scenes. A love triangle on an ocean liner places the modern Delilah between the new philistine, a degenerate and violent aristocrat, and a young opera singer whom she uses and then rejects. He is later revealed to be an anarchist who has planted a bomb on the ship. Clearly representing class conflicts and cultural/moral shifts of the new century's modernity, the film points toward the anxiety regarding technology and the inevitability of nature in the Austrian/German *Bergfilm* or mountain film of the 1920s to 1940s. Korda also made two other films dealing with the sea that same year: *Herren der Meere*/Lords of the Seas (1922) and *Eine versunkene Welt*/A Sunken World (1922). The latter, based on Lajos Biros's novel *Serpolette*, offered a fictionalized version of the disowned

Habsburg archduke, who rejected his heritage, renamed himself Johann Orth and escaped Vienna with his mistress, a dancer. On a ship bound for what Orth believes will be a new world with classless utopian possibilities, he is eventually crushed by the dancer's libertine relationship with the crew and steers the ship to its doom.

Vienna had reached a near-saturation point in film production by 1922 and was among the world's leaders in the industry. In addition to the majors — Sascha-Film, Astoria, Dreamland, Listo-Film, Schönbrunn-Film and Vita-Film — approximately twenty other independent companies produced around seventy-five feature films in addition to about sixty one-act comedies, cultural and educational films per year. Although various associations already existed for directors, projectionists and actors, there was no single organization that would represent this rapidly growing industry. Heinz Hanus, who had started his prolific writing and directing career with the Kolms and Fleck and who had become head of the Austrian Association of Film Directors, promoted the idea of a union among his colleagues. After long negotiations, Hanus and the founder of the Austrian Stage Association, Alfons Bolz-Feigl, called the first general assembly of the Vereinigung aller am Film Schaffenden Österreichs (Union of the Austrian Film Industry), more commonly known as the Filmbund on December 31, 1922. The organization soon set standards for protection of the industry's interests as a whole as well as for copyright protection and labor arbitration. A fund was established for the emergency support of the film industry's unemployed members, and free medical and legal assistance for industry workers and their families was instituted. Additionally, laws were set for minimum pay, labor conditions and contractual relationships with foreign corporations. This progressive organization was soon to be put to the test in an almost overwhelming task of assisting much of Austria's film personnel.

The financial crisis of 1923, which caused runaway inflation in Germany, Hungary and Austria, contributed greatly to the downward spiral in Vienna's film production that lasted until after sound was introduced. Austrian cinemas were inundated with American films because their studios used the crisis as an advantageous climate for export and came to nearly dominate the country's cinemas. Major Austrian production firms declined from about twenty to a scant three. Despite the fact that Austria could boast the most technically advanced film site in Europe with the Vita-Film Rosenhügel Studios, by 1925 only five films were produced, while twelve hundred films of American origin had been made available to the Austrian censor. Nearly three thousand Austrians working in the film industry became unemployed.

Kertész answered this crisis with another monumental epic, *Die Sklavenkönigin*/The Slave Queen (1923–24). From its inception, the film was conceived as a challenge to Hollywood, where Cecil B. DeMille was in production with his own biblical epic, *The Ten Commandments* (USA 1923). In addition to this, several factors also influenced Kertész's choice of an Egyptian theme for his next picture. He had made two other films since *Sodom und Gomorrah* that, although successful, did not receive the international attention accorded his biblical epic. Having just completed the Sascha-Film production of *Harun al Raschid* (1924), with Henry Black-

A cast and crew of thousands: Mihály Kertész's monumental biblical epic *Die Sklavenkönigin* 1923–24.

burn and Mary Kid, and riding the international Egyptian fad brought on by the discovery of the tomb of Tutankhamen in 1922, Kertész turned to H. Rider Haggard's novel *The Moon of Israel* as the basis for his new spectacle. Adapted for the screen by Ladislaus Vajda, who had previously scripted *Sodom und Gomorrhah*, the film tells the tale of the Israelite maiden Merapi (Maria Corda), who falls in love with the son of the Egyptian king (Adelqui Millar) against the backdrop of the Ten Commandments story. Moses (Hans Marr) leading the Israelites through the parting of the Red Sea would be the climax to the sprawling costume drama. Competing with DeMille for brilliant new effects, Kertész created a miniature set for the manipulation of the Red Sea sequence and, through an astoundingly successful early matte-process, placed the actors between the parted and closing waves of the Red Sea. The film was a critical and popular success internationally and led to Kertész's contract with Warner Brothers (and his career as Michael Curtiz), which he immediately signed in the midst of directing Kolowrat's *Der goldene Schmetterling*/The Golden Butterfly in Berlin in 1926.

Kolowrat's Hungarians and the epic film may have dominated Austrian cinema during the first half of the 1920s with sheer mass and publicity, but the majority of films produced in Austria at the time were still literary adaptations, romantic tales and socially critical melodramas. Neoclassical writer Franz Grillparzer remained a popular source in Austrian and Austrian/German co-productions with *Die Jüdin von Toledo*/The Jewess of Toledo (1919), the aforementioned *Die Ahnfrau*/The Medium (1919), and *Das Kloster bei Sandomir*/The Convent at Sandomir (1919). The 1922 film of Grillparzer's *Die Beichte eines Mönchs*/The Confession of a Monk managed to stylistically straddle the Austrian monumental epic and German expressionist film. Giant sets contrasting with intimate scenes, atmospheric and near-abstract lighting, unique costumes designed by Remigius Geyling all led the wave of semi–expressionism (it was less strictly stylized than its German counterpart) in Austrian cinema. Literary works by Romantic and Poetic Realist authors were employed to expand this new stylistic synthesis. Most popular was the work of E. T. A. Hoffmann, whose writings provided the basis for Hugo Held's *Elixiere des Teufels*/Elixirs of the Devil (1920) and Josef Malina's *Hoffmanns Erzählungen*/The Tales of Hoffmann (1923). Films were based on novels and stories by Heine, Balzac, Dumas, Twain, Flaubert, Swift, and the Brothers Grimm, but often the themes of these writers were transferred into original scripts such as *Der Rebell*/The Revolutionary (1919) and *Die arge Nonne*/The Wicked Nun (1920). Despite the global popularity of the German *Caligari* film, true cinematic expressionism never took root in Austrian film, and only two works stand out as an attempt to bring "Caligarism"[50] to Vienna: an obvious reworking of the original in *Das Haus des Dr. Gaudeamus*/The House of Dr. Gaudeamus (1921), which also utilized other stylistic elements such as *Jugendstil* and Italian Futurism in its heady mixture, and Robert Wiene's *Orlacs Hände*/The Hands of Orlac (1925) with his *Caligari* star, German actor Conrad Veidt. Despite the monumental films, technological rather than stylistic experimentation was of greater interest to most Austrian filmmakers at this juncture. Beginning in 1921, attempts at color films by "Hnatek und Leyde" were shown in Vienna. Emil Leyde, who had directed the 1915 propaganda film *Das Kriegspatenkind*, offered tricolor (blue/green/red) films such as *Fatmes Erretung*/Fatme's Rescue (1922), written and directed by Hans Marschall, and *Fiat Lux* (1923), directed by Wilhelm Thiele. In 1924 Leyde founded Leyde-Buntfilm (Leyde Color Film) in Vienna, to continue the development of color motion pictures, but the failed enterprise shut down in 1926 and Leyde returned to his native Germany in 1927.

Biographical dramas about figures from Austria's long imperial history also provided satisfying entertainment for a new republic attempting to locate national identity. Eighteenth-century flourish was represented by Wolfgang Amadeus Mozart in *Mozarts Leben, Lieben und Leiden*/The Life, Loves and Sufferings of Mozart (1921), directed by Otto Kreisler. But the most popular era by far was the post–Napoleonic Biedermeier (1815–48), which offered escapism from the economic crisis with its images of a stable and orderly Old Austria and its impressive mix of nineteenth-century heroes, legends and myths: *Der Graf von Cagliostro*/The Count of Cagliostro (1920), *Beethoven* (1927), *Ein Walzer von Strauss*/A Waltz by Strauss (1925), and *Vater Radetzky*/Father Radetzky (1929). These period films helped develop the field of film costume design by such artists as *Cagliostro*'s "discovery," Oskar Freidrich Werndorff (1886?–1938), who became a noted costume and set creator in Vienna and later in New York.[51] Beyond the biopics, general historical epics also figured heavily in the production output of the early 1920s. Arthur Schnitzler's *Der junge Medardus*/The Young Medardus (1923), Kertész's non-biblical monumental film with Karl Lamac and Anny Hornik, featured two set designers, Julius von Borsody and Artur Berger, who recreated war-torn Vienna during Napoleon's occupation. But Schnitzler was not the only contemporary author who enjoyed cinematic treatment. There was also Alfred Deutsch-German's *Alte Zeit-Neue Zeit*/Old Times–New Times (1919) and *Oh, du lieber Augustin*/Oh, You Dear Augustin (1922), based on the novel by H. K. Breslauer. The brother of Filmbund president Heinz Hanus, Emmerich Hanus (1889–1956), directed two Astoria Film productions —*Erde*/Earth (1920) and *Glaube und Heimat*/Faith and Homeland (1921)— based on dramas by Austrian playwright Karl Schönherr (1867–1943) and also scripted by the author. Both films utilized the actors of the Exl-Bühne and were made on location in the Tyrol and in the Zillertal. The Exl-Bühne, a Tyrolean theater company, was formed as an amateur group in 1902 and originally specialized in peasant plays. By 1910, they had assumed a high level of professionalism and gave their productions an authentic quality the traditional theaters could not replicate. Ultimately, the Exl-Bühne would come to represent the best aspects of the provincial *völkisch* (folk) culture in a dramatic world dominated by Viennese cosmopolitanism and would therefore continue to be popular under National Socialism after the Anschluss in 1938.[52] *Glaube und Heimat* also featured one of Austria's most important early cinematographers, Eduard Hoesch. Franz Kranewitter's drama, *Um Haus und Hof*/Around the House and Courtyard (1921), was directed by Eduard Köck, a leading figure in Tyrolian film into the 1950s.[53] The film was also shot in the Tyrol with members of the Exl-Bühne and produced by the regional Tiroler-Heimatfilm company.

Jewish historical and biographical topics were also an important aspect of the cinematic output. Otto Kreisler's *Theodor Herzl* (1921) featured both Rudolf and Josef Schildkraut, while *Ost und West*/East and West (1924), directed by Sidney M. Goldin, showcased future American Yiddish cinema and Hollywood character actress Molly Picon. Additionally, there was *Der Jude von Granada*/The Jew of Granada (1923), written by Felix Salten; *Jiskor* (1924), directed by Goldin; and *Der Fluch*/The Curse (1925), directed by Robert Land, written by Walter Reisch (who would script for Ernst Lubitsch and Billy Wilder in Hollywood) and featuring Hungarian (and later Hollywood character) actor Oskar Beregi and the English-born star of German film, Lilian Harvey. Two films based on novels by Hugo Bettauer (1872–1925) have become unique cinematic and sociopolitical documents. *Die Stadt ohne Juden*/A City Without Jews (1924), directed by H. K. Breslauer from a script he co-wrote with Ida Jenbach, featured Anny Milety, Hans Moser (Jean Julier, 1880–1964) in his second film role as the anti–Semitic official Volbert, and future Hollywood character actress Gisela Werbezierk. The film was not shown in Germany until after Bettauer's murder in 1925 by a young National Socialist. The film depicts a chilling foreshadow of the Holocaust, as various classes deal with the expulsion of Jews from the city of Utopia. Bettauer's novel was more direct, placing the action clearly in Vienna and subtitling the work, "a novel of tomorrow."[54]

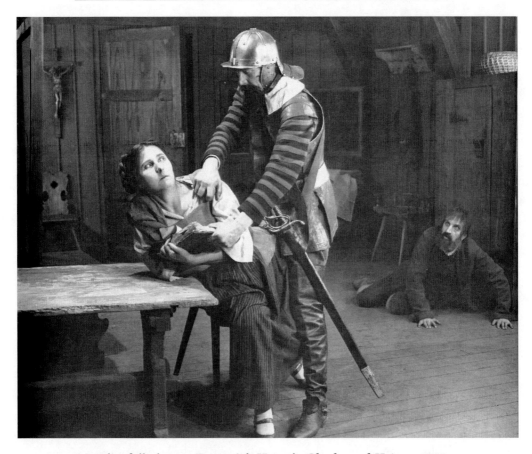

Moralist folk drama: Emmerich Hanus's *Glaube und Heimat*, 1921.

Die Stadt ohne Juden was considered lost until 1990, when a disintegrating nitrate print found in the Netherlands was restored by the Austrian Film Archive and shown at the Viennale Film Festival.[55] Bettauer's *Die freudlose Gasse*/The Joyless Street (1925) was directed by G. W. Pabst (1885–1967), a social-realist Austrian filmmaker who would find his greatest fame in German cinema. Echoing the early proletarian dramas of the Kolm/Fleck team, Pabst's look at poverty in inflation-ridden Vienna was filmed in a Berlin studio rather than on the city's streets, but it offered Greta Garbo, Asta Nielsen and Werner Krauss an early cinematic triumph. Comedy was the most neglected genre during the mid–1920s glut of American films, which provided enough Chaplin, Harold Lloyd, Laurel and Hardy, and others, for Austrian tastes, although there was still Kolowrat's homegrown team of Cocl und Seff.

Pabst was not the only Austrian director to gain fame in German cinema. Vienna-born Fritz Lang (1890–1976) began his career writing short stories and scripts while he recuperated from a war injury. These works were made into German silent features directed by Austrian director Joe May (1880–1954). By 1919, Lang had been hired by Erich Pommer, head of Decla-Bioskop Studios in Berlin.

His script of *Lilith und Ly*/Lilith and Ly was filmed by Erich Kober the same year. The story deals with a mystical Sanskrit manuscript and the creation of a dangerous artificial woman (a foreshadowing of the destructive robot Maria in Lang's 1928 *Metropolis*) that fit perfectly into the occult film fad. Paul Czinner (1890–1972), the husband and mentor of international film and stage star Elizabeth Bergner, also created Austrian film prior to his work in Germany and later for Korda in England. He considered the most important work of his Vienna period to be the 1919 *Inferno*, a film that offers the first images filmed on a moving camera, which Czinner built on a tricycle.

Following the Vita-Film board's accusations of Anton Kolm's overspending in the construction of a new studio complex in Vienna's Rosenhügel area and his subsequent death in 1922, Louise Kolm and Jakob Fleck disassociated themselves from the company and relocated to Berlin in 1923, where they married and continued to produce and direct as Jakob and Louise Fleck. Some of their German silents were made at Berlin's UFA studio, but most of their close to forty features between 1923 and 1933 were produced by the Hegewald-Film company owned by Liddy (aka Lydie) Hegewald, Germany's female silent film mogul. These films continued in the socially critical melodrama vein of the Kolm–Fleck Vienna productions, but Louise Fleck was sensitive to the changing tastes of the audiences and added a few operettas and imperial-era romances in the mix; "Viennese films that were so popular in Berlin."[56] Among these films was the Flecks' second version of *Der Pfarrer von Kirchfeld* in 1926 featuring a young German actor who was to become a major Hollywood director, Wilhelm (William) Dieterle. Also during this period, Louise's son Walter Kolm-Veltée completed his training as a sound engineer at another major Berlin studio, Tobis-Film. The new Vita-Film studio built by Anton and Louise Kolm opened without them in 1923, boasting the largest and most advanced soundstages in Central Europe. Unlike Kolowrat's involvement with American production to shore up his empire during the inflation, Vita-Film turned to France to "internationalize" its product and arranged for French-Austrian co-productions and several Vienna-filmed French projects. Among the French directors who created Austrian films for Vita were Germaine Dulac, Jean Legrand, Severin Mars, M. Liabel and Edouard-Emil Violet. Dulac's 1923 *Die sterbende Sonne*/The Dying Sun is considered a basis for her future work as a leading French surrealist. Additionally, the Vita-Film studio played host to Belgian director Jacques Feyder, who filmed Jules Romain's script *Das Bildnis*/The Portrait there in 1923. In 1924, France's most famous comic actor, Max Linder, reportedly a significant inspiration to Charlie Chaplin, shot *Der Zirkuskönig*/The Circus King with soon-to-be American film star Vilma Banky in Vienna. Linder's reputation as a difficult actor was supported by his tantrumlike appearances at the studio and the project was to be one of his final films. The unhappy Linder committed suicide with his wife at the end of the year. International co-production did little to solve the Austrian film crisis brought on by the wild inflation, but with the installation of a radio broadcasting center, the Vita-Film studio became home for another major technical advance which was to have as much of an influence on Austrian and German sociopolitics as the medium of film had.

Austria can claim three pioneers in animation during this period. Although the genre never played a significant role in the national cinema, early work did briefly influence European and American cartoonists. Ladislaus Tuszynski (1876–1943), Peter Eng, and Louis (or Luis) Seel experimented with animation techniques during the 1920s and with the combination of animation and live-action film. But the most uniquely Austrian cinema creation of the mid–1920s was the collaboration between film and a name synonymous with Old Vienna, its literature and opera: Hugo von Hofmannsthal (1874–1929). The author, librettist and essayist had shown a keen interest in film since the early silents and in 1921 published *"Der Ersatz für Träume"* (The Replacement for Dreams), one of the first essays in Austrian film theory. Von Hofmannsthal understood the popularity of the medium as a mass psychological phenomenon of dreamlike escape into darkness and silence from the boredom and misery of the daily urban existence. By 1924 he had scripted *Daniel Defoe* and *Lucidor*, neither of which were filmed. But it was his libretto for Richard Strauss's opera, *Der Rosenkavalier*/The Cavalier of the Rose that became one of the final grand-scale films of the silent era. His bittersweet romantic and comic intrigues among the nobility during the eighteenth-century reign of Empress Maria Theresia was produced in 1925 by Pan-Film and directed by Robert Wiene. The film boasted both location shooting at Schönbrunn Palace (the empress's beloved home) and lavish sets recreating rococo Vienna created by the director of set design for the Vienna Opera, artist Alfred Roller (1864–1936). Approximately ten thousand extras were used in the film, which starred an international cast: Michael Bohnen as Baron Ochs von Lerchenau, the boorish suitor to the young Sophie (Elly Felice Berger), who is desired by the "Cavalier of the Rose," Octavian (Jacques Catelain), the young lover of the beautiful wife of the Field Marshall (Huguette Duflos). Von Hofmannsthal soon disassociated himself from the project, regarding it to be an "extremely amateurish and clumsy film."[57] Nonetheless, the film's lavish visuals were both critically and popularly triumphant, and Pan-Film planned on an American tour of the film with composer Richard Strauss conducting a large accompanying orchestra. But the introduction of sound film in 1927 removed any further interest in the project.

Der Rosenkavalier had an equally sumptuous rival in 1925, the Austrian-French co-production of Gustav Flaubert's *Salammbo*. This last of the grand Sascha-Film productions was filmed in Vienna studios with a partial French crew and starred French actress Jeanne de Balzac in the title role. Also filmed with a "cast of thousands," the Punic War–era costumes were designed by Remigius Geyling. This exotic epic of slaves, courtesans, and military camps premiered in Paris in October 1925 with a music score by French composer Florent Schmitt, a colleague of Maurice Ravel who specialized in the trendy Orientalia. In 1929, Austrian composer Arnold Schönberg (1874–1951) created alternate music for the production, but it has instead entered the concert repertoire without ever having been used for the film.

Two large-scale attempts at dealing with the more recent Austrian past were attempted in 1925. *Oberst Redl*/Colonel Redl, directed by Hans Otto Löwenstein

Austrian rococo and the high art silent film: Robert Wiene's *Der Rosenkavalier*, 1926.

(1881–1931), presented the story of the homosexual Austrian army officer Redl (Robert Valberg), who was blackmailed into spying for the Russians during the Great War and who subsequently was compelled by his superiors to commit suicide to save the empire embarrassment. It was the first of many international versions of the story, which was eventually turned into a successful English stage play, *A Patriot for Me* by John Osborn and the 1985 film *Oberst Redl*/Colonel Redl, by Hungarian director István Szabó. Löwenstein also capitalized on the nostalgia for the imperial past with *Das Geheimnis des Leibfiakers Bratfisch*/Royal Coachman Bratfisch's Secret (1925), which reworked the details of the mysterious death of Austrian Crown Prince Rudolf and his mistress, Baroness Marie Vetsera, at Mayerling in 1889. The director had previously attempted to bring the scandal to the screen in 1919 in *Mayerling*, but the film was banned after a group of monarchist aristocrats campaigned against it. The new film included scenes from his abandoned 1919 effort. These were not the only films dealing with the monarchical past. Löwenstein had previously offered the stories of Napoleon's doomed young son in *Der Herzog von Reichstadt*/The Duke of Reichstadt (1920), scandals of the Serbian crown in *Königin Draga*/Queen Draga (1920) and Austria-Hungary's last monarch in *Kaiser*

Karl/Emperor Charles (1921). Otto Kreisler, who had previously brought Mozart and Herzl to the screen, filmed the mysterious life and death of Bavaria's most memorable king in *Ludwig II* in 1922. By 1928, Löwenstein had gained a reputation as a director of historical costume epics, and he remade Louise and Anton Kolm's 1915 *Der Traum eines österreichischen Reservisten*/The Dream of an Austrian Reservist, which launched a Great War genre in film analogous to the popular war and imperial collapse novels of the era. Max Neufeld (1887–1967) gave a more critical view of that world in *Die Brandstifter Europas*/The Arsonists of Europe (1926), and finally a royal rejection of the past in favor of the Jazz Age was delivered with *Seine Hoheit der Eintänzer*/His Highness the Slave (1926), in which the sociopolitical anxieties of the 1920s are mixed into a blending of romantic and criminal genres. Directed by Karl Leiter and written by Walter Reisch, the film traces the scandalous misadventures of several members of a fictionalized Austrian dynasty and other noble families sent into exile in 1918, as they reemerge in a world where money and sex are overt tools of power. Two of the final silent films to be made in Austria looked back into the Habsburg past as a world of open possibilities, at least in the realm of love: Max Neufeld's *Erzherzog Johann*/Archduke Johann (1929) lavishly dramatized the popular tale of the Habsburg Prince's (Igo Sym) love for and marriage to the commoner Anna Plochl (Xenia Desni), and *Erzherzog Otto und das Wäschermädl*/Archduke Otto and the Laundress (1930), which trivializes a similar misalliance.

While Vienna became the undisputed film metropole for the Austrian Republic after 1918, there were small regional production companies that deserve recognition for their contribution to the development of the Austrian silent film. Between 1919 and 1924, Alpin-Film, Opern-Film and Mitropa-Musikfilm were established in Graz. The Tiroler-Heimatfilm was founded in Innsbruck and Salzburger-Kunstfilm emerged in Salzburg. The most experimental of these regional studios was the Mitropa-Musikfilm, which produced three pictures in 1921, all directed by Ludwig Loibner.[58] Of these three, *Die schöne Müllerin*/The Fair Maid of the Mill, from the song cycle by Franz Schubert, and *Czaty*, based on a ballad written by Polish national poet Adam Mickiewicz, required vocal accompaniment at screenings. *Czaty* is also known for its accomplished emulation of Romantic style painting in its images of castle chambers, forests and moonlit glades. Bruno Lötsch offered Styria's contribution to Austrian film in the form of a documentary series, *Steirischen Filmjournal*/Styrian Film Journal (1920). The first documentary of the Salzburg Festival, *Die Festspiele*, was produced by the Salzburg-Kunstfilm in 1921, and it included scenes from the now traditional performance of Hugo von Hofmannsthal's *Jedermann*/Everyman, featuring German-language film and theater stars Alexander Moissi, Werner Krauss and Hedwig Bleibtreu. Additionally, the firm offered the drama *Die Tragödie des Carlo Pinetti*/The Tragedy of Carlo Pinetti, which starred Alphons Fryland and was shot in Salzburg in 1924.[59]

Although the runaway inflation had abated somewhat after 1925, poverty and questions regarding national identity still dominated the embattled First Republic. The final phase of the silent era once again belonged to the social-critical films, in the particular blend of realism and diluted expressionism that could only be found in Austrian cinema. The titles speak for themselves: *Haifische der Nachkriegszeit*/Sharks of the Postwar Era (1925), *Sacco und Vanzetti* (1927), *Gefährdete Mädchen*/Endangered Girls (1928), and *Eine Dirne ist ermordet worden*/A Whore Was Murdered (1930). Heinz Hanus's *Frauen aus der Wiener Vorstadt*/Women of Vienna's Suburbs (1925) was subtitled *Fünfzehn Jahre schweren Kerker*/Fifteen Years at Hard Labor and presents an unyielding dramatization of the abuse of working-class women. After a foray into lighter fare with Alexander Girardi and music by Franz Lehár in the 1927 feature *Der Rastlbinder*/The Tinker, which he wrote and directed with Arthur Gottlein and Maurice Armand Mondet, Hanus returned to social drama. His *Andere Frauen*/Other Women (1928), which deals with lesbianism, might also be counted as among the most accomplished of a particular subgenre, the "enlightenment" film. These works blend documentary information with exploitation melodrama and range in subject matter from hereditary illness in the early Kunstfilm production of *Die Geisel der Menschheit*/The Hostage of Mankind (1918) to *Alkohol, Sexualität und Kriminaliät*/Alcohol, Sexuality and Criminality; *Wie sag' ichs meinem Kinde?*/How Do I Tell My Child?; *Die Tuberkulose*/Tuberculosis; *Moderne Laster (Narkotika)*/Modern Vice (Narcotics); and *Was ist Liebe?*/What Is Love? All of these were directed by Dr. Leopold Niernberger (1884–1940) between 1920 and 1924. But it was Hans Otto Löwenstein who created the most controversial film of the genre by taking on the illegal act of abortion in *Paragraph 144* (1924). Films that simply exploited nudity and sexuality also appeared, such as *Irrlichter der Tiefe*/Will-o-the-Wisp (1923) and *Tänze des Grauens und des Lasters und der Ekstase*/Dances of Horror, Vice and Ecstasy (1923), which featured performer Anita Berber who often danced partially clothed or completely nude on the cabaret stages of Berlin and Vienna, and who expired from excessive drug and alcohol abuse at age thirty. Even more exploitative versions of the "enlightenment" drama appeared a few years later. They were imported from Germany where the style had been successful, but only a few of these, such as *Vom Freudenhaus in die Ehe*/From the Bordello into Marriage (1927) and *Eros in Ketten*/Eros in Chains (1930), would be produced in Austria. Löwenstein moved back into narrative film but continued with erotic terror in *Landru, der Blaubart von Paris*/Landru, The Bluebeard of Paris (1923), a sexploitation film that is noteworthy for having been co-written by a woman, Rosa Wachtel (1900–?). Like Ida Jenbach, the co-writer of *Die Stadt ohne Juden*, Wachtel began her career as a journalist and film critic and ultimately scripted eleven Austrian films between 1921 and 1929 for such directors as Josef W. Beyer, Max Neufeld, and Robert Wohlmut. In 1929, Fritz Weiss directed *Vagabund*/Vagabond, a look at the condition of the homeless tramp in contemporary society, which mixed documentary and fiction in a style that foreshadowed Italian neorealism of the late 1940s and furthered the art of montage technique influenced by early Soviet film and German expressionism.

Not all films dealing with contemporary urban dysfunction were forays into vice, poverty and disease, or were sensationalist "B" films. In 1927, Sascha Kolowrat offered a sophisticated look at the new morality and sexual freedom brought on by

Modern sophistician and anxiety: Willi Forst and Marlene Dietrich in Gustav Ucicky's *Café Elektric,* **1927.**

the Jazz Age with his *Café Elektric* (subtitled: "When a Woman Loses Her Way"), directed by Gustav Ucicky. It stars two extraordinary Kolowrat discoveries: Willi Forst as the small-time gigolo and Marlene Dietrich as the "lost woman." The already dapper Willi Forst would become one of Austria's great romantic leads and its leading film director during the 1930s and 1940s, while Dietrich shows signs of the seductive physicality that was to make her an international sensation in Austrian director Josef von Sternberg's *Der blaue Engel*/The Blue Angel (Germany 1930), Germany's first sound production. This sophisticated contemporary drama was not the first to feature Kolowrat's female discoveries. His 1925 film *Das Spielzeug von Paris*/The Toy from Paris introduced a new French actress named Lily Damita. In 1926, she appeared in Kolowrat's Austrian-German co-production of *Fiaker Nr. 13*/Coach No. 13. While many filmmakers had fled the industry crisis to studios in Berlin, London and Hollywood, Kolowrat remained in Austria to create expensive and large-scale productions. In 1927 he produced *Die Pratermizzi*/Mizzi of the Prater, which he hoped would become a success due to the film's traditional Viennese tale and the all-star technical talents: Gustav Ucicky directed from a script by Walter Reisch; Eduard von Borsody was cinematographer; Karl Hartl, the future head of Austria's Wien-Film company, was assistant director; and the team of Artur Berger and Emil Stepanek created the impressive sets. The film had proven to be one of Kolowrat's most difficult productions due to the excessive drinking habits and temperamental displays of its central performer, American silent-screen siren Nita Naldi.[60] It was also Kolowrat's final production. He died of cancer at age 42 on December 4, 1927, and seemed to take the silent era in Austria with him.

The flow of Austrian film talent to Berlin and, most important, Hollywood was something that was already evident and promised to influence the state of international co-productions by the end of the silent era. One might even speak of diasporic Austrian film in Berlin, London and Hollywood, which utilized many Austrian actors and technicians but also provided work for such directors, writers and producers as Josef von Sternberg, Fritz Lang, Erich von Stroheim, Paul Czinner, Carl Mayer, G. W. Pabst, Mihály Kertész, Karl Hartl, Gustav Ucicky, Alexander Korda, Jakob and Louise Fleck, Fred Zinnemann, Joe May and Billy Wilder. But Austrian film, which had only partially recovered from the inflation crisis, and had to deal with a brain drain of its cinema talents, political instability, and the world economic depression brought on by the 1929 American stock market crash, was met with yet another blow. As early as 1928, the new American "talkies" were being screened in Vienna, but Austria would only slowly create its own sound features. Austria's last silent picture appeared as late as 1930: *Die Tat des Andreas Harmer*/The Deed of Andreas Harmer, a crime drama featuring a police dog, Lux (similar to Rin Tin Tin), written and directed by Alfred Deutsch-German. Unlike American and other European cinemas, Austrian theaters continued to show silent films into the mid–1930s. Although production had greatly declined, Austrian film talent continued to hold world recognition, but often for their work outside Austria. A new Viennese cinematic style would refocus international attention on this national cinema, following yet another crisis in its film industry during the early era of sound.

2

Sound and Diverging Visions: 1929–1938

The Viennese Film; Hollywood Beckons;
Two Industries; Fading Freedoms

The development of sound film in Austria was immediately met by two opposing forces: a moderate upswing in Austrian film production and the sudden world economic crisis led by the American stock market crash of 1929. The first German-language sound film experiments were previewed in Vienna as early as 1928. These were, like the very early silents, short non-narrative clips of trains in motion, political speeches, singers vocalizing, factories at work, and were created by the German Tri-Ergon firm, which utilized an early sound-to-film transfer known as the Lichttonsystem (Light-Sound System). That same year, director Hans Otto Löwenstein premiered his Ottoton format, a synchronized phonograph recording system he named after himself, with his short film *G'schichten aus der Steiermark*/Stories from Styria, which he created in four days. It was shown in June at Vienna's palatial theater of popular culture, the Urania. Its success encouraged Löwenstein to return to the Listo-Film studio to expand the film into a feature-length sound production, which premiered in September 1929.[1] By that time, the Americans had won the international race to create "talkies" with Alan Gorland's synchronized phonograph sound feature, *The Jazz Singer* (USA 1927). This partial sound sensation had had gained immediate international acclaim upon its premiere in October 1927 and beat Löwenstein's feature-length revision of his sound short to Vienna's Central-Kino theater by several months.

The hesitation in Austrian sound film production was primarily due to the instability of the slowly recovering film industry, which caused Viennese studios to lag two years behind other European film companies. Producers were simply unable to commit to such an expensive new technology. Studios had to be freshly equipped, directors and actors had to understand the new medium, and the various systems simply did not allow for an easy choice. Just as Löwenstein was presenting it, the synchronized phonograph had been surpassed by sound transfer systems, but use

41

of these was hampered by foreign control and disputed patent cases. Ironically, Austria had created one of the first sound transfer processes in the world. Between 1905 and 1913, Heinrich Stefan Peschka developed such a system but failed to convince filmmakers of its value. The Austrian brand of sound-to-film transfer, the Selenophon system, had been in development since the mid–1920s by the Vienna Selen Research Company, which included Oskar Czeija, Paul Bellac, Otmar Hampel and Leopold Richter.[2] Selenophon was on its way to international utilization alongside the American Western Electric and the German Tobis-Klangfilm processes when the 1938 German Anschluss ended Austria's sound system presence in cinema.

It was not until 1930, however, that an Austrian studio, Schönbrunn-Film, was actually adapted for Selenophon sound production. By this time, the world economic depression had made investment in Austrian film production difficult and the refitting of studios for sound production became nearly prohibitive. Theaters only hesitantly decided to invest in the expense of sound projection conversion. Sascha-Film managed to convert and produce the first Austrian sound transfer feature film in co-production with the German firm of Fellner and Somlo. *Geld auf der Strasse*/Money on the Street (1930) was directed by Georg Jacoby (1882–1964), who had helmed a war propaganda film about Austria-Hungary's ally Bulgaria, *Bogdan Stimoff* (1916), and assisted Löwenstein in the making of the controversial abortion film *Paragraph 144* in 1924. Sound film, however, meant an increase in production costs by approximately 300 percent. This contributed to the shuttering of the remaining small and medium-size companies that could not afford conversion and caused production (most films continued to be silent) to decline by half of the previous year's releases. In 1931 sound finally surpassed silent production in Austria, but the latter did not completely cease until 1933.

The fate of Sascha-Film was indicative of the future of the entire Austrian film industry in the 1930s. Having lost its artistic and financial leader, Sascha Kolowrat, in 1927, it was floundering both economically and creatively through the depression, the new sound technology, and ever-rising production costs. By the end of 1931, a consortium made up of the Austrian Pilzer Group (the brothers Oskar, Kurt, Severin, and Victor Pilzer) underwrote the studio. A switch from the Austrian Selenophon sound system to the German Tobis-Klangfilm was immediately undertaken to make the Sascha productions more appealing to the German market. This resulted in substantial German Tobis investment and subsequently changed the name of the company to Tobis-Sascha-Film. In 1933, the Vita-Film Studio at Rosenhügel was bought by the renamed company and was adapted to sound production, but this move did not halt the slow demise of the firm as a production company. Between 1934 and 1938, it leased out its studio facilities to other firms and ultimately moved into the business of releasing and distributing films rather than making them. Nonetheless, two of Tobis-Sascha's final productions, plotted out by the Hungarian-born Felix Salten (1869–1945), who would script his novel *Bambi* into an animation classic in Hollywood in 1942, are to be counted among the classics of the era: *Maskerade* (1934), which will be examined in the section dealing with the Viennese Film genre; and *Hohe Schule*/Haute École (1934), directed

by Erich Engel (1891–1966), scripted by Josef Than and Albrecht Joseph from the
screen treatment by Alexander Lernet-Holenia, and featuring Paul von Hernried,
who would become Hollywood's wartime leading man, Paul Henreid. The film
credits Heinrich Oberländer rather than Josef Than as the co-writer, but, according to a 1975 West German interview with Than, this was only camouflage designed
to meet Germany's racial laws (following Hitler's election as German Chancellor
in 1933) for export purposes. These laws forbade the presence of Jewish artists in
German arts and culture. It is important to understand that the German investment and involvement that saved Sascha-Film and much of the Austrian film industry in the early 1930s, and might have strengthened both cinemas to certain
European dominance, instead damaged Austrian cinema after German firms were
nationalized and "aryanized" by the Nazi regime from 1933 onward.

The early short sound films, like the early silents, made use of the audience's
fascination with the new medium and managed to entertain without offering
significant cinematic art. Filmed comedy sketches such as *In der Theateragentur*/In
the Theatrical Agency (1930); the one-act stage play *In Ewigkeit, Amen*/Forever in
Peace, Amen (1930); and even a reading by the former opponent of the industry,
Karl Kraus, editor of the famed critical journal *Die Fackel* (The Torch) was filmed
with sound in 1934. Director Arthur Gottlein (1895–1977), who had worked with
Heinz Hanus on his silent films, collaborated with Viennese cabaret star and writer
Karl Farkas on *Justizmaschine*/Justice Machine (1931), *Unter den Dächern von
Wien*/Under the Roofs of Vienna (1931) (referencing French director René Clair's
1930 *Under the Roofs of Paris*), and *Lampel weiß alles*/Lampel Knows It All (1932).
Farkas continued by scripting the feature romantic comedy *Sehnsucht 202*/Longing
202 (1932) with Emmerich Pressburger. The film was directed by Max Neufeld,
produced by one of the few new sound production companies, Allianz Filmfab-
rikation, and featured Magda Schneider, Hans Thimig and Attila Hörbiger
(1896–1987), the dramatic half of the two Hörbiger brothers who would become
Austria's greatest male film stars for over twenty years beginning in the 1930s. Farkas
followed this project with another feature romance, *Abenteuer am Lido*/Adventure
on the Lido (1933), for Pan-Film, which was directed by Richard Oswald and
included music by future Hollywood film composers Walter Jurmann and Bronislaw Kaper. The film showcases Alfred Piccaver, Annie Rosar, Hungarian character
actor Szöke Sakall (1882–1955); later Hollywood's S. K. "Cuddles" Sakall, and Nora
Gregor. Gregor (1901–49), who also made films in Hollywood and France, and pre-
dated Grace Kelly in abandoning her film career for a "royal" marriage with Prince
Ernst Rüdiger von Starhemberg (1899–1956), a paramilitary leader and vice chancellor in Austria's clerico-authoritarian regime of the mid–1930s. Their son, Heinrich Starhemberg (a.k.a. Henry Gregor, 1934–97) would gain attention as a writer
and dramatist in Spain and South America in the 1970s and 1980s and as an infre-
quent stage and screen actor in Austria. Farkas and his collaborator Fritz Grünbaum, who had also worked as a film writer and actor in Germany until the Nazi
regime deported him as a Jewish "undesirable" in 1933, created a comic serial entitled *Metro Grünbaum — Farkas tönende Wochenschau*/Metro Grünbaum — Farkas's

Talking Newsreel as a parodic jab at the bombast of Hollywood imports. Farkas departed Austria at the Anschluss in 1938, and after working in France and in the United States (on Broadway and in Hollywood), returned to Austrian film in 1946. Grünbaum unfortunately remained in Vienna and was deported to Buchenwald concentration camp by the Nazis, where he is reported to have died in 1940.[3]

The employment of motion pictures for political campaigning was in full swing by the early 1930s, and it was the Social Democratic Party that made the most effective use of the new medium. There had been several workers' films during the silent era, which had advertised various leftist movements and culminated with the 1930 silent film directed by Frank Ward Rossak, *Das Notitzbuch des Mr. Pim*/Mr. Pim's Trip to Europe. This anti-capitalist comedy, strongly influenced by the 1924 Soviet silent directed by Lev Kuleshov, *The Extraordinary Adventure of Mr. West in the Land of the Bolsheviks,* tells the story of a conservative American who arrives in Vienna to discover his daughter has fallen in love with a socialist. This conflict precipitates the American's exploration of the progressive and humanistic "Red Vienna," which dispels his prejudices. Ultimately, he approves of his daughter's marriage to the young socialist, and comes out in favor of socialism. An animated film was also created to serve Social Democratic propaganda — the silent *Die Abenteuer des Herrn Antimarx*/The Adventures of Mr. Anti-Marx (1930). By 1926, the Social Democratic government of Vienna had established its own film association, the Kinobetriebsgesellschaft, known as Kiba, which, in addition to its attempt to improve the film industry along socialist lines, produced and distributed films and acquired theaters.

The move towards, sound had only exacerbated the impoverished state of the Austrian film industry in the Central European economic strife that followed the U.S. stock market crash. The Hollywood industry utilized this crisis to increase its presence in Austrian cinemas. But its films and filmmakers did not appear without controversy. Charlie Chaplin came to Vienna in March 1931 for the premiere of his new feature *City Lights* and blatantly attacked sound in favor of the silent film in newspaper interviews. Earlier that year, *All Quiet on the Western Front*, the 1930 sound film directed by Louis Milestone and based on the antiwar novel by German author Erich Maria Remarque, received its Vienna premiere at the Apollo Kino, a Social Democratic Kiba theater. Due to the obvious anti–Central Powers propaganda of the work, various political groups, as well as Defense Minister Carl Vaugoin, had attempted to have the book banned in Austria since 1929. The film's premiere and subsequent screenings were met with protests and disturbances from the conservative Christian Social party and the more right-wing paramilitary *Heimwehr* militia, as well as from the Austrian National Socialists. Another Hollywood connection began in Vienna in 1931: Otto Preminger's (Otto Ludwig Preminger, 1906–86) first directorial effort, *Die große Liebe*/The Great Love, with Hansi Niese, Attila Hörbiger and Betty Bird, placed him in the roster of talented young filmmakers who would have to prove they could repeat their first successes. Preminger would certainly manage to do that, albeit abroad. His single Austrian film is a fable of second chances but it manages to movingly articulate the economic hardships, unemployment and social inequities of the First Republic. A prisoner of war returns to a gray and enervated Vienna ten years after the end of the empire. His mother, whom he mistakenly believes is long dead, has never given up hope for her son's return and finds him by accident. She attempts to buy him a future as a taxi owner through financial deceit, but her son finds love and the mother's deed is resolved with an incongruous happy ending. The web of subplots and the interaction of different social spheres typical for Preminger's American films are already present here.

Nothing during this period, however, can compare with the unique blend of futuristic science fiction and party politics that is the 1932 Social Democratic film *Die vom 17er Haus*/Those of the 17th House. Written by Siegfried Bernfeld and Artur Berger, designed by Emil Stepanek and Artur Berger, and directed by Berger, it depicts Vienna in the year 2032 with spectacular model sets (the symbol of Vienna, the gothic St. Stephan's Cathedral, is engulfed by Bauhaus-style steel and glass skyscrapers), futuristic costumes and what are ostensibly computer monitors. Although the film evokes a more rational future than its obvious influence, Fritz Lang's *Metropolis*, its plot is far less complex and more overtly political: in answering a request from China, an archivist explains the "historical" developments in Austria to his grandson. The film's alternate past suggests a civil war between the political camps as well as terrorism by the Austrian National Socialists, but a typical class-conflicted love story allows for a happy ending and a future firmly grounded in socialism. The Social Democratic mayor of Vienna appears at the conclusion of the film, encouraging the audience to vote for his party. The unique and successful Social Democratic program of erecting city-run apartment complexes (the famed Karl Marx Hof among them) for the workers notwithstanding, one questions why the claustrophobic and regimented skyline of the film should appeal to the working class. One answer might be that the images of such a futuristic Vienna would blot out nearly all that is old and elitist — the buildings, monuments, and landmarks associated with the aristocratic or imperial (read: reactionary) past.

The early 1930s saw the brief but potent emergence of Austrian film and theater pioneer Leontine Sagan, who is often mistaken as German because of her landmark film, *Mädchen in Uniform*/Girls in Uniform (Germany 1931). Born Leontine Schlesinger in Vienna in 1889, she began her career as an actress under the auspices of theater director Max Reinhardt. Sagan soon defied the male-dominated world of theater with her work as a stage director in Austria and Germany in the 1920s. After promoting several female dramatists, Sagan decided to base a film on the drama *Gestern und Heute* (Yesterday and Today) by German playwright Christa Winsloe, which had already gained notoriety for its all-female cast. Sagan adapted the stage work into her 1931 film, which she directed in Germany. In addition to the female cast, it was also the first German-language film to be produced cooperatively, whereby those involved with the production obtained shares in the film rather than a salary. The obvious financial and creative empowerment of the female performers and crew as co-owners of the film should rank as a unique and progressive development in international film production history, but its revolutionary value has largely been forgotten.

Sagan's *Mädchen in Uniform* is remarkable on an ideological level as well. The story, which takes place in an aristocratic girls' boarding school, parodies Prussian military values and male social constructs. The result is not only a criticism of these aspects in German and Austrian culture but also a criticism of the displacement of women, their lack of identity, and their problematic self-definition along male norms. In her 1979 study *Sexual Stratagems*, Nancy Scholar considers the film all the more remarkable "when we consider the historical context in which it appeared":

> By 1931, Hitler was in the ascendancy.... In this milieu, Sagan's film appeared overtly anti-nationalistic, anti–Prussian, anti-authoritarian, and surprisingly, a separate ending, which was pro-fascist, was shown in Germany, and eventually Goebbels had the film banned as unhealthy.... The film departs radically from convention in its open presentation of the possibilities of love between two women.[4]

Perhaps the film's most fascinating aspect is the humanist nonconformism of the teacher, Fräulein von Bernburg (Dorothea Wieck), who rejects the notion of being a male manqué to her female charges. The value of nurturing over a regimented sense of discipline and the "difference" of the female persona as a desirable human condition is a protofeminist statement that remains provocative even today. The subsequent censorship of the film ultimately forced the director and her crew to leave Germany, but in 1932, Sagan was asked by Austrian silent film director Alexander Korda, then based in London, to direct *Men of Tomorrow* in England. Sagan also eventually edited the film, which was intended as a star vehicle for Merle Oberon, Korda's protégée. It was a box-office failure, but Sagan's maverick work precipitated a call in 1934 from Hollywood producer David O. Selznick. Unfortunately, a possible Hollywood practice of importing female film directors, patterned after the cultivation of such expatriate female actors as Greta Garbo, Marlene Dietrich, Luise Rainer and the Austrian Elisabeth Bergner, did not materialize. With the Selznick call failing to develop into a serious offer, Sagan moved to South Africa with her husband in 1939, returned to theater direction and co-founded the National Theater of Johannesburg, with which she was still associated at her death in 1974. She returned to film only once and in a minor capacity in George King's collaborative musical *Showtime* (GB 1946).[5]

Motion picture study and training also gained a respectable foothold in Austria during this time. In 1933, the Lehrinstitut für Tonfilmkunst (Instructional Institute for the Art of Sound Film) was founded in a former silent picture studio housed in a large *Jugendstil* building on the Bauernmarkt in Vienna's first district. The building would later be used during the Wien-Film era as a secondary studio site and in 1946 as the home for the first new Austrian studio in the postwar era, Belvedere-Film. The film institute offered courses in film dramaturgy, film acting, vocal technique, and sound film direction taught by several important names of the period: among them were Artur Berger, Heinz Hanus, Karl Farkas, Franz Herterich and

Hans Theyer. Even the German-Hollywood director Ernst Lubitsch was known to have given guest lectures and taught a few courses. Despite its detractors, sound film had become the medium of the day, and the seminars on sound film performance and production were filled to capacity. Even Arthur Schnitzler, who had often missed opportunities to bring his work to the Austrian screen in the silent era, now attempted to have various texts filmed with sound. In 1930, he reworked his 1926 *Traumnovelle* (Dream Story) for a possible sound film under the direction of G. W. Pabst. The project remained unrealized, but the work would finally receive a controversial adaptation at the end of the century in Stanley Kubrick's final film, *Eyes Wide Shut* (GB 1999). Schnitzler's novella, *Spiel im Morgengrauen* (Game at Dawn) was adapted for an American sound film, *Daybreak* (1931), which was directed by Jacques Feyder. Following Schnitzler's death in 1931, Max Ophüls brought the author's famed *Liebelei* to the German sound screen with Austrian stars Luise Ullrich, Willy Eichberger and Paul Hörbiger, but the 1933 release, which might have been a major success in the German-language realm, was doomed because of political realities. Hitler's racist laws meant that work by both Ophüls and Schnitzler was banned. An Austrian-Czechoslovakian co-production also made headlines that year: *Ekstase—Symphonie der Liebe/Ecstasy—Symphony of Love*, directed by Gustav Machaty, might have been praised for its experimentally abstract film vocabulary and symbolic plot, but it was the nude scenes by the young Austrian actress Hedwig Kiesler, later Hollywood's Hedy Lamarr (1913–2000), that made it a sensation. Henry Miller compared Machaty's film with the experimental literary work of D. H. Lawrence, and Machaty followed this cinematic provocation with one of the great visually stylized films of the era, *Nocturno* (1934), which blends an elegant Art Deco sensibility and minimalism into startling compositions that have been inexplicably forgotten by film artists and theorists. No less controversial than *Ekstase*, *Nocturno*'s tale of a woman who finds sexual fulfillment and luxury far from the confines of her lower-class marriage and family dared to suggest that female sexual desire was repressed by a male dominated society and that money can indeed triumph over love.[6]

Since live orchestras were no longer needed to accompany films, they were overused on screen in the new genre of the musical. Austrian cinema once again managed to cultivate world-class talents, this time with vocalists borrowed from its formidable opera and operetta stages, cabarets and concert halls: Jarmila Novotna, Maria Jeritza, Joseph Schmidt, Adele Kern, Jan Kiepura, and Marta Eggerth were among those who gained instant fame as musical motion picture stars. Films such as Wilhelm Thiele's *Grossfürstin Alexandra/Crown Princess Alexandra* (1933), with music by Franz Lehár and featuring Maria Jeritza, Joseph Schmidt, and Leo Slezak, and Paul Fejos's *Frühlingsstimmen/Voices of Spring* (1933), with music by operetta composer Oskar Straus, began a second career for many singers and operetta composers. Despite the popularity of these films, the other important Austrian genre, the social-critical drama, was not neglected in early sound production. The economic crisis and unemployment found resonance in Hans Steinhoff's *Scampolo* (1932) with Dolly Haas and Paul Hörbiger. Billy Wilder (credited as *Billie* Wilder,

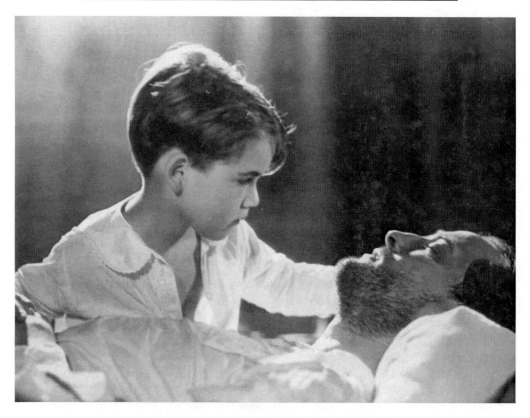

The victims of materialism: Gustav Machaty's *Nocturno*, 1934.

a.k.a. Samuel Wilder, 1906–2002) authored the script for the film and for the following Steinhoff comedy (also with music by Walter Jurmann and Bronislaw Kaper)
named *Madame wünscht sich keine Kinder*/Madame Does Not Prefer Children
(1932), a vehicle for Austria's original movie star, Liane Haid. Wilder's unique iconoclastic Hollywood style is already obvious in *Scampolo*, because his comedy dared
to attack party politics, racism and political oppression with witty, double enten-
dre–laden dialogue. Following these two films, Wilder, who had been born in imperial Austro-Poland and originally worked as a journalist in Vienna, moved to Berlin
productions and ultimately to Hollywood. Another specific Austrian genre of the
period utilizing the new sound technology was the musical melodrama of the small
town or the old Vienna suburb in *Das Lerchel vom Wienerwald*/The Little Lark of
the Vienna Woods (1931), *Wiener Zauberklänge*/Magical Viennese Sounds (1931),
Lang ist es her/It's Been a Long Time (1932), and *Das Glück von Grinzing*/The Happiness of Grinzing (1933). The titles of these films clearly suggest their sentimental and nostalgic content.

   Crime and historical drama also gained some box-office attention in early
sound. Notable are the proto-noir *Der Hexer*/The Sorcerer (1932), based on a text
by Edgar Wallace and directed by Paul Lamac, and *Unsichtbare Gegner*/Invisible
Adversaries (1933) directed by Rudolf Katscher (later a British director under the

name R. Cartier) and featuring Raoul Aslan, Oskar Homolka, and Peter Lorre. Emil Jannings, the star of *The Blue Angel* (Germany 1930), appeared in both the 1933 Austro-French co-production *König Pausole*/King Pausole, directed by Alexis Granowsky, and an Austrian-Hungarian co-production that same year, entitled *Rakoczimarsch*/The Rakoczi March, which showcased and was co-directed by Gustav Fröhlich (1902–87), a German-born leading man in Austrian film.

Having left Berlin and returned to Vienna after Hitler's assumption of power in 1933, Jakob and Louise Fleck brought the icon of the lost empire to sound film in *Unser Kaiser*/Our Emperor (1933), with Karl Ehmann as Emperor Franz Joseph. The title seems to dismiss the republic, and the film was an obvious attempt to define sovereign Austrian identity along nostalgia for a benevolent symbol of a great polyglot empire. The romanticized biopic positioned itself against the pan–Germans of the past (e.g., "their Emperor") and the newsreel image of the Austrian who had become German chancellor of a "new empire" (the Third Reich) in the present. The film also features Hansi Niese, who had gained fame on the stage but had only a brief run as a film lead in the early 1930s. In addition to the aforementioned Otto Preminger debut film, Niese was also seen in Max Neufeld's Sascha-Film class-conflict comedy *Purpur und Waschblau*/Royal Purple and Washday Blue (1931) with comedian Richard Eybner and later Hollywood émigré Lilia Skala, as well as in *Sturm im Wasserglas*/Storm in a Waterglass (1931), directed by Georg Jacoby and scripted in part by Felix Salten. Another female star of the early 1930s — Anni Ondra — had the pedigree of having been discovered by Sascha Kolowrat himself. Unlike Niese, Ondra specialized in dramatic heroines and was a favorite of director Karl Lamac (1897–1952), appearing in his *Die grausame Freundin*/The Cruel Mistress (1932) and *Die Regimentstochter*/The Daughter of the Regiment (1932).

A specific blend of historical and aesthetic sensibilities melded into a unique style in Austrian cinema during this period. It soon became known as an entirely new and geographically focused genre in European cinema: the Viennese Film. The artist responsible more than any other for this concept was Willi Forst (Wilhelm Frohs, 1903–80). Forst was an actor who had begun in Austrian silent pictures (*Sodom und Gomorrhah* and *Café Elektric* among them) and had made his sound debut in *Atlantic* (Germany 1929). Within the early sound era, he had become known for his distinctive voice and "charming Viennese" persona[7] in German films usually directed by Geza von Bolvary. He appeared in two of the best Viennese comedies of the early 1930s: first with film icon Liane Haid and the first lady of the Viennese stage, Hedwig Bleibtreu, in Karl Hartl's *Der Prinz von Arkadien*/The Prince of Arcadia (1932), written by his future production partner Walter Reisch and with music by Robert Stolz; and in what Forst considered the best learning experience for his future role as director, *So ein Mädel vergisst man nicht*/An Unforgettable Girl (1933) directed by expressionist film-actor-turned-director Fritz Kortner. Forst actively developed his reputation as a great screen lover, but his directorial debut in *Leise flehen meine Lieder*/The Unfinished Symphony in 1933 brought to Austrian cinema one of its greatest filmmakers and influential industry figures, whose lack of presence in the international film canon of important directors today

Romanticizing Schubert (Hans Jaray) for the first Viennese Film: Willi Forst's *Leise flehen meine Lieder*, **1933.**

is one more casualty from the negligence that has greeted Austrian cinema since the 1950s. *Lieder* was so popular throughout Europe that it was reshot in a 1934 British version (co-directed by Forst and Anthony Asquith) for the English-language market as *The Unfinished Symphony*. The co-author of the original was Walter Reisch (1903–83), who in Hollywood exile would script *Ninotchka* (USA 1939) and *Gaslight* (USA 1944) and would work with Billy Wilder. In *Lieder*, Reisch took on the love affair between composer Franz Schubert, ostensibly Austria's favorite dramatized musical figure, and the Countess Esterhazy. With Hans Jaray as Schubert, Luise Ullrich — fresh from Ophül's *Liebelei* — as Schubert's innocent love, Hans Moser as her father and Marta Eggerth as the seductive Czardas-dancing countess who disrupts the composer's life, Reisch attempted to subvert the clichés of previous Schubert films and stage works. Forst's impressionistic images of Biedermeier Vienna, costumed by the "Edith Head of Austrian film," Gerdago (Gerda Gottstein, a.k.a. Gerda Iro, 1906–),[8] whose opulent and often startling designs made her more comparable to Adrian at MGM, and framed by the lavishly detailed and stylized sets by Julius von Borsody, were underscored almost continuously by selections of Schubert's music, arranged by Willy Schmidt-Gentner (1894–1964), the leader in the new art of Austrian film composition, and performed by the Vienna

Philharmonic and the Vienna Boys' Choir. Schmidt-Gentner was among the most prolific Austrian film composers and music arrangers in the 1930s, participating in no less than twenty pictures during the decade. The orchestration of image, lighting, music and performance in *Lieder* suggests a unique personal style that had not been previously seen in the new musical film. Although traditional melodrama would also be avoided, the genre was certainly Viennese from its very roots. Theatrical and visual values of the Baroque, the near-operatic equality of dialogue and music, and the balanced blending of all aspects of the film into a seamless *Gesamtkunstwerk*, or total work of art (a goal of the Romantics and turn-of-the-century Viennese artists who attempted aesthetic, even spiritual transcendence) are at work here. Forst's greatest influence as director was René Clair,[9] which suggests the style Forst hoped to adapt and transform: "As the melody of Paris resounds through all the films of René Clair, which one can hear and feel, so the films of Willi Forst offer a Vienna in which the music, the atmosphere, the essence of the city is nourished by and grows from its past, from the tradition of music and history, from theater and culture."[10]

But Forst's Schubert film, which was a success in both German- and English-language versions, also represented a specific sociohistorical ideology. Set in the Biedermeier era—that repressive, bourgeois-centered period between the Napoleonic era and the failed revolutions of 1848—the film celebrated the average man and woman and the values of love and hard work as opposed to the Romantic idealism that had brought about the French Revolution and the Napoleonic Wars. The spirit of the Biedermeier offered perfect escapism for the anxiety-laden year of 1933 as it had done in previous troubled times. It was also very typically Viennese in its enshrinement of art above even love. Walter Fritz sums up the style and success of the Forst/Reisch Viennese Film:

> Why was it that the Viennese Film emerged as a widely discussed concept in the wake of *Leise flehen meine Lieder* and burst forth so suddenly from its bewildered dormancy during the silent film era? The reason is not to be sought in the soundtrack alone but in the use of music as an essential element of the dramatic impact. Even the presentation of the figures was permeated by the dramatic structure of the music. The real effect of the film derived from the blending of music and plot, whereby these films managed to avoid resuscitating the mannerisms which had crept into the acting tradition of the silent film era. The screen exuded highly personal chamber music, the images were in soft focus, the acting was restrained, the landscape endless and the palace settings sumptuous. The sun set over the fields and the golden light was caught in the folds of the curtains, the language was soft and informal, and the music played and played.[11]

Forst's follow-up in this new genre, *Maskerade*/Masquerade (1934), secured his reputation as a significant director and gave him the international recognition he did not quite have as an actor. It also made an instant star of Paula Wessely (1908–2000) in her lead debut. A foremost figure in German-language motion pictures and theater for five decades and the wife of Attila Hörbiger, Wessely was considered

Paula Wessely and Adolf Wohlbrück strike an iconic pose in a publicity motif from
Willi Forst's *Maskerade*, 1934.

by Laurence Olivier to be the greatest film actress of the twentieth century, and Bette Davis was known to have studied her performances. Wessely's role as the impoverished but morally upright art student Leopoldine in the decadent atmosphere of turn-of-the-century Vienna set the tone for the female lead (along with Luise Ullrich in *Lieder*) in the Viennese Film, and it also typecast Wessely as the innocent or "good" woman for most of her work in the 1930s and 1940s. The centerpiece of *Maskerade* is Leopoldine's meeting with the society painter Heideneck (Adolf Wohlbrück) at a lavish carnival ball. Its strikingly Romantic and decadent, even erotic, mood can be credited to the soft camera work of Franz Planer and to the seductive music arranged and composed by Willi Schmidt-Gentner. *Maskerade* received an award for best screenplay at the Venice Film Festival and ultimately proved to be so successful internationally, that Hollywood "borrowed" the story for a new but less welcomed version entitled *Escapade* in 1935, with the German-born and nonconformist Hollywood star Luise Rainer.

Only six film companies formed during the silent era managed to survive the 1930s: Allianz (founded 1913), Sascha-Filmindustrie (founded 1918), Mondial (founded 1920), Konrad Wiene Internationale Filmgesellschaft (founded 1921), Projektograph-Oskar Glück (founded 1925), and Excelsior (founded 1925). Of these, the Konrad Wiene and Excelsior companies produced only one film each, Allianz turned solely to distribution after 1933, and Sascha-Film, which had become Tobis-Sascha, ceased all involvement in film production aside from the rental of its large and technically advanced Rosenhügel studio lot. Most Austrian sound film production companies had been founded between 1934 and 1936. These included Forst-Film, Walter Reisch-Filmproduktion, Pan-Film Leopold Meissner, and Gloria-Film.[12]

The political developments between 1933 and 1934 placed Austrian cinema under governmental control more than it had ever been, even during the World War I. The July 1927 torching of the Justice Palace in Vienna by leftist demonstrators in protest of the Schattendorf Trial,[13] and the subsequent police and army intervention that resulted in the deaths of eighty-nine people became the subject of two powerful 1927 documentaries by Gustav Mayer. The looming civil war and the growing power of the Austrian National Socialists, who demanded Anschluss or annexation of Austria to Hitler's new Reich, was countered by Austria's new chancellor, Engelbert Dollfuss (1892–1934). Disbanding the embattled parliament on the basis of an obscure law and instituting a "non-party" clerico-authoritarian corporate state, often referred to as Austrofascism, he hoped to stabilize the country and disallow any merger with Nazi Germany. Although Dollfuss's Fatherland Front movement was to have been a national force sans party politics, it was, in fact, led by the conservative, Catholic-oriented Christian Social Party. The subsequent laws, which made all political parties illegal, may have temporarily silenced the National Socialists, but it also alienated a substantial portion of Austria's electorate, the Social Democrats. Dollfuss, who admired Mussolini and benefited from his support, based his corporate state on the Italian model and flatly rejected Nazism and its racist, expansionist policies. He strove to make Austria the "better Germany" and chose the symbol of the crusader's cross as a counter to Germany's pagan swastika. Although his Fatherland Front may have had external fascist traits — uniforms, mass meetings, leader-cult imagery — it never had a cohesive platform. Its one-sided collection of Christian Social Party members, centrists, monarchists, conservatives, military officers, aristocrats, capitalists, Catholic youth, and anti-leftists/anti–German nationalists of all hues found their ideology in the Catholic-based philosophy of Othmar Spann, Habsburg nostalgia, anti-socialism, and Central European cohesion against German Nazism, a laudable but hopeless concept given the anti–Austrian sentiment in most of the new republics freed from Austria-Hungary in 1918. The anti-socialist stance also corresponded with the rejection of German expansionism, since prior to Hitler's ascendancy to power in 1933 various Social Democrats had agitated for union with Germany.

Dollfuss's authoritarian regime immediately turned to film, appreciating its immense value for spreading political, cultural and economic propaganda. Rather than work with the industry, the new regime, which was officially proclaimed by decree in May 1934, decided to take the film industry totally under its "protection."[14] The first step in this new political relationship was the transference of the ownership of film theaters in the possession of the outlawed Social Democratic Party. The socialist-led Kiba organization passed to the city of Vienna and came under the leadership of Karl Imelski (1887–1938), who had been active in film production since 1919 and who had held various positions at MGM in Austria after 1924. Although he also worked as a producer and director, the corporate regime brought him to the leadership of several film organizations and he became one of the most powerful men in the Austrian film industry up to the Anschluss in 1938. The new Austrian nationalism supported not only the Austrian camera and projector industry — the regime decreed that all films must be shown on Austrian equipment — but also dictated what was to be shown on that equipment. Weekly newsreels were to be solely Austrian productions promoting the country's achievements, so that the public would come to identify with the modern, sovereign Austria, rather than to find promise in projected German hegemony. To this end, the Vaterländische Tonfilmgesellschaft (Fatherland Sound Film Company) was founded, which absorbed the *Österreich in Bild und Ton*/Austria in Image and Sound productions run by the Selenophon Company.

Official censorship, which had fallen with the empire and had been difficult to apply in the First Republic even on an ad hoc basis (*Ekstase* in 1933, for its Hedwig Kiesler nude scenes; *All Quiet on the Western Front* in 1931, for its anti–Central Powers stance, etc.), was re-instituted by decree on March 9, 1934. Additionally, all independent or various political party–associated film organizations and societies were disbanded and replaced by a large state-controlled umbrella association, the Österreichische Filmkonferenz (Austrian Film Conference). It was to be responsible for representing the film industry inside and outside the country, as well as for mediation between different professional branches of the industry. The Conference organization would be advised by the Ministry of Education, as well as by official departments that were responsible for financing and censorship.[15] The

Catholic Church was not left out of this new structure. Vienna's Cardinal Innitzer so praised the idea of an organization that would guide filmgoers that, in October 1934, the Institut für Filmkultur (Institute of Film Culture) was created out of a previous German-Austrian youth culture group. The new state cinema publication, *Der gute Film* (The Good Film), would allow for the Church's input regarding film production and presentation in Austria. It was issued in two versions: one for teachers, academics, and clergy; the other for the public. The Institute also set the criteria for topics and scripts that might be made into Austrian films in the service of the "Christian, German and corporate state."[16] A rating system was created by the Institute, which divided films into five categories: (I) general artistic or technical acceptability were rated "valuable entertainment"; (II) limited artistic or technical acceptability were rated "conditionally valuable entertainment"; (III) films that were generally well made but without particular cultural or ideological value were rated "non-objectionable entertainment"; (IV) films of a problematic theme, artistic or technical nature were to be "viewed with reservation"; and (V) films of little artistic or technical value or with negative cultural and/or ethical effect were "to be avoided." Given governmental control and censorship, the two final categories were never applied to any Austrian film and were only meant to satisfy the format of the system. Most filmmakers rejected, if nothing else, the regime's vague notion of a "good" film, and thus also the work of the Institute. Nevertheless, the public seemed to appreciate the "advice" and made the publication of *Der gute Film* a measured success.

The greatest disruption in the Austrian film industry, however, was neither the dire economic situation nor the authoritarian Austrian regime, but Nazi Germany. Following Adolf Hitler's assumption of power in Germany in January 1933, the National Socialist Party began the *Gleichschaltung*, or changeover of society and culture, to its ideology. The first indication of the nationalization and aryanization of the German film industry was given in Propaganda Minister Joseph Goebbels' speech to the German Organization of Filmmakers on March 28, 1933. From that point on, the German film industry would be subordinate to Goebbels's ministry and the goals of National Socialism. Germany's largest film studio, UFA, immediately severed contracts with all Jewish talent and organizational staff. In April, Goebbels called for the boycott of all Jewish businesses, and the emigration of Jewish and anti–National Socialist film talent began (mostly to Vienna and Hollywood), and by July, the government had officially pronounced that employment in any field was no longer just dependent on citizenship but on ancestry. Jews or, in Nazi terms, "non–Aryans," were thus non–Germans and would have to be granted a work permit like foreigners received. In the case of Jewish film talent, additional approval would have to come from the Propaganda Ministry. Few permits were given and all were terminated prior to the end of the year in preparation for the Nuremberg Racial Laws, which were announced in September 1935 and laid the foundation for a total aryanization of Germany and the Holocaust.

The Austrian film industry became the haven for German-speaking talent fleeing Germany. Vienna might have benefited from such an influx if it were not for the plans Hitler had set in motion from his first days in office — to isolate, impoverish and bring Austria to its knees in order to foster a Nazi coup and accomplish annexation. Even tourism, Austria's most important industry, was to be hampered: Nazi Germany instituted the *1,000 Mark Sperre* (the 1,000 Mark barrier), which required a deposit of 1,000 Marks for each German who desired to travel to Austria for either business or pleasure. Austria's film market was highly dependent on Germany for production and distribution. Many German companies had bought into Austrian firms during the early years of sound and Austrian film's largest export audience was Germany. Austrian films that were made with Jewish or with known or perceived anti–German/anti–National Socialist talent were officially refused German release beginning in March 1933. Of the fourteen Austrian films in distribution at the time of the first National Socialist German film industry guidelines (March 1933 to February 1934), five were blocked from release, one was pulled from distribution, and three that had just been sold to Germany —*Abenteuer am Lido*/Adventure on the Lido (1933), *Frühlingsstimmen*/Voices of Spring (1933), and *Wenn du jung bist, gehört dir die Welt*/When You Are Young, The World Belongs to You (1934) — were rejected in such an evasive manner that it provides particular insight to the process. The new arm of the Propaganda Ministry, the Reichsfilmkammer (Reich's Film Chamber), known as the RFK, flatly dismissed the well-made Viennese Film *Frühlingsstimmen* due to its "poor quality." The actual reason was that some of the film's music had been composed by operetta composer Oskar Straus, who was Jewish. Both *Abenteuer am Lido* and *Wenn du jung bist ...* had been directed by an Austrian long active in German film, Richard Oswald (1880–1963), who was Jewish, and whose filmography was made up of socially critical, progressive, anti-war interpretations condemned by the National Socialists long before their assumption of power: *Dreyfus* (Germany 1930); *Der Hauptmann von Köpenick*/The Captain of Koepenick (Germany 1931); and *Die letzten Tage vor dem Weltbrand*/The Last Days Before the Immolation of the Earth (Germany 1931). These films include singers Joseph Schmidt and Alfred Piccaver and actor Szöke Sakall, who were all considered non–Aryan by the RFK and thus labeled "unacceptable." The irony is that the production company of *Wenn du jung bist...*, the Haas-Film company, founded by Heinrich Haas (1890–1953) in 1933, was acceptable to the Nazi regime since Haas himself was considered Aryan.[17] Believing he comprehended the new limitations of Austrian film in Nazi Germany, Haas even contacted the RFK during the making of the film and offered them the script for censorship. The RFK insisted on several changes, which Haas prepared, but their central criticism regarded Joseph Schmidt, whom they advised was too unattractive to help motivate such an uninteresting plot.[18] The Austrian cabinet council for film, Eugen Lanske, naïvely avoided the obvious and blamed the ban not on the director's "non–Aryan" status but on a vaguely "negative personal reputation," stating that other "non–Aryans" did not support Oswald or his situation in any recognizable manner.[19] Prior to his escape from Austria on the heels of the German annexation, Oswald made one more film, again with singer Joseph Schmidt, *Heut' ist der schönste Tag in meinem Leben*/Today Is the Most Beautiful Day of My Life (1936), which features Felix Bressart, who would also quit Austria to become one of Hollywood's most prolific character actors. Oswald, however, found little artistic opportunity in Hollywood.

The Film Agreement of 1934 placed the Austrian film industry under strangulating external pressure by Nazi Germany, which forbade the importing and showing of any Austrian film that included among cast or crew "non–Germans" (émigrés from Nazi Germany) or "non–Aryan" Austrians. That this was specifically aimed at destabilizing the Austrian economy and aryanizing Austrian cinema from outside, in preparation of annexation, was clear to Oskar Pilzer (1882–1939) the director of Tobis-Sascha and president of the Austrian Association of Film Production, a branch of the corporate state's official film culture establishment. His Pilzer Group had part or direct ownership of many Austrian film companies including Vienna-Film, Gloria-Film, Viktoria-Film, Walter Reisch-Filmproduktion, and Tobis-Sascha. Pilzer maintained that the Third Reich was not as insistent on Aryan talent in other foreign films as it was in Austrian product:

> The Austrian productions featuring Franziska Gaal are not allowed to approach the censors in Germany, but when such a film would be produced in Hungary, there is no trouble at all. Prominent Jews in French or British films pass through German censorship with ease, but in the case of an Austrian film, a Jewish third camera assistant would be objected.... Meanwhile, the Aryan Paragraph (of the Nuremberg Racial Laws) has been enacted. Now, for example, Herr Reich is allowed to be a producer but not a director.... We must demand that there should be no limitations in the use of "Austrians"; only those specifically mentioned in the contract should be so avoided.[20]

Pilzer and others in the Austrian film industry believed that the Germans were not targeting Austrian citizens, only ex–German ("non–Aryan") nationals in Austrian film, and that the racial laws of Germany did not apply to Austria nor would Austria institute an *Arierparagraph* (Aryan Paragraph) of its own to suit Germany. Unfortunately, Austrian film did exactly that with its concessions to Germany for the sake of film distribution. Film credits were edited to remove the "undesirable" names and by 1935, the previous agreement was replaced with a new one that put the now seriously disadvantaged and dependent Austrian film industry one step closer toward mandatory aryanization. Austria was limited to the distribution of twelve films annually in Germany through German companies, whereas Germany could export an unlimited amount to Austria. Cases involving permission to work no longer needed German citizenship, Austrian citizenship would be acceptable, but this was a worthless concession because the German proof of Aryan status, the *Ariernachweis*, was still demanded. This gave Germany substantial control in the creation and casting of Austrian films. Exceptions would be approached on an individual basis, but only in the same manner that Berlin dealt with its own film talent, meaning that this was nearly impossible.

One of the very rare instances of an exception was for Walter Reisch, who had scripted and directed a new film for Paula Wessely, *Episode* (1935). His credit on

Paula Wessely and Otto Tressler in Walter Reisch's Viennese Film *Episode*, 1935.

Willi Forst's *Maskerade* had been removed in printed programs and advertisements in Germany. In what appears to have been another tactic to confuse and destabilize the Austrian industry, this widely anticipated film was not passed by the German censors until an Austrian delegation met with the RFK, and the German distributor complained of lost investments should the film be banned. *Episode* revisited the formula of *Maskerade*, but this time a socially critical aspect regarding the economic and class struggles of the First Republic seasoned the romantic fantasy. Set in Vienna in 1922, Paula Wessely once again played an impoverished art student, Valerie, who becomes involved with the arts patron Torresani (Otto Tressler). She learns that a banker who has committed suicide had misappropriated her mother's small savings. This threatens Valerie's art studies until Torresani comes to her rescue. After operetta-like confusions involving Torresani's wife and the tutor of Torresani's sons, Valerie discovers her love for the tutor and ultimately finds her way toward her artistic goals. The work is pure Viennese Film, not only stylistically but with regards to plot and *Weltanschauung*. Its impressionistic story of the flow of life and love seems to have been influenced by the work of Arthur Schnitzler, particularly his famous play *Anatol*. The film broadened Paula Wessely's visibility throughout Europe, and she subsequently received a best actress award for the role at the following year's Venice Film Festival. Walter Reisch created one more film prior to his Hollywood emigration, the 1936 *Silhouetten*/Silhouettes, which is set in the world of ballet and features his wife Lisl Handl. Reisch left Vienna in 1936 and that same year directed the film *Men Are Not Gods* in London prior to his arrival in Hollywood.

The discord that Germany caused the Austrian film industry and practically every other aspect of Austria's economy and culture was no doubt intended to be a brief and fruitful policy by the National Socialists. On July 25, 1934, Austrian Nazis assassinated Chancellor Dollfuss in an attempted coup that was to enable the Anschluss. But no internal collapse occurred and Kurt von Schuschnigg (1897–1977), the minister of education in Dollfuss's government was named chancellor. Although von Schuschnigg continued the corporate state, he was quite different in many ways from his predecessor, and his regime, which lasted until the German Anschluss in 1938, intended to reduce the government's authoritarian aspects. An aristocrat and monarchist who maintained good relations with the Habsburg family, von Schuschnigg downplayed the rural-oriented propaganda of Dollfuss and desired to see Austria recover its cosmopolitan reputation as the reborn center of *Mitteleuropa*. With no great admiration for Mussolini or his fascism, von Schuschnigg allowed the Fatherland Front to fade somewhat as a national movement. Its militia lost power and the regime became less specifically ideological and more pragmatically bureaucratic. Von Schuschnigg even considered rapprochement with the Social Democrats, who had been imprisoned and killed in the civil war that brought Dollfuss to power, in hopes of creating a true national front against the threat of German Anschluss. He could, however, still count on Mussolini's protection, at least until the Berlin-Rome Axis of 1936, which gave Mussolini a powerful ally at the cost of abandoning Austria to its inevitable German annexation. To that end, Austrians who were illegal members of the Austrian National Socialist Party openly aided Germany's involvement in the Austrian film industry. German producer Serge Otzoup and Austrian banker Wilhelm Gaik founded a company that would help Austrian productions ensure that their cast and crew is Aryan and therefore allowed for German distribution and presentation without problems. Austrian producers were encouraged to make bilateral agreements with the Otzoup firm and the leader of the outlawed Austrian National Socialist Party, Josef Leopold. The former president of the Filmbund and head of its authoritarian successor organization, silent film pioneer Heinz Hanus, assisted in providing racial information about the talent being employed. Several major Austrian companies made use of this Faustian agreement, among them Gloria-Film and Pan-Film.

Willi Forst, arguably the most famous of all Austrian directors at the time, and considered to be Aryan by the National Socialists, could ignore much of this political intrigue and founded his own film production company in Vienna in 1936, followed by a branch in Berlin. He intended to continue to make films for the entire German-speaking world and beyond. Although he had lost his collaborators due to German racial laws, Forst developed himself into a world-class four-way talent, as producer, director, writer and actor in films made in Germany: *Mazurka*

(Germany 1935), *Allotria* (Germany 1936), *Serenade* (Germany 1937), *Bel Ami* (Germany 1939), and *Ich bin Sebastian Ott*/I Am Sebastian Ott (Germany 1939). Forst returned to Vienna in 1936, however, to film *Burgtheater*/The Court Theater, with music by Peter Kreuder, who created an evergreen standard with one of his songs in the score, "Sag' beim Abschied leise Servus" ("Whisper Goodbye When You Leave"). The film starred German actor Werner Krauss as a great stage actor whose life is altered by one late love. As usual in Viennese Film, renunciation of passion and its sublimation into art is offered as the dramatic conclusion.

Another Austrian who found fame in Germany prior to the Anschluss was director E. W. Emo (1898–1975), who had made several notable Austrian films during the 1930s, such as *Zirkus Saran*/Circus Saran (1935), a celebrated vehicle for Hans Moser. In 1936, Austrian actor Paul Hörbiger (1894–1981), who had first gained fame in productions by Germany's UFA prior to his recognition in Austrian film, formed a company in Berlin with the Austrian Consul, Karl Künzel, and E. W. Emo, known as Algefa-Film, which attempted to introduce Austrian talent and themes into German cinema. Its most successful film was also one that suggested, albeit in a subrosa manner, the "difference" between Germany and Austria. Hörbiger explained in a 1971 interview that *Das Fiakerlied*/The Cabbie's Song (1936) was a work that utilized imperial nostalgia (reviled by the National Socialists) and Viennese dialect to its fullest. The script was written by the banned Austrian-Hungarian author Ödön von Horváth, who used the pseudonym H. W. Becker, and the song that Hörbiger sings was written by a Jew. Rather than "sanitize" the film, Hörbiger merely stated that the song was composed from motifs by nineteenth-century dramatist Ludwig Anzengruber. Hörbiger believed the German censors knew little about literature and would believe this absurdity — and they did. Another Austrian director in German film at this time was Arthur Maria Rabenalt (1905–93), who insisted on complete control over his films and often ran into trouble with censorship.

The German-Austrian co-production *Die Pompadour*/The Pompadour Woman (1935) offered what was perhaps the most peculiar blend of officially sanctioned and banned talent in one film. The script was written by Veit Harlan, the later director of Nazi Germany's most propagandistic feature films (*Jud Süß*/Jew Suess, 1940; *Kolberg*, 1945), and von Horváth under his H. W. Becker pseudonym. Harlan co-directed with Austrian film composer Willy Schmidt-Gentner, and the film starred Käthe von Nagy as Madame Pompadour and Willy Eichberger (who would soon emigrate to London as Carl Esmond) in the role of the painter Boucher. The lavish period sets were designed by Julius von Borsody. Composer Schmidt-Gentner added only one more film to his stint as a director: *Prater* (1936), a love story against the backdrop of Vienna's famous amusement park with Magda Schneider, Willy Eichberger and Annie Rosar. Herbert Selpin, a German director who had scored a hit in Austria with his Viennese Film *Romanze*/Romance in 1936, returned to Germany and UFA, where he was interrupted in the 1942 filming of *Titanic* for having uttered criticisms about the German Wehrmacht.[21] He was removed from the film, expelled from the RFK, and imprisoned, and later he reportedly committed suicide. The South Tyrolean–born director Luis Trenker (1892–1990) found fame in German cinema as one of the exponents of the *Bergfilm*. In 1931, he co-directed the World War I mountain epic *Berge in Flammen*/Mountain in Flames with Austrian director Karl Hartl. Trenker's teacher and mentor in the mountain film genre had been Arnold Fanck, the father of the German *Bergfilm* and the director of Leni Riefenstahl's early silent starring roles. One might argue that this genre of snow-bound climbing adventures and melodrama actually began with the audience-pleasing war documentaries from Sascha-Film dealing with the conflict in the Dolomites, such as the 1917 *Ein Heldenkampf in Schnee und Eis*/A Heroic Battle in Snow and Ice.

Forst's only true rival in the Viennese Film genre was the Hungarian-born Geza von Bolvary (1897–1961), who had at one time been his director. Von Bolvary had also worked in Berlin, but the quality of his few Austrian films ranked him at the top of any list of Viennese directors. Beginning with the lush *Frühjahrspa-rade*/Spring Parade in 1934, one of a series of Franziska Gaal vehicles to be discussed later in this chapter, von Bolvary managed to provide a more dramatic edge to the Viennese Film. His 1936 drama *Ernte*/Harvest, co-scripted with Philipp Lothar-Meyring and shot by Franz Planer, provided an early dramatic vehicle for the pairing of Paula Wessely and Attila Hörbiger. His *Lumpazivagabundus*/Lumpaci, The Vagabond (1936) was based on the work by Austrian folk playwright Johann Nestroy (1801–62), and attracted the trio of Paul Hörbiger, German comedian Heinz Rühmann and rising Austrian leading man Hans Holt. The film has since been regarded as providing the three actors' finest performances. Also in the film is actress Hilde Krahl, who so impressed Marlene Dietrich's director/mentor Josef von Sternberg on a visit to Vienna in 1937 that he considered bringing her to Hollywood. Krahl, a cool actress with a chiseled look, would not, however, fulfill her screen promise until the mid–1940s. Von Bolvary's most important film of the period was *Premiere* (1937), a contemporary musical. Written by Max Wallner, photographed by Franz Planer and scored by Schmidt-Gentner, the film was the first German-language film for a Swedish singer and actress, Zarah Leander, who had become known for her unusually deep voice in many appearances on the Viennese stage. In film she developed a striking persona that combined the eroticism of Marlene Dietrich, the appearance of Greta Garbo, the strong dramatic presence of mid-career Joan Crawford, and her own intelligent style. In short, she was a major film talent on the horizon and, following the film's success (it also featured Attila Hörbiger, Theo Lingen and Karl Skraup), Carl Froehlich of UFA signed her to a contract which led to her becoming the greatest female star in the films of the Third Reich. In Germany and Austria today, she has become a cult figure along the lines of Judy Garland in the United States and is mostly remembered for her work as a singer and for her portrayals of relatively independent women rather than for her ambiguous relationship with the Nazi regime.

Von Bolvary returned to a more traditional Viennese Film style with his 1938 *Finale*, written by Ernst Marischka (1893–1963), who would later translate the genre into the imperial epics of the 1950s. The Italian director Carmine Gallone

(1886–1973) attempted a Viennese musical with his 1936 *Opernring*/Opera-Ring (a portion of Vienna's grand Ringstrasse boulevard passing the opera house is known as the Opernring), featuring Polish singer Jan Kiepura, Luli von Hohenberg, Fritz Imhoff and the music of Schmidt-Gentner. The film, which was produced by Horus-Film and released by Gloria-Film, was not for German distribution. The success of such large-scale films also brought the grand period film back into vogue. There was the above-mentioned *Pompadour* film, but also the Hans Moser vehicle directed by Erich Engel, *Nur ein Komödiant*/Only a Comedian (1935); the Olga Tschechowa starrer, *Maria Walewska* (1936); and *Der Postillon von Lonjumeau*/The Postillion of Lonjumeau (1936). The most lavish of these, *Das Tagebuch der Geliebten*/The Diary of the Beloved (1935), directed by Hermann Kosterlitz (1905–88) with Lili Darvas, Hans Jaray, Szöke Szakall and Attila Hörbiger, featured 1,200 costumes designed by Ladislaus Czettel. Kosterlitz became Henry Koster in Hollywood, directing Deanna Durbin's early films as well as *Harvey* (USA 1950), *The Robe* (USA 1953), and *Mr. Hobbs Takes a Vacation* (USA 1962).

In his documentary on film talent emigration from Germany after 1933, Günter Peter Straschek reports that the racial laws made about nine hundred members of the German film industry unemployable in Germany and ultimately stateless.[22] Many of these headed to Hollywood but a substantial portion sought out Vienna and Budapest, to be able to work in the German language and often because Austria or Hungary had been their country of origin. Since they were not able to work with most of the major Austrian film companies, a secondary or independent film industry developed around this talent. These new companies were not dependent on Germany for investment or distribution and therefore rejected Germany's racial guidelines. Their *Emigrantenfilm* (emigrant film) utilized émigré and Austrian non–Aryan talent, co-produced their films with foreign studios and in multilanguage versions, and marketed them across Europe. The first of these production houses to open in Vienna in 1934 was Wiener-Film/Morawsky, founded by two former employees of the German Terra Company, Rudi Loewenthal and Erich Morawsky. Their first production, *Salto in die Seligkeit*/Salto Finds Happiness (1934), was directed by Fritz Schulz and featured Schulz, Felix Bressart and Olly Gebauer. Loewenthal and Morawsky intended to follow the style of the original United Artists company in Hollywood, where the performers were essentially shareholders in their film.[23] But their plans for a follow-up, *Letzte Liebe*/Last Love (1935), also to be directed by Schulz, suffered from financial constraints and set the United Artists angle to the test. A member of one of Austria's important business families, Julius Meinl II, eventually bankrolled the film by trading financial support for his Japanese wife's (Michiko Tanaka-Meinl) leading role in the film. Meinl's tireless promotion of his wife as a film star echoed William Randolph Hearst's involvement with Marion Davies. In addition to the film, Meinl commissioned an operetta for Tanaka from composer Paul Abraham.[24] His generosity attracted major names to the *Letzte Liebe* project: Hans Jaray, Albert Bassermann, Oskar Karlweis, and opera singer Richard Tauber. Although the expensive film managed a return on its expenditures, it forced the producers to consider international investment, particularly

Scandinavian partnerships, for future projects. But the company never managed to produce another film, and Morawsky emigrated to France in 1936.[25]

Despite its failure, Wiener-Film/Morawsky opened the doors for what became a major mode of Austrian film production in the 1930s. It also gave significant careers to Hans Jaray (1906–90) and Hungarian-born Franziska Gaal (1901?–72), one of the important but forgotten comediennes in Austrian and German-language film. Also brought to wider fame were Szöke Sakall and rotund former UFA comedian Otto Wallburg (1889–1944), who fled to Holland after 1938, where he survived underground until his deportation to Auschwitz in 1944. Actor Fritz Imhoff (Friedrich Jeschke, 1891–1961), who was not Jewish, continued his work in Austrian film after the Anschluss and into the postwar period. From behind the camera there were director/actor Fritz Schulz (1898–1972), who fled to Switzerland in 1938; director Max Neufeld (1887–1967), who had helped found the silent Vita-Film company in 1919 and fled to Italy after the Anschluss; and producer Joe Pasternak (1901–91), who continued his work in Hollywood as producer of Henry (Kosterlitz) Koster's first Deanna Durbin film, *Three Smart Girls* (1936), which saved Universal Pictures from grave financial crisis, and a number of MGM musicals.

There were no less than three independent films not made for German distribution showing in Austrian theaters in 1934: the Hermann Kosterlitz comedy *Peter* (1934), an Austrian-Hungarian co-production for the Vienna branch of Universal Pictures filmed in German at the Budapest studios of Hunnia-Film with Franziska Gaal, Hans Jaray, Felix Bressart, and Otto Wallburg; Fritz Schulz's *Ende schlecht, Alles gut*/Bad Ending, Good Everything (1934), also shot in German and Hungarian at Hunnia and featuring Szöke Szakall and a primarily Hungarian cast; and Max Neufeld's *Ein Stern fällt vom Himmel*/A Star Falls from the Sky (1934), produced by the Austrian company Styria-Film, the second production firm founded by Heinrich Haas, and shot at Vienna's Tobis-Sascha/Rosenhügel studio. The latter film showcases opera recording star Joseph Schmidt, who was also in the 1936 British remake directed by Paul Merzbach, called *A Star Fell from Heaven*. As previously mentioned, Haas's other Joseph Schmidt starrer, *Wenn du jung bist, gehört dir die Welt*/When You Are Young, The World Belongs to You (1934), had been rejected by Germany, and a film tentatively titled "Wehe dem, der lügt" (He Who Lies Shall See) was so quickly rejected by the RFK that the project never made it beyond the planning stage. He subsequently turned his back on mainstream German-language productions to work in Austria's independent film industry. In 1935 he co-produced his first Austrian-Hungarian feature, *4½ Musketiere*/4½ Musketeers, with Budapest's Hunnia-Film (and shot at their studios), directed by Ladislaus Kardos and offering the usual blend of German émigré, Austrian, and Hungarian talent.

Another major player in the independent Austrian film phase was Panta-Film, a company founded by Eduard Albert Kraus, a wealthy oil businessman who had decided to increase his fortune through motion picture production. His first project, *Bretter, die die Welt bedeuten*/Theater World (1935), was helmed by UFA actor and director Kurt Gerron (1897–1944), a physician and theater star who had come to fame as the cabaret manager in Josef von Sternberg's *The Blue Angel* (1930). His emigration to Paris in 1933 had led to only two film roles, and Gerron hoped to continue his work in Austria. *Bretter* was to have enabled Gerron to make a more important feature, but, following the box-office failure of Panta-Film's Lili Darvas and Hans Jaray romance, *Tagebuch der Geliebten*/Diary of the Beloved (1935), directed by Hermann Kosterlitz, Kraus decided to end his foray into independent film and produce more lucrative material for German distribution. The three films that Kraus's new RFK-approved firm, Horus-Film, produced for the German market — Erich Engel's *Nur ein Komödiant*/Only a Comedian (1935), Carmine Gallone's *Opernring* (1936), and Arthur Maria Rabenalt's *Die weiße Frau des Maharadscha*/The White Wife of the Maharaja (1936) — were financial disappointments. Kraus ended his new role as producer in near ruin. Gerron left Austria for the Netherlands where he directed two Dutch films but soon found himself back on the theater and cabaret stages. Following the German invasion of the Netherlands, Gerron ran the Jewish theater Joodsche Schouwburg in Amsterdam, but in 1943 he was arrested and sent to Westerbork internment camp. From there he was transferred to Theresienstadt, the "paradise camp," comprised of an entire city of Jewish and other inmates often too well known or needed for propagandistic exploitation to simply disappear. The façade of a civilized urban setting was also intended to placate protests from outside the Reich regarding rumors of death camps. In 1944, Gerron was commanded to direct the fictionalized "documentary" *Der Führer schenkt den Juden eine Stadt*/The Fuehrer Gives a City to the Jews, which was to present a picture of humane treatment of the Jews to the International Red Cross and the world press. Once the film had been delivered, the "set" was no longer required and by the end of the year, Kurt Gerron and most of the inhabitants of Theresienstadt were deported to their deaths at Auschwitz.

The most successful independent production company in Austria prior to the Anschluss was, in fact, not really an Austrian firm at all. It was the Vienna branch of Hollywood's Universal Pictures, which had departed Berlin following the nationalization of the film industry. The branch set up new headquarters in Vienna and Budapest and made good use of the Tobis-Sascha Rosenhügel venue. It was responsible for making the talented Hungarian actress Franziska Gaal into an internationally recognized film personality and for creating the romantic on-screen duo of Gaal and Hans Jaray. Gaal, who was born of Jewish ancestry between 1901 and 1909 (she always claimed to have forgotten her birth date)[26] as Franziska Zilverstrich in Budapest, began her colorful career on the Hungarian theater and cabaret stages. Her film debut in 1921 in the Hungarian *Az Eger* led to her "discovery" by producer Joe Pasternak, who headed Universal's Berlin productions. Her subsequent first German-language film, *Paprika* (1932), was met with critical and financial success and cast her image as a naïve gamin. Pasternak recalled that his new star could not speak a word of German and "played her part by learning her speeches phonetically. She never knew what she was saying."[27] In contrast, critic Paul Ickes praised her control of the German language along with her acting expertise.[28] With four films in two years — *Gruß und Kuß-Veronika*/Love and Kisses, Veronica (Germany 1933); *Skandal in Budapest*/Scandal in Budapest (Germany/Hungary 1933);

Csibi, der Fratz/Csibi (Austria 1934); *Frühjahrsparade*/Spring Parade (Austria/Hungary 1934)—Gaal had become a star in Germany, just as the Nazi propaganda machine instigated its hate campaign against her.

Gaal's first Austrian film, *Csibi, der Fratz*, was one of the largest and most successful productions of the era. Directed by Max Neufeld, the film was shot at Rosenhügel and in Hungary (to avoid the film being "Austrian" or an "émigré film" in hopes of German distribution) in late 1933 or early 1934 and features Hermann Thimig, Tibor von Halmay, and character actress Leopoldine Konstantin, who left Vienna for the United States in 1938 with writer husband Geza Herczeg. (In Hollywood Konstantin became famous for her single film role as Madame Sebastian in Hitchcock's neo–Nazi spy thriller *Notorious* [USA 1946], but returned to Vienna in 1948.[29]) As a Hungarian film, the Gaal starrer had no difficulty with German release, which supported the view of Tobis-Sascha head Oskar Pilzer, that the RFK's aryanization demands of foreign film distribution in Germany were intended to destroy the Austrian film industry in preparation for German control and were not meant as guidelines for other European films. Geza von Bolvary's entry in the Viennese Film genre, *Frühjahrsparade*, made the following year, also succeeded in gaining German distribution by using the façade of a Hungarian production. Aside from Gaal, it was also a film made up of what was considered top-ranking Aryan Austrian and German talent: the film was scripted by Ernst Marischka and includes actors Wolf Albach-Retty, Paul Hörbiger and Adele Sandrock.

Despite it being advertised as a Hungarian production, Franziska Gaal's next Pasternak/Universal Pictures feature, *Peter* (1934), directed by Hermann Kosterlitz, had no hope for German distribution. It became her first "émigré film," shot with Felix Bressart and Otto Wallburg at the Hunnia Studios in Budapest, and her first romantic paring with Hans Jaray. The film's progressive class-conscious tragicomedy is couched in the economic and social upheaval of the times. Franziska Gaal plays Eva, a poor young girl who is evicted with her father from their apartment for lack of rent payment and becomes a homeless street musician. Forced to exchange her clothes with a fleeing thief, she finds it easier to live as a boy named Peter. A confrontation with a doctor (Hans Jaray) lands her before the youth authorities, but her impoverishment earns her the doctor's help, who finds Peter a job at a local garage. Eva re-introduces herself to the doctor as Peter's sister and attempts to help his failing practice with disastrous results. An adventure at a dance hall involving a stolen necklace unmasks the role playing and love, although the financial problems remain unresolved. Gaal's *Peter* pre-suggests Katharine Hepburn's trouser-role in *Sylvia Scarlett* (USA 1935) and even the gender-ambiguous image and naïveté of Giuletta Masina's Gelsomina in Fellini's *La Strada* (Italy 1954), for whom miracles happen "which are denied to more intelligent beings."[30] *Peter*'s romantic comedy-of-poverty was a re-vision of the Austrian socially critical melodrama genre, and its progressive style, unusual script and fine performances earned it the award for Best Comedy of the Year at the 1935 Moscow International Film Festival. Film historians Armin Loaker and Martin Prucha compare it to the Depression-era fables of Hollywood's Frank Capra, noting that Pasternak may have been intentionally following a Hollywood trend for success, particularly the witty, quick-fire language of the screwball comedy. *Peter* certainly demonstrates aspects of this Hollywood genre, which had life in Austrian film between the 1930s and the 1960s. It was essentially a hybrid creation, which continuously evolved between the aspects of American social comedy and the sensibilities of Austrian film–associated talents, such as Billy Wilder, Ernst Lubitsch, and a host of expatriates and exiles who originally brought their cinematic impulses to Hollywood in the early 1930s. Their development is analogous to that of film noir, which transferred German expressionism and sociopolitical pessimism to the American gangster and social realist genres, although, unlike screwball comedy, noir never truly developed in German and Austrian film. Because these foreign artists spoke German and many had worked in Berlin during the era of expressionist film (even if this style had nothing to do with the artist's work), film noir is labeled a "German influence." Paul Schrader's 1972 article set this standard for subsequent research on the topic, and no one has bothered to question his conclusion that Hollywood was "bursting" with a "large number of Germans and Eastern Europeans working in film noir: Fritz Lang, Robert Siodmak, Billy Wilder, Franz Waxman, Otto Preminger, John Brahm, Anatole Litvak, Karl Freund, Max Ophüls, John Alton, Douglas Sirk, Fred Zinnemann, William Dieterle, Max Steiner, Edgar G. Ulmer, Curtis Bernhardt, Rudoph Maté."[31] Most of the foreign talent Schrader credits with creating the genre are obviously not "German or Eastern European" as he notes, but Austrian.

Hans Jaray (1906–90) began his career in Viennese theater, where he was also active as a writer and director. His film career began in the silent era, but it was Willi Forst who gave him his first major role as composer Franz Schubert in *Leise flehen meine Lieder* in 1933. Like Gaal, the new National Socialist German press damned him just as he was achieving popularity. His subsequent film roles between 1934 and 1937 made a star of him nevertheless, and he would emerge as the romantic leading man of the émigré/independent film. Jaray's subtle acting style and elegant appearance, much in the tradition of Forst, could not help establish him in Hollywood exile after 1938. Jaray suffered from depression and only worked sporadically in American film and theater. He managed the lead in Alexander Korda's production of *Lydia* (1941) opposite Merle Oberon, but his rejection of a Lubitsch project at Paramount in 1942 had serious ramifications for his relocated career. He turned again to the stage and co-founded (with Grete Mosheim, Lili Darvas, Oskar Karlweis and Felix Gerstmann) The Players from Abroad, a New York–based theater group of exiled actors, and he returned to Vienna in 1948 to resume his theatrical career as actor, director and teacher. His final appearance in film was in *Fedora* (USA/West Germany 1978), Billy Wilder's Hollywood-skewering mystery (and late follow-up to his 1950 *Sunset Boulevard*) about a seemingly never-aging European movie diva. Based on a short story by Otto Preminger's Hollywood protégé-turned-author, Thomas Tryon, Wilder transforms the title character (performed by both Hildegard Knef and Marthe Keller) into a rich pastiche based on Marlene Dietrich, Gloria Swanson, Greta Garbo, Pola Negri — and even a bit of Franziska Gaal.

When Pasternak realized that director Hermann Kosterlitz, writer Felix Joachimson, and actors Gaal and Jaray made for a winning formula, he followed *Peter* with the Austrian-Hungarian co-production of *Kleine Mutti*/Little Mother (1935), which was shot in Hungary, although without Jaray. Felix Joachimson recycled his script about the orphaned girl Marie, the foundling she mothers, and a happy ending with the son of a banker in Hollywood twice (as Felix Jackson)— in 1939 for Garson Kanin's *Bachelor Mother*, with Ginger Rogers, and in 1956 as Norman Taurog's *Bundle of Joy*, with Debbie Reynolds. Critics at the time compared Gaal's Marie to the best of Mary Pickford. Indeed, the role allowed her to showcase her innocent spitfire persona and was tailor-made for Gaal, in more ways than just to suit her acting style. As a film about an outcast victimized by society's confusion about her identity, who, through determination and luck, manages to turn the odds in her own favor, it clearly reflected Gaal's life.

Katharina, die Letzte/Katharina the Last and *Fräulein Lilli*/Miss Lilli, both made in 1936, were Gaal's final films in Europe. In *Katharina*, opposite Hans Holt, Gaal brings her talents to what is essentially a Cinderella story clothed in the social-economic crisis of Austria in the 1930s. The film once again deals with changing, confused and misunderstood identity, a national anxiety at the time. The story focuses on an aristocrat, Hans von Gerstikow (Holt), who, rejected by the industrialist father of the woman he loves, is forced to sneak into the industrialist's villa disguised as a chauffeur. There he meets the illiterate servant girl, Katharina (Gaal), whom he uses to achieve his goals. The self-sacrificing Katharina helps Hans and protects him from the industrialist's machinations until Hans realizes that it is Katharina he truly loves. *Katharina* also marked the only Austrian film appearance of the German male singing group The Comedian Harmonists, who enjoyed major popularity at the time despite their Jewish members. They toured Europe and the United States before the German racial laws (which had been late in application to the group because of vast popular regard) finally forced them to disband. Another notable aspect of *Katharina* is the image of the nobleman as a strong and ultimately good figure. Unlike Weimar Germany, Austria's constitution of 1919 forbade the use of noble titles, including the noble particle of "von" (of). Although artists in film and elsewhere continued to use "von" as part of an artistic name and therefore managed to circumvent the law, the blatancy of "Hans von Gerstikow" is unusual for the times, even during the more pro–Habsburg Austrofascist period. The allegory of Gaal's innocent heroine finding a happy end with a transformed aristocrat suggests a sort of class negation that was never possible in the German–language theater genre of the bourgeois tragedy. In fact, such a theatrical class conflict–based misalliance usually destroyed the woman, inevitably the member of the weaker and more vulnerable lower class. The film's positive spin brings to mind German author Gotthold Ephraim Lessing's (1729–81) seminal Enlightenment-era play *Minna von Barnhelm* (1767), in which an aristocratic officer learns from his betrothed that there can be no gender-based double standards and that love and rational thought can co-exist. On a political level, *Katharina's* unity of the representatives of the upper and lower classes against injustice provides an allegory for

The socially critical comedy: Annie Rosar and Franziska Gaal in Hermann Kosterlitz's *Kleine Mutti*, 1935.

the idealized authoritarian state staving off social and economic hardships as well as German expansionism. After his emigration to Hollywood, Felix Joachimson produced a remake of his *Katharina* script as *Because of Him* (USA 1946), a Deanna Durbin (his wife at the time) vehicle, once again for Universal Pictures.

Fräulein Lilli reunited Gaal and Jaray but marked the end of Universal's involvement in Austrian film production. As Universal had withdrawn in early 1936, *Lilli* was already in production before it was announced which firm would be producing it. Opus-Film, founded by the brothers Ladislaus and Zoltan Vidor, sons of Tobis-Sascha administrator Ludwig Vidor, finally took control of the troubled picture, which had already seen one director, Hans Behrendt, depart due to conflicts with Gaal, and which had suffered schedule setbacks due to constant bickering on the set and legal issues involving Gaal's salary. Robert Wohlmuth (1902–87), later the Hollywood short film author-director Robert Wilmot and founder of Pathescope Productions, eventually took the directorial reins, but the Gaal-Jaray romance about an unemployed beauty and a playboy involved in jewelry theft in Monte Carlo, filmed on location in Monaco and Deauville, was a financial failure. Opus-Film quickly disappeared, and Gaal was branded a difficult actress of such magnitude that Austrian insurance companies refused to deal with any future Gaal film. There were to be no more in Austria.

Gaal came to Hollywood with the publicity of being a new Garbo or Dietrich, but she made only three films: Cecil B. DeMille's *The Buccaneer* (1938), Frank Tuttle's *Paris Honeymoon* (1939), and Norman Taurog's *The Girl Downstairs* (1939). Her surprising lack of popularity, despite her considerable talent, was double-edged. Apparently, the audience of the time did not care for her Hungarian accent and filmmakers did not appreciate what had already been suggested in the *Fräulein Lilli* project, namely her temperamental, egocentric manner. It may have been nothing more than what was tolerated with any other star of the time, but Gaal was no Hollywood creation and found it difficult to fit into the dictates of the studio system. Astonishingly, she chose to leave the United States and return to Hungary, Nazi Germany's ally in 1940, in the midst of the war in Europe. It is unknown how she survived the Holocaust, but by 1946, she was back on the now Soviet-controlled soundstage at Hunnia Studios, contracted for a project known as *Der König Streikt* (The King Strikes), a comeback film created for her by Austrian director-producer Karl Hartl. The film, directed by the Hungarian Akos von Rathonyi (1908–69), was to have launched a rebirth of the independent Austrian-Hungarian films of the 1930s. Franziska Gaal's difficult nature also returned, and when she appeared late or not at all to her calls, the Soviets who were bankrolling the film suspended the project. The work was completed without her as *Ohne Titel*/Without Title (1946). Gaal eventually returned to the United States and died in 1972, without making another film.[32]

In addition to the Gaal films and the aforementioned Fritz Schulz's *Ende Schlecht, Alles Gut*/Bad Ending, Good Everything (1934), there were other important Hungarian co-productions. The lavish *Ball im Savoy*/Ball at the Savoy (1935), directed by Stefan Székely (1899–1979) and written by Hermann Kosterlitz with

Rosy Barsony in a Busby Berkeley–influenced musical number from Stefan Székely's art deco *Ball im Savoy*, 1935.

Geza von Cziffra (based on the operetta by Alfred Grünwald and Fritz Löhner-Beda, with music by Paul Abraham), paired Hans Jaray with Rosy Barsony (1909–77), a Hungarian-born dancer who had scored some success in operetta and film of the early 1930s. Barsony's German career ended after the racial laws went into effect and her roles went to another Hungarian, the new UFA song-and-dance star Marika Rökk. Székely attempted an Austro-Hungarian adaptation of the Warner Brothers' musical style, particularly that of Busby Berkeley, and he succeeds admirably with *Ball im Savoy*. The film offers stunning art deco sets, well-orchestrated dance numbers, and Székely's own flair in melding Central European operetta, complete with its aristocratic fantasies, into Hollywood spectacle. He followed this film with a comedy, *Hochzeitsreise zu 50%*/Honeymoons 50% Off (1937), a more solidly Hungarian production shot in Budapest in both Hungarian and German. Cabaret actor and writer Fritz Grünbaum, who had previously written the Jakob and Louise Fleck film, *Die Csikosbaroness*/The Csikos Baroness (Germany 1930), authored the script. Having left Germany in 1932 to work in Austria, Grünbaum was deported to Dachau after the Anschluss and died there in 1941. Székely and his wife, actress Iren Agay, left for Hollywood in 1938 where they both continued to work in their disciplines as Steve Sekely and Irene Agay. In 1937, Johann Vaszary directed the Zoltan and Ludwig Vidor production of *Die entführte Braut*/The Abducted Bride, also known as *Roxi und Ihr Wunderteam*/Roxi and Her Wonder Team, and *3:1 für Liebe*/3 to 1 for Love. This musical comedy with Hans Holt and Rosy Barsony relocated an operetta by Paul Abraham to the unusual milieu of the soccer world. But it did little to mask a tired formula, which even the state-run *Der gute Film* publication did not fail to note.[33] But the film is significant for other reasons beyond its sport setting. It was to have been the start of Ludwig Vidor's Budapest-based film productions but it would in fact be the final Austrian independent co-production with Hungary prior to the Anschluss. Austrian soccer star Matthias Sindelar, who later refused to kick for the German team and died under mysterious circumstances, also appears briefly in the film. *Die entführte Braut* received its premiere in February 1938, a scant month before the annexation of Austria by Nazi Germany.

The musical comedy *Bubi,* also known as *Der kleine Kavalier*/The Little Cavalier (1937), was directed by Béla Gaal and produced by Romuald Rappaport, the former business director of Universal Pictures in Vienna, who had set up his own company, RORA-Film. The film features Szöke Szakall, Otto Wallburg, Lizzi Balla and Hans Holt, but it was intended as a dramatic showcase for radio and recording child star Mirscha, in an attempt to siphon audiences away from the Hollywood child-star films arriving at the time. The only Rappaport/RORA-Film production, *Bubi* was not able to repeat the popularity and success of the previous year's musical, *Singende Jugend*/Singing Youth (1936), one of the few Austrian/Netherlands co-productions (where German talent had also fled after 1933 and 1938), which was directed by Max Neufeld, shot by Hans Theyer and featured the Vienna Boys' Choir. *Jugend* begins as a neorealistic Austrian social drama about an orphaned boy Toni (Martin Lojda) living in poverty with his street-musician friend (Hans Olden). Toni dreams of joining the Choir and his friend convinces the rector of the Choir's school (Ferdinand Maierhofer) and a nun, Sister Maria (Julia Janssen), to accept the boy. During a summer trip to the Tyrol with the Choir, Toni risks his life to defend Sister Maria, who has become his mother figure, from suspicion of theft. He recovers from his injuries to find himself welcomed into his new life and home. The film is very much in tune with the authoritarian Christian-Social ideology, suggesting the benefits of discipline, folk culture and Catholicism. Set against Austria's highest mountain, the Grossglockner, the film also managed to display the public works of the regime, the newly constructed Grossglockner highway.[34] *Singende Jugend* may well have influenced the troubled-but-good orphan-boy theme in Hollywood films, such as in Norman Taurog's *Boys Town* (USA 1938) and Michael Curtiz's *Angels with Dirty Faces* (USA 1938). It was the nun- and child-laden *Sound of Music* of its day, finding success with audiences in France, England, and Czechoslovakia, where it was voted Best Foreign Film of 1936.

In addition to *Singende Jugend,* there had been an Austrian/French/Netherlands co-production, *Alles für die Firma*/Everything for the Firm (1935), the single work produced by the Austrian-Dutch company B.M.S.-Film. *Firma* was shot at the

Vienna Selenophon studio in simultaneous German and Dutch versions. This satire set in the world of business included Felix Bressart, Alfred Neugebauer, Oskar Karlweis, Otto Wallburg, Fritz Imhoff, and Annie Rosar and was directed and written by Rudolf Meinert (1882–1945), a Vienna-born theater director who had entered into film in the silent era, directing over forty German films before his dismissal on racial grounds. Meinert emigrated to England in 1938.

Austrian co-productions with Czechoslovakia were primarily the work of Jakob and Louise Fleck, who co-directed two films in Prague (with Walter Kolm-Veltée), both produced by the Brno-based company Terra-Film: the marriage farce *Csardas* (1935) and *Heimatfilm, Der Wilderer von Egerland*/The Poacher from Egerland (1935). Both were simultaneously filmed in German and Czech versions. It is clear that the Flecks, who had been so instrumental in developing the progressive and critical social film dramas in Austrian cinema history, had continued their ideology in other genres, where, according to official criticism of the time, it had certainly no business being. *Csardas* was criticized as a tasteless comedy due to the too liberated persona of the female lead role, and *Egerland*, despite its accomplished nature photography, was taken to task for its artificial characterizations and plot contrivances.[35] Louise Kolm-Fleck had now clearly moved beyond the troubled images of women in her previous films, where they were repressed and rescued or destroyed. *Csardas* deals with a newlywed couple, Dolly (Irene von Zilahy) and Helwig (Max Hansen), who decide to go "on the town" when their relatives do not arrive for a planned visit. While they are enjoying themselves, their house is robbed, their relatives appear, and the couple is ultimately arrested. All is resolved through an alcoholic haze at the police station. Despite the screwball comedy formula of rapid dialogue and action, growing confusion and wild misadventures, Dolly's desire to be entertained, her rejection of expected behavior, and her manipulation of her husband expose the absurdity of traditional gender concepts and archaic social constructs that make this less a "harmless comedy" and far more a satire with protofeminist aspects. Kolm-Fleck's *Csardas* deals with possibilities of the woman as individual rather than with the male expectations for the female role.

One other major film was made with Czech partnership: Max Neufeld's 1935 *Hoheit tanzt Walzer*/Highness Dances a Waltz, based on the operetta of the same name by Julius Brammer and Alfred Grünwald with music by Leo Ascher. The film, previously made as a silent by Fritz Freisler in 1926, was simultaneously filmed in *three* different language versions (German, Czech and French) at Prague's Barrandov studio as *Romance Viennoise* or *Valse Eternelle*. This independent and poorly imitative attempt at Viennese Film is set in 1820 and offers the story about the creation of the first waltz, not by one of its true composers, Josef Lanner, but by Hans Jaray's "Josef Langer," Beethoven's fictional assistant by day and a bandleader at the Prater amusement park by night. Disguising her royal identity, Princess Marika (Irene Agay) becomes involved with Langer and attempts to promote his new dance music with dire consequences. Ultimately, the resulting scandal helps to popularize the waltz, which Beethoven now also composes, and Marika declares her love for Langer. The critics dismissed this contrived film, which had none of the originality or production details that made the Forst/Reisch product so unique and appreciated. Even so, it managed to find an audience because of the popular presence of Hans Jaray.

Independent Austrian film also created a single co-production with Sweden, the 1936 Fritz Schulz comedy *Rendezvous in Paradies*/Rendezvous in Paradise. Produced by Nationalfilm and Götafilm of Stockholm, it was filmed simultaneously in German and Swedish versions. It was a failed attempt by director Schulz and producer Rudi Loewenthal to establish Austrian independent film co-production beyond Hungary and Czechoslovakia, and it was not shown in Austria until after the war.

By 1936, there were strong contradictions regarding the condition of the Austrian film industry. The state-led Austrian Film Conference was held that year and, suggesting that film had certainly come into its own as a major national art form, made impressive plans for a film academy as well as for an archive and a museum. But the possibilities of independent Austrian filmmaking had begun to fade. The new film agreement between Germany and Austria in March of that year stipulated that the agreement would have to be renewed annually and the Germans now demanded that all German performers and crew (except the extras or atmosphere players) in Austrian films bound for German release would have to present their *Ariernachweis*, or documentation of Aryan status. Only fourteen Austrian films would be allowed into Germany each year. The involvement of Universal Pictures in Austrian film after the studio's exile from Berlin led the government's film council, Eugen Lanske, to seek stronger American involvement in Austrian film production and to open the U.S. market to independent films. His consultations in New York and Los Angeles led to a surprisingly positive response. American studios were more than just interested in co-production. Both MGM and Twentieth Century Fox promised solid investment in the Austrian film industry and planned on five Hollywood/Vienna co-productions in the foreseeable future as well as around fifteen dubbing commissions per year. That May, the *London Reporter* boldly offered the news of the coup: the Lanske/MGM/Fox negotiations had already led to pre-production status for two films to be made in 1937.[36] Even more astonishing was the communication from Joseph Breen, the administrator of Hollywood's Production Code (which guided studios in self-censoring films), who informed Lanske that "as a Catholic, [he] is greatly sympathetic to Austria" and prepared to promote Austria's desires in the Hollywood industry.[37] But German demands for a reduction of American films in Austria and the importation of more German-made features made Lanske withdraw his plans. By January 1, 1937, the duty charges for American and "all English language films" were raised by 50 percent. The opportunity to create Hollywood/Viennese co-productions had been dashed. Given the Austrian talent in Hollywood such a joint effort might have led to a unique chapter in international cinema art, which would have certainly influenced film after 1938 (as a true Austrian exile cinema?) and encouraged the return of Austro-Hollywood film talent to the postwar Viennese film industry. The attention to German demands and the dismissal of the American interests caused such a deterioration in the relationship between the Austrian government and Hollywood that Paramount Studios withdrew its Austrian release of *Champagne Waltz* (USA 1937), an imperial

Vienna-themed musical comedy that counted Billy Wilder among its writers, as well as the studio's weekly newsreels. The distribution of American film in Austria sank to its lowest level since sound was introduced.[38]

The Berlin-Rome Axis of 1936 lost Austria its erstwhile protector, Mussolini, who aligned with Hitler and abandoned Austria to Hitler's goals of Nazi infiltration and the eventual annexation of his former homeland to the German Reich. The removal of the Pilzer brothers from the board of the German/Austrian Tobis-Sascha concern had already indicated the extent of German influence within the Austrian film industry. Tobis-Sascha was transformed into a German "scout," which swallowed up many Austrian production companies by purchase rather than through merger, in an attempt to control the industry landscape and prepare it for *Gleichschaltung*, or a switch over to National Socialism. The summit meeting between Hitler and Chancellor von Schuschnigg at Berchtesgaden in February 1937 was to have normalized the German-Austrian situation, but it was in fact a major step for the Nazification of Austria. Although the Austrian corporate state was to be a non-party or national front system, Hitler demanded and received concessions to allow Austrian National Socialist representation in the government. Members of the mainstream film industry seemed to ignore the ominous possibilities, perhaps because they had already been aryanized and their productions found talent and distribution in Germany with little problem. A roster of fascinating projects was announced for 1938, all, of course, unrealized due to the annexation and redesign of the former Austrian film industry according to Propaganda Minister Goebbels's dictates. Several projects were to have revisited the Habsburg past: Mondial-Film announced a film about the young Empress Elisabeth, known as Sissi, "Die kleine Prinzessin" (The Little Princess). Eventually produced by the aryanized Mondial-Film as *Prinzessin Sissi* in 1939 under the direction of Fritz Thierry, it was not until the Ernst Marischka trilogy of Romy Schneider "Sissi" films of the 1950s that this theme would become synonymous with Austrian film. Styria-Film announced a biopic on Archduke Johann (also not made until 1950) and two Hilde Krahl starrers; Donau-Film presented plans for a film version of Eugene d'Albert's opera *Tiefland* to be directed by Karl Hartl (the film was eventually made by Leni Riefenstahl between 1942 and 1945). But Intergloria announced the most impressive plans of all: German leading man Hans Albers in "Casanova" directed by Karl Hartl; Paula Wessely in "Radium" (a biopic on Madame Curie to be filmed in Paris and Vienna); and Marta Eggerth in "Tatjana," a film written by Thea von Harbou, the co-author of *Metropolis* and former wife of Hollywood director Fritz Lang.

The final Austrian film release was Geza von Bolvary's *Spiegel des Lebens*/Mirror of Life (1938) with the husband and wife team of Paula Wessely and Attila Hörbiger. It did not receive its premiere until after the German annexation in July of 1938. The polarized nature of Austria at the end of its sovereignty is, however, best displayed in two other final films made just prior to the Anschluss. The 1937 Austrian/Czechoslovakian co-production by Jakob and Louise Fleck, of *Der Pfarrer von Kirchfeld*/The Priest from Kirchfeld was the third cinematic treatment of Anzengruber's drama by the couple, who had first filmed it as a silent in 1914. For

Catholicism and folk traditionalism: Hans Jaray, Fred Hülgerth and Hansi Stork in Louise Kolm-Fleck and Jakob Fleck's *Der Pfarrer von Kirchfeld*, 1937.

that version, author Friedrich Torberg scripted the adaptation (using the pseudonym "Hubert Frohn") and the film features Hans Jaray, Hansi Stork, Frida Richard and the Vienna Boys' Choir. The story, played against the backdrop of Austria's breathtaking alpine scenery, revolves around the reputation of a priest who has taken up an orphaned girl as his housekeeper. The man responsible for the hateful gossip, which turns the parish against the good priest, is ultimately transformed thorough personal tragedy. With the housekeeper finally wed to her beloved, the town learns from the experience and the priest can move on to do God's work elsewhere. The film promotes a strong Catholic/Austrian folk ideology in the face of looming National Socialism. It was to be Jakob and Louise Fleck's final Austrian film. Due to their pro–Austrian cinematic stance and Jakob Fleck's Jewish ancestry, the couple was forbidden from making films following the Anschluss. For income, Jakob Fleck briefly offered a photo retouching service from his home. The couple was arrested in 1938 and interned for sixteen months at Dachau and Buchenwald concentration camps. The financial intervention of a German émigré director in Hollywood, William Dieterle, who had launched his career in the couple's 1926 version of *Der Pfarrer von Kirchfeld* (and whose sympathies to "old Austria" is evident in his 1939 Hollywood film *Juarez*, where he presents a benevolent image of the doomed Habsburg Emperor Maximilian of Mexico), allowed the Flecks their release and they ultimately fled to Shanghai. There they created the first Austrian-Chinese film — *Söhne und Töchter der Welt* a.k.a. *Kinder der Welt*/Sons and Daughters of the World a.k.a. Children of the World (1941), co-directed with Chinese filmmaker Mu Fei. The film premiered on October 4, 1941, in the Jindu Theater in Shanghai and ran until withdrawn from circulation following the Japanese occupation in December 1941.[39] Plans for new productions upon their return to Vienna in 1947 were ended with Louise Kolm-Fleck's death in 1950, followed by her husband and creative partner three years later. Her son by Anton Kolm, director Walter Kolm-Veltée, who had been drafted to serve in the Wehrmacht during his mother and stepfather's exile, would, however, continue the long family tradition into the Austrian Second Republic as a noted director and the founder of the Film Academy at Vienna's University of Music and Performing Arts.

The counterpoint to the Fleck's pro–Catholic Austrian imagery was the denigration of imperial Austria, its historical development outside of the German Reich and the cosmopolitan and Habsburg associations of the current Austrian government. *Hotel Sacher* (1938), which by its very name evokes the social center of the imperial Viennese world, was directed by the Reich-approved Erich Engel and written by Friedrich Forster-Burggraf. The film's leads are German actors Willy Birgel and Sybille Schmitz, and they are joined by an Austrian contingent made up of Wolf Albach-Retty, Elfie Mayerhofer, Fritz Imhoff, and Hedwig Bleibtreu as the cigar-smoking Hotel Sacher proprietress, a fictionalized version of the no less provocative Anna Sacher. The film manipulates the World War I Redl scandal in which a homosexual Austrian officer was blackmailed into giving military secrets to the Russians. Here, the officer character's lure is the femme fatale spy played by Schmitz, who weaves intrigue and betrayal around her victim during the New Year's Eve celebration of 1913. Engel's film was meant to "demonstrate" the historical corruption of the multicultural and "Slavic-oriented" Austrian culture, which betrayed Germany and its "true German roots." The Anschluss is pre-justified in the sensationalist commentary of the film's publicity, which asks: "Is this old Austria really rotten at its core and ripe for collapse? Then there is only one choice for a straight and decent man, who chooses not to be a traitor: Escape from this world."[40] As a nominally "Austrian" production aimed against the country of its creation, the film also signaled the end of its production firm, Mondial-Film, which was suspended by the new Nazi government following the entry of Hitler's army on March 12, 1938. *Hotel Sacher* was also subsequently "annexed" and distributed internationally by Germany's national film company, UFA in 1939. Similarly, Tobis-Sascha, the great German-controlled Austrian studio-turned-conglomerate, which had grown from the very beginnings of Austrian cinema, was absorbed by the new National Socialist establishment. Founder Sascha Kolowrat's name vanished from film between 1938 and 1945. Austria disappeared as well, but only from the maps of the world.

3

The Wien-Film Era: 1938–1945

Nazism, Subversion, and the Entertainment Film

The future of the film industry in a country that was to become a province of the German Reich was conceived throughout most of the 1930s, long before Chancellor von Schuschnigg would make his decision to hold a national referendum on the German Anschluss in order to make England and France take notice of Austria's victimization. The policy on what became known as "former Austrian" film was also achieved long before the chancellor's heartrending radio speech to Austria accepting Hitler's preemptive invasion of Austria on March 12, 1938. Hitler's arrival speech, given from the balcony of the imperial Hofburg palace, announced the "return" of his homeland into the Reich and thus marked Austria as the first national victim of Nazi aggression (although given the significant numbers of Austrian National Socialists, Austria could also be seen as a collaborator). Systematic infiltration of Austrian film production through German investment, racial dictates, and blatant corporate absorption since 1933, had so prepared the industry for its new form and role that Berlin was in complete control in a matter of days following annexation.[1]

The first transports of Austrians bound for Dachau concentration camp began on April 1, 1938. Nine days later, von Schuschnigg's referendum was held after the fact by Hitler's new interim "chancellor" of Austria, Arthur Seyss-Inquart. In best ballot-fixing tradition, the results gave a 99 percent vote in favor of Anschluss. Von Schuschnigg was dispatched to a Gestapo prison and later Sachsenhausen concentration camp as the *Gleichschaltung* of the former sovereign nation was undertaken. Austria disappeared from the map and was integrated into the Third Reich as the *Ostmark* or Eastern March. Dissatisfied with this new name, which still recalled "Austria" in German (*Österreich*), Hitler later degraded the annexed country into the even more fragmented and vague *Alpen- und Donaugau* (Alpine and Danube District). In response to the New Order, the Austrian film publication *Mein Film* insisted that "true" Viennese films had always been examples of good "German" cinema, both in theme and execution. That they were Viennese because of "a certain something that one could not place into words"[2] no longer made them Austrian. At first, this statement seems to attempt an absurd sense of continuity for Austrian film coupled with acceptance of German leadership, but one can certainly read between the lines. The idea that despite all external appearances of Nazi pan–Germanization, the spirit of what was Viennese film, indeed what was Austria, would live on in memory and in subtle, even subversive, cultural elements, was the hope and intention of many in this Berlin-controlled film world. With the dissolution of all film organizations and the transfer of their activities to the Reichsfilmkammer or RFK (Reich's Film Chamber), *Mein Film* was soon obliged to call for loyalty to and confidence in Propaganda Minister Joseph Goebbels, the man who would be in charge of the film talents of the *Ostmark*. It was important to him that the industry and the public know their beloved stars also welcomed this "homecoming" to the Reich, and several personalities, including Paul Hörbiger, were quoted in print as encouraging the "yes" vote in April's sham referendum.

All aspects of filmmaking and presentation would now be controlled by the RFK, and membership was required for a "former Austrian" to work in the unified all–German industry. This was, of course, only possible with the documentation of Aryan status. All production plans were suspended, although two comedy films were allowed to proceed before the official announcement of the creation of the basis of Vienna's specific cinematic contribution to the Reich, Wien-Film. Both these works would have ironic tangential connections with the Jewish-American film culture in Hollywood: director E. W. Emo (Emmerich Josef Wojtek, 1898–1975), who had often worked in Germany and was to hold a leading position in the new film hierarchy, produced both of these films through his own company, Emo-Film. *Der Optimist*/The Optimist (1938), a curiously titled film that might have well been suggesting how one should look at the Anschluss, includes Gusti Huber among its cast. After the war, Huber emigrated to the United States with her American officer husband and gained fame on the stage and screen with her portrayal of the mother in *The Diary of Anne Frank* (USA 1959), and as the real-life mother of American actress Bibi Besch. The other Emo film that bridges the brief period between the Anschluss and the establishment of Wien-Film is *Dreizehn Stühle*/Thirteen Chairs, featuring the two great German-language comedians Heinz Rühmann and Hans Moser as two untrustworthy "friends" searching for a lost treasure hidden in one of a set of widely scattered chairs. A remake of the 1936 British film *Keep Your Seats Please*, this film has been adapted several times internationally since and was most recently remounted for the large screen by director/producer Mel Brooks as *The Twelve Chairs* (USA 1970).

The Tobis-Sascha group was transformed into the new Wien-Film (Wien is German for Vienna) firm on December 16, 1938. As the Reich's centralized production unit in the *Ostmark*, it would control the great Rosenhügel studio lot, the secondary Schönbrunn and Sievering facilities, and additional small venues such as the Bauernmarkt building that had housed the Lehrinstitut für Tonfilmkunst in the early 1930s, as well as all film transfer plants and post-production sites. Only three quasi-privately owned production companies were permitted to operate: Emo-Film, Willi Forst's Forst-Film and Styria-Film, but these were in actuality nothing more than satellites of Wien-Film. Managing director of the new studio was Fritz Hirt and the production head of the company was Austrian director Karl Hartl (1898–1978), who utilized his power to keep Vienna's film industry as autonomous as possible from the dictates of Berlin and the influence of its sister studio UFA, which would release all Wien-Film productions. Goebbels foresaw a specific mission for Vienna as one of the three production centers (along with Berlin and eventually Prague) of the Reich. Wien-Film would employ the Viennese Film genre and produce operetta films and musicals as the more entertainment-oriented and more exportable aspect of the Reich's film-making, while UFA Berlin (and the other nationalized German studios, Tobis, Terra, and Bavaria) would focus on dramas, historical spectacles, and propaganda "documentaries." Even the logo of the new company, a treble clef, blatantly associated Wien-Film with the mythos of musical Vienna. Viennese-associated traditions and images, even the dialect, were to be utilized as indications of the Reich's Germanic cultural multivalence, to appeal to the audiences of allied and occupied lands, and most important, to cinematically annex the historical/cultural Vienna (and by extension, Austria). But as I will discuss later, this co-opting of the Viennese myth (intended to contain and exploit) actually allowed Wien-Film to distance itself from, and to some extent subvert, the dictates of the pan–German ideology. One of the primary missions of the Reich's film industry was the production of biographical features (known as the genius genre), which would suggest the importance of Germans in world history and not only "enlighten" but elevate the public's sense of national superiority. Wien-Film would also have to produce its share of films about Austrian musicians, composers and writers who had now become historical figures of the Greater Germany.

Centralization and expansion of film theaters was also instituted. As early as July 1938, all Austrian film theaters, including those owned by UFA prior to the Anschluss, were absorbed into Propaganda Ministry control. Given its specific cultural mission, the new Vienna mega-studio Wien-Film echoed the concept of the Hollywood studio system more closely than had been normal in previous Austrian cinema development. Many Austrian talents at UFA in Berlin (Forst, Moser, the Hörbiger brothers) returned home to participate in this new phase of Vienna's industry. Although such products were films of the German Reich, many of its talents hoped that their efforts would continue to be seen as nothing less than subcultural Austrian cinema. In addition to production head Karl Hartl, Wien-Film's directors were all Aryan Austrians who had established themselves in German film prior to the Anschluss or were leading exponents of the Viennese Film: Willi Forst, Geza von Bolvary, Eduard von Borsody, E. W. Emo and Gustav Ucicky. Like the Hollywood star system, particularly that of MGM, Wien-Film cultivated and promoted the fame of its screen talent, and this roster was composed of internationally recognizable names: Paula Wessely, Attila Hörbiger, Willi Forst, Hans Moser, Paul Hörbiger, Hans Holt, Maria Holst, Hermann Thimig, Leo Slezak, Hilde Krahl, Curd Jürgens, Wolf Albach-Retty and Marte Harell (Karl Hartl's wife). Supporting and character actors were also selected from a specific pool of well-known pre–Anschluss stage and screen talent: among them were Rudolf Carl, Oskar Sima, Annie Rosar, Hedwig Bleibtreu,

Erik Frey, Siegfried Breuer, Karl Skraup, Winnie Markus, Pepi Glöckner, Egon von Jordan, and Rosa Albach-Retty. Also like Hollywood, pairings would be created to "sell" a film: the comedies of Paul Hörbiger and Hans Moser were among the most popular, followed by the dramas of Paula Wessely and Attila Hörbiger, and director/ leading man Willi Forst with almost any leading lady. Although Forst's coupling with Maria Holst in his Viennese Film *Operette* (1940) became a romantic classic, it was Hörbiger and Moser that became known as film's "dream pair," and there was no comparable and lasting romantic male/female pairing.[3] The overwhelming male dominance — even phallocracy of the Nazi ideology — and the reduction of women to subordinate roles had ultimately influenced audience demand and reception.

Conversely, strong unpaired female leads were also popular, but the female stars of Nazi cinema were never quite the paragons of Aryan womanhood the regime would have preferred. Here, the audiences ignored ideology and entrusted their entertainment fantasies to the sultry Dietrich/Garbo/Crawford image of the Swedish Zarah Leander, the exotic Hungarian dancer Marika Rökk, and the Viennese cosmopolitanism of Paula Wessely, Elfie Mayerhofer and Maria Holst. Only the blond Swedish-born actress, Kristina Söderbaum, wife of UFA director Veit Harlan, who created some of Nazi cinema's most anti–Semitic features, managed to essay the self-sacrificing Aryan child-woman in such films as *Das unsterbliche Herz*/The Immortal Heart (Germany 1939), *Die goldene Stadt*/The Golden City (Germany 1942), *Opfergang*/The Great Sacrifice (Germany 1944), and the final Third Reich epic, *Kolberg* (Germany 1945). The box-office "magic" of certain stars also allowed some concessions to their private lives that would run counter to ideological dictates, as in the case of comic superstar Hans Moser, whose Jewish wife was exiled from the Reich to Budapest but was allowed weekend visits from her husband.[4]

The great technicians that had made Viennese Film a success in the pre–Anschluss era were also co-opted by Wien-Film, to ensure that the high quality of film production would continue, perhaps even be surpassed by the new studio. As music was so important to this genre, Willy Schmidt-Gentner continued to contract most of the musical direction assignments. Anton Profes may have been known as the secondary composer of the Wien-Film productions, but both Schmidt-Gentner and Profes conducted the Vienna Philharmonic as the "Wien-Film Studio Orchestra" in the newly built recording hall (part of the studio expansion and state-of-the-art technological upgrading between 1939 and 1941) at Rosenhügel. Truly important figures from pre–Anschluss musical film and operetta were no longer part of this industry phase, since most — Paul Abraham, Ralph Benatzky, Oskar Straus, and Robert Stolz among them — had emigrated or were forced into exile. Wien-Film was thus forced to rely heavily on the music of nineteenth-century composers. Gerhard Menzel was among the most prolific of the studio's screenwriters, usually paired with director Gustav Ucicky. Among cinematographers, Hans Schneeberger, Sepp Ketterer, Günther Anders and Karl Kurzmayer would be most often seen in Wien-Film credits, as was editor Arnd Heyne, who taught many of the new Wien-Film (and later postwar) editors the craft.

With only four exceptions, the more than fifty features produced or distributed by Wien-Film between 1939 and 1945 were not overtly political, although this entertainment angle completely suited the designs of the Propaganda Ministry, especially as it later provided a diversion from the war. Nonetheless, Wien-Film productions, which were to support the National Socialist public directive of *Kraft durch Freude* (Strength through joy) were almost continuously at odds with the censors in Berlin, suggesting that the Vienna-based creations have very little in common with the stricter National Socialist cinema of UFA. Most Wien-Film product found box-office success and remain classics today primarily because of their avoidance of National Socialist ideology and because of their significant artistic and technological aspects. The industry launched its program for escapism through regression into a romanticized Viennese past immediately: the first Wien-Film production (although produced as an Emo-Film) was E. W. Emo's Strauss family saga *Unsterblicher Walzer*/Immortal Waltz (1939), with Paul Hörbiger as Johann Strauss Sr., Fred Liewehr as Johann Strauss Jr., Fritz Lehmann as Eduard Strauss and Hans Holt as Josef Strauss. The lavish imperial setting and the memorable Strauss waltzes might have been claimed by the regime as parts of the Reich's history and the film as a work displaying a family of "German geniuses," but the film generates nothing if not sentimentality for a lost imperial Austrian world. Some of the early productions of Wien-Film, however, were anything but the sort of film the studio has become known for. Two of these productions foreshadowed aspects of neorealism: *Frau im Strom*/Woman in the River (1939) was a curiously gritty film for the period, which echoed the social dramas of the 1930s. Written by Gerhard Menzel and directed by Gerhard Lamprecht, it tells the tale of a suicidal woman rescued from the Danube Canal by a working-class man — a man who becomes involved with a band of smugglers from Southeastern Europe. *Donauschiffer*/Danube Navigator (1940) was directed by Robert A. Stemmle from a script written by Wien-Film dramaturge Hans Gustl Kernmeyer with Philipp Lothar Mayring and Werner Hochbaum, a writer who had been banned by the Nazis. In this film Attila Hörbiger, Hilde Krahl and Paul Javor provide the love-triangle centerpiece for the *Grand Hotel*–style passenger vignettes on a steamship en route to the Black Sea. These unusual lapses in providing lavish musical entertainment were, however, geopolitically motivated and display Wien-Film's secondary mission in reaching an audience in the allied or conquered lands of Southeastern Europe. Another unlikely film is the inventive comedy *Das jüngste Gericht*/Judgment Day (1940). Based on the play by Friedrich Lichtenegger, director Franz Seitz put Karl Skraup, Hans Holt and Susi Nicoletti into this small-town love story set around the appearance of Halley's Comet in 1919 and the belief that it signaled the end of the Earth. The dismissal of apocalyptic notions was aimed at public anxiety about the war, which was palpable despite the victory in Poland. Franz Antel, one of the major Austrian film director/producers of the Second Republic, served as production coordinator for the film. Antel would remake *Krambambuli* (1940), after the novella by Marie von Ebner-Eschenbach, twice in the postwar era. Josef Freidrich Perkönig, an author who supported the regime and became one of its artistic giants, scripted this first version. It was directed by Karl Köstlin, scored by Willy Schmidt-Gentner, and among the film's cast was silent film star Paula Pfluger, last seen on the screen in 1929, in her sound "comeback" role.

There was a strict hierarchy among the actors and directors regarding assignments and studio promotion at Wien-Film and its semi-autonomous satellites. Willi Forst and Geza von Bolvary helmed the musical and the Viennese Film; another actor-turned-director, Hans Thimig, created theater- and literary-based features; and E. W. Emo made comedies and two of Wien-Film's four political-propaganda features.[5] By far the most interesting 1939 release was Gustav Ucicky's *Mutterliebe*/Mother Love, which was written by his usual collaborator, Gerhard Menzel, and was awarded the highest rating in Nazi cinema: "of particular political and artistic value." Both Ucicky and Menzel tended to "specialize" in the themes that managed to achieve such high government ratings.[6] *Mutterliebe* was the first in several Ucicky Wien-Film productions that, although not blatantly political, expounded on the themes of self-denial, self-sacrifice, and the concept of a greater destiny. In the Wien-Film constellation, Ucicky's specialty was a contrived form of social drama, which, with one exception, was not overtly propagandistic but did offer melodramatic allegories on the general values of the Reich. This unique style had already been apparent in Ucicky's films for UFA as early as *Das Flötenkonzert von Sanssouci*/The Flute Concert at Sanssouci (Germany 1930), in which he perfected the blending of literary character types, folktales, and romantic idealism that Siegfried Kracauer considered to be the roots of Nazi culture and film in the Weimar Republic. Set at the court of eighteenth-century Prussia's King Frederick the Great, *Flötenkonzert* espouses the importance of messianic political leadership, male dominance (women are depicted as weak and disloyal), military might, and organized mass culture. Moreover, the film's conclusion suggests that failures in German history can and will be corrected.[7] Ucicky's *Mutterliebe*, which featured Käthe Dorsch as the mother; Hans Holt, Wolf Albach-Retty, Rudolf Prack and Susi Nicoletti as her grown children; and Paul Hörbiger, Frieda Richard, Winnie Markus, Pepi Glöckner and Siegfried Breuer in supporting roles, presented the saga of a self-sacrificing "natural" mother, and this character was intended as a role model for women as war approached.

Ucicky followed with *Ein leben Lang*/For a Lifetime (1940), a melodrama of self-sacrifice, which managed to make its ideological statement without ever once evoking World War II. A pregnant country girl, Agnes (Paula Wessely), is abandoned by her aristocratic lover Hans von Gallas (Joachim Gottschalk), who becomes a diplomat in China. He returns briefly to Vienna and upon meeting her, he tells of his marriage and son, but Agnes remains silent about their child, Hansl. While Hans finds himself in the Great War, Agnes builds herself a life without him and buys a restaurant. With the loss of the empire, the aristocratic world gives way to capitalism and an industrialist buys Hans's family palace. Injured in battle and having lost nearly everything, Hans returns to Vienna in a wheelchair, a broken man who welcomes death. In Vienna's City Park he meets Agnes again, and upon discovering his unknown son, he steps from his wheelchair into a new life. By 1940, Hansl would be old enough to be a soldier of the Reich.[8] He therefore signifies the leveling of the aristocratic world and the failure of the Habsburg Empire but also the ascendancy of the common man under National Socialism. The story of family reunion at any price is a tragically ironic one given the lead actor's life following the film's release. Gottschalk's popularity was not of the magnitude of Hans Moser, but like Moser, Gottschalk also had a Jewish wife. The SS representative at the Propaganda Ministry, Hans Hinkel, insisted Gottschalk divorce his wife and abandon her if he wanted to continue working. Instead, the thirty-seven-year-old actor, his wife and son committed suicide in 1941. His name and image were henceforth banned from the cinema of the Reich.

Ucicky's version of Pushkin's novella *Der Postmeister*/The Postmaster (1940), with Hilde Krahl, Siegfried Breuer, and Heinrich George in the title role, is today considered the director's most accomplished work. The intensely detailed period story of love, tragedy, and the self-sacrifices of a father set in imperial St. Petersburg could have only been made in accordance with the particular demands of the Nazi war machine. In 1940, Ucicky was praised for showing a "different" Russia, one without Communism. Pushkin and other Russian writers were still allowed while Hitler and Stalin celebrated a non-aggression pact, but following the invasion of the Soviet Union in 1941, the film was banned, as was most Russian literature and art. Ucicky's most infamous and still controversial Wien-Film production is *Heimkehr*/Homecoming (1941), with Paula Wessely and Attila Hörbiger, which deals with the supposed abuse of Germans in Poland and "validates" the Nazi destruction of the country. One of the four *Tendenzfilme*, or overt propaganda films of the studio and its satellites, it damaged Wessely's reputation after the war. I will examine this film in the later section on the Wien-Film propaganda cinema. Other Ucicky films of the era also maintained the director's themes of self-sacrifice, loyalty and a form of private heroism: *Schicksal*/Fate (1942), which was set in Bulgaria (a member of the Axis since 1941) and examined the loyalty of the servant; *Späte Liebe*/Late Love (1943) dealt with the sacrifices in a marriage; and *Ein Blick zurück*/A Look Back (1944) presented the fate of an upper-class family. Ucicky created two medical dramas; *Das Herz muß schweigen*/The Heart Must Be Silent (1944), which framed the story about the pioneers of the x-ray with the entreaty that all physicians do their "duty in the total war,"[9] and *Der gebieterische Ruf*/The Calling, a love triangle featuring Maria Holst as a female physician (such a professional female role was truly rare in Third Reich cinema), which was not completed until 1947. Ucicky and Menzel ended their inseparable Wien-Film collaboration with *Freunde*/Friends, which followed the long friendship of two men into marital and social conflicts. The banning of the film upon its completion for its lack of either pure escapist or serious heroic qualities in November 1944 demonstrates the increasing vigilance of Berlin over Wien-Film product as the Reich collapsed.

It was Willi Forst, however, that led and even dominated Wien-Film's reputation and style. He had secured his reputation as a major star, director, screenwriter and producer with his 1939 Forst-Film production of *Bel Ami*, based on the novel of the soon-to-be-banned Guy de Maupassant, and followed it with the test of any great film actor — the double role — in *Ich bin Sebastian Ott*/I Am Sebastian

Ott (1939). Unlike the other directors, he preferred to use relatively untested talent as co-stars and thus managed to create stardom for several leading ladies: Lizzi Waldmüller and Ilse Werner in *Bel Ami*; Trude Marlen in *Sebastian Ott*; and later Maria Holst, Dora Komar and Judith Holzmeister. His most important work of the period is known today as his Wien-Film trilogy: *Operette*/Operetta (1940), *Wiener Blut*/Viennese Blood (1942), and *Wiener Mädeln*/Viennese Girls (begun in 1944 but not completed until 1949). While he certainly used the Reich to further his career, Forst was nonetheless aware of the distinct opportunity he had to continue Austrian content and style in such entertainment films while appearing to satisfy the official mission of Wien-Film. He would later reflect on his involvement with the Nazi propaganda machine and the effort to create both personal and "Austrian" cinema in such a totalitarian state:

> I never wasted much thought on the kind of films I was making. They came about by themselves, born of my relief at no longer having to "reproduce," and of the growing pressure exerted by the Nazis. My native country was occupied by the National Socialists, and my work became a silent protest. Grotesque though it may sound, it is true that I made my most Austrian films at a time when Austria had ceased to exist. I hit upon exactly the things people yearned for: distraction, joy. What I began doing — I would again say, with almost unerring accuracy — turned into a program, was fashioned ever more consciously into a program. Of course, we couldn't go looking for what we wanted in the present, which is why virtually all of my films are set in the past. I created films reviving the spirit of an age in which charm, sophistication, delicacy and courtesy were important qualities. I freely concede that this was the product not just of a mental attitude, but also and to a significant degree of the need to ward off the interference of the Reich Propaganda Minister. Indeed, at a time when the Nazis had just abolished the final remnant of a once vast empire from the map, there was a certain mischievous appeal and gratification in demonstrating to people what an intellectual power Austria had been — albeit in the guise of lightheartedness, music and humor.[10]

Gertraud Steiner suggests that this commentary was no simple hindsighted self-justification. Forst's Wien-Film projects managed to provide a subtle resistance to the dictates of Nazi socioculture. His popular success in presenting what seemed to be harmless excursions into a romanticized Viennese culture of the past provided him an escape from having to create an overt propaganda film, but his allusions and references often contradicted National Socialist dictates and became a point of friction with the censors: "One step further and he would have been barred from making films."[11] Sabine Hake, however, finds such a subversive aesthetic strategy little more than "fantasy resistance," since the unreal and the masquerade, which now might represent difference, had always been part of the Viennese operetta construct. Nevertheless, she concedes that, transformed through Forst's "deceptive lightness and ironic self-awareness, the Vienna myth became a game between the filmmaker and his audience."[12]

Operette/Operetta (1940) has become Forst's best-known work. It is certainly a high point in the Viennese Film genre and brings together all of Forst's talents as auteur. As the film's leading man, writer, director, producer, also responsible for overseeing the artistic and music direction, his superbly orchestrated and uniquely detailed Romantic/decadent style can only be compared to the baroque silent films of Erich von Stroheim, to the elegant comedies of French director René Clair, and to the later operatically orchestrated style of Italian director Luchino Visconti's nineteenth-century period films (*Senso, The Leopard*). Returning to the place and time best suited for the Viennese Film — imperial Austria between the Congress of Vienna and the Belle Époque — Forst's images are photographed with an eye toward nineteenth-century court paintings by Hans Schneeberger and Sepp Ketterer and are underscored by the music of Johann Strauss Jr., Karl Millöcker and Franz von Suppé, as arranged by Willy Schmidt-Gentner and performed by the Vienna Philharmonic and State Opera Choir. One of the most famous songs in the film sung by Forst, "Ich bin ja heute so verliebt" ("I Am So in Love Today"), was reportedly based on song material sketched by Forst during an infatuation with actress Zsa Zsa Gabor, who had once briefly appeared on the stage in Vienna.[13] Forst's script, written with Axel Eggebrecht, offers the backdrop of the historical Viennese theater world (with all Jewish personalities missing) at the end of the nineteenth-century for the genre's typical theme of love that is sacrificed for art. Forst gives an intelligently nuanced performance as the historical Franz Jauner (1832–1900), a provincial theater director who rises to the heights of Viennese society as its opera director but who falls when he is imprisoned for his responsibility in the catastrophic 1881 Vienna Ringtheater fire.[14] His rival, the diva and director of the Theater an der Wien, Marie Geistinger (Maria Holst), adores him, but has renounced love for a successful career in the more elevated world of opera, and she resists both Jauner's advances and his promotion of Viennese operetta. Although he successfully stages the new entertainment form, he is only forgiven and able to reclaim his place in society because a fatally ill Geistinger persuades the audience to welcome his "revolution of the operetta." Following Geistinger's death, it is the naïve singer Emmi (Dora Komar) who earns Jauner's true love. But Geistinger, like Austria in the Reich, maintains a spectral, influential presence, and Jauner sees a vision of her face at the triumphant conclusion of the operetta. The film includes portrayals of personalities that are not simply cameos, as is often the convention in such historical romances but are convincingly woven into Jauner's story: Leo Slezak as operetta composer Franz von Suppé, Paul Hörbiger as Alexander Girardi, Edmund Schellhammer as Johann Strauss Jr., Viktor Heim as the painter Hans Makart, and Curd Jürgens as composer Carl Millöcker. Although *Operette* suggests that artistic fulfillment and fame is available only to men, it is nevertheless unique in its portrayal of a nineteenth-century woman who was as powerful behind the stage as she was on it. Such an image was hardly harmonious with the woman-as-mother dictates of National Socialist ideology. Sabine Hake also considers that gender and sexuality are central to the representation of Austrian cultural superiority in Forst's work in the figure of the composer/conductor, whose threatened masculinity "resonates with larger concerns about Austrian culture and its own emasculated condition"[15] under the Third Reich.

Forst followed the immense success of *Operette* two years later with the second of his Wien-Film trilogy, *Wiener Blut*/Viennese Blood, this time based on an actual operetta, which was created posthumously from Strauss's music. Forst was again director, writer and producer, and brought on Jan Stallich as cinematographer and Schmidt-Gentner as music director. The film takes place during the Congress of Vienna (1814-15), which attempted to restore European "order" following the final defeat of Napoleon (and where the early waltz was supposedly given one of its first public presentations). It is a romantic comedy regarding Count Wolkersheim (Willi Fritsch), the ambassador of a fictional German principality (the remnants of the many states of the Holy Roman Empire in the post–Napoleonic German Confederation were not united into an empire until 1871), and his beautiful Viennese wife (Maria Holst), whose marriage is imperiled by her attempts to reconnect with Vienna and by the Count's bored flirtations with a chorus girl. The film became a proving ground for the film dynasty that would translate the Viennese Film for the

postwar era. Georg Marischka served as assistant director, and Ernst Marischka was co-writer along with Forst and Axel Eggebrecht. Wien-Film's master of sound, Alfred Norkus, offered state-of-the-art work in his field. But as exquisitely mounted and performed *Wiener Blut* may be, its formulaic quality often seems to parody the Viennese Film. Moreover, the central allegory of the historical "love" between the Germans and the Austrians is so contrived and enforced as to border on sarcasm. While the Count distances himself from a Vienna that "is not for us" and from the "noise" of its musical culture, it is the introduction of the new dance — the waltz — that ultimately reunites husband and wife, the Germans and the Viennese. Although the utterance "Viennese blood cannot be denied" explains the film's conceit of a pseudobiological impulse to dance, it also

A Wien-Film period musical romance: Maria Holst and Willi Forst in Forst's lavish *Operette*, 1940.

provides a statement of unyielding difference. *Wiener Blut* was received as one of the most popular films in the Reich and throughout axis Europe in 1942, receiving the "artistically valuable" rating from the RFK. Forst's next film was a rare contemporary salon comedy set aboard a luxury liner, *Frauen sind keine Engel*/Women Are Not Angels (1943). Although not a Viennese Film, Forst made this high-society romp about the creation of a musical a similarly stylized entertainment that existed as far from the realities of the time as was possible.

Forst waited until nearly the end of the Reich and the war to create the final film in his Viennese trilogy. *Wiener Mädeln*/Viennese Girls was begun at Rosenhügel during the bombing raids of 1945, but the nearly continuous exodus of the lead actors and more than 1,700 costumed extras from set to air-raid shelter necessitated the production's move to the Schönbrunn studio facilities and finally to Barrandov Studio in Prague. The film is remarkable as the first color Viennese Film and for expressing the process of resignation, exile, and reemergence that suggests Austria's experience under the Third Reich from an already *postwar* perspective. Forst again takes the leading role, this time as troubled Viennese composer Carl Michael Ziehrer, whose attempt to find fame alongside the already legendary Johann Strauss Jr. meets with some early success, but he abandons the rise after his love, Klara Munk (Judith Holzmeister), rejects him for the diplomat Count Lechenberg (Curd Jürgens). Ziehrer goes into self-imposed exile and gains prominence abroad. Upon his return, he settles for a more accessible love interest and is strengthened by this relationship and his new celebrity. Sent to "defeat" the film's stand-in for John Phillip Sousa, John Cross (Fred Liewehr), at a highly fictionalized 1894 Chicago World's Fair, Forst's Ziehrer at first rejects the competition, but in due course emerges as the proud representative of Viennese culture, as his band appears in old Austrian uniforms and performs his now-famous *Wiener Mädeln* waltz. The reconciliation of Ziehrer, Klara and Lechenberg at the Fair in support of Vienna and to dispel the pain of the past, allegorizes a future Austrian reconstruction through the return of Vienna's culture (Ziehrer) to Vienna's state (Lechenberg).

Sousa's music was not used for the film because he was thought to be Jewish. Instead Schmidt-Gentner and Karl Pauspertl composed several Sousa-esque numbers for Cross's band to play. The large cast includes Hans Moser as Ziehrer's collaborator and friend, Edmund Schellhammer repeating his Johann Strauss Sr. characterization from *Operette*, and Leopold Hainisch as music publisher Haslinger. Alfred Kunz designed the opulent Viennese and American period sets, Stallich served as cinematographer, Hans Wolff as editor, and W. Fred Adlmüller designed the countless costumes. Despite the continuous interruptions from air raids and location changes, production was reportedly near completion by February of 1945. Negative material was stored in Prague and Berlin, but the color processing could only be accomplished at the Berlin facilities, which was nearly impossible given the bombings. By March, the costumes and equipment for the film were removed from the studios and stored in the countryside. The film's music recordings, lost in the final months of the war, had to be re-recorded by Schmidt-Gentner and the Vienna Philharmonic at Rosenhügel Studios during the Allied occupation. Forst's Wien-

Film color extravaganza would not be completed until 1949, and then in two distinct versions: an East German print assembled without his permission from the material stored in Berlin, and the later director's cut completed in Vienna.

Curd Jürgens (1915–82), whose early career ascent was due to Wien-Film but whose criticism of the regime prompted Goebbels to label him "politically unreliable," resulting in labor camp internment in late 1944, commented about Forst's ideological bent in 1971:

> Willi Forst would have made these films anyway, even if there had not been a Ministry of Propaganda; and he made them although there was a Propaganda Ministry. I know for a fact that the authorities kept asking Forst to make a political film. He refused to do anything of the kind. He took refuge in the dream factory, as it were. Dr. Goebbels was quick to take advantage of his good fortune: these films were shown in those parts of Europe under German occupation — and in some unoccupied countries — and conveyed the enchantment of Austria as being a [Nazi] German enchantment. Nevertheless, in my view, Willi Forst put up an unparalleled resistance to the regime and protected us all to the extent that I — and many of my friends — will owe him a debt of gratitude all our lives. He told us exactly what to do. In 1941 he said to me, "Curd, never ever make a film which says anything political. One day you'll have to account for it."[16]

Of course, Forst refers to blatant propaganda, since all films are political statements of some kind. But since the entertainment films Wien-Film specialized in were not understood to be overtly political, this could allow them to be subversively so, by evoking a great deal of material that ran counter to National Socialist ideology and even the regime's cinematic conventions. How this was possible or presentable aside from Forst's specific Viennese Film genre can be best understood in an examination of the work of Karl Hartl. Berlin had chosen him to head Wien-Film, since from the point of view of his previous work, he suited the role perfectly. Hartl was a Vienna-born director who had begun his career as assistant to Sascha Kolowrat, and whose output at UFA in Berlin included two science fiction/fantasy films, *FP1 antwortet nicht*/FP1 Does Not Answer (Germany 1932) and *Gold* (Germany 1932); a *Bergfilm* with Luis Trenker, *Berge in Flammen*/Mountain in Flames (Germany 1930); and the patriotic/Romantic *Ein Burschenlied aus Heidelberg*/A Student Song from Heidelberg (Germany 1930). Hartl clearly understood specific German film genres and tastes but also had exploitable credibility in the Austrian industry.

The Vienna-based cinema of the Third Reich provided a cultural-theoretical counterpoint to the Berlin style that ultimately divided rather than united. Film historian Linda Schulte-Sasse finds either direct use of or influence from the literature, history and philosophy of the eighteenth-century Enlightenment as a strong basis for the German narrative films of the Reich, ranging from the iconization of Prussia in *Fredericus* (Germany 1935) to the blatant anti–Semitism of *Jud Süß*/Jew Suess (Germany 1940) to the genius genre of *Friedrich Schiller, Triumph eines Genies*/ Friedrich Schiller, Triumph of a Genius (Germany 1940) to contemporary themes in films like *Hitlerjugend Quex*/Hitler Youth Quex (Germany 1933), *Robert und*

Bertram (Germany 1939), and the Zarah Leander mega-hit, *Die große Liebe*/The Great Love (Germany 1942).[17] These distorted versions of Enlightenment paradigms offer security to the viewer through familiar material, the valorization of bourgeois culture, and the illusion of classical harmony and wholeness. In a similar fashion, Wien-Film product can be read to find a comforting underlying cultural-historical paradigm in the Viennese Biedermeier and its message of small victories: love, family, modest creativity — all in the service of social harmony. The selective affinity Nazism has with the Enlightenment is mirrored by the ideology's exploitation of the bourgeois-centered culture of the Viennese Biedermeier, particularly its repressive moralist notions and the synthetic-classicism, which promoted reactionary notions of wholeness. Most of the important Wien-Film biographies are set in the Biedermeier milieu: Author Ferdinand Raimund in *Brüderlein fein*/Dear Brother (1942), the Strauss family in *Unsterblicher Walzer*/Immortal Waltz (1939), operetta composer Carl Michael Ziehrer in *Wiener Mädeln*/Viennese Girls (1945–49), and the folk figure of the Fiakermilli in *Schrammeln* (1944). Regardless of how one interprets the concept of a Greater German Reich and negates Austria with the idea of a provincial *Ostmark* and the even more culturally diluted notion of the *Alpen- und Donaugau*, the very success of Wien-Film's mission rested on the conjuring of "an *Austrian* past, not a greater German one."[18] Despite the aryanization of the past, Vienna's Belle Époque could not offer the same pro–German messages as Prussian historical or German literary models might. Lingering imperial-era class consciousness and multiculturalism as well as Catholicism had made the creation of a leveled and homogeneous interwar German-Austrian an impossible challenge that was inherited by the race-based illusions of Nazism. Notions of an autonomous role for the annexed Austria, such as the early *Ostmark* Governor Artur Seyss-Inquart's concepts of naming a future district the "Prince Eugene Gau" (referring to one of the heroes of the liberation of Vienna in the Turkish Siege of 1683) and "The Reich Fortress of Belgrade" (conjuring up images of Austro-Hungarian designs in the Balkans) were immediately dispelled by a Habsburg-detesting Hitler who rejected such a "quasi-imperial and royal [Austrian] National Socialism." Nevertheless, Austria's history and culture continued to impede pan–Germanism in the Austrian territory.[19]

Perhaps the most interesting intentional failure of Nazi ideological *Gleichschaltung* in Wien-Film product occurs in Karl Hartl's 1942 Mozart biography *Wen die Götter lieben*/Whom the Gods Love, written by Eduard von Borsody from a well-known novella. It is important to the comprehension of film creation in annexed Austria to examine this film in order to offer a clear example of the subtle undercurrents that played against National Socialist or pan–German ideology. Hartl, who had been known to scoff at Nazi cultural doctrines,[20] began work on the composer's story with an obvious disregard for ideological realities. He initially hired Elfi von Dassanowsky, a young opera talent and music student at Vienna's Academy of Music, to instruct actor Curd Jürgens in piano and music for his role as Emperor Joseph II. Hartl was aware that Dassanowsky had refused to join Nazi youth and music organizations and her education and fledgling career was subsequently suspended for extraordinary labor service.[21]

Schulte-Sasse includes Hartl's film in her roster of the Nazi genius genre, a category that she analyzes as National Socialism's "biologistic celebration of Leader, Genius, or Personality."[22] The fact that most German genius films, and Hartl's Mozart work as well, are set in the eighteenth century suits Nazism's distorted affinity with the Enlightenment, since the decay of that period eventually generated the "aesthetic of genius." As public attention shifted from the work of the Enlightenment to the deification of authors such as Goethe and Schiller, the genius aesthetic, or what Jochen Schmidt considers an "increasingly reactionary genius-religion,"[23] developed. The connection of this worship to Romantic notions of the poet-leader transposed into a National Socialist messiah who would rescue the *Volk* from industrial mass society is strong. Among the genius films Schulte-Sasse discusses that demonstrate the ideology of the genre is Herbert Maisch's *Friedrich Schiller* (Germany 1940). Schulte-Sasse investigates how this biopic could be understood as both the story of a German "superman" and an indictment of the oppression of the spirit. Among its many ruptures is the "ambivalent critique of disciplinary tyranny ... the necessary Other against which he [the genius] realizes himself."[24]

To read Hartl's *Wen die Götter lieben* as a genius film is to realize the difficulty of an Austrian cultural *Gleichschaltung* with Nazi German norms. Like Schiller, Mozart represents the genius that can be reflected on both high and popular cultural planes, the mixing of which, as philosopher Theodor Adorno posits, frees the observer from critical understanding of the art in favor of accepting the "kitsch-biography" as the ennobling force. For Nazi purposes, it becomes a "narcissistic mirror"[25] for the masses in their identification with the German genius. Also like Schiller, Mozart is known for his commonness and his role as a rebel hero against forces that do not understand his greatness. But this is where the similarity ends. Unlike Schiller or the other German genius figures in Nazi cinema, Mozart had no true Other against which he needed to realize himself. He composed for, against, and regardless of the authority that he attempted to manipulate and which could not deal with him. Whether employed by the Archbishop of Salzburg or facing the Emperor's courtiers in Vienna, Mozart composed music to order, but also music for himself and for the masses, often simultaneously. Mozart may be interpreted as a genius who rises from the people and falls to them again, but his transcendence is in his art rather than in a "heroic" life, and Hartl's film emphasizes this quite directly. Despite the posturing of the title, Hartl's Mozart appears as the unruly target of a regimented world that would have him be appropriately submissive or disappear—much like Austrian cultural identity in the Nazi Reich.

Maisch's *Friedrich Schiller* shifts the biographical emphasis of family and interpersonal relationships in Schiller's life to the subject as pure creative ego. The Nazi genius aesthetic nullifies such banalities as parents to fulfill the idea of an artist's self-birth through the creation of a masterwork.[26] Hartl's film goes distinctly in the opposite direction: Hans Holt's slightly effeminate Mozart dispels any notions of the creative German superman or even of the clichéd masculine hero. His Mozart is a playful child-man, a doting son and friend. Unlike the Schiller biopic, Hartl opens his film and births his creator in the gentility of familial love. And unlike the parents in *Schiller*, Mozart's mother and father are not spectators to greatness; they are an integral and nurturing aspect of his self-realization. Following the panoramic opening shot of Salzburg, we are met with gossips that study the coach waiting to take Mozart and his mother (Rosa Albach-Retty) to Paris. We witness the loving farewell between Mozart's parents, follow Mozart's father (Walter Janssen) as he searches for his missing son, and we discover Mozart excitedly showing a miniature portrait of the woman he is infatuated with to a friend. The film's opening hardly suggests pro–German propaganda or even sympathy: when the gossiping women begin to criticize the impending trip, a man corrects them and praises the decision, suggesting how much better a life in Paris would be compared to Mozart's present situation. The journey is sealed with "Adieu," the first of a roster of French words Mozart uses throughout the film — "succès," "soirée," and "compositeur" among them. In an ideological atmosphere where foreign loan words are dispelled with often archaic and odd-sounding *Reichsdeutsch* and professional titles are strictly translated into proper German, and given the poetic license of Hartl's biography, such constant French flourishes might have easily and expectedly been removed.

The nationalistic content is often incongruously obvious or else playfully subverted. On the journey to Paris, Mozart convinces his mother to stop in Mannheim to see Luise Weber (Irene von Meyendorff) whom he met on a previous tour. He produces the miniature again and comments on "her blue eyes and blonde hair." At the Weber family meal, Mozart's desire to become the royal court conductor is deflated by Luise's sister Sophie (Thea Weis), who suggests the Mannheim court is saturated with "intrigue." Instead of a German self-definition, Mozart frames himself as a foreigner and replies, "Wird man schon deixln, wie man bei *uns* sagt" (We'll manage it somehow [using a term in dialect], as *we* say). It is Luise's singing talent and beauty that appeals to the Prince instead of Mozart's conducting, and he is thanked for the discovery and dismissed on behalf of the monarch by the foppish, French-speaking Baron von Gemmingen (Richard Eybner). Although this royal rejection of Mozart might be interpreted as the repressive Other by which he might harden his genius, what effect it could have on the audience reception of the character's heroism is immediately negated by the following scene. Mozart, awaiting Luise's farewell with his doting mother, is met instead by the attentive Constanze, who arrives with flowers and food for the travelers. The composer is literally surrounded by women who adore him, not for his genius but for his boyish helplessness.

Following the death of Mozart's mother and his return to Salzburg then Vienna, which is conveyed only by title card, the viewers join a coffeehouse conversation by Mozart's friends held in unabashed Viennese dialect. Kramer and Prucha call the cinematic cultivation of this dialect during the Anschluss "Viennese Film's most important trump card."[27] Gertraud Steiner finds that "a kind of hidden resistance shimmers" in the use of such dialect.[28] The Viennese patois in Hartl's film spares no one unfamiliar with the sound and suggests a difference with Mannheim nearly equal to that of France. The waiter underscores a cultural difference in his attempt to rally support for Austria's son by reminding everyone that they are in Vienna — as if this suggests something quite different from the rest of the (German) world.

„Wen die Götter lieben"

Mozart as Austrian memory: Winnie Markus and Hans Holt in Karl Hartl's *Wen die Götter lieben*, 1942.

In view of Hitler's hatred of the Habsburg dynasty and the multicultural Austrian Empire, Hartl's Emperor Joseph II, portrayed here by Curd Jürgens, offers another conflicting element to Nazi German (e.g., anti–Austrian) film propaganda. With great respect, the court official von Strack (Paul Hörbiger) reminds the court musicians that the monarch is to be addressed "not as the Emperor but as His Majesty." Jürgen's violin-playing Emperor who unknowingly performs Mozart's composition with his string quartet is attractive, talented, intelligent, and, given Jürgen's "Aryan" leading-man visage, the quintessential Nazi cinema image of a strong leader. His conversation with von Strack ridicules both German cultural superiority and the dialect problems of Wien-Film. Although the Emperor speaks a gentler form of Viennese dialect, he does not understand von Strack's thick accent and the courtier has to repeat himself. The dialogue seems calculated to call attention to the difference in the language. Moreover, although the match of the German Constanze Weber and Mozart might symbolize a German-Austrian union, Constanze is anything but the model for proper German womanhood. Her meeting with Mozart in Vienna shows her to be untalented in the kitchen, vain about her appearance and coquettish. The sequence immediately following the Emperor's approval of Mozart is a love scene with Constanze in Frau Weber's kitchen, which emphasizes Mozart's frivolous sensuality, a trait not appropriate to a "German genius."

Vienna, and by association Austria, is evoked as different from Germany and as having an important history in the discussion of the libretto for Mozart's new opera *Die Entführung aus dem Serail* (The Abduction from the Seraglio). This story of European women kidnapped for a harem recalls the Turkish Sieges of Vienna and one of the participants remarks, "That is something exotic, something that the Viennese always like." The libretto's seduction scene helps Mozart decide on marrying Constanze against the wishes of her mother, and he subsequently sets out his bourgeois expectation of life, which hardly inspires a narcissistic mirror or biologistic celebration of genius: moderate fame, saving money, raising a family. The scenes that convey the "birthing" of the genius through his work — Mozart conducting the premiere of the *Serail* opera — is intercut with the birth of Mozart's son. But this parallel of genius production is rendered ambiguous by Mozart's departure from the opera house in view of the Emperor (who does not protest) to find even greater joy with Constanze and son. If genius movies "are pervaded by the same opposition between a centralized social form and the 'heart,' under which lies a more fundamental opposition between everyday constraints and aesthetic elevation,"[29] then Hartl's Mozart only pays lip service to this concept. His genius finds the physical life far more compelling than notions of immortality. This is underscored by the sequence that presents a peaceful Biedermeier tableau of a Mozart family scene, interrupted and threatened not by unenlightened forces but by two very base attractions: money and sex. Constanze's complaint that the baker will no longer give credit forces the squandering Mozart to go to a moneylender, and sister Luise's seductive appearance rekindles his early attraction and Constanze's jealousy.

The outdoor party sequence in Prague, where Mozart celebrates his new opera *Don Giovanni* (Don Juan), hints at the ideal of the Romantic creator, particularly as Mozart and Luise perform an impromptu aria in nature. But the scenes are calculated to motivate Constanze's alienation and to suggest the multiculturalism of the Austrian experience. Mozart drinks a toast to his hostess and praises the friendship and kindness of his Bohemian friends for giving him "a life without cares." Mozart is equated with his own Don Juan creation and, similar to the previous birth scene, his conducting of *Don Giovanni* is intercut with a fantasy of Constanze's departure. Once again, genius production is subsumed by basic, even banal, human needs and relationships. Habsburg Austria is evoked again as Mozart composes both his *Zauberflöte* (The Magic Flute) opera and his final and unfinished work, the *Requiem*, during which he recalls in montage the successes of his childhood. The images replay the anti-genius aspects of the film and idolize Old Austria: the child Mozart playing with other children and cuddled in his mother's arms; a shot of the Gloriette colonnade announcing Schönbrunn Palace; his piano performance for Empress Maria Theresia; a tour of Europe with his father. The nostalgia for a happy and prosperous past is so sutured to images of the empire that viewer identification with Mozart would manipulate members of an *Ostmark* audience to conjure their own memories of the lost Austria.

The most fascinating scene of Hartl's film is Mozart's fictionalized meeting with an unknown young musician, Ludwig van Beethoven (René Deltgen), who is the film's closest approximation of a genius genre type. He appears as if out of nowhere with a visage already hardened into a tortured seriousness that suggests his rage at the ordinary and his overwhelming passion for art. His piano perform-ance of a pastiche of themes from future work presents him to the audience as an already triumphant and transcendent musical deity even in this embryonic state. Moreover, he cannot fathom Mozart's warning that he will have a difficult time of overthrowing tradition. Beethoven mythically retreats into the night, but not before asking Mozart if he might call again. Nominally, the chain of genius continues, the torch is passed, but the obsessive, egocentric German must first learn from the more human and pragmatic Austrian.

Mozart's death as he is composing his *Requiem*, including his imagination of the soprano choir voices in the Confutatis, was lifted to great extent and without credit by Czech-American director Milos Forman for his 1984 film *Amadeus*. The connection of Mozart's greatness with the public ("he will live on in us ...") and the avoidance of Christianity in the deathbed scene seem artificial given the set-ting and is contrived to suit Nazi ideology. The dying Mozart envisions being wel-comed by the descending Queen of the Night from his *Magic Flute* rather than by a Christian deity, and Constanze is consoled with pantheistic spiritualism: "Those whom the gods love, they take back early." The closing title shot repeats the motif of the opening credits — a lyre and an intertwined laurel branch — framing the story in classical notions of eternal greatness. The heroic tone of this death is also accom-plished by the avoidance of Mozart's pauper's funeral and the indifference of the court and the public. Ironically, such a true depiction might have enforced the image of Mozart as a maligned, misunderstood genius, who is condemned by the repres-sive Other, but the contrived closure of a hero's death was more effective for the home-front of 1942. This fictional enshrinement of Mozart by the Austrians at his deathbed only underscores the film's subversive message. Mozart is associated with a great Old Austrian culture in his youth and again at his death. The geopolitical points of Mozart's life in Hartl's film are neither convincing of German cultural superiority nor of some precursor of a unified (National Socialist) Europe. Hartl tends toward a realistic con-veyance of a divisive, dynastic Europe in which Germany, as represented by Mannheim, pales in its unimportance to both Paris and Vienna. Although the former is never seen, its counter–German influence haunts the film in language and aristocratic style.

Similarly, the film's Austria, represented by Salzburg, Vienna, and Prague, with its heavy dialects, exotic elements and sophisticated urbanity seems foreign in com-parison to provincial Mannheim. The suggested superiority of France and the difference of Austria are clearly the filmmaker's choices and a subversion of the pan–German anti–Habsburg historiography is the result. Hartl's film should not be considered a resistance film in the strict sense of the term, nor is it intended as an affront to the German viewer. Rather, the work represents the best of what may be called Wien-Film's cinema of hidden identity — reminding those of the *Ostmark* what Austria was and might still be under the propaganda of the Reich.

Karl Hartl's 1955 remake of *Wen die Götter lieben*, titled simply *Mozart,* provides an informative intertext with the 1942 film. It underscores the director's earlier work as one yielding to nominal dictates of Nazi cinema but also omitting the calculated aspects found in the typical genius genre. The 1955 Mozart hagiography, however, clearly follows the ideology of the genius film. As portrayed by the introspective Oskar Werner, Hartl's second Mozart has few childlike attributes. Gone are the composer's parents and his wife and son vanish early, while his mother-in-law's presence provides no significant plot purpose. Werner's Mozart lives only for his artistic creation and is surrounded by admiring performers and fawning women — particularly the femme fatal Luise, portrayed by the exotic-looking Nadja Tiller, who attempts to seduce him, and by Johanna Matz as Annie Gottlieb, the first to perform the leading role of Pamina in *The Magic Flute*. Unlike Hartl's earlier Mozart, this one seems incapable of love for anything but his own work. His relationship with Annie, although possibly physical, remains primarily one that focuses on her voice and his music. The women of Mozart's life are given more functional roles in the Wien-Film opus than in the postwar remake, where they have little bearing on the central genius character and recognize that they must accept his lack of attention. Additionally, the French are labeled revolutionaries and Mozart is called a "very German" composer.

The remake also plays heavily to what Adorno calls the "bourgeois vulgar-consciousness" that is satisfied by the representation of art through a genius icon rather than the art itself,[30] a strong aspect of the genius genre. Hartl pads this film with so many often awkwardly inserted excerpts from Mozart's works, that Hartl's second Mozart seems to have no life or purpose beyond the operatic stage. The anti-imperial Austria sentiment that might have suited the 1942 version is apparent in the 1955 remake. Here the Emperor never appears, but his Lord Chamberlain displays an arrogant attitude toward Mozart, which is also presented in the film's early music store scene. There, members of a decadent aristocracy ridicule Mozart and praise composers of foreign origin: Chimerosa, Scarlatti, and Salieri. The more common singers, musicians, and inn patrons, however, worship this German-speaking son of the *Volk*.

The genius genre attributes in Hartl's 1955 version, however, do not dispel the image of Mozart as a childish, nonconformist and selfish artist. That is precisely what Mozart is called upon to represent in Milos Forman's *Amadeus*, which is based on Peter Shaffer's stage play and uses the fantasy of a fatal rivalry with Salieri taken from Alexander Pushkin's drama and the Rimsky-Korsakov opera, *Mozart and Salieri*. Forman also lifts aspects directly from Hartl's 1955 film, notably the now famous "too many notes" line and the entire burial scene. Forman's Mozart, a vulgar father-fearing autodidact who wears flamboyant wigs, may be a genius but he is strongly informed by the anti-patriarchal counterculture of the 1960s and the punk influences of the early 1980s. Reading the two Hartl Mozart films against each other, it is apparent that the director knew that Mozart could never represent dominant culture even in the nominal ideological manipulations of his 1942 opus. It can only have been for the addition of the general image of Mozart to the Nazi cinematic cultural canon that *Wen die Götter lieben* was awarded the RFK rating "of particular political and artistic value" as the film offers no compelling propaganda in the service of German culture or the heroic genius cult. Instead, Hartl's film presents a very human figure whose uniqueness is less due to his genius than to his childlike persona, banal desires, and what can only be described as often startling Austrian "national traits." Goebbels praised the film by suggesting that Mozart's music was symbolic of the great culture Germany was defending against the "wild invasion of the barbarians of the East."[31]

Willi Forst's concept of the elegant musical inspired a new generation of directors at Wien-Film and led to hybridization of the original Viennese Film genre. Geza von Bolvary's contemporary comedy *Wiener G'schichten*/ Viennese Tales (1940) paired the "dream team" of Hans Moser and Paul Hörbiger as waiters in Vienna's posh Café Fenstergucker, a celebrated meeting place of opera stars, artists and members of high society. The film, written by Ernst Marischka and Harald Bratt, featured most of the prominent character actors of the time and blended both the stylized atmosphere of the Viennese Film with the witty dialogue and physical humor that went to Hollywood with Ernst Lubitsch and Billy Wilder. Von Bolvary followed up this Wien-Film brand of the screwball comedy, with *Dreimal Hochzeit*/Marriage Times Three (1941), again written by Ernst Marischka, this time with Axel Eggebrecht, from an idea by the very non-comedic Gerhard Menzel, and featuring the Austrian and German mix of Marte Harell, Willy Fritsch, Hedwig Bleibtreu and Theo Lingen. In 1941, Hubert Marischka decided to try his own hand at directing this genre and did so quite admirably with *Wir bitten zum Tanz*/Will You Dance?, which reunited Moser and Hörbiger as two rival dance school directors. The film is considered a classic today, not only for its adroit comedic performances but also for Moser's hit song, which, sung in dialect, certainly suggested the nostalgic undercurrent of the Wien-Film productions: "Ich trag im Herzen drin ein Stückerl altes Wien" ("In my heart I carry a little piece of Old Vienna").

As a director, Hans Thimig (1900–91) concentrated on stage-to-screen translations and quickly surpassed his already impressive skills in front of the camera. His breakthrough came with the romantic comedy *So gefällst du mir*/That's How I Like You (1941), which he co-directed with Rudolf Schaad. He followed this with two Wien-Film classics: the 1942 biopic (if not to say genius genre) film on Austrian author Ferdinand Raimund, entitled *Brüderlein fein*/Dear Brother with Hans Holt, Marte Harell, Hermann Thimig, and Paul Hörbiger, and the 1943 film *Die kluge Marianne*/Wise Marianne, which gave dramatic diva Paula Wessely her only romantic comedy role as a peasant girl who transforms herself into a sophisticated lady for the love of a writer (played by Thimig rather than by her husband, Attila Hörbiger, who co-stars). It was the theater biography of *Brüderlein fein* and his 1944 *Die goldene Fessel*/The Golden Bond, based on the play by the nineteenth-century Austrian folk writer Johann Nestroy, that gave Thimig his reputation as the counterpoint to Willi Forst at Wien-Film. Both auteurs dealt with the culture of the *Biedermeier* era, but whereas Forst focused on the operetta and music world in the Viennese Film genre, Thimig concentrated on theatrical translation. Much like Forst, Thimig loved the seemingly endless possibilities of the medium. Unlike Forst, however, who attempted to stylize music and drama into "pure cinema," Thimig desired to find a unique balance between theater and film, for the sake of expanding theater into a more realistic visual realm.[32] To accomplish this, Thimig allowed writer Franz Gribitz to update Nestroy's difficult and dated dialect and to add realistic development to some of the playwright's more abstract tableaux, which required the creation of original scenes and dialogue. Given the high regard for Nestroy in Austria, this might have spelled disaster, but Thimig succeeded in remaining loyal to the spirit of the original work. Rather than an adaptation, Thimig created a cinematic re-vision — as if Nestroy had been able to write for film. The alterations made this cautionary comic tale about the nouveau riche, designed by Alfred Kunz and Fritz Jüptner-Jonsdorff and skillfully shot by Hans Schneeberger, a popular success.

Brüderlein fein utilized costume designs by Ernie Kniepert (1911–90), whose unusual career journey between Vienna and Hollywood has been forgotten and is even today missing from studies attempting to recover women in film history. Her early creations in her native Austria were for popular dance artists and Viennese operetta productions. These brought her to the attention of Hollywood scouts and resulted in a six-month contract with MGM in 1938. Kniepert assisted both Adrian on his designs for *The Wizard of Oz* (USA 1939) and Orry-Kelly on the film about the tragic involvement of the Habsburg dynasty in Mexico, *Juarez* (USA 1939). She returned to Vienna after the conclusion of the contract and joined the group of the most popular costume designers at Wien-Film: Hill Reihs-Gromes (*Der Postmeister*) Alfred Kunz (*Operette*), Albert Bei (*Der weiße Traum*), W. Fred Adlmüller (*Wiener Mädeln*), and Herta Broneder (*Die goldene Fessel*). Period costuming was often a collaborative project at the studio, but Kniepert's designs for *Wen die Götter lieben*/Whom the Gods Love (1942) and *Brüderlein fein* were considered among the best of the individual efforts. Following the war, Kniepert created the costumes for the production of Beethoven's opera *Fidelio*, which reopened the Vienna State Opera House in 1955 after a decade of painstaking repair from Allied bombing, for the Salzburg Festivals, and for Austrian film into the 1960s.

Hotel Sacher creator Erich Engel attempted to soften his heavy-handed propagandistic reputation with the 1942 romance film *Sommerliebe*/Summer Love, which was based on Otto Erich Hartleben's Hungarian-themed novella, *Die Serenyi* (The Serenyi Woman) for O. W. Fischer and Susi Nicoletti. That same year, Geza von Bolvary directed one of the studio's more costly (1.8 million Reichsmark) projects, *Die heimliche Gräfin*/The Secret Countess, with a script by Geza von Cziffra. The lush period comedy takes place during the final years of the Danube monarchy. Created by two men of the Austro-Hungarian nobility, the film displays an odd contradictory relationship to the era, denigrating the imperial court and its aristocracy (in a fictionalized setting in Bohemia) in an almost mechanical nod to National Socialist ideology, while at the same time celebrating its culture and elitist atmosphere. Elfriede Datzig appears as the Countess and Marte Harell as a thief who switch roles and save the Archduke (Paul Hörbiger) from a scandal invented by the coup-minded Kubasta (Oskar Sima). The film was rated "artistically valuable" but also "educational." Also in 1942, Geza von Bolvary directed Gerhard Menzel's screenplay, *Schicksal*/Fate, which attempted to bridge the Ucicky social melodrama and the Viennese Film and was set in von Bolvary's more familiar milieu of royalty.

Geza von Cziffra created one of the most famous of the entertainment films from Wien-Film in 1943. *Der weiße Traum*/The White Dream was intended to be Wien-Film's answer to the novelty musicals starring Hollywood's Sonja Henie. This was Austria's first ice revue film and the only one during the Wien-Film era, although the genre would be revisited again after 1945. At a cost of more than 2 million Reichsmark, the film was among the most expensive of the era, but also one of the most successful throughout the Reich and occupied Europe, eventually earning back 35 million Reichsmark. It placed star ice dancer Olly Holzmann and Olympic ice skater Karl Schäfer into dance numbers and sets that rivaled Hollywood's mania for backlot bombast. Anton Profes composed the score and created three classic songs that are still popular today including "Kauf dir einen bunten Luftballon" ("Buy Yourself a Colored Balloon"). The film was so strikingly entertaining and apparently so nonpolitical that prints obtained during occupation of Vienna ran in Soviet cinemas for several years.[33] The director followed this immense success with one more Olly Holzmann vehicle, the comedy *Hundstage*/Dog Days (1944), which put Holzmann on roller skates. *Der weiße Traum* subsequently inspired the founding of the Vienna Ice Revue in 1945, which then in turn appeared in feature films of the 1950s and 1960s.

Next to the Viennese Film and musical extravaganzas, the main draws of Wien-Film were the comedies of E. W. Emo. Following his unimpressive attempt at mounting a Forst-like Viennese Film on the Strauss family, *Unsterblicher Walzer*/Immortal Waltz in 1939, Emo quickly returned to the contemporary character-driven comedies he excelled at before the Anschluss, such as the Magda Schneider/Fritz Imhoff musical comedy *Musik für Dich*/Music for You and the Hans Moser/Trude Marlen crime spoof *Die verschwundene Frau*/The Vanished Woman, both from 1937. His first comedy in the Wien-Film era, produced under his Emo-Film banner, was *Anton der Letzte*/Anton the Last (1939), written by Fritz Koselka who would script most of his films, and features Hans Moser, O. W. Fischer and Elfriede Datzig. A contemporary satire that plays on several social taboos, which were considered obsolete under National Socialism and therefore not deemed offensive, it is primarily known for allowing Moser one of his most manic performances as the irascible servant to a count (Fischer) who has an illegitimate child with a local peasant girl (Datzig). The film was partially shot at the Klessheim Castle near Salzburg, which enabled Moser to complete rehearsals for that year's Salzburg Festival. Emo followed this with *Der liebe Augustin*/Beloved Augustin (1940), with music by Schmidt-Gentner, a star vehicle if ever there was one for Paul Hörbiger, who appeared as the seventeenth-century folk legend and minstrel Augustin (the subject of a famous folk song) who miraculously survived the Black Plague after having spent the night in an open mass grave. The film, which features

Wien-Film's ice-revue sensation: Olly Holzman in Geza von Cziffra's *Der weiße Traum*, 1943.

Maria Andergast, Richard Romanowsky, Rudolf Prack, and opera singer Michael Bohnen as Emperor Leopold I, takes critical shots at the Habsburg Empire by portraying Augustin as a German rebel who criticizes the aristocratic French influence at Vienna's court. Aside from the official praise for his two propaganda films, this was the only Emo picture to receive a state rating of "valuable to popular culture." His comedies suffered the same biased reception found in all Western cinema; they were not considered particularly important as film art, despite the fact that they are highly accomplished films and represent Emo at his most honest creativity. Returning to modern times, Emo once again provided Hans Moser with a suitable role for his comic curmudgeon in *Meine Tochter lebt in Wien*/My Daughter Lives in Vienna (1940), with Elfriede Datzig, O. W. Fischer, and a host of character actors. The frantic comedic structure of the film follows a *commedia dell'arte* style and historian Walter Fritz believes that Moser's portrayal of Florian Klaghofer, who mistakenly believes his daughter is the wife of a rich man in Vienna, is to be considered Moser's best nonpartnered performance on film. In 1941, Emo and Moser would pervert this successful artistic collaboration by creating Wien-Film's only comedic propaganda film, a political satire called *Liebe ist Zollfrei*/Love Is Tax-Free. After directing yet another propaganda feature, a biographical drama on the final days of famed Vienna mayor Karl Lueger, *Wien 1910*/Vienna 1910 in 1943, Emo left politics behind to again cast Moser in the type of film that allowed the actor his best bluster in *Reisebekanntschaft*/Travel Companion, a screwball comedy that has Moser on the trail of a missing suitcase filled with lottery winnings.

As the war progressed, official criticism of the nonconformist aspects of the Wien-Film product increased. Although Propaganda minister Goebbels appreciated Willi Forst's work as a director, he found his presence as a leading man too soft for the times and believed that there was perhaps even something "Jewish" about his on-screen persona.[34] Forst's cinematic gentlemen did not present the ideal of a National Socialist hero and Goebbels lamented that *Operette* was actually hindered by Forst's performance. He had no knowledge of Forst's bisexuality, which was a secret widely known and kept in the industry, and if exposed would have immediately ended Forst's career and imperiled his life. In 1942, all film production in the Reich, including the nominally autonomous Wien-Film studio, was consolidated as part of the UFA concern, the UFI Trust. Director subsidiaries such as Forst-Film or Emo-Film, regional satellites such as Styria-Film, and all independent post-production facilities were absorbed by a unified industry that was ideologically and financially controlled by the state as an actual branch of the government. Although it was still answerable to Goebbels's Propaganda Ministry, Fritz Hippler, creator of one of the most virulently anti–Semitic "documentaries" of the Reich, *Der ewige Jude*/The Eternal Jew (Germany 1940), was appointed as the new Reichsfilmintendant (Reich Cinema Director). Goebbels explained this reorganization as increased recognition for the great achievement of film in and for the Reich, but he also asked that the industry become more budget-minded. Unless previously approved, no film could be longer than 2,500 meters and cost more than 1 million Reichsmark. The Wien-Film costume epics and musicals seemed to have standing permission to overspend, but by 1943, only minimum pay would be forthcoming to the talent of the Reich's film industry.

Measures were taken to subordinate film more strictly to the requirements of the ideological, economic and propagandistic aspects of the "total war" effort. The following were among the subjects prohibited from any feature film: persons smoking, the caricaturing of teachers or academics, members of the Habsburg dynasty, Austrian imperial uniforms, marriages without children, illegitimate children, negative images of Berlin, and any type of catastrophe. Undesired but not entirely forbidden concepts bordered on the absurd: espionage involving army personnel, low-class Berlin dialect, scripts featuring a chain of coincidences, and names associated with commonness, parody, or with the culture of old Austria such as Lehmann, Schulze, Müller, Meier, Krause, Anna, Emma, Berta, Marlies, August, Emil and Gustav. Among the aspects encouraged were positive images of teachers and authority figures, families with many children, upper-class Berlin images, and attractive names.[35] The "majesty of death" as Hippler put it, was an important artistic aspect in film, particularly in the biographical or genius genre films, but he suggested that these death scenes be avoided for the sake of "piety and respect" for such great figures. Of course, the avoidance of death scenes had far more to do with the war than with artistic tastes, and Wien-Film presented only three such deathbed scenes: Johann Strauss Sr. in *Unsterblicher Walzer*, Mozart in *Wen die Götter lieben*, and the actress Therese Krones in *Brüderlein fein*.[36] Propaganda minister Goebbels and *Ostmark* governor Baldur von Schirach made an official visit to Wien-Film's Rosenhügel studios on March 14, 1942, to see the new sound recording facilities and to reaffirm the role of Wien-Film within the Reich's cultural goals. It was the director of the studio facility, Fritz Hirt, rather than production chief Karl Hartl, who received the political leaders. Hirt, a German who had emphasized Wien-Film's readiness and ability to serve National Socialism from the very founding of the company, was the studio's liaison man with the Party. Soon thereafter, the regime informed Wien-Film that any false reports about the war in film or by industry personnel would be punishable by imprisonment and even death. Although their subversive power was never truly understood, the heavy Viennese or Austrian dialects of Wien-Film productions finally did become too much for Berlin to take. In 1944, Wien-Film head Karl Hartl informed Forst, Ucicky, Thimig, Hainisch and von Cziffra that the authorities expected them to be "particularly careful that the Viennese dialect or the dialect of the Alpine and Danube province in our films should be so regulated, i.e., to suit the generally understood High German speech and writing style of the Greater German Reich, so that our films will be understood by a German public of all regional origins."[37] Suiting general speech meant at the most an accent or perhaps a flavoring, but not the full-blown dialects that had been so flagrantly used in Wien-Film product to that point.

Much of this dialect inclusion was also due to the few instances of regionalism permitted prior to the centralization moves of the UFI Trust. Ernst Marischka's *Sieben Jahre Pech*/Seven Years of Bad Luck (1940), a vehicle for Hans Moser and German comic actor Theo Lingen, was a production of the semi-autonomous Styria-Film, and its success, primarily due to Moser's performance of a hit song by Karl Föderl, insured a 1942 sequel — something not common in German-language film of the era — entitled *Sieben Jahre Glück*/Seven Years of Good Luck. Moser also starred in the 1943 *Ferienkind*/Holiday's Child, which was written by Fritz Koselka but not directed by his usual partner E. W. Emo. Karl Leiter helmed this Styria-Film production, which dealt with the practice of sending disadvantaged children on vacations to the estates of the wealthy. Moser's character discovers that the *Ferienkind* he has taken on is his own grandson. Film historian Karsten Witte understands the film to be not only an attempt at dealing with the lingering class conflict between the working class and the rich but also as a propagandistic allegory of Austria's "return" to the German Reich.[38] Between 1943 and 1944, director Leopold Hainisch filmed *Ulli und Marei*/Ulli and Marei in several Viennese studio facilities and in the Tyrolean Ötztal. The film was based on a book by the writer Eduard Köck, who appears in the film along with Attila Hörbiger and Ilse Exl, the last director of the Exl-Bühne theater group. This rare opportunity of a partial on-location production utilizing regional talent fostered a desire by the filmmakers to explore how cinema might be freed from the bounds of studio artificiality and propaganda constraints. But this mountain tale, which sought a more authentic look at the rural life and human experience, was deemed unacceptable for entertainment or propaganda purposes and therefore not released until 1948. Hainisch's progressive film echoes the more radical Italian break from the soundstage that occurred a year earlier in the nascent neorealism of Luchino Visconti's class-conscious *Ossessione* (Italy 1943), which was also banned. Hubert Marischka's comedy *Ein Mann gehört ins Haus*/A Man Belongs at Home (1945) was another semi-location production, shot at the Schönbrunn studio facility and at Zell am See. But unlike the unique *Ulli und Marei*, Marischka's film was created as a comedic variant of the *Heimatfilm* and its emphasis on the simple and healthy life of the country population. This genre was perfectly suited to the National Socialist cultural concept of *Blut und Boden* (blood and soil), which romanticized and celebrated the folk culture of the racially pure and soil-bound German in opposition to the decadent urban culture of the Weimar Republic and the Austrian First Republic. Still, the *Heimatfilm* would become a far more popular genre in postwar Austrian and West German film. Stripped of National Socialist ideology, such films would be relatively inexpensive to produce and would provide escapism from the ravages of life in the ruins and under occupation. But there was another, more practical reason for the increase of on-location mountain and country films in 1944 and 1945 — the avoidance of interruption by Allied bombing raids.

Wien-Film had retained its semi-autonomy not only because it was so adept at creating highly entertaining and escapist box-office successes, but because it also made good on fulfilling the order for an occasional *Tendenzfilm* or ideological propaganda film to show that it was not totally lost in Viennese nostalgia and soft on the ideas of the Reich. UFA and its stars were mostly responsible for this type of film, but there were also Wien-Film talents that found these projects to be worthy cinematic art. Most, however, did not. Axel Eggebracht, who wrote *Bel Ami*, *Operette,* and *Wiener Blut* with Willi Forst, recalled in a 1989 interview that German director Veit Harlan, known for his propagandistic films, had requested Forst do the lead role in his anti–Semitic *Jud Süß*/Jew Suess feature. Forst apparently responded with an amazing set of artistic "reasons" why he could not be available for this "important" project.[39] When Hans Thimig was asked by Berlin to direct a propaganda film following his last comedy for Wien-Film, *Wie ein Dieb in der Nacht*/Like a Thief in the Night (1945) with Wolf Albach-Retty and Gusti Huber, studio head Hartl suggested he simply disappear and that he would cover for Thimig by claiming illness.

Heinz Helbig (1902–) directed the first of the four Wien-Film propaganda features. His period film, *Leinen von Irland*/Linen from Ireland (1939), written by Harald Bratt and Philipp von Zeska for Otto Tressler, Irene von Meyendorff, Oskar Sima, and Siegfried Breuer, tells the story of Dr. Kuhn (Siegfried Breuer), a Jewish secretary at the Prague (then in the Austro-Hungarian Empire) Libussa textile firm, who attempts to sabotage the Bohemian industry by importing Irish linen. His plot, supported by a Jewish uncle, also involves the seduction of Lilly (Irene von Meyendorff), the daughter of the firm's president. A heroic weaver ultimately exposes Kuhn's intrigue and the corruption of the Trade Ministry. The industry is saved and Lilly finds love with the only honest civil servant in the Ministry (Rolf

Wanka). The film, which unites the Aryan population against the "Jewish intrigue," curiously enforces a class distinction that although strongly present in the Reich, was not something propaganda films normally evoked. According to National Socialism, class conflict ceases to exist when the *Volk* is united by blood. Moreover, racial excellence was to be the only criteria of a new aristocracy, displacing the degenerate ruling castes of the past. The film asks its audience to accept a social–Darwinist process to support the existence of lingering class distinctions. It implies that class conflict is not about socioeconomic inequality but about racial impurity. Like the racist texts warning of the assimilated Jew who attempts to fit into German society in order to abuse it, the Jewish figures here display an external façade of urbane sophistication, which is unmasked by the "true German worker." The film, which cost a modest 744,000 Reichsmark, earned back double its outlay in two years of release.

The aforementioned 1941 Emo comedy *Liebe ist Zollfrei*/Love Is Tax-Free is also considered a *Tendenzfilm*. Written by Fritz Koselka from a play by Fritz Gottwald, it was designed as a vehicle for Hans Moser, who portrays Lorenz Hasenhüttel, a customs officer in a fictionalized First Republic Austria led by an incompetent chancellor (Oskar Sima). In his famous curmudgeon manner, Moser's insignificant but honest civil servant exposes a corrupt regime while attacking democracy, capitalist bureaucrats, and practically every aspect of the former Austrian Republic, as well as several other targets, including foreigners, the English language and even Swiss-Germans. The survival of Moser's Jewish wife was at the mercy of the regime, so he never protested the Reich's film politics or official plans for his career. In addition to this brazen satire, Moser also made several films with German producers and directors between 1939 and 1945. Emo returned to the propaganda feature in 1943, with the biographical drama *Wien 1910*/Vienna 1910. These two political concessions to Berlin at Wien-Film earned him the gratitude of the regime and the short-lived position as production head of the Reich's film industry in Prague at Prag-Film in 1944. Like *Liebe ist Zollfrei* and *Leinen von Irland*, *Wien 1910* returns to the particular focal point of the few *Tendenzfilme* at Wien-Film — the defamation of the sociopolitics of imperial or republican Austria. Unlike Emo's other *Tendenzfilm*, however, the targets here are actual historical figures. The film is set during the final days of Vienna's popular mayor, Karl Lueger, and attempts to display the roots of German nationalism (read Nazism) in imperial Vienna vis-à-vis the "corrupt" (and Habsburg-loyal) Christian Social and "Jewish" Socialist political movements prior to World War I. Known for his progressive urban concepts, which favored the working classes, Lueger attained near-legendary status among the Viennese population. He is still a controversial figure today because of his pragmatic anti–Semitism, which he used to achieve his political aims. The film, however, presents Lueger and his politics in such distortion as to make the film subversive of its own aims. Despite Hitler's measured praise of him in *Mein Kampf*, the dying Lueger (Rudolf Forster) is the villain of Gerhard Menzel's script. With a deathbed oath in support of the Habsburg Empire, Menzel's Lueger damns the two forces he believes will destroy his imperial world: the Social Democrats led by the Jewish Victor Adler (Herbert Hübner) and the Pan-German Nationalists led by the intended hero of the film, Georg von Schönerer (Heinrich George). Although the anti–Semitic treatment of Adler, complete with a "positive" depiction of physical violence against him, is to be expected in such a film, the attempt to suggest a precursor to Hitler while being selective and reductive about Lueger's politics confuses the representations. Although Lueger is condemned for his Catholic and Habsburg-loyal worldview, in which he rejects a greater German Empire, his portrayal by Forster is very Hitlerian, particularly in speech and gesture. Historically, von Schönerer, who founded the Pan-German Party in 1885, led a violent anti–Semitic assault in 1888, which resulted in his loss of noble title, deprivation of his parliamentary seat, and imprisonment. Menzel's script portrays him as a hero who sacrifices his social standing and nearly himself for the cause against a "Slavic-Jewish" Austrian Empire. But Forster's Lueger appears to be the more sympathetic and interesting character. Was this an intentional sabotage of a propaganda film? The director never commented on the matter, but the expensive (approximately 2.5 million Reichsmark) historical drama was ultimately deemed unacceptable for showings to "former Austrians" in the *Ostmark*, and after re-editing, it was only screened in distant Reich territories and in Axis states. In the postwar world, the confused film has had the opposite effect: it has hurt the historical reputation of Karl Lueger and the re-evaluation of him as a pioneer of urban planning. The emotional reactions to Lueger, especially filtered through this curious work, had long hindered the possibilities of examining either the film or the history it manipulates. A screening of the film in Vienna in 1970 was met with protests that escalated into a near riot.[40]

Although the Gustav Ucicky/Gerhard Menzel series of heroic and self-sacrificial melodramas suited the ideology, they were not blatantly propagandistic. Ucicky took the ultimate step into such filmmaking with his 1941 *Heimkehr*/Homecoming, the most notorious of the four overtly political features from Wien-Film. Curiously, the film has nothing to do with Vienna or even former imperial or republican Austrian history, although it does borrow from the style of Austrian social dramas of the 1920s and 1930s. It might well have been made by UFA Berlin, given its German/Polish setting. It was honored as few films of the Reich had been, achieving official recognition from the Italian Ministry of Culture and receiving the highest German rating directly from Goebbels as "Film der Nation" (Film of the Nation) as well as the additional kudos, "of particular political and artistic value" and "valuable for youth." The film contrives the plight of a German minority in Polish territory prior to the 1939 "liberation" to justify the attack and destruction of Poland. Released in 1941 during the start of the war with the Soviet Union, it was aimed at presenting the Slavic peoples as subhuman and suggesting that the Germans who live in Eastern Europe are to be united with the Fatherland through conquest, giving Germans *Lebensraum* (living space) and promoting racial purity through German colonization. The film focuses on a group of Germans abused and imprisoned by Polish and Jewish townspeople whose acts are depicted as wholly supported by the Polish government. Resisting bravely, they are about to be executed when the invading German army saves them. The film was shot at Rosenhügel and also on location in the town of Chorzele in East Prussia, where there had actually been a Polish population prior to the war. Paula Wessely and Attila Hörbiger would never escape the criticism for having portrayed the lead characters in the film, which also included a mostly German supporting cast, the Vienna Boys' Choir and for the sake of authenticity, several Polish actors and Jewish actor Eugen Preiss, who was forced to do an anti–Semitic characterization. The film has long been avoided in Austrian popular and academic discourse and has only recently become the subject of detailed semiotic analysis by Gerhard Trimmel in his 1998 text *Heimkehr: Strategien eines Nationalsozialistischen Films* (Heimkehr: Strategies of a National Socialist Film). It was one of the most expensive projects undertaken by Wien-Film at 3.7 million Reichsmarks, but it earned far less (4.9 million) than more popular and far less costly entertainment films like *Operette,* which earned a 5 million return for the cost of 2.1 million, and *Wiener Blut,* which earned 7 million for a cost of 2.7 million. Paula Wessely was offered the heretofore unheard-of salary of 150,000 Reichsmark to portray the character of the schoolteacher Marie Thomas in the film.[41] It was hoped that Wessely, who could be relied upon to give a tour-de-force performance in such a dominant and suffering role, would give high-art credibility to the simplistic hate film. She was given such sentimental monologues as the following, which transforms a universal emotional reaction to displacement into a nationalistic exultation:

> Don't doubt that we'll get home.... Just imagine how it will be when there are only Germans around us; and when you go into a shop they don't speak Yiddish or Polish but German. And not just the whole village will speak German but everything far and wide will be German. And we'll be in the very center of it, in the heart of Germany. Just imagine what that will be like! And why shouldn't it happen? We will live on the good, warm soil of Germany. At home and in our homes. And at night, when we wake up, our hearts will be seized by the delicious shock of knowing we are sleeping in the middle of Germany, at home and in our homes, and all around us is the comforting night, and round and about us is millions of German hearts are quietly beating. Then you will be at home, in the company of your fellow beings.[42]

As the mouthpiece of the film's messages, Wessely's character, obviously intended to encourage the stamina of women on the homefront, actually transcends the secondary, passive role for women dictated by National Socialism and becomes the film's dominant leader. Although she managed to convince the audience of her ideological bent on screen, she acted quite differently behind the camera, especially if the subject was personal. When Eugen Preiss, the Jewish actor who had been forced to participate in this film, became ill with typhoid fever during the shooting and was interned, Wessely visited Preiss daily and blocked his deportation to a concentration camp. The premiere of *Heimkehr* in Vienna on October 10, 1941, was a spectacle in itself. *Ostmark* governor Baldur von Schirach joined Ucicky, Menzel, several of the performers and high ranking representatives of the Party, State and

Paula Wessely as the victimized German in Poland: Gustav Ucicky's notorious
Heimkehr, 1941.

the army, to see the film, which was preceded by a performance of Beethoven's
Coriolan overture by the Vienna Philharmonic conducted by Rudolf Moralt to set
the emotional mood of the picture. Expectedly, the reviews heralded the screening
and the film as significant contributions to German film art.[43]

Paula Wessely's relationship with Nazi propaganda and the regime itself is one
of contradiction and opportunism, which continues to be controversial even after
her death. Her actions to defend Preiss as well as Walter Reisch while being touted,
used and well paid as the great dramatic heroine of National Socialism were first
questioned by Austrian writer Elfriede Jelinek's play *Burgtheater* in 1982 and later
by Maria Steiner's book *Paula Wessely: Die verdrängten Jahre* (Paula Wessely: The
Suppressed Years). After 1945 Wessely went on record to condemn *Heimkehr*, but
her fame in the Reich along with the problems of the postwar Austrian film industry made her eventually turn to theater for the balance of her long career. Wessely's
political taint is neither unique nor excusable, but the limitation or loss of career
after 1945 is something that appears to be specifically gender related. It is a fact
that cannot be denied in even the most contrived arguments on talent, fame, and
political favoritism that male directors, actors, and writers continued to work in

postwar Austria, Germany and Europe, whereas the end of the Reich was also the film career fade-out for many female cinema artists of equal popularity — not only Paula Wessely but also such German film icons as Zarah Leander, Lilian Harvey, Marika Rökk, and Lil Dagover.[44] Male artists that tolerated or supported European fascism often increased their fame in the postwar era: Céline, Roberto Rossellini, Salvador Dali, G. W. Pabst, Douglas Sirk, Richard Strauss, Herbert von Karajan, Gottfried Benn, Ernst Jünger, and Gustaf Gründgens, among others. Even Veit Harlan, the director of the anti–Semitic *Jud Süß*/Jew Suess, who worked closely with Propaganda minister Goebbels and whose films were "more in tune with the political interests of the Nazi government"[45] than most, was able to revive his career in the 1950s, while his wife, actress Kristina Söderbaum, could not. Fritz Hippler, creator of the most vicious Nazi propaganda film, *Der ewige Jude*/The Eternal Jew, was apparently "denazified" in 1951 and employed by the U.S. Army as a translator.[46]

In 2002, a dossier compiled by exiled Jewish author Carl Zuckmayer (1896–1977) for the American OSS, or Office of Strategic Services, the forerunner of the CIA, was finally published. The secret report from 1943 to 1944, in which the famed Austrian writer provided his impressions of 150 German and Austrian cultural personalities, was to have been used as a basis for cultural renewal during postwar occupation. Although the information was apparently never applied to Allied cultural "reeducation" in Germany or Austria, Zuckmayer's writings might have spared several stars their long-standing controversy. He strongly defends Paula Wessely as being "free of Nazi influence" and having supported the sovereignty of Austria into the Anschluss. He maintains that in the mass arrests during the first days of the annexation, Wessely and husband Attila Hörbiger defended colleagues against condemnation and had personally driven a Jewish friend to the border to help him escape. According to the author, the brothers Hans and Hermann Thimig, and actors Heinz Rühmann, Theo Lingen, Käthe Gold, Alma Seidler and Käthe Dorsch all distanced themselves significantly from National Socialism and the racist political culture. Zuckmayer claims that Dorsch, a friend of Hermann Göring in her youth, used the relationship to save several concentration camp inmates. Perhaps the most interesting information aside from the Wessely/Hörbiger defense is Zuckmayer's take on Willi Forst, whose statement about his resistance in making the most "Austrian" films during the period of the Reich has often been dismissed by critics despite the danger Forst faced regarding his sexuality. The fact that he had easily risen to stardom in the Aryanized German and pre–Anschluss Austrian film industry has often counted against him, despite the obvious Austrian messages in his Wien-Film product. Zuckmayer praises Forst for having "bravely fought" to protect his non–Aryan colleagues and relates that he had planned on emigrating to the United States in 1939, when the onset of the war removed the opportunity. The dossier reports Emil Jannings's Nazism to have been one of pure career opportunism and self-aggrandizement and also suggests that a "seriously alcoholic" Heinrich George, who shifted from being a staunch Communist to an equally fervent National Socialist, and began his theater performances with a Nazi salute, was aware of the possible future consequences for his political actions. Other personalities Zuckmayer considered to be either opportunistic or convinced supporters of the regime were Oskar Sima, Fred Hennings, Friedl Czepa and Leni Riefenstahl.[47] Differentiating the active Nazi supporters by their varied personal agendas (career or financial motivation, cowardice, revenge, etc.) Zuckmayer regards only a relatively small percentage of the notables of the time to be ideologically motivated Hitlerians.

Of course, the most controversial case of career taint involved film director, writer, producer and actress Leni Riefenstahl (1902–2003). Although she is not an Austrian filmmaker, she is briefly examined here because her final work in the Reich, *Tiefland*/Lowlands (1945–54), is considered an Austrian film because of its location and cast and because it was completed as a Tobis-Sascha production. Riefenstahl's company also fostered a secondary film firm specializing in ski adventure features and shorts, which featured largely Austrian talent. Considering the ongoing interest in Riefenstahl and recent attempts to find something in her work that would have satisfied her critics or released her from cinematic exile, it is inexplicable that Riefenstahl's final dramatic film, *Tiefland,* has received so little attention. In 1992, German feminist filmmaker Helma Sanders-Brahms bluntly asked, "How is it possible that after fifty years the fear of dealing with this film is still so great that just the refusal to view it is considered a correct attitude for German intellectuals?"[48] Certainly here is a film feminists ought to examine in discussing Riefenstahl's eventual consideration of the female and the female artist in patriarchal society. It is the only dramatic film of Riefenstahl's career other than *Das blaue Licht*/The Blue Light (Germany 1932) and the only one made during the Third Reich. As a project which Riefenstahl has defended as an attempt to escape making a propaganda or war film, it should be considered as much a work of "inner emigration" as that of the writers who remained in Nazi Germany and who came to reject the Reich. To consider that Leni Riefenstahl changed her mind about fascism is not to rehabilitate or excuse her monumental National Socialist propaganda exercise *Triumph des Willens*/Triumph of the Will (Germany 1934). *Tiefland* certainly reflects, confronts and distances itself from the ideology that rooted her earlier work.

The film had originally been announced as a 1938 Donau-Film production and was then shelved due to the Anschluss and the dissolution of the company.[49] An adaptation of the Eugen d'Albert (1864–1932) opera with libretto by Rudolph Lothar (based on the 1896 Spanish play *Terra Baixa* by Angel Guimera) was reconsidered in 1939 when Riefenstahl's highly stylized adaptation of Heinrich von Kleist's drama *Penthesilea* (1808) was deemed too costly a project.[50] Due to the escalating war, Goebbels insisted on nationalistic material or pure entertainment film. Riefenstahl predicted that *Tiefland* would only take a few months to film, but since it was not considered valuable for propaganda purposes, it was given no financial support. Although Riefenstahl first welcomed the project as a brief respite from current events and as an alternative to the assignment of a propaganda film or war coverage, it was not until the project became increasingly protracted, with endless filming in Spain, the Austrian Alps, the Dolomites, and at the Barrandov studio in Prague, that she used the film as a permanent refuge from Nazi Germany, until production was finally ended in 1944. *Tiefland* was confiscated by the French government after the war and finally returned, with footage missing, to Riefenstahl after her several years in detention camps and her final clearance by French courts.

Despite the enthusiasm of postwar Italian neorealist directors for the film, *Tiefland* has either been ignored in previous discussions of Riefenstahl's oeuvre, or else it has been attacked as an example of Riefenstahl's anachronistic or egocentric filmmaking. Much of this criticism is aimed at Riefenstahl's starring role, the result of her apparent inability to find a suitable actress to portray the lead character, Martha. This beautiful gypsy dancer who creates her art for the wealthy Spanish Marquez Don Sebastian, played by the Goebbels-esque Bernhard Minetti (a brutal dictatorial lord to his suffering peasants), similar to how Riefenstahl created her art for Hitler, however, is a cinematic admission of her own opportunism and the inability to escape the "leader" when conditions are not ideal. Riefenstahl also "scripted" her own transcendence from her unavoidable fall with the Reich by emphasizing the destruction of the Marquez by his own *Volk* and Martha's escape into the mountains with the innocent and passive shepherd and defender of the weak, Pedro (Franz Eichberger), the very opposite of the National Socialist warrior-hero image. Additionally, Riefenstahl suggests the capitalist-fascist connection in the Marquez's loveless marriage with the wealthy and vain daughter (Maria Koppenhöffer) of the mayor (Karl Skraup) and in the intrigues at court led by the Marquez's administrator, Camillo (Aribert Wäscher), who has more than a passing semblance to the girth and voluptuary nature of Hermann Göring. In her memoirs, Riefenstahl wonders why she insisted on completing the film amid personal tragedy, illness, and the collapse of the Reich. Sensitive to analyses of her work undertaken for the sake of accusation, she finally trivialized her own visions and impulses, whether it was the messianic image of Hitler floating above the crowds in *Triumph des Willens* or the need to resolve her disillusionment with fascism.

The company Riefenstahl founded to create the *Olympia* documentary continued after the film's completion as a production firm for second features in the very *Bergfilm* traditions that had given Riefenstahl her start as actress and director. Joachim Bartsch headed the company, and its product usually featured producer Walter Traut, cinematographer Guzzi Lantschner, and the skiers Heli Lantschner and Trude Lechle. Born in Innsbruck in 1919, Lechle began her cinema career as an actress in the Olympia productions, which focused on her skiing prowess rather than on her dramatic ability. Her first film was the 1939 *Osterskitour in Tirol*/Easter Ski Tour in the Tyrol, in which she co-starred with Heinrich Harrer, the Austrian mountaineer whose friendship with the young Dalai Lama is the subject of the 1997 American film *Seven Years in Tibet* (with Brad Pitt as Harrer). The winter ski adventures of *ABC im Schnee*/ABC in the Snow in 1940 and *Jugend in Sonne und Schnee*/Youth in Sun and Snow in 1942 followed. But, like Riefenstahl before her, acting and athletics in front of the camera were not satisfying enough for Lechle and in 1941, she took on the role of production assistant and also became assistant to cinematographer Sepp Allgier in an unfinished ski/army epic known only as *Wehrmachtsfilm* (army film). The production, which was interrupted by the German invasion of the Soviet Union, lost much of its cast and crew to the war and was never completed.[51] Having wed Hans Dreihann-Holenia, a relative of author Alexander Lernet-Holenia in 1943, Lechle also became professionally known as Trude Dreihann, assisted cinematographer Albert Benitz in Riefenstahl's *Tiefland*, and had a short acting career after the war.

Willi Forst's unfinished *Wiener Mädeln* may have been the only color feature to come out of Wien-Film, but the studio had used color since 1943 in its program of culture and nature films produced by Otto Trippel. The Propaganda Ministry considered these short documentaries, known as *Kulturfilm,* a service in the "enlightenment" of the public. Unlike the disappointing box office of the propaganda films, the *Kulturfilm* enjoyed great popularity. Not only did they highlight cultural and nature subjects of the *Ostmark*, they also did their southeastern European duty in co-productions with Romanian (and in planned films with Bulgarian and Greek) studios. Although Wien-Film produced nearly sixty of these documentaries for the Reich between 1939 and 1944, more serious newsreel production was only entrusted to UFA in Berlin. The film that has come to represent the "final" work of the studio, and which was in fact the last one to be completed, was Geza von Bolvary's Viennese Film *Schrammeln* (1944), based on the life and times of the famed Schrammel Quartet, which helped bring Vienna's folk and waltz music to international fame in the nineteenth century. The film, scripted by Ernst Marischka and Hans Gustl Kernmayer, focuses on the creation of the quartet by the violin-playing brothers Johann and Josef Schrammel (Paul Hörbiger and Hans Holt), guitarist Anton Strohmayer (Hans Moser), clarinetist Georg Dänzer (Fritz Imhoff) and the legendary folk singer known as the "Fiakermilli" (Marte Harell), who mediated the many quarrels of the quartet's members. The music style of this historic group is still known today as *Schrammelmusik* (Schrammel music) and is considered one of Vienna's important contributions to Austrian folk culture. The choice to make such a film as the war front and Nazism collapsed is a final demonstration of the dissident quality of Wien-Film productions. While *Schrammeln* offered nostalgia for old Vienna, dance music and romance, Berlin's UFA was producing its final film, *Kolberg* (Germany 1945), a color epic depicting the heroism and self-sacrifice of one small Prussian town that resisted Napoleon, which exhorted the audience to fight the enemy to the death. By the time *Schrammeln* was shown in theaters in the Austrian province in 1944, the messages Wien-Film slipped in between the lines or the waltzes were no longer just quietly appreciated. The name of Austria (*Österreich*) had been forbidden in film even as a historical reference. This required a rewriting of one of the Schrammel Brother's songs, *"Was Öst'reich ist"* (What Austria Is) as *"Wie schön das ist"* (How Beautiful That Is). During the screenings in Vienna and other Austrian cities, the audiences would break into wild applause each time the masked line was sung. The ideological Anschluss, at least, had ended with unmuzzled reaction in the cinemas. In Berlin, Goebbels had apparently become more interested in winning a war on film than in the survival of the Germans, and he ordered soldiers off the Soviet front to be military extras in the epic battle scenes of UFA's *Kolberg*. Wien-Film, however, entered pre-production for a film with a

Nostalgia as subversion: Hans Moser, Hans Holt, Marte Harell, Paul Hörbiger and Fritz Imhoff in Geza von Bolvary's *Schrammeln*, 1944.

title that revealed interests far removed from the final battles: *Liebe nach Noten*/Love According to the Notes.

By 1944, the war had altered the Reich's film industry significantly. Bombings had destroyed studio facilities and cinema theaters. Fritz Hippler was replaced by Hans Hinkel as the Reich's Cinema Director. This new head of film culture in the Reich, a staunch National Socialist and a self-proclaimed expert in the aryanization of the German film industry since 1933, believed that film should be a war industry and that the various production chiefs of the Reich would now be totally under his military-style command. Although a one-year labor service had been mandatory in the Reich for youth, members of the artistic sector were often excused, given their contribution to the culture of the Reich. Hinkel saw to it that, beginning in 1944, even members of the film industry should perform such labor service. Not only youthful members were expected to participate, and only major stars like Paula Wessely or the elderly, such as Rosa Albach-Retty, were excused.[52] Additionally, he decided that the manpower of the industry might better serve the war effort and conscripted a majority of its male personnel into the army and later as the Reich's territory quickly decreased, into the home defense. Fritz Hirt, the regime's trustworthy liaison at Wien-Film, protested against this total drain of the industry, but to no avail. Resistance to self-annihilation in the cause of a hopeless war was particularly strong in Austria and found resonance among the filmmakers. In February 1945, Paul Hörbiger was arrested by the Gestapo for alleged involvement with an Austrian resistance group. Rumors of Willi Forst's death in the final bombing raids on Vienna circulated. According to Marte Harell, plans were made by Hinkel's office to detonate the Rosenhügel studio prior to the Soviet arrival as part of the general "scorched earth" policy Hitler ordered as the Reich disappeared, but her husband and his staff managed to derail this plan.[53] The liberation of Vienna by Soviet troops scattered members of the industry into the western region of Austria in hopes of escaping the brutality of the Red Army and surviving the final days of the war. Like the captain of a sinking ship, Karl Hartl decided to remain with the remnants of Wien-Film in Vienna and was arrested by Allied occupation officials in August 1945.

4

Postwar and Second Republic Boom: 1946–1959

Reconnections and Re-Visions

There was a long accepted fallacy in Germany and Austria, known as *Stunde Null* or zero hour, which suggested that the landscape of arts and culture, primarily literature, was so tainted by Nazism that there could not be any continuity between the Third Reich and the postwar world, perhaps not even between the German and Austrian interwar republics and what 1945 was to foster. While the fact remains that the arts had been perverted to suit National Socialist ideology, and language was particularly affected by racism, the simple rejection of this past did not result in a tabula rasa. Not only did authors return from exile to continue their work and reconnect the culture with the pre–Nazi era, but authors living in Germany and Austria — those that had continued to publish and those in "inner emigration" — also provided a fractured continuity with their experiences under Nazism. While occupation forces held various studio facilities and influenced what immediate postwar cinema was to be about in the reestablished Austria, only very few who fled the Anschluss returned to Vienna and the Austrian film industry. Most of this vital talent had made their way to London and Hollywood and the English-language film industries. While some had continued their relative fame, a few becoming legendary, others had failed to reinvent themselves. As the years distanced the Reich and the war, these talents also became distanced from their identity as Austrians. They were now "Hollywood Europeans," and ironically, when their origin was discussed, they were and are often still regarded as Germans. For Austria this was not as devastating as some would have it, since, like with literature, there was important talent that had remained in the country. Along with the ideas and talents of a new generation of directors, actors, writers and technicians, it was primarily the Wien-Film legacy that brought Austrian cinema to the level of excellence and popularity it enjoyed in the postwar era. Genres were cleansed of National Socialist dictates or limitations, and reinvented for an audience that could again experience the qualities of American, French, and British film. While severely hampered in the early years of occupation by the wartime destruction of facilities, material shortages, and strict Allied control, technological aspects managed impressively and soon caught up with Western European state-of-the-art practices.

What effect did the banishment of a significant portion of the film industry have on the development of Austrian cinema? Their talent and abilities, which helped make American film the leader of the art in the Western if not the entire world, were certainly loss enough. But there was a more subtle consequence, one that was not immediately understood, and which ultimately proved to be more devastating: the total disconnection of Austrian film from its exiled and diasporic talent, their concepts, and their work. The distant result was that subsequent film-making generations suffered an amnesia that would influence the creation and reception of Austrian film into the 1990s. The strong influence of Austrian cinema and its talents in Western national cinemas, particularly in the American industry, was forgotten; the "independent film" of the 1930s was literally lost; and the Wien-Film era, which was relegated entirely to "Nazi cinema," was ignored. The pressure for commercial success (television would siphon off cinema audiences as it did elsewhere) or for the creation of a New Wave as a rejection of traditional genres and styles only served to make Austrian film derivative and inorganic. Most of the blame, however, for allowing Austrian cinema to nearly vanish from national and international screens in the 1960s and 1970s must be borne by successive Austrian national governments, which had little interest in cinema art and provided none of the expected financial support mechanisms found in other Western European film industries. More than any other reason, this inhibited cultivation of new talent and the continuation of a worthy cinematic tradition.

The immediate postwar era, however, still recalled what had come before, and the reborn industry managed in the first decade after the war to train a new generation of Austrian film talent that would bring the cinema to another creative peak in the 1950s. Some of these filmmakers would even assist in the basic survival of the industry during its later nadir. Unlike the *Vergangenheitsbewältigung*, or "coming to terms with the past," which the West Germans had pursued since 1945 in most aspects of society and culture (but curiously not with any significance in film), Austria, which had been labeled a victim of Nazi Germany by the Moscow Declaration of 1943, preferred to close the subject. Along with having distanced itself from the unique cosmopolitan sensibilities of the empire in all ways except to serve tourist kitsch, and avoiding the Dollfuss-Schuschnigg period rather than dealing with it as a flawed but heroic stance against Hitlerian aggression, the early Second Republic also rejected the fact that it had been both a victim and perpetrator of Nazism. It chose to step out of history, reinvent itself as another Switzerland (with which it shares no important historical or sociocultural developments) and flounder as a vague bridge between the cold war blocs. This made critical viewpoints difficult to come by in the arts. Hubert Klocker, writing about the development of performance art in Europe, observes that the Second Republic's dislocation also adds another aspect to the mix of postwar Austrian cultural influences — the desire to evoke the "better" albeit trivialized past while totally avoiding the "bad":

A conception of art that operated more in retrospect and from the desire to retain traditional values emerged from the intellectual ruins. One clung to the past and longed for the fair, collective memory of a monarchical-centralized Habsburg world. It was the task of postwar art to create a link back to the intellectual tradition at the turn of the century, when the energies released by the fragility of the Austro-Hungarian empire and the entire Europolitical structure had been transformed in Viennese modernism into trail-blazing achievements in art and science. Furthermore, the postwar generation had to find its own identity through an intensive international exchange of ideas. It was faced with the problem of finding answers to the recent aberrations of the National Socialist phase and to the intellectual and cultural inclinations, rooted far in the previous century.[1]

What did succeed amid all this, however, was the establishment of the concept of an Austrian Nation. The Anschluss had forever destroyed historical notions that Austria might be part of a larger German nation or would want to ever again consider itself as such. The multicultural heritage of the imperial Austrian empire was not only the stuff of romanticized nostalgia, but it became very selectively useful to the reconstruction of neonational (read: non-Germany–associated) identity. But what exactly the Austrian Nation would represent was another matter altogether.

It seems almost a cinematic cliché about the Viennese love of artistic saturation that artistic life succeeded in reestablishing itself within days of the end of the Third Reich and the war. The Allied bombing of Vienna had taken its toll on the city and its most beloved cultural edifices had not been spared: much of the Opera House had been destroyed by a direct hit and the building continued to burn for days; the Burgtheater was severely damaged, as was the neoclassical Parliament building and a portion of the sprawling imperial Hofburg palace. But most disturbing of all was the bombing of the immense gothic St. Stephan's cathedral that had always represented not only the center of Vienna but of Austria as well. It was now a rubble-filled gaping shell; the Pummerin, its over ten foot high, twenty-one-metric-ton bell which had been cast from the captured cannons of the 1683 Turkish Siege of Vienna, lay smashed as if to indicate that the zero hour was indeed at hand. Approximately 8,000 buildings had been destroyed, 40,000 were damaged (28 percent of the city's structures) and 270,000 people were homeless. It seemed as if there could be no turning back, no avoidance of what had happened, no retreat into trivialized history or the "beauty" of art. On April 25, 1945, two days before Karl Renner, the chancellor of the provisional government, announced the reestablishment of an independent Austria (the return of actual sovereignty did not occur until 1955), Vienna's oldest radio station, RAVAG, returned to the air. The Burgtheater mounted its first postwar production in temporary housing on April 30, 1945 (the day of Hitler's suicide), and the Volksoper offered a performance of Mozart's *The Marriage of Figaro* the following day. On May 29, the University of Vienna once again opened its doors to students and the new independent newsreel *Österreichische Wochenschau*/Austrian Weekly Show flashed on in cinemas. This was soon exchanged for the more propagandistic U.S./U.K. co-production, *Welt im Film*/World on Film, which was in turn replaced by the *MPEA Tönende Wochenschau*/MPEA

Sound Weekly Show. Salzburg established its *Rot-Wiess-Rot* (Red-White-Red; the colors of the Austrian flag) radio station on June 6, 1945, and by August, the first postwar Salzburg Festival was in full swing.[2] On October 26, 1945, the publication *Mein Film*, which had been founded in 1926 and had been so popular until its suspension, resumed weekly publication. The lack of printing paper resulted in a very limited circulation, but the new publisher found a waiting audience. And many audiences were indeed left waiting: the few cinemas that were operational were often closed due to power shortages.

The first Austrian film to be shown following the war premiered on August 3, 1945. It was E. W. Emo's *Freunde*/Friends (1944), which had been forbidden for distribution by the Nazi regime. It would be the first of a series of *Überläufer*, or overrun projects that were made in the Reich but were either not completed until later or had been shelved after completion. Following *Freunde*, Austrians would also finally see Gustav Ucicky's *Am Ende der Welt*/At the End of the World (1943–47), written by Gerhard Menzel and starring Brigitte Horney as a woman who wants to finance her cabaret with the destruction of a forest. The film had an eclectic supporting cast: Attila Hörbiger; a German cabaret legend of the 1920s and 1930s, Trude Hesterberg; second-string leading man Alexander Trojan; and the ever-popular comedian Karl Skraup. The other *Überläufer* were a mix of unfinished and banned films: Hans Thimig's *Umwege zu Dir*/Detours to You (1944–47); the final Wien-Film project, Geza von Cziffra's *Liebe nach Noten*/Love According to the Notes (1945–47); the Exl-Theater Group film, *Ulli und Marei*/Ulli and Marei (1944–48); Hubert Marischka's comedy *Ein Mann gehört ins Haus*/A Man Ought to Be in the Home (1945–48); Hans Hass's *Menschen unter Haien*/People among Sharks (1945–48); Luis Trenker's *Im Banne des Monte Miracolo*/Banned from Monte Miracolo (1943–48); Hans Thimig's *Wie ein Dieb in der Nacht*/Like a Thief in the Night (1944–49), which was the last picture actually completed at the Wien-Film studio; Willi Forst's color musical *Wiener Mädeln*/Viennese Girls (1949); and Leni Riefenstahl's *Tiefland*/Lowlands (1945–54).[3] By December 1945, Austria saw the founding of its Society of the Friends of Film, and Paula Wessely, who had been forbidden to perform as punishment for her collaboration with the National Socialists, was quickly released from her artistic limbo, but she did not appear in film again until 1948.[4]

Viktor Matejka, the new cultural councilor for the city of Vienna, immediately promoted the idea of a reborn film industry. Having been persecuted by the Nazis, Matejka began his rebuilding of Vienna's artistic environment by defining "Austrian culture" and by praising its cinema for having made the world aware of the nation's history, art and society, "which distinguish and differentiate us from other peoples."[5] But the actual continuation of the industry was difficult, given that Wien-Film and other production facilities defined as "German property" had been confiscated by the Allies. With Austria and Vienna divided under four-power administration since July 9, 1945, the facilities of the Austrian film industry were equally disunited and passed to Allied ownership on June 17, 1946: Wien-Film's Rosenhügel studio found itself under Soviet administration, the Schönbrunn studio facilities were controlled by the British, and the Sievering soundstages and Grinzing copying facilities were under U.S. administration. Although the other Allied powers soon returned the administration if not the actual ownership of these facilities to the Austrian government, the Soviet Union continued to administer Wien-Film/Rosenhügel for another ten years under its USIA law, which provided for the administration of "Soviet property" in Austria. This foreign control, coupled with the increasing cold war tensions between the Western Allies and the Soviets, fractured and hampered film production in Austria and wasted what might have been salvaged from Wien-Film's reputation and tradition. Not only production but export was also hindered, and this delayed Austria from reintroducing itself in the global film market. As with the former UFA Babelsberg studios in Berlin, Wien-Film/Rosenhügel was to become the production site for Soviet propaganda in what might well have become the Communist half of a divided Austria. Karl Hartl, who returned to his Wien-Film offices as the firm's business manager after having been released from custody in late 1945, reported to the Western Allies that the Soviets were plundering the studio, dismantling and removing equipment which was being shipped to the Soviet Union. The Western Allies were able to halt some of this, but soon Hartl met Colonel Lonin, who declared himself the new head of the facility. Hartl recalls that, at first, the Soviets did not consider a reborn Austrian film industry of any importance to their propaganda goals. The new Soviet chief of Wien-Film asked him directly if he preferred American or Russian film, to which Hartl replied that he preferred American, and with this comment, he departed the remnants of the film company he had helped build for work at the U.S.-controlled Sievering facility.[6] Hartl, however, remained the manager of the reconstructed non–Soviet controlled aspects of the now fragmented Wien-Film company, and he also headed the reconstituted Tobis-Sascha production and distribution firm as well as the new Austria-Film production company.

Rolf Schmidt-Gentner, who was to begin work as a sound technician at the Soviet-controlled Rosenhügel studios, was shocked to discover that all sound equipment, except for material requisitioned by the Nazis from the Cinecittá studio in Rome, was missing: "The Russians had not only removed the small instruments but the large machinery as well by simply cutting them from their floor anchor and sending them on to the Soviet Union. No one knows if this equipment was ever used there."[7] The Rosenhügel studio became known as "Wien-Film East" and was avoided by most immediate postwar filmmakers because of its Communist image and control. The many new production companies that formed in the era used the Schönbrunn or Sievering facilities or shot "on-location."

Despite their plunder, the Soviets soon came to understand the economic and propagandistic advantages in restarting production with Austrian talent. They set up their own distribution firm, Sovexport, for Soviet-financed Austrian film, which was soon matched by the British Eagle Lion company, the French OEFRAM and the American ISB, later known as MPEA. But postwar distribution was ultimately dominated by the United States and by the Soviet-Austrian productions at Rosenhügel. Despite the cold war polarization of Vienna's studios, the shortages of film stock, electricity, coal for heating and, of course, food, it is remarkable that four films were actually produced and distributed in Austria in 1946. The first true post-war film was *Glaube an Mich*/Believe in Me (1946), directed by Geza von Cziffra. The film was financed by a new company called Loewen-Film, which took its name from businessman Carl Albert Loewenstein, who had generated his financial back-ing on the black market. Von Cziffra credits several members of the Loewenstein family, among them a coal merchant and a sugar producer, with financing the start of both postwar Austrian and German film.[8] Obtaining the permission to create such a company was difficult given the four-power administration and the division of the mostly inactive film industry. Von Cziffra's application submitted to the American Film Officer Eugene Sharin produced no reply until Karl Hartl's wife, actress Marte Harell, appealed to the U.S. High Commissioner's representative, General Brand. Sharin's hesitation was not only politically motivated but intended to serve what was to become the American dominance in postwar Austrian and West German cinemas. He claimed that he had been ordered to block any Austrian film development until U.S. distributors could establish themselves in Vienna. Sharin also admitted that Erich Pommer, the former production head of UFA in the 1920s, who had returned to Occupied Germany at the behest of the United States to reor-ganize the production facilities in Hamburg (the U.S. Zone), had the same task in Germany. The approval of the von Cziffra/Loewen-Film license was never intended and only occurred because "General Brand is a soldier, who has no concept of the economic fronts of a war."[9] For the Americans, the restarting of the Austrian film industry had been accidental and politically premature. Unlike Germany, where returning émigrés had found an "old boys' network" that was largely hostile to Allied and other "outside" interference in their film tradition and industry,[10] the Austrians had no such illusions. Exiles did not return and much of the industry was in some way considered "tainted" simply because it had worked in an indus-try that represented Germany. Willi Forst attempted to convince the government that it should actively pursue a return policy for filmmakers and other artists in exile, but the provisional and early Second Republic governments had what amounted to a blind eye toward the national film industry and dismissed any such potentially expensive initiatives.

Von Cziffra's *Glaube an Mich* utilized much of the old Wien-Film talent behind the camera: von Cziffra and Kurt Nachmann wrote the script, Hans Schneeberger was cinematographer, Anton Profes scored the film, and Marte Harell, Ewald Balser, Rudolf Prack, Erik Frey, and Senta Wengraf (in her first film appearance) performed the lead roles. Making this slight musical comedy set at the harmless location of a ski resort proved to be a difficult challenge. The location of Zürs am Arlberg was situated in the French occupation zone and was being used as a rest and recreation area for the French military. Obtaining permission for filming was nothing less than a test; the script was heavily censored by the French officials, and von Cziffra's wife, Petra Trautmann, was ordered to leave Zürs before her work on the film was completed due to some unflattering comment she had made about the French flag.[11] Early shooting was lost because the film stock that von Cziffra had bought on the black market had already been used. The rushes provided an unplanned metaphor on the indelibility of the past: the double exposure showed an interesting montage of the film's ski scenes over a previous shoot of German soldiers on parade. Hans Schneeberger later managed to obtain fresh stock from the Soviets.

The film's plot is pure escapist formula and deals with a music professor (Balser), who, with his nephew as bait, constructs a scenario to test the loyalty of his future wife (Harell). She is not swayed by the cabal but ultimately falls for another. A curious blend of salon comedy and ski film, with American-style swing music from Anton Profes that liberated Austrian film from the limitations of the Reich's musical dictates, the work was carefully contrived to avoid creating any types that might be perceived as racial parody. Dramatic conflicts were easily resolved by the film's conclusion. The premiere of the film on November 15, 1946, was enthusiastically received by the public, which still recalled von Cziffra's Wien-Film triumph, *Der weiße Traum*, and seemingly ignored modest production values of this first postwar film. Critics were less forgiving and found the film to be a simplistic, kitsch-laden nonevent that would be uninteresting to audiences in Austria and abroad.[12] Von Cziffra agreed that the film was somewhat anachronistic and that it had been an "old script," but while the director agreed with criticisms regarding technical quality, he certainly found no problem in continuing to create such light entertainment and emerged as one of the leading exponents of the continuation of the lavish Wien-Film style in the postwar era.[13]

Glaube an Mich also touched on the *Heimatfilm*, the important Austrian and German genre that originated in the silent era and has continued in one form or another to the present day. *Heimat*, which can be translated as "homeland," also suggests an untranslatable emotional/spiritual value "implying both a return to imaginary or real origins and roots, and a totalizing, acquisitive gesture."[14] It was a concept based in the Romantic era's celebration of the land, the common folk, peasantry, and the mythical, often mystical, powers of nature. Even prior to the Third Reich, the notion of *Heimat* had sociopolitical connotations. It was a term used to represent the idealized unification of German/ic culture, language and geopolitics. National Socialism added a racist component to the formula and thereby perverted both the literary/cinematic genre as well as the concept itself. The word *Heimat* was so overused by the National Socialists that it was too rife with racist and expansionist values to be used in German-language speech without suspicion for decades following the war. It was not until German director Edgar Reitz's eleven-part television miniseries of 1984, *Heimat*, a response of sorts to the American NBC network *Holocaust* miniseries, which was shown on West German television in 1979,[15] that the word itself was reintroduced to new generations, but not even the reunification of Germany has rehabilitated the concept completely. In Austria, the word was also unpopular but was detached from its National Socialist taint rather quickly, given the general avoidance of Austria's role in the Reich and because *Heimat* had also been used by various anti–German political forces to conjure an idealized Austrian homeland in the interwar period. The postwar *Heimatfilm* in Austria cleansed itself immediately of any previous pan–German notions. Austrian landscapes, particularly Alpine settings, were again highlighted, along with the rural and Catholic population. The *Bergfilm* also returned and was modernized by the ski romance/comedy/adventure plots, and the *Bauernschwank*, or broad peasant comedy, a subgenre of the *Heimatfilm*, evolved into the farcical "tourist film," which featured urbanites who find a happy ending in rural surroundings.

The second postwar film was *Der weite Weg*/The Long Way (1946) and was directed and produced by pioneering silent film cinematographer Eduard Hoesch (1890–1983) via his Donau-Film company. Hoesch was allowed the needed film stock in exchange for Soviet distribution with Sovexport and the film thus became the first postwar project to be permitted use of the Rosenhügel studio. A melodrama about the plight of the returning soldier, in this case a released prisoner of war who learns that his wife may have been unfaithful, it also evokes the suffering of those on the homefront during the war. The plot development, however, relies too heavily on trite Wien-Film melodrama, rather than a connection with the progressive Austrian socially critical films of the 1930s or nascent Italian and East German neorealism.

The third film of 1946 was *Schleichendes Gift*/Slow Poison, an "enlightenment" film by German director and cinematographer Hermann Wallbrück on the post-war venereal disease epidemic. It was rather incongruously followed into the few working Austrian cinemas by a musical comedy, *Praterbuben*/Prater Boys (1946), another Soviet-sponsored and Sovexport-released production, this time produced by the new Vindobona-Film company and directed by Paul Martin (1899–1967). It reintroduced Wien-Film's composer Willy Schmidt-Gentner to postwar audiences and marked the return of director Hermann Thimig as an actor in a tale of a carnival announcer at the famed Prater amusement park who becomes a father figure to a group of street boys. The film manages to re-frame such troubled youth films as the musical *Singende Jugend*/Singing Youth (1936) and Michael Curtiz's *Angels with Dirty Faces* (USA 1938) with life among the ruins and an overt class consciousness that was certainly welcomed by the Soviet occupation. The Prater amusement park was so damaged (the giant 1897 Ferris wheel was inoperable, its cabin-size gondolas having been set ablaze during the final days of the war) that much of it was recreated at Rosenhügel's backlot.

Willi Forst, who returned to the postwar film scene with the intention of reestablishing Austrian film as an internationally important cinema, founded a new publication in April 1946. *Film* was edited by Josef Malina and was as much a sounding board for Forst's tireless encouragement as it was a serious cultural magazine. The first issue showcased a new song by Peter Wehle, who would become a film composer in the 1950s, entitled *"Steh auf, liebes Wien"* ("Stand Up, Dear Vienna"), and Forst rejected notions of the "Zero Hour" and of the hardships of reestablishing an industry in a four-power occupation by declaring, "The Viennese film is dead — long live the Viennese Film!"[16] His premature optimism faded in later issues, particularly given the fact that none of the Austrian films produced in 1946 were exported to Western Europe, and the hopes for a reestablished American connection resulted only in the subsequent purchase of a few films by the Casino Film Exchange in New York for limited showings at minor "art house" cinemas.[17] The

The soldiers come home: Hans Holt, Thea Weis and Rudolf Prack in Eduard Hoesch's *Der weite Weg*, 1946.

missed opportunity to link the Austrian and Hollywood film industries in the late 1930s had not been forgotten, and the fact that so many Austrian film exiles had established themselves there after 1938 made this a reborn goal for many producers.

The Austrian Creditanstalt Bank, which had been majority owner of the Tobis-Sascha concern prior to the 1938 nationalization and the creation of Wien-Film, sued both the Allied occupation administration and the representatives of what was UFA Berlin for restitution of its property. This normalization was not something that would rapidly occur. Wien-Film would ultimately pass to Austrian control upon the 1955 State Treaty that returned Austria to sovereignty, but the Creditanstalt Bank was instrumental in founding two new film entities in 1946, which would utilize the revered name for the sake of continuity: Sascha-Filmproduktion and its distributing arm, Sascha-Film. In addition to his figurehead administrative position with the fragmented Wien-Film, Karl Hartl was also appointed head of a third new production firm made possible by the Creditanstalt, the Neue Wiener Filmproduktiongesellschaft (New Viennese Film Production Company), in July 1947. Later that year a fourth new company was formed with help from the bank, the Salzburg-based Österreichische Filmgesellschaft (Austrian Film Company), which also had offices in Innsbruck. This company, known as ÖFA, and headed by Guido Bagier, had been formed specifically outside of Vienna and in the American Zone so that the independent Austrian film industry would survive if the country remained divided and Vienna fell into total Soviet control. Since there were no studios in these regions, makeshift soundstages were set up and both the Salzburg Festival Theater and the Innsbruck Festival Theater in Thiersee were utilized.

By 1947, 110 individual production companies had registered their existence, although only about thirteen ever produced any films. These short-lived independent production companies continued to spring up and disappear throughout the first ten years of the postwar era. Nonetheless, over three hundred films were eventually created in this new cinematic world of independent companies, established and emerging talents, and foreign influences between 1946 and 1959. To decode the various artistic and sociopolitical forces at work during such a prolific phase, it is necessary to shift the methodological structure in this particular chapter. Rather than the previous organization along genres, directors or actors, a stricter chronological order is necessary for examining the rapid hybridization of style and genre, the influence of commercial competition on such mutations, and the generational imprint on the arc of the period's productivity.

One of the most significant early postwar companies, Belvedere-Film, founded in 1946, was not just a production firm but was conceived as Austria's first new traditional studio responsible for and housing all aspects of its product. The immediate postwar film industry attracted several former silent film talents who had little to do with the cinema of the 1930s or the Wien-Film era. At Belvedere-Film, two of its founders began their careers during the infancy of the industry: August Diglas, who had been involved with the Dreamland-Film company, and silent actor/director Emmerich Hanus, the brother of silent film pioneer and later Filmbund president Heinz Hanus. In addition to several investors, the company was also co-founded by the twenty-two-year-old opera singer, pianist and actress Elfi von Dassanowsky (1924–), who had been hired by Karl Hartl to teach Curd Jürgens piano for his role in *Wen die Götter lieben* (1942). Her refusal to join National Socialist organizations derailed her studies at Vienna's Academy of Music and Performing Arts, which she had entered at age fifteen as the youngest female student in the history of the institution. After extended labor service, UFA Berlin rather than Wien-Film sought her out as a possible new musical film ingenue, but she declined the offer. With her operatic debut in 1946, von Dassanowsky also became involved with the reconstruction of the Austrian cultural identity and performed in a series of self-produced concerts for the Allied High Command and worked with the Allied Forces Broadcasting and the BBC in Vienna. Von Dassanowsky had been introduced to Emmerich Hanus by operetta and musical composer Alfred Gerstner, who believed that her youthful desire to see a reborn Austrian cinema was echoed in Hanus's intention to create a new generation of film talent working in an entirely new film studio. Hanus had acted in silent films in addition to directing the folk drama films *Glaube und Heimat* (1920) and *Erde* (1920). With the advent of sound, he entered banking and distanced himself from the pro–National Socialist activities of his brother, making only a few minor character-role appearances in film.[18] Although she co-founded the studio, von Dassanowsky was not an invested owner but rather was employed as producer in charge of creative development. Her association with Emmerich Hanus at this new juncture in Austrian film recalled the work of Louise Kolm with Heinz Hanus at the beginning of the industry. It also made her the second female studio founder and fourth female producer in Austrian cinema history, following Kolm, silent film supporting actress Carmen Cartellieri (1891–1953), who formed her own production company in 1920, and Anna Berg-Schwarz (1894–1977), who co-produced (with husband Leo Berg) the 1937 Kolm/Fleck film *Der Pfarrer von Kirchfeld* with her short-lived Excelsior company.

As a new studio, Belvedere-Film was not hampered by either occupation control or the problems other production companies had in renting facilities or locating suitable soundstage replacements. The 1903 *Jugendstil* building in the heart of Vienna's first district[19] that became Belvedere Studios in 1946 had been utilized in the early 1930s as the Institute for Sound Film, where Heinz Hanus was among the faculty members. Previously it had been used as a silent picture studio and during the Wien-Film era it served as a secondary rehearsal and production site. The building had been plundered and abandoned, but within a year it was adapted to the needs of what Marielies Füringk called "Vienna's film studio *en miniature*."[20] In addition to the small offices, dressing rooms, construction rooms, wardrobe storage, sound recording facilities, and editing space, there were two medium-sized soundstages, obviously enough to make Belvedere Film one of the cultivators of new talent in the postwar era. Helping "kick-start the revival of the Austrian film industry,"[21] as John Walker puts it, the studio also attempted to reconnect with the provocative entertainment of the interwar period and to adapt the Wien-Film musical and comedy style. It also hoped to reinvent genres that had been tainted by Nazi cinema — the *Heimatfilm*, provincial comedies, and operetta — for an audience now exposed to British, French and American productions. The studio only produced seven films, but it satisfied its goals in presenting new and important talent on both sides of the camera, exporting its work, and attaining, if not always critical praise, then certainly a measure of popular appeal. Production began modestly in 1946 with two culture films: *Symphonie in Salzburg*/Symphony in Salzburg, an extended visual/aural poem to the city, Mozart and the Salzburg Festival, and *Kunstschätze des Klosterneuburger Stiftes*/Art Treasures of Klosterneuburg. *Die Glücksmühle*/The Mill of Happiness (a.k.a.: *Das Erbe von Mülhof*/The Inheritance of Muelhof, 1947), Austria's first postwar *Heimatfilm* comedy, followed. It was directed by Emmerich Hanus, who had returned to direction earlier that year with a Viennese Film–style Franz Schubert biopic entitled, *Seine einzige Liebe*/His Only Love (1947), the only film produced by Royal-Film. *Glücksmühle,* which featured Wien-Film secondary stars Thea Weis and Karl Skraup, also set the pattern for Belvedere-Film's development of technical talent with cinematographer Hans Nigmann and set designer Sepp Rothaur. The interiors of this film, which tells the story of a rich farmer who purchases a worthless mill to get even with his stingy female cousin only to discover that the mill is of substantial value, were shot at the Belvedere-Film studio facility with exteriors done at Alt-Aussee. Although the film was a success with audiences, critics derided it as an overly simplistic village comedy.

Belvedere-Film followed this with more escapist entertainment, the period provincial comedy *Wer küsst wen?*/Who Is Kissing Whom? (1947), a film written as a vehicle for emerging lead Wolf Albach-Retty and Trude Marlen, then husband

and wife. Albach-Retty ultimately pulled out of the project and was replaced by Alexander Trojan, whose work on this film gave him a brief career as a secondary romantic lead in Austrian and West German film. *Wer küsst wen?* was directed by Wolf-Dietrich Friese, lensed by Wien-Film's Sepp Ketterer and Hans Nigmann, and included set design by Sepp Rothauer and music by Belvedere's in-house composer, Oskar Wagner. The reestablished Sascha distribution company released both of these first two Belvedere feature films.

The film event of 1947 should have been the return of comic star Hans Moser in J. A. Hübler-Kahla's (1902–65) episodic parody of Austrian history, *Die Welt dreht sich verkehrt*/The World Turns in Reverse. Despite Moser's welcome bluster and the postwar moral of the film, which suggested "good times lie ahead, if we make it so,"[22] the film was hampered by stagy direction and poor production values. A more dramatic film evocative of the cinematic expertise of Wien-Film productions rose to the occasion. *Triumph der Liebe*/Triumph of Love (1947) was Alfred Stöger's (1900–62) first Austrian feature in a career that would span into the 1960s. An adaptation of Aristophanes' *Lysistrata*, it stars O. W. Fischer (Otto Wilhelm Fischer, 1915-2004), who had been a secondary lead in Wien-Film productions and was to become, due in part to this film, one of the major actors in Austrian and West German cinema. He is pared with Judith Holzmeister and supported by theater star Josef Meinrad, who would also later find roles in international productions. Leopold Hainisch and Tirol-Film remade the folk drama *Erde*/Earth shot as a silent in 1920. The new version again featured the participation of the Tyrolean Exl-Theater Group. Also recalling the silent era was a documentary on Austria's postwar political reconstruction, *Sturmjahre*/Storm Years, directed by Frank Ward Rossak (1897–1957), who had performed in silent film as "Francis Ward" and had made short films for the Social Democratic Party in the 1920s and early 1930s.

It was also a comeback year for the remnants of the Viennese Film genre, or rather the musical subgenre it had evolved into during the last years of Wien-Film. Hubert Marischka and German comic actor Theo Lingen co-directed the musical comedy *Wiener Melodien*/Viennese Melodies (1947), a Donau-Film production shot at Rosenhügel with sets by Julius von Borsody and performances from many Wien-Film regulars. The film, released by Sovexport, was a lavishly produced but thin yarn about the confusion surrounding twin sisters. It was the first postwar Austrian film to be included in an international film exhibition, the 1947 Locarno Film Festival. More in the traditional mold of Wien-Film's composer dramas was O. W. Fischer's second film of the year, *Das unsterbliche Antlitz*/The Immortal Face, which was directed by Geza von Cziffra, produced by his new company Cziffra-Film, and released by Sascha. With sets by Jüptner-Jonstorff and cinematography by Ludwig Berger, the film is a deftly orchestrated fantasia on the life of German neoclassical painter Anselm von Feuerbach (1829–1880). Conceived as an abstract/symbolic advancement of the Viennese Film, a "total work of art," even Gerdago's startling costume designs are based on the subject's paintings.[23] Unfortunately, like so many worthy experiments to come, it failed to seed a new formalistic or stylistic direction.

Gustav Ucicky returned to filmmaking after having been declared "politically neutral" by the Allies, with a thoroughly Viennese, if not to say intentionally "patriotic" Austrian, work after the pan–German excesses of his propagandistic *Heimkehr*. *Singende Engel*/Singing Angels (1947), scripted by Ucicky and Rolf Olsen, was a lavishly mounted biopic of the Vienna Boys' Choir "as told" by composer Joseph Haydn. Shot at Rosenhügel with an all-star cast that recalled Wien-Film spectaculars and with music arranged and composed by Schmidt-Gentner, the film, not surprisingly, was a major box-office draw. Ucicky donated the proceeds of the film to the reconstruction of Vienna's St. Stephan's Cathedral and the film was shown at the Hannover Film Festival in 1948. But the greatest popular success of the year and ultimately the early postwar era was a semimusical version of the *Heimatfilm*, *Der Hofrat Geiger*/The State Councilor Geiger, which was also known as *Mariandl* in Germany and *The Blue Goose Inn* in English-language release. Produced by Willi Forst and Paul Hörbiger, it was directed by the German-born Hans Wolff (1911–79) and co-scripted by Wolff and Martin Costa from the stage musical by Costa. It reunited the "dream pair" of Paul Hörbiger and Hans Moser and introduced the urban presence and song interludes into the *Heimatfilm*. Here, the countryside and its inhabitants provide an escapist backdrop for the character-driven plot (which touches on the Austrian social drama) and served as a form of escapist "vacation" for an audience tired of the war-torn occupation. The credits announce that the film will not show any trace of the impoverishment and troubles of the time, but the plot, which revolves around the financial rescue of the Blue Goose Inn run by the old innkeeper (Josef Egger), his assistant Marianne (Maria Andergast), her daughter Mariandl (Waltraud Haas), and the servant Hans (Louis Soldan), cannot completely evade the realities of 1947. Speaking to his servant Lechner (Hans Moser), the Hofrat Geiger (Paul Hörbiger) relates his retirement from public service in 1938 as a protest against Nazism. Marianne also conveys her bitterness from years of having raised her illegitimate daughter. On a vacation, Geiger, the father of Mariandl, meets Marianne and wants to make amends, even proposes marriage. She rejects him and refuses to share the daughter she alone has raised. The film never explores the reasons for Geiger's abandonment of Marianne but one can surmise it may have been class related. Mariandl enjoys the company of Geiger although she has no idea that he is her father and eventually Marianne is forced to wed Geiger in a sham marriage because it is discovered that although she is an "Austrian" she was not born in Austria and needs citizenship. Geiger regains his pre–Anschluss civil service position and returns to Vienna. Marianne attempts to secure her citizenship in Vienna for several months, which results in her meeting with Geiger, who corrects the bureaucratic blunders that might have denied her the sought-after citizenship. In the meantime, Mariandl has married Hans, who has become the new director of a refurbished hotel that Geiger secretly financed. The film finds restoration of harmony in different aspects of traditional domestic order: the exponent of the ruling class (Geiger) protects the servant (Lechner) who is loyal to him; man (Geiger) rescues woman (Marianne); and marriage is promoted as the ultimate goal (for both couples). The film is also an allegory of national reconstruction in the renewal of the hotel, and of rapprochement between the classes (recalling the antagonism

The rural idyll during cold war occupation: Josef Egger, Maria Andergast and Paul Hörbiger in Hans Wolff's *Der Hofrat Geiger*, 1947.

between the ruling Right and working class Left of the Austrofascist period) in the marriage of Mariandl and Hans, which also results in a child — a new and innocent beginning.

In addition to *Hofrat Geiger*'s representation of the "quality" of the Austrian persona and of national values to audiences through a hybridization of the *Heimatfilm*, it was also a new type of musical, given its contemporary melodies, which reflected the somewhat realistic setting. The film found adulation at the 1948 Hannover Film Festival, and the song "Mariandl" became a sensation not only in Austria and West Germany but in the Netherlands and Belgium as well, countries that had so rejected German-language arts since 1945. In fact, the premiere of this film in Antwerp was met with a bomb threat. The title had to be changed to *Weense Harten/* Viennese Hearts to underscore its non–German origin so that it could be shown.[24]

Unlike the West Germans, who in addition to their entertainment films reconnected with some aspects of their Weimar-era realism and socially critical cinema in order to approach the condition of the present, postwar Austrian film did not often revisit the 1930s social-critical drama genre. Instead, the reinvention or rediscovery of the Austrian identity and cinema was largely to be found in the biographies of its great composers, in imperial nostalgia, and in the variations of the *Heimatfilm*. Although these popular films displayed a return to technical excellence and can be regarded today as classics of their type, film criticism questioned this tradition-laden direction as one suitable for postwar Austrian cinema.

Karl Hartl's *Der Engel mit der Posaune*/The Angel with a Trumpet (1948) was the most significant production of the early postwar era for several reasons. The film marked the return of director Karl Hartl and actress Paula Wessely, introduced actor Oskar Werner to international stardom, provided a much-needed example of new dramatic filmmaking in a glut of escapist pictures, and most significantly, was a rare, if reductive, attempt at examining the problems of recent Austrian history. The saga of the Alt family and their piano-building firm (the "angel with the trumpet" is the company's symbol) begins in nineteenth-century imperial Vienna and concludes in the rubble of the postwar world. Although the film does not offer a critical exploration of the Nazi era, it does not entirely avoid the period. Its piano-building dynasty also functions microcosmically as the development of the Austrian nation in the twentieth century. Central to this allegory is the character of Henriette (Wessely) whose unrequited love for Emperor Franz Joseph's son, Crown Prince Rudolf (whose love-pact suicide at Mayerling has been the subject of several German, French and American films) is exchanged for middle-class marriage and family with Franz Alt, as the empire is lost and replaced by a small republic. Their two sons, played by Hans Holt and Oskar Werner, represent the division of Austria regarding Hitler and annexation, and Henriette's arrest and suicide due to her Jewish ancestry brings a too-late realization of the meaning of Nazism to this once important family. Wessely's performance ranks among her finest, yet the obvious apologia for her association with Nazi cultural politics in making this particular role her cinematic comeback has often been criticized. Maria Steiner, who has written a provocative study of Wessely's Third Reich career, maintains that the actress's relationship with Nazism was one of pure opportunism for both parties, even prior to the Anschluss.[25] Steiner also notes that aspects of anti–Semitism and race hatred in the original *Posaune* novel by Ernst Lothar (Ernst Lothar Müller, 1890–1974) were minimized in the screenplay by Karl Hartl and Franz Tassié.[26] Lothar fled to the United States in 1938 but returned to Vienna as a U.S. cultural officer in 1946 and resumed his career as a writer and theatrical director. Film historian Gottfried Schlemmer finds the casting of Wessely as a Jew to be an "affront," particularly given Lothar's Nazi persecution (he was nearly arrested by two actors from his theater who had joined the Storm Troopers). Moreover, Schlemmer considers the production's avoidance of Lothar's persecution and exile in publicity on the film deplorable. Nevertheless, he professes an appreciation for the extraordinary cinematic quality of the film, particularly its fine editing style.[27]

Posaune was shot by Günther Anders at Rosenhügel (but produced by Vindobona-Film and Hartl's non–Soviet influenced Wien-Film stand-in, the Neue Wiener Filmproduktion) with music by Schmidt-Gentner and was not only one of the major box-office successes of the postwar era but also clearly, and without much credit, an influence on the family saga film internationally. Hartl's dynastic melodrama

Austria as family saga: Karl Hartl's *Der Engel mit der Posaune*, 1948.

of Central European family tradition, opportunism and disaster in National Social-
ism began a trend, which continued with such international films as Vincente Min-
nelli's *The Four Horsemen of the Apocalypse* (USA 1962), Luchino Visconti's *The
Damned* (Italy/West Germany 1970), Vittorio de Sica's *The Garden of the Finzi-
Continis* (Italy 1970), and István Szabó's *Sonnenschein/Sunshine* (Hungary/Ger-
many/Austria 1999), among many others. Hartl's cast, which, in addition to Wessely,
Holt and Werner, features both Attila and Paul Hörbiger, Hedwig Bleibtreu, Fred
Liewehr, Curd Jürgens, Maria Schell, Helene Thimig, Erni Mangold and Karlheinz
Böhm, was intended to be the quintessential high-art reintroduction of Austrian
cinema to world audiences. It proved to be only a limited triumph in that respect,
since the wide popularity of the film and its cast did not subsequently translate into
a new global awareness of the contemporary Austrian motion picture. *Posaune*
received several Austrian honors including the Sascha Pokal award and was the first
postwar Austrian film to be presented at the Venice Film Festival. Former Austro-
Hungarian silent director Alexander Korda, who had become a major British film
producer during the war, convinced Hartl to create an English-language version in
1950, which immediately brought Oskar Werner and Maria Schell into the London and Hollywood film industries.

The work of Austrian author Alexander Lernet-Holenia provided the basis for two dramas in 1948. Despite his love for military pomp, this former imperial officer had written antiwar novels and indirectly criticized the First Republic with his mourning of the loss of the Habsburg world and Austria's (and his own aristocratic) identity. Although he took part in the attack on Poland as a Wehrmacht officer, he was wounded and quickly avoided reassignment by working in the Berlin film industry. Aspects of his literary work had been banned for its pro–Habsburg sentiments, and his tenure in film production was also truncated due to concerns about his ideological reliability, but he managed to write the first draft of the Third Reich's most successful film, the 1942 Zarah Leander starrer *Die große Liebe*/The Great Love. Withdrawing to the Austrian countryside, he wrote, among other works, a cryptic novel dealing with the concepts of resistance, *Mars im Widder* (Mars in Aries). Although it had been published in serialized form in a magazine, the book was forbidden by order of Propaganda Minister Goebbels on the day of its release. In the postwar era, Lernet-Holenia regained the popularity he had in the 1930s and was the first Austrian writer to deal with the Anschluss and war guilt in his novels *Der Graf von Saint Germain* (The Count of Saint Germain, 1948) and *Der Graf Luna* (Count Luna, 1955). He also criticized the sociopolitical atmosphere of the Second Republic in satirical novels and in essays.[28] Considered the literary heir to Hugo von Hofmannsthal and Rainer Maria Rilke, Lernet-Holenia's often ambivalent mix of neo–Romanticism and criticism, his ruminations on Austrian and personal identity, and his celebration, even "between the lines" of Old Austria and cosmopolitan Vienna, made his work a natural for the similarly ambivalent direction of postwar Austrian cinema. His novella *An klingenden Ufern*/On Resonant Shores (1948), produced and directed by Hans Unterkircher (1895–1971), was praised by critics for its stylistic updating of the Viennese Film form.[29] Lernet-Holenia's *Maresi* (1948) marked the return of Hans Thimig as film director, who intended to satisfy several generations of filmgoers at once by blending Wien-Film regulars with a new generation of postwar talent. One of the box-office successes of 1948, the film featured music by Anton Profes and sets by Julius von Borsody. Lernet-Holenia's 1947 novella, *Der zwanzigste Juli* (The 20th of July), which dealt with an aristocratic Austrian woman who gives her identity papers to save a Jewish acquaintance only to be left without an identity, was brought to the screen as the film noir–like *Das andere Leben*/The Other Life (1948) by Rudolf Steinböck, the director of Vienna's Theater in the Josefstadt and its ensemble.

Resistance to Nazism was also the subject of Eduard von Borsody's *Frau am Weg*/The Woman on the Path (1948), based on the play by Austrian writer Fritz Hochwälder, *Der Flüchtling* (The Refugee), which was itself based on an unfinished sketch by German expressionist playwright Georg Kaiser. The film was labeled by critics impatient for a radical stylistic break and international acclaim as a healthy and creative "milestone," a film "the world expects of us."[30] Anti-Semitism was the theme of only one dramatic epic of the era, G. W. Pabst's *Der Prozess*/The Trial (1948). The director had followed his early German successes (*Die freudlose Gasse*/The Joyless Street, 1925; *Die Büchse der Pandora*/Pandora's Box, 1929; *Die*

Dreigroschenoper/The Threepenny Opera, 1931) with productions in Paris and an unsuccessful stay in Hollywood. He subsequently returned to Berlin, where he made three films that were among the most interesting of the Third Reich but which damaged his reputation in the postwar world.[31] In this first Austrian film for the Austrian-born director, Pabst examined the roots of Nazi genocide through the not-so-latent Central European prejudices in a Hungarian town in 1882, and his work was, like Paula Wessely's role in *Engel mit der Posaune*, immediately attacked by the press as a safe attempt to "cleanse" his career. The timing and non–Austrian setting of the film may suggest this, but it was hardly the sole reason for its creation, since Pabst had already planned the material for production in his Berlin period during the 1930s. The plot explores the opportunism behind racism: with the help of an opportunistic lawyer (Josef Meinrad), a landowner (Heinz Moog) claims a missing girl was the victim of a Jewish "ritual murder" for the sake of personal gain. He incites the villagers into a potential lynch mob, but the defendant's council (Ewald Balser) ultimately reveals the fabrication and the manipulation of "witnesses" to the public. The film's period mood recalls aspects of German expressionism and the brooding atmosphere of the Viennese social-critical films of the 1930s. But its rapid departure from theaters underscored the unpopularity of this subject with postwar audiences. The film would be heavily referenced in Woody Allen's tribute to the angst of German Expressionism and the writings of Franz Kafka in his *Shadows and Fog* (USA 1992).

There were several entertainment films to see in 1948 to avoid such a "coming to terms with the past"—or even with the present. Geza von Cziffra reassumed his position as heir to Willi Forst with the operetta film *Der himmlischer Walzer*/The Heavenly Waltz. He followed this with a circus story, *Königin der Landstrasse*/Queen of the Landstrasse, with music by Anton Profes, cinematography by Hans Schneeberger and sets by Fritz Jüptner-Jonstorff. E. W. Emo also returned to direction with *Kleine Melodie aus Wien*/Little Melody from Vienna, a period musical that reintroduced operetta composer Robert Stolz, whose work had been banned in the Reich. *Heimatfilm* comedies were always popular: Actor Rudolf Carl (1899–1987) took up the directing reigns for the first time in Belvedere-Film's *Der Leberfleck*/The Freckle (1948), notable for reuniting his comedic talents in front of the camera with those of Oskar Sima and Hans Olden. Carl Kurzmayer (1901–74) also directed Carl that year in another peasant comedy, *Die Schatztruhe*/The Precious Chest (1948). The former cinematographer who had earlier that year lensed actor Theo Lingen's directorial work on the comedy *Hin und Her*/To and Fro (1948), based on a work by Austro-Hungarian playwright Ödon von Horvath, also directed *Die Sonnenhofbäuerin*/The Sonnhof Farmer's Wife (1948). Newcomer Harold Röbbling directed *Die Verjüngungskur*/The Rejuvenating Cure (1948) as well as the less rural musical revue film *Fregola* (1948), starring the tap-dance sensation of the Third Reich, Marika Rökk, who had been allowed by the Allies to resume her film work in 1946. Alfons Benesch (1924–) wrote, directed and produced the *Bergfilm* drama *Gipfelkreuz*/Peak Cross (1948), and Max Neufeld, one of the independent filmmakers of the 1920s and 1930s, returned to Vienna from Italian and Spanish exile to direct two films: a marriage drama set in the world of horse racing, *Verlorenes Rennen*/The Lost Race (1948), and a sentimental yarn about a famous pianist who returns to Vienna only to discover he has a daughter, *Anni, eine Wiener Ballade*/Anni, A Viennese Ballad. The illegitimate child theme of *Hofrat Geiger* would be used throughout the postwar era, as it could broach the subject of responsibility for the past without alienating the audience or causing critical controversy as the few actual historical-political films had done.

Eduard von Borsody managed to interweave the topic of the returning soldier (who was here differentiated from his more serious German counterpart by being a musician) with a crime drama in *Arlberg-Express* (1948). It was one of the very few examples of Austrian film noir in the early postwar era and the final film for pioneering cinematographer Hans Androschin, who had begun his career in silent film. Hubert Marsichka offered Hans Moser one of his best postwar comedy vehicles (an interesting mix of salon comedy and "tourist" *Heimatfilm*) as a misogynist who falls in love with the wife of an industrialist (Susanne von Almassy) and follows her on her vacation in the countryside in *Der Herr Kanzlierat*/The Councilor. Franz Antel (1913–) directed his first film, *Das singende Haus*/The Singing House in 1948, a revue comedy with new jazz-flavored songs by popular composer Peter Kreuder. The unique sets were designed by Jüptner-Jonstorff, who used ingenuity to compensate for the severe lack of materials. Among his more inspired creations was a background curtain made up of toilet paper rolls.[32] The film's modest financial success was also brought about by Antel's knack with publicity and launched the most famous and prolific director of the Second Republic. The truly progressive film of the year, however, had none of the promotion of an Antel production and remains neglected by Austrian film scholarship. *Zehn Jahre später*/Ten Years Later (1948) was directed by ski film expert Harald Reinl (1908–86), who had helmed many of the Riefenstahl Olympia-Produktion second features. This blend of *Bergfilm* and neorealist drama stars Trude Lechle, also of the wartime Olympia films, double amputee skier Sepp Zwicknagel, Herbert Matt and Jan Boon. The first film to use disabled athletes as its central actors, *Zehn Jahre später* offers a unique coming-to-terms-with-the-past plot: two former friends — one British, the other Austrian — had fought as soldiers on opposite sides in the war, suffered severe injuries, and are reunited in postwar Kitzbühel where they reclaim their self-respect and their friendship. One reviewer praised the film for its symbolic portrayal of the damage of war and the desire for peace on "both sides" through sport and for creating "a new artistic style that will influence the world."[33] Attending the 1948 Austrian premiere of the film was Hollywood actor Tyrone Power, who was reportedly so impressed by the work that he attempted to personally release the film in the United States *Zehn Jahre später* is an ensemble film in every respect. Its very creation was due to the combined efforts of Lechle, Zwicknagel, and the other actors who wanted to convey hope for disabled war victims and for Europe as a whole. A unique work in Western cinema at the time, it has since attained limited cult status and is shown annually on regional Austrian television.[34]

Despite the criticism surrounding his return to direction, Pabst was on the screen again the following year with *Geheimnisvolle Tiefe*/Mysterious Depth (1949). The anti-capitalist film, albeit not supported by, or in support of the Soviet occupation, was written by his wife, Trude Pabst with Walter von Hollander, shot by Hans Schneeberger, and starred German actress Ilse Werner as a woman who departs her introverted scientist lover for marriage to a wealthy businessman and a life of luxury. The objectification and abuse she suffers soon sends her back to her passive lover. The film, an entry in the 1949 Venice Film Festival, was Pabst's second box-office flop in two years, but it has recently been rediscovered as a document of social and gender relationships in the postwar era, one which also supports individuality, partnership without marriage, and the possibility of female dominance. Also approaching the problems of marriage and love was *Liebe Freundin*/Dear Friend (1949), the second and final film production of the Josefstadt Theater. Directed by Rudolf Steinböck and written by Curt Johannes Braun, it features Johannes Heesters, Erik Frey and Vilma Degischer as characters psychologically scarred by Nazism and the war who attempt to fit into the new postwar society. The film was of critical if not popular interest, especially for its "exquisite ensemble acting,"[35] which seemed refreshing after so many new star vehicles. Film criticism and scholarship gained renewed influence in the industry that year through the founding of the journal *Filmkunst* by Ludwig Gesek, which continues in various formats into the present day. G. W. Pabst was one of the contributors to the first issue, and ignoring the poor reception of his new Austrian "problem" films, insisted that the future of the medium lay not in entertainment but in enlightenment.[36] Pabst invested much in making this future a reality, but like Forst, government support was not on his side. His Pabst-Kiba-Film production firm had been founded in late 1947 in order to create artistic films with the financial support of the city of Vienna. Four films were produced before the city withdrew its support and the company was disbanded.

The son of Luise Kolm-Fleck, Walter Kolm-Veltée made his directorial debut with the Beethoven biopic *Eroica* (1949). The most expensive postwar film to that date, it presents Ewald Balser as the composer supported by both the Vienna Philharmonic and the Vienna Symphony Orchestra under the direction of Hans Knappertsbusch, as well as the Vienna State Opera chorus, the Vienna Boys' Choir, and several vocal and instrumental soloists. The film's story of Beethoven's rejection of Napoleon, an avaricious nephew (Oskar Werner), and even love for the sake of his art, follows Viennese Film form, but the realistic rather than stylized performances, outstanding production values, and technical excellence helped make it the greatest critical success of the postwar era. Its popularity, like the composer biopics before and after it, demonstrates that the cinematic rediscovery of Austrian culture, even identity, was to be found in adapting the same genre that held the forbidden identity in trust during the Reich — the Viennese Film. While *Eroica* truly reintroduced the high quality and unique style of Austrian cinema to the world (the film was hailed at both the 1949 Cannes and 1951 Sao Paulo Festivals) for a brief time, it failed to encourage state support of filmmaking at home.

Along with the audience approval of Beethoven's return, there was applause for the cinematic re-teaming of wife and husband Paula Wessely and Attila Hörbiger,

The historical biopic as cultural reconstruction: Ewald Balser as Beethoven and Oskar Werner as his nephew in Walter Kolm-Veltée's *Eroica*, 1949.

this time in an uncharacteristic marriage comedy, *Vagabunden*/Vagabonds (1949) directed by Rolf Hansen. By 1949, the presence of Wien-Film directors actively shaping postwar film was complete: Willi Forst refrained from directing and produced again, as he had the previous year, this time a comedy directed by Walter Firner, *Der Kuckucksei*/Cuckoo in the Nest (1949); E. W. Emo returned with a realistic drama, *Es lebe das Leben*/Long Live Life (1949); Geza von Cziffra offered the film noir *Lambert fühlt sich bedroht*/Mr. Lambert Feels Threatened (1949); and Eduard von Borsody directed the *Bergfilm*, *Weißes Gold*/White Gold (1949). Max Neufeld recalled the *Emigrantenfilm* of the 1930s in style, content, and creation with the Austrian/West German/French co-production of *Liebling der Welt*/Beloved of the World (a.k.a. *Seine Hoheit darf nicht Küssen*/His Highness Must not Kiss, 1949), a musical about the romance of an exiled king and a chanteuse filmed at Rosenhügel. The story bears more than a passing similarity to Erich von Stroheim's more decadent albeit incomplete silent epic *Queen Kelly* (USA 1929). Alfred Stöger, whose *Triumph der Liebe* (1947) success was followed with a light romance in *Rendezvous in Salzkammergut* (1948), returned with a drama about the Catholic priesthood, *Das Siegel Gottes*/The Seal of the Lord (1949) and showcased Josef Meinrad, Inge Konradi and Susi Nicoletti in his comedy *Mein Freund der nicht "Nein" sagen kann*/My Friend Can't Say No (1949). Former actor Hans Schott-Schöbinger

(1901–84) directed Curd Jürgens in one of the first regional projects from Graz (which along with Innsbruck and Salzburg would become the centers for actual non–Viennese production beyond the location shooting of *Heimatfilms*), a romantic drama entitled, *Hexen*/Witches (1949). Hans Wolff offered a musical comedy vehicle for Wolf Albach-Retty composed by Robert Stolz, *Ein bezaubernder Schwindler*/A Fascinating Deceiver (1949). Harald Reinl directed a *Bergfilm*, based on the story by nineteenth-century author Adalbert Stifter, *Bergkristall*/Mountain Crystal (1949), which features Franz Eichberger, Riefenstahl's discovery for her 1945–54 *Tiefland*. The film was strikingly realistic in comparison to the sound-stage-produced films of the time and reintroduced the on-location quality of the early *Bergfilm*. The film also managed to explore in a folktale manner what the more topical or realistic dramas dared not approach — the concept of the scapegoat. Here a man and his family is shunned by the town for his supposed murder of a vanished hunter. He is finally understood to be innocent when his imperiled children discover the corpse of the accidentally killed man in the icy mountains on Christmas Eve.

Belvedere-Film ended its production run with two of its most interesting and costly films in 1949. *Dr. Rosin*, a sprawling drama about a turn-of-the-century Viennese physician who becomes a victim of the opium trade, was the ultimate back-lot epic, which recreated old Vienna, Marseilles, Chicago, San Francisco, Shanghai and other locales in the confines of Belvedere's small soundstages. Despite the obvious technical limitations, the film has a sweeping visual and dramatic style that suggests the future filmmaking of David Lean. The casting is unusual, even bizarre: along with first film appearances by Alfred Schnayder as the doomed Dr. Rosin and Lyn Astor as his femme fatale, Josef Hübner and Adolf Ario impersonate Chinese characters, and Beryl Roberts, who appeared in silent Hollywood second features such as *The Soda Water Cowboy*, (USA 1927) and *Just Off Broadway* (USA 1929), has a cameo as a Josephine Baker–like cabaret dancer. A. (Arthur) de Glahs, a previously unknown name in Austrian cinema, directed the film. Studio co-producer Elfi von Dassanowsky maintains that the film was actually co-directed by Belvedere-Film heads Emmerich Hanus and August Diglas under the "de Glahs" pseudonym.[37] Certainly the overwhelmingly strong visuals and the brevity of dialogue in this film and in the following "de Glahs" opus suggest the work of a silent director (Hanus was a silent actor and director; Diglas began his career in silent production). In this respect, the Hanus/Diglas films have interesting correspondences with the essentially "silent" sound films made by Charlie Chaplin late in his career.[38] Like Chaplin, the Hanus/Diglas team offered extended visual scenes or tableaux that have little or no dialogue. The plots tend to progress through the physical action of the characters rather than from their almost incidental language. According to von Dassanowsky, the creation of "de Glahs" emerged from Emmerich Hanus's fear that his work was being dismissed by the critics because of the Nazi collaboration of his brother Heinz Hanus,[39] and from the admiration August Diglas had for American director Cecil B. DeMille and for the aristocratic Wien-Film auteurs Geza von Cziffra and Edmund von Borsody.[40]

The final Belvedere film, *Märchen vom Glück*/Kiss Me, Casanova (1949), also directed by de Glahs, may have been envisioned as a light, star-studded musical comedy destined for audiences tired of what had become a long postwar occupation trauma as its fanciful title suggests, but its risky, even progressive form and style makes it a standout in Austrian postwar cinema. Leading man O. W. Fischer, who had wanted to move into the musical genre, was given the only singing role of his career in this film, and it also provided the comeback role for Maria Holst. The film gave prolific Austrian comedic performer and writer Gunther Philipp (Gunther Placheta, 1918–2003), his first film role, and Miss Austria of 1949, Nadja Tiller (1929–), who would rapidly move on to European film stardom, made her film debut as well. Additionally, the film was the actual start of the long careers of both German singer, actress and cabaret artist Evelyn Künneke (1921–2001), who had fleetingly appeared in two wartime films, and cinematographer Hanns Matula (here as editor). It was the most expensive picture Belvedere produced (which included scenes shot at the giant sound stages of Rosenhügel), one of the factors that contributed to the shuttering of the studio.

The plot is a simple one, designed to allow a maximum of cinematic excursions providing song-and-dance numbers, comedy set pieces and satire. In Utopistan, a country with South American dictatorial overtones, shy but wealthy Fernando (Fischer), rejected by the bored socialite Danielle (Holst, in a parody of the UFA and Hollywood icons complete with that ubiquitous cinematic symbol of luxury, the white telephone) for being unexciting and weak, concocts a Don Juan–like persona who kidnaps women for three days in order to fulfill their personal romantic fantasies. The members of the government panic but fail to capture this love bandit. Ultimately, it is Danielle's turn but Fernando ultimately reveals himself, proving he could be "dangerous" but also that she misunderstood what she truly wanted in a man. Using elements of the screwball comedy, its swipe at an arrogant but incompetent authoritarianism is an obvious reaction to the Nazi past and the Allied occupation of Austria, and the film deals with officialdom in an iconoclastic manner reminiscent of the Marx Brothers' *Duck Soup* (USA 1933). In overall conception, however, *Märchen vom Glück* is a sociopolitical comedy precursor to such manic cold war satires as Billy Wilder's *One, Two, Three* (USA 1961), itself a product of an original Austro-Hungarian text by Ferenc Molnar and a famed Austrian-American director, and the kaleidoscopic all-star international sex comedies of the mid–1960s, such as *What's New Pussycat?* (USA/France 1965), *Bedazzled* (GB 1967), *The Honey Pot* (USA/GB 1967), and *Candy* (USA/Italy 1968). The episodic structure, cameo appearances, and the anarchic feel of such "experimental" pastiches of the mid–1960s can already be found in *Märchen vom Glück*, which made it an unpopular film with the critics who expected a more traditional comedic structure and a move toward stylish neorealism rather than surrealism. It is not surprising, however, that the roots of psychedelic cinema can be found in such a postwar fantasy/satire/neo-screwball comedy, given the crisis societies they spring from.

The film is subversive of static "cultural tradition" from the start. A pre-title vignette features a cameo of producer Emmerich Hanus putting aside a copy of

Escapist fantasy and political satire: O. W. Fischer and Nadja Tiller in Arthur de Glahs's *Märchen vom Glück*, 1949.

Goethe's *Faust*, to read the tale that is the film. Obviously deflating the cliché male-power role of the Nazi period and the lingering militarism of cold war Europe, Fischer's Fernando is a bespectacled intellectual, a gentle-man, who is able to slip into an aggressively sexual pose at will. His character suggests that gender roles are chosen but also that society prefers to uphold archaic ideals. He is no less a man of many costumes than the women he targets, but his alter ego, a foretaste of Jerry Lewis's Buddy Love in *The Nutty Professor* (USA 1963), alters himself to suit the personality of the particular woman. He even rejects the amorous notions of the too young daughter of the president, giving her instead a three-day return to the simple pleasures of childhood. The "victims" appear to be strong, intelligent and independent women in comparison to the addled men. The film's revision of the notion of a "leading man," as well as its recognition of female sexual desire and self-realization reach far beyond its era. It briefly inspired other forays into experimentation in mainstream entertainment films, most notably Wolfgang Liebeneiner's *1. April 2000* (1952), but its unfortunately long disappearance from the screen has denied it a deserved classic status. The studio's films had been missing since the withdrawal of Soviet occupation forces in Austria in 1955 and were deemed lost. In 1998, a print of *Märchen vom Glück* and an incomplete copy of *Dr. Rosin* were found in the Austrian Film Archives. As many so-called lost Austrian films, particularly from the pre–Anschluss era have recently turned up in Russia and Eastern Europe, there is now an effort to locate the rest of this maverick studio's creations.

Finally completed, Willi Forst's color Viennese Film about composer Carl Michael Ziehrer, *Wiener Mädeln*/Viennese Girls, premiered in Vienna in 1949. It was instant nostalgia, but it also reminded postwar filmmakers of the technical quality of the Wien-Film productions and of the vanished era of the auteur — Forst being the film's director, producer, writer and lead actor. His relic, however, seemed preferable to many postwar visions. Its popularity with the audience of the period was second only to *Hofrat Geiger*,[41] and it became an official entry at the 1949 Cannes Festival. Realizing musical diversion was in more demand than ever, Franz Antel wasted no time in following up on his debut with a musical *Heimatfilm* subgenre he invented known as the "summer-comedy." *Kleiner Schwindel am Wolfgangsee*/The Little Swindel at the Wolfgangsee (1949) was filmed in Linz and on location in Vienna and at the Wolfgangsee with Waltraud Haas, Hans Holt, Susi Nicoletti, as well as Gunther Philipp and Nadja Tiller, fresh from their *Märchen vom Glück* debuts. The multitalented Philipp also co-wrote the script with Antel, which was produced inexpensively and set the cast and tone for a good deal of Antel's work, which, aside from his later imperial epics, tended toward airy and lighthearted musical comedies.

Forst's long-awaited *Wiener Mädeln* was followed by the first color film of Austrian postwar cinema, the socialist-tinged working-class musical *Das Kind der Donau*/The Child of the Danube (1950), with Marika Rökk. The film was directed by her husband, Georg Jacoby, who had made several Austrian silent pictures and had directed the first UFA color film, *Frauen sind bessere Diplomaten*/Women Are Better Diplomats (Germany 1942), which also features Rökk. Shot at the Soviet-controlled Rosenhügel, the production demonstrated the extent to which Stalin's representatives were willing to utilize the cinema icons of the Nazi past in order to influence the future. The film ran for years in Soviet and Eastern European cinemas. It was also one of the first contributors to the growing market in recordings of film music and songs. Other hits of the period were a swing number by Anton Profes from the Paula Wessely/Attila Hörbiger *Vagabunden* film and a Peter Kreuder song from Franz Antel's *Das singende Haus*.

With the physical reconstruction of Vienna in full swing by the turn of the decade, audiences seemed to be ready again for more serious or high art fare, and there was a sudden shift toward the production of literary films. Gustav Ucicky directed two in 1950. The first was *Der Seelenbräu*/The Soul's Brew, based on a novella written by Carl Zuckmayer during his American exile, which presented the rivalry between two Alpine towns and their breweries. The film was breathtakingly shot by *Bergfilm* specialist Hans Schneeberger and featured music by Willi Schmidt-Gentner. As with his previous *Singende Engel* (1947), Ucicky once again proclaimed this film as a "typical Austrian film" and one that would show the world what Austria represents.[42] He followed this with *Cordula* (1950), based on a 1927 work by

Anton Wildgans. The script, written by the director with Austrian author Max Mell, was also shot by Hans Schneeberger. Set in a rural village during World War I, it provided Paula Wessely (who also produced the film) with one of her best post-war roles as the inn servant Cordula who is seduced and left with a child by an officer (Erik Frey). The original work by Wildgans portrayed the moral collapse of the town as represented by different characters. Here, the other "sins" are given life by Attila Hörbiger, Jane Tilden, Alma Seidler, Fritz Imhoff and Karl Skraup. Despite the allegorical aspect of the film, it was welcomed by both Austrian and foreign critics as another "first step" toward a stalled Austrian neorealism and as an anti-dote to the typical comic or sentimental *Heimatfilm*.

Another literature-based village drama that year was Alfred Stöger's *Das Jahr der Herren*/The Year of the Lord (1950), based on the 1933 novel by Karl Heinrich Waggerl, the most popular author of the Dollfuss/Schuschnigg era. Waggerl co-wrote the script with film actor and writer Ulrich Bettac; the story follows a year in the life of a town and focuses on the illegitimate child (Karl Haberfellner) of a woman (Käthe Gold) who is forced to leave the town while a local priest (Ewald Balser) cares for the boy. Ultimately the woman returns with a father (Josef Mein-rad) for the boy. This atmospheric film, shot on location, was unmistakably a rep-resentation of the Catholic and folk ideology of the 1933-38 Austrofascist state, but rural idyll and Catholic morality still played well in the early Second Repub-lic, which attempted to redefine specific Austrian values in an occupied land caught between the ruins of the Nazi Reich and hope for returned sovereignty. Religion and high art were also represented in two documentaries: *Das große Geheimnis*/The Great Mystery (1950), Alfred Lehner's catechism film, commissioned by the Catholic Film Guild; and *Das Salzburger Welttheater*/The Salzburg World Theater (1950), directed by Max Zehenthofer, an entry in the 1950 Venice and 1951 Berlin Film Festivals.

The new crossover of the musical into the *Heimatfilm* was much in demand, and the catchword drawing in audiences had evolved from the simple concept of *Glück* or "happiness" in the titles of the immediate postwar films, to more erotic desires such as kissing and outright sin with Franz Antel's *Auf der Alm, da gibt's ka Sünd*/In the Pasture There Is No Sin (1950), Hubert Marischka's *Küssen ist keine Sünd*/Kissing Is No Sin (1950), and Fritz Schultz's *Gruß und Kuß aus der Wachau*/Love and Kisses from the Wachau (1950). The Habsburg drama and Habs-burg-era biopic also emerged in 1950, beginning a theme that would snowball through the decade. These genres were as important to the reconstitution of Aus-trian identity as the genius genre had been in defining the Third Reich's pan–Ger-man "master race." But such cinematic hagiographies were also astonishingly hypocritical given the nation's official banning of the leading members of the House of Habsburg, including the last Emperor's son, Otto von Habsburg, who had escaped Hitler's grasp in American exile and had there influenced a positive Allied postwar policy regarding Central Europe and the reestablishment of an independ-ent Austria. Between 1950 and 1955, filmmakers concentrated on the lives of Tyrolean patriot Andreas Hofer, Empress Maria Theresia, ex–Habsburg prince

Johann Orth, Archduke Franz Ferdinand, Empress Elisabeth (in a series known as the "Sissi" films), World War I spy Colonel Redl, and the composers Mozart, Schubert, and Johann Strauss. *Erzherzog Johanns große Liebe*/Archduke Johann's Great Love, directed by Hans Schott-Schöbinger, was a sentimental fictionalization of the rebellious Habsburg prince (O. W. Fischer), a progressive and beloved figure in the province of Styria during the nineteenth century, whose marriage to a postmaster's daughter, Anna Plochl (Marte Harell), is known as one of the great romances in Austrian history. This formula of escape into Austria's imperial past coupled with the struggle and victory of true love over social constraints would be the most popular of all the imperial period films.

Battling hopelessly against the glut of film noir imports from Hollywood, two Austrian crime dramas and one crime comedy attempted to attract an audience in 1950. The first was a directorial turn for actor Curd Jürgens with *Prämien auf den Tod*/A Bonus for Death (1950), a film produced by the regional Alpenfilm-Austria company of Graz. But the real crime film attraction of the year was a British film, directed by Carol Reed in Vienna in 1949, *The Third Man*. Penned by Graham Greene, the film offers Joseph Cotten as American writer Holly Martins, who is seeking traces of his friend, Harry Lime (Orson Welles), a cynical black marketer of diluted penicillin (which has caused the deaths of several children) who apparently was killed in a traffic accident. Helping him discover a gray, exhausted Vienna and ultimately Lime's fate are British officer Major Calloway (Trevor Howard) and Harry's mistress, Anna Schmidt (Alida Valli), a self-destructive actress who becomes a pawn between Martins and Lime. The film, produced by Alexander Korda, was so heavy with Austrian talent that many still consider it a British/Austrian co-production. With the exception of Ernst Deutsch who became an exile actor in the United States and Britain and who has a supporting role here, major Wien-Film stars Siegfried Breuer, Paul Hörbiger, Annie Rosar and Hedwig Bleibtreu appear in cameos, functioning as signifiers for Austria's popular culture, for the Anschluss, and thus for the Allied occupation as well. The technical side of the film also has a significant Austrian contingent with art direction by Ferdinand Bellan, editing by Oswald Hafenrichter, as well as the now-classic zither compositions by Anton Karas. Karl Hartl helped Reed assemble the cast and crew and took the British director to a *Heurigen* (a suburban Viennese wine garden) where he first heard Karas perform. Despite American co-producer David O. Selznick's insistence that the film be scored with a traditional orchestra, Reed opted for Karas (whom Selznick considered a mere "banjo player"[43]) and his zither, which helped underscore the mix of tension, danger and sentimentality. More than any other film, *The Third Man* smashed the cliché image of imperial Vienna[44] with its ruins and its cold war embattled four-power occupation forces, while it made cinematic icons of the giant Prater Ferris wheel, the Hotel Sacher, the sprawling Central Cemetery, and Vienna's catacombke sewers. The film received the Grand Prize at Cannes in 1949, won the 1950 BAFTA (British Academy Award) Best British Film title, and garnered Oscar nominations in 1951 for Best Director, Best Film Editing and Best Black and White Cinematography by Robert Krasker (it won the latter). Today, tourist demand to relive this bleak and haunting film has prompted Vienna to provide a guided tour to *The Third Man* locales, which includes a stroll through, of all things, its historic sewers.

The rapid construction of new theaters, including the impressive Forum cinema in 1950 and the large Metro cinema, which had been converted from a legitimate theater space in 1951, combined with the increase in film production necessitated an agreement on general conditions of film supply between the professional associations of distributors and exhibitors. By the climax of the film "boom" in 1958, there would be 1,244 cinemas in Austria, or about one cinema for every 5,600 people.[45] As part of this structure, a new agreement was struck with West Germany regarding the exportation of Austrian films to West Germany and vice versa, which was to be renewed annually. The amount varied only slightly between this period and the height of the production boom in 1958, but Austrians were allowed thirteen to fifteen film exports against seventy-five to ninety-five West German films.

In addition to *The Third Man*, two other foreign "Austrian" films received international attention in 1951. The Swiss director Leopold Lindtberg, whose postwar work was calling attention to an emerging Swiss cinema, directed *Die Vier im Jeep*/Four in a Jeep (Switzerland 1951) about the tense four-power administration in Vienna as seen through the eyes of four patrolling officers. Forst's West German production of *Die Sünderin*/The Sinning Woman (West Germany 1951) caused the largest scandal in postwar German-language cinema. The film starred German actress Hildegard Knef, who had been a draughtswoman for UFA Berlin's special effects department and had attained star status with her leading role as a concentration camp returnee in Germany's first postwar film, *Die Mörder sind unter uns*/The Murderers Are Amongst Us (Germany 1946), which was produced by the Soviet-controlled replacement for UFA at the Berlin-Babelsberg facility, DEFA. After several other productions, it was Forst's film, which cast her as Martina, a woman who becomes a prostitute to support her artist lover and ultimately commits suicide with him, that brought her to the attention of Hollywood. It resulted in a Twentieth Century Fox contract, and a subsequent neo–Dietrich star build-up that made her the best known European film personality in Hollywood on Broadway during the 1950s. *Die Sünderin* was a major departure for Forst, who desired to spearhead a new German-language neorealist style with a frankness and adult subject matter that reflected the times as art. The film's stylized metaphoric imagery and a narrative structure made up of random flashbacks lashed together by Martina's monologue were revolutionary for the time and the genre. It is influential in the late 1970s and early 1980s "women's pictures" of New German Cinema auteur Rainer Werner Fassbinder and in current postmodern filmmaking. In addition to the character's "immorality," Knef's brief nude scene caused protest, particularly by the Catholic Church, which condemned the values presented in the film. All this helped make it a lucrative production, but it also had interesting repercussions in Austria. Forst, whose reputation had become too associated with the past when his final Wien-Film *Wiener Mädeln* finally appeared in 1949, had reinvented his career and German-language cinema with one film. It was a shock to the industry that Forst, who found such promise in a reborn Austrian cinema after 1945, made his "comeback" film in West Germany with a German star. Although Forst would return to make his final films in Vienna, *Die Sünderin* demonstrates that his loyalty was always to his art and not to political or national interests, a fact already apparent in his participation in both independent and "aryanized" productions of the 1930s and in his work for Wien-Film. He had been greatly disappointed by Austria's dismissal of his attempts to recall exiled film talents from Hollywood and the overall lack of support and recognition due him (compared with the national promotion of directors in Italy and France) as Austria's historically important and world-class filmmaker. *Die Sünderin* also reawakened the debate regarding censorship in Austrian film. "Schmutz und Schund" (smut and trash) in the arts became national discourse during the 1950s and audiences as well as distributors encouraged a voluntary control for films, similar to the West German model, since actual censorship was a matter dealt with by the occupation forces.

A significant portion of the many releases of 1951 was based on literary works to provide safe territory for the national box office while underscoring the art of the Austrian Nation. A portion of these were from *Bauerntheater* or peasant theater: Arthur Maria Rabanalt's *Hochzeit im Heu*/Wedding in the Hay (1951), Paul Löwinger's *Valentins Sündenfall*/Valentin's Fall from Grace (1951), and J. A. Hübler-Kahla's *Der Fünfminutenvater*/The Five-Minute Father (1951), all pandered to the audience's desire for provincial escapism. *Das gestohlene Jahr*/The Stolen Year (1951), based on an unpublished novella by Stefan Zweig and Berthold Viertel, showcased authors who had been banned during the Nazi era. *Der Weibsteufel*/The She Devil (1951) returned to traditional folk literature by Karl Schönherr — the second postwar lensing of his work after *Erde* (1947). The 1914 drama was scripted for the screen and directed by Wolfgang Liebeneiner (1905–87) a German-born actor who had risen in the ranks of the Reich's film bureaucracy to become a professor and director of the Berlin Film Academy and governor of the RFK. He had directed several important German films of propagandistic nature, such as *Bismarck* (Germany 1940) and the notorious film advocating euthanasia, *Ich klage an*/I Accuse (Germany 1941). After the war, he claimed he had protected many opponents of the Nazi regime through his pretense at party loyalty. He returned to filmmaking in West Germany in 1949 and in Austria with *Das Tor zum Freiden*/The Gate to Peace (1951). His second film, the Schönherr drama, had major production difficulties, not because of Liebeneiner's Nazi past but because producer Heinrich Haas had a problematic Allied "denazification" process. This was ironic given the fact that Haas was one of the independent Austrian film producers of the pre–Anschluss era, had produced the two Joseph Schmidt films that had been banned by Nazi Germany in 1934 to 1935 and had worked with director Max Neufeld whose work had also been banned. But in 1937, Haas had founded a sister Styria-Film firm in Berlin, obviously to distance himself from the independent Austrian film, producing among other German/Austrian films, Liebeneiner's *Der Mustergatte*/The Model Husband (Germany/Austria 1937). *Der Weibsteufel*, which stars Liebeneiner's wife, actress

Hilde Krahl, deals with an aged smuggler (Hugo Gottschlich) who uses his wife (Krahl) as a lure for a young rival (Kurt Heintel), but her desire to have children and the resulting love affair instead leads to disaster. When the wife realizes that both men have exploited her, she commits suicide and her husband is murdered by the young rival. In a character constellation typical of the *Bergfilm* (woman between two opposing men of differing age or class), the irrational female force is deemed responsible for the disruption of the (male-dominated) order. The critical and popular interest in such a moralistic even reactionary *Heimatfilm*, which warns against decadence and disrupted social and gender role orders, reflected a conservative backlash in an Austria tired of Allied occupation and foreign cultural influences. It also suggests why Willi Forst may have found his *Sünderin* film too heady a project for Austria at the time. The film was praised as high art by many critics and awarded the Sascha Pokal prize.

A true *Bergfilm* was Harald Reinl's 1951 *Nacht am Mont Blanc*/Night on Mont Blanc, a near remake of Arnold Fanck's classic silent mountain adventure, *Der heilige Berg*/The Holy Mountain (Germany 1927). Reinl had previously worked with Fanck on his most famous film of the genre, *Stürme über dem Mont Blanc*/Storms Over Mont Blanc (Germany 1930), and attempted to recreate not only the audience-pleasing formula but its original crew as well. Fanck's cinematographer, Walter Riml, lensed the film, while Fanck's house composer, Giuseppe Becce, provided the atmospheric Wagnerian score. But the film also managed concessions to the times: the love triangle and mountain danger of the original Fanck plot was updated with marijuana smugglers and substantial comic relief. *Nacht am Mont Blanc* also avoided presenting the mountain as a mystical elemental force, an aspect that played so well into the National Socialist Romantic nature bound *Blut und Boden* ideology. As the decade progressed, the setting would increasingly be used only as a picturesque backdrop for sport.[46]

Franz Antel's *Der alte Sünder*/The Old Sinner (1951), written by the author of *Hofrat Geiger*, Martin Costa, exploited the early cinematic interest in the Habsburg era with expertise. It was a perfect vehicle for Paul Hörbiger's lovable Viennese father characterization, and translated much of the traditional Biedermeier film vocabulary of the Wien-Film era into an allegory for the new Austrian Nation. Hörbiger portrays a famous and wealthy couturier to the aristocracy in nineteenth-century Vienna, whose career is quickly ended by the 1873 stock market collapse. With the help of the rational bookkeeper played by Maria Andergast and her several daughters, Hörbiger manages to rebuild his life and shop, which becomes a more modest, middle-class establishment. The single new aspect added to this exercise in cinematic Biedermeier is the image of a woman as being emotionally secure and intellectually capable, certainly a result of the increased public role of women during postwar reconstruction. Although critical of the empire's class-based society, the pointed inclusion of a Hungarian nobleman and a French entertainer in the plot favorably suggests Austria's multiculturalism. With a vast change in genre and period, the director returned to his formula of the summer vacation as backdrop for a contemporary musical in *Eva erbt das Paradies*/Eva Inherits Paradise

(1951). The film was designed to draw audiences who liked traditional operetta as well as those who sought escape from the urban squalor of occupation and the daily pressures of being a country on the edge of the cold war volcano. The story is a simple but effective fable of reconstruction: Eva (Andergast) inherits the run-down Hotel Paradise in the resort area of the Salzkammergut. With the help of her friend (Susi Nicoletti), the hotel's servant (Rudolf Carl), the conductor of a jazz band (Gunther Philipp), and several near–bikini-clad girls, she is able to bring fame and fortune back to the inn. Ultimately, she even marries the son (Josef Meinrad) of her rival (Annie Rosar). This film was not only officially recognized and praised at its Apollo theater premiere in Vienna on September 20, 1951, but Antel's skillful blending of two highly commercial genres was also rather foolishly raised to comparison with the work of Roberto Rossellini, in a desperate attempt to locate an exportable new national cinema style.[47] Even Hollywood comedy expert Billy Wilder criticized what had now become an overly simplistic direction for German-language film, claiming that if the German and Austrian audiences are given "a mountain in the background and Paul Hörbiger in the foreground, they are satisfied!"[48] But Antel's mix made money and bore imitation. Georg Marischka returned to what first appeared to be a more traditional blend of *Heimatfilm* and musical in the cinematic treatment of the 1907 operetta by Victor Leon and Leo Fall, *Der fidele Bauer*/The Merry Peasant (1951), but the film was given music with new jazz tempos and the plot was adjusted to suit the geopolitics of the times: the ingenue who wins the heart of the leading man, was originally the daughter of a Berlin official but was now a visiting American. The retailored hybrid with, as Wilder had suggested, a spectacular Tyrolean backdrop shot by Hans Schneeberger and the presence of the redoubtable Paul Hörbiger succeeded with the audiences and the critics as a form of "New Wave" operetta.

The industry welcomed back Austria's last great traditional operetta composer, Robert Stolz, from his exile with a cinematic treatment of his stage work, *Tanz ins Glück*/Dance into Happiness (1951), directed in color by Alfred Stöger and starring a mostly German cast. The film attempted to fuse the operetta/revue film with high art in its plot about a South American opera singer and director (Johannes Heesters) who finds love during his work at the Bregenz Festival. Johann Strauss, Jr. also returned, albeit as the subject in the Austrian/Liechtenstein co-produced biopic *Wien Tanzt*/Vienna Dances (1951), directed by Emile Edwin Reinert (1903–53), and starring Adolf Wohlbrück. Austrian actor Wohlbrück (1900–67) had a significant post–Anschluss career as Anton Walbrook in London and Hollywood and was perhaps best known for his role in the British film *Gaslight* (GB 1939), which was remade by MGM in Hollywood with Charles Boyer and Ingrid Bergman in 1944. Ernst Marischka, who would define this era, offered his first postwar look at Old Vienna in *Verklungenes Wien*/Faint Melodies (1951) with music by Ralph Benatzky. The ice revue film introduced by Geza von Cziffra's wartime classic *Der weiße Traum*/The White Dream (1943), spawned postwar imitations and the live Vienna Ice Revue. It was a natural step to bring the revue itself into cinema with Georg Jacoby's Agfacolor *Frühling auf dem Eis*/Spring on the Ice (1951). The ultimate

Vienna's translation of a Hollywood novelty genre: J. A. Hübler-Kahla's *Seesterne*, 1952.

creation in the trend of revue films, however, was J. A. Hübler-Kahla's *Seesterne*/Sea Stars (1952), a water-based musical extravaganza shot at giant tank sets at Rosenhügel, which interpreted the style of Hollywood's Esther Williams films with imaginative results.

Despite the popularity of escapist entertainment, several dramas risked approaching the problems of contemporary Austrian society: there was Georg C. Klarens's *Ruf aus dem Äther*/Call from the Air (1951); Harald Reinl's religious drama *Gesetz ohne Gnade*/Law Without Mercy (1951); and the Hubert Marischka–directed *Stadtpark*/City Park (a.k.a. *Kleiner Peter, große Sorgen*/Little Peter, Big Problems 1951), based on the theater work by Hans Schubert, a bittersweet, Italian neorealist-flavored film about the relationship between an old woman (Annie Rosar) who rents chairs in the park and a young boy (Peter Czeike) dealing with his divorced parents. But the most provocative work of the contemporary drama genre was Harald Röbbling's neorealist *Asphalt* (1951), with Johanna Matz in an episodic film dealing with the social and sexual fate of its young characters. The work echoes aspects of films by Rossellini, de Sica and Visconti in its gritty, on-location working-class milieu, while Walter Partsch's unapologetic black-and-white camera work captures the postwar fatigue of its many supporting nonactors. The central story focuses on a naïve seventeen-year-old nightclub dancer, whose desire for a better life is used and abused by a sophisticated young man who promises love but demands sexual servitude. Fleeing him, she suffers arrest and hospitalization, but finally returns to the club to accept her fate. Matz brings a heartbreakingly bruised quality to the character of the child-woman Erika, whose emotional and intellectual development, social possibilities, even beauty are all inhibited by an inescapable world of brutishness and poverty. Although the film hardly approached the adult frankness of Forst's *Sünderin*, Röbbling's *Asphalt* was condemned as smutty and sexually sensationalist by critics. It was certainly no more "adult" than Arthur Schnitzler's famous turn-of-the-century play *Reigen*, which had just been filmed in France by Max Ophüls as *La Ronde* (1950). Not surprisingly, the Ophüls version of the play was also subsequently banned as too sexually frank for Austrian audiences.

Decades before leading actors began cultivating their own film properties, Paula Wessely had formed her Paula Wessely-Filmproduktion with *Cordula* in 1950, in an effort to create star vehicles tailored to her age and talents. Like Bette Davis, who at this same time was suffering career decline due to the lack of film roles in a Hollywood increasingly interested in ingenues and sex symbols, Wessely found little opportunity in either the *Heimatfilm* or musical comedy in an industry that soon heralded the young Romy Schneider and Johanna Matz as box-office icons. She subsequently tailored the growing imperial nostalgia in cinema to her own talents by developing and starring in the historical drama *Maria Theresia* (1951). As Austria's empress, social reformer, and mother of French Queen Marie Antoinette (in addition to fifteen other children), who balanced her affairs of state with her passionate but often difficult marriage, Wessely briefly found a suitable role for the mature phase of her career similar to that of Bette Davis's in *The Virgin Queen* (USA 1955). Wessely remained with the imperial trend in her 1955 royal comedy *Die Wirtin zur goldenen Krone*/The Hostess of the Golden Crown, directed by Theo Lingen. This comedy of errors arising from the exchanged identities of a princess and the hostess of an inn featured costumes designed by Austria's society couturier, W. Fred Adlmüller, and co-starred one of Wessely and Attila Hörbiger's three actor daughters, Christiane Hörbiger. Although Wessely's company produced eleven films (not all were Wessely vehicles), it did not reactivate her former status in film.

The pairing of Hans Moser and Paul Hörbiger in a comedy of errors, *Hallo Dienstmann!*/Hey Messenger! (1952), gave Franz Antel his most successful film to that time. The title song of the film became one of the pop hits of the decade, and the film was so imbedded in the audience's mind that quoting Moser's wisecracking lines became a national fad. Although the critics of the time attacked the film for its simplistic expansion of Moser's old comedy sketch into a feature film, his superb performance has made it one the classics in Austrian film comedy. But 1952 would go down in Austrian cultural history as the year of a most unusual controversy in its postwar arts. It arrived in the form of a film unique not only to Austrian but to all European and Western cinema in its creation and intended goals *1. April 2000,* the government-produced all-star science-fiction-fantasy/romantic comedy, was commissioned by the federal chancellery, written by Ernst Marboe, directed by Wolfgang Liebeneiner, and produced as an unabashed "state film." Hilde Krahl, Josef Meinrad, Curd Jürgens, Hans Moser, Paul Hörbiger, and most of Austria's

MARIA THERESIA

Paula Wessely holds court in Emile Reinert's *Maria Theresia*, 1951.

film stars of the time appear in the film, so it is perhaps easier to detail who was *not* in the film and only Paula Wessely and Attila Hörbiger were conspicuously absent. The couple may have been still too associated with Nazi cinema to be useful to a film intended as an extravaganza bound for export to the United States and the world.[49] The reason for the project could not be disparaged: Austria had languished under its four-power occupation longer than Germany, which was returned to sovereignty as two separate states in 1949. The fact that the Moscow Declaration of 1943 had promised the reconstitution of Austria's sovereignty at the conclusion of the war had little effect on the actual occupation and there were growing fears of Austria's permanent cold war victimization. The film would plead Austria's plight and desire for the return of full sovereignty. Both Willi Forst and G. W. Pabst had originally been considered as the director (or co-directors) of this essentially epic propaganda project, which had been planned since 1948. By 1949, a government-sponsored script competition was announced for the creation of a film to promote Austria to the world, and by 1950, the film was envisioned as a blockbuster with an extraordinary budget involving Hollywood investment, and with projections of large international box-office earnings. Both Forst and Pabst considered co-direction impossible given their differing styles (Forst wanted to re-vision the

The comedic "dream pair": Hans Moser and Paul Hörbiger in Franz Antel's *Hallo Dienstmann!*, 1952.

Viennese Film here as an "Austrian Symphony" of music-dominated images[50]) and their concerns about the Ernst Marboe script. Walter Kolm-Veltée was briefly considered and rumors still circulate that Billy Wilder was also approached, but in late 1951, it was announced that Wolfgang Liebeneiner was to direct the "Austria film" as it was advertised. This was undoubtedly the oddest choice given the director's German origin and his National Socialist past. But the government's selection was rationalized with the idea that national cinemas do not require native directors and that Liebeneiner had created successful Austrian films and had publicly stated his love of the country.[51] Universal attraction to the film was the primary goal for Liebeneiner, who no doubt also saw the possibility to gain international visibility with this grand production. Prior to casting wife Hilde Krahl in the female lead, he had actively considered Ingrid Bergman for the role of the leader of a futuristic United Nations, the World Protection Commission or WPC. An offer was made, but the government considered the risk of using Bergman, who had been exiled from Hollywood at the time for her adulterous relationship with Roberto Rossellini and found the choice too daunting for a project intended for American audiences.[52]

Liebeneiner's earlier career was, after all, unknown in the United States, but there was no way around Bergman's international scandal-sheet notoriety (condemnation by the Catholic Church would also have serious repercussions in Austria) and the government dropped the plan. Hopes for creating an American box-office success were already dampened by the end of 1951, during the negotiations for a simultaneously filmed English-language version. German-Hollywood producer Wolfgang Reinhardt was tapped for this co-production, but he immediately rejected what he believed was the reverse process of the script's creation — a thin plot built around Austrian imagery — and suggested that the historical excursions be dropped in favor of a romantic scenario that would use contemporary artistic sites (the Salzburg Festival, the Vienna Opera, etc.) as backdrops. Script author Marboe tended to agree with this viewpoint, but there was no time to rework the script, and Liebeneiner launched into filming with a version he apparently readied himself.[53]

The film takes place in the year 2000, as Austria continues to languish under four-power occupation. The new president (Meinrad) refuses to accept this fact and orders the Allied representatives to leave the country. His demand is understood to be a threat to world peace and precipitates the visit of the WPC chairwoman (Krahl) and her international board to investigate the provocation. She immediately labels Austria a belligerent nation and orders the country to be destroyed or emptied of its population and used as a museum like resort. The president retorts by presenting the board with a pageant of Austrian history to emphasize the benevolent and progressive nature of the Austrians. The WPC board is soon swayed by the delights of Austrian culture, and the chairwoman, surprised by her own attraction to Vienna's beauty and the president's charm, and aided by the rediscovered Moscow Declaration, rescinds the order to destroy Austria and removes the occupation forces. She is also united with the president in a wry display of the empire's old geopolitical motto, *Bella gerant alii, tu felix Austria nube* (Let others fight wars, you lucky Austria, marry), coined by the Emperor Maximilian I on the occasion of the double marriage of his grandson and granddaughter to the heirs of Hungary and Bohemia in St. Stephan's Cathedral in 1515. The event is spectacularly recreated as a silent film insert with music, to demonstrate how marriage and inheritance, not bloodshed, formed the basis for Habsburg world power. Other historical and cultural tableaux range from Paul Hörbiger's monologue as the famed Augustin of the Black Plague, to a performance featuring the Lipizzaner Stallions of the Spanish Riding School, to a montage of excerpts from Viennese operetta. But a recreation of the liberation of Vienna from the Ottoman Siege of 1683 is aborted due to the government's lack of funding for the project. Coffee, the spoil of that war, and another Austrian contribution to the world, is symbolically served to the WPC board instead. The overriding message of Austria's historic munificence is underscored when Prince Eugene of Savoy, one of the heroes of the liberation (the more significant leader of the allied Christian forces, King Jan Sobieski of Poland, is not mentioned), insists that his plans for conquering Southeastern Europe were blocked by an emperor who "loved peace and music." All this is framed by a science fiction vision of Vienna circa 2000, complete with futuristic electronic and television devices, flying saucers

A plea for sovereignty through science fiction: the President of the World Protection Commission (Hilde Krahl) arrives to meet the leader of a still occupied futuristic Austria (Josef Meinrad, third from right, with sash) in Wolfgang Liebeneiner's *1. April 2000*, 1952.

descending on Schönbrunn Palace, and death-ray laser rifles. Although the historical references end with Emperor Franz Josef and Empress Elisabeth who are waiting in the wings to defend their land (the twentieth century is ignored and neither world war is evoked), in-jokes and topical political humor abound. Hans Moser gives one of his most hilarious turns as the composer of a new Austrian hymn that might inspire the WPC and which is subsequently learned by the entire population overnight. The WPC's flying saucer landing in Vienna seems influenced by scenes from Robert Wise's *The Day the Earth Stood Still* (USA 1951), where an alien spacecraft arrives in Washington with warnings for an embattled cold war world.[54] The grotesque "Michelin Man" guard uniforms may recall countless Hollywood sci-fi films, but the other futuristic costumes designed by Elli Rolf suggest late twentieth-century fashion with uncanny accuracy. Scholars point to the film's overriding emphasis of Austria's musical heritage to prove the nation's historical pacifism, and indeed the WPC is ultimately won over by the various musical elements of Austria, including representation of all its great composers and music styles.[55] Only Irwin Allen's Hollywood historical fantasy pageant, *The Story of Mankind* (USA

1957), which examines aspects of world history and culture in an all-star cosmic trial deciding the fate of humankind, has ever attempted to recast Liebeneiner's vision. But the idea of music as a language of peace and the indelible image of the giant WPC flying saucer disappearing over the spire of St. Stephan's Cathedral also have an interesting correspondence with the human/alien musical communication and spaceship lift-off conclusion in Steven Spielberg's *Close Encounters of the Third Kind* (1977).[56]

Unfortunately, the film's political intentions were too transparent for a foreign market that expected an entertainment film. It was criticized in the United States for the lack of audience appeal in its esoteric and contrived "satire and fictionalizing," and it fared only somewhat better in European release.[57] American author Thornton Wilder, who had seen the film in Innsbruck in December 1952, had a very positive reaction to the work and expressed an interest in creating an English-language version. He was prepared to donate his work as a gesture of admiration for Austria, but plans were abandoned after the film received mixed reaction in the international press.[58] *1. April 2000* received the Sascha Pokal prize and was the nation's official entry at the 1953 Cannes and San Sebastian Festivals and the 1954 São Paulo and Mar del Plata Film Festivals. It was subsequently distributed in twenty-two countries into the mid–1950s by the Sascha-Film firm and had a distant final premiere in Chile in August 1955. The nine-million-Schilling film never became the export sensation its makers had gambled on, earning back only 4.6 million Schillings.[59] Ernst Marboe, who wrote a book about the production in 1954, indicated that the film was also intended as the starting point for a government fund for film production. Indeed, the film unions requested that the earnings of the film be earmarked for that purpose, but the government immediately rejected this.[60] Despite the official production of the film, the response was an ominous indication of disinterest in financial support for filmmaking, which contributed to the ruin of Austria's commercial industry in the following decade.

The desire of Austrian releasing companies to see an indigenous neorealism take root in the wake of Italy's fame with the style was aimed more at creating export demand than at influencing organic development of Austrian cinematic identity. Because of this, nearly any film that attempted gritty reality was heralded as the harbinger of the long-awaited neorealist trend. When Kurt Steinwender, a sculptor who had made Austria's first postwar experimental film, *Der Rabel/The Raven* (after Edgar Allan Poe) with Wolfgang Kudranofsky in 1951, offered the bleak urban soap opera *Wienerinnen/Viennese Women* (1952), he was immediately labeled the leader of Austrian melodramatic neorealism, or neo-verismo style, which ostensibly began with this film (and with some aspects of Röbbling's *Asphalt*) and sputtered through the 1950s. The film, which follows the fate of four young women, borrowed from Forst's *Sünderin* but also from Giuseppi De Santis's *Bitter Rice* (Italy 1949), which was shamelessly exploited by its reconstruction-aimed publicity: "From Bitter Rice to Bitter Bricks" announced the caption of the poster, which featured a scantily clad Silvana Mangano from *Rice* alongside a similarly posed Hilde Rom from *Wienerinnen*, suggesting that the film was an urban rubble-film translation of

De Santis's landmark rural drama. Despite this sensationalism, the film was indeed worthy of attention as a filtering of Italian neorealism through Austrian cultural values, and like the Italian films, it launched several new acting careers. Cinematographer Elio Carniel promoted his new moving camera technique, which gave the film its unique feel, in publications like *Mein Film*, but this unstructured style failed to find appeal among the mainstream of Austrian filmmakers of the time. *Wienerinnen* would, however, become an influential cult film among young filmmakers at the close of the century, who sought to reconnect with Austrian narrative cinema traditions that might be applicable to experimental and "dogma" aesthetics.

Drawing more of an audience that year than artistically shot squalor was, of course, an operetta film (there was at least one annually), Ernst Marischka's *Saison in Salzburg*/Season in Salzburg (1952) with Johanna Matz and Adrian Hoven. Based on Fred Raymond's 1938 operetta and shot on several soundstages at Rosenhügel, it led the re-vision of Wien-Film style with its lavish costuming by Gerdago and set design by Jüptner-Jonstorff. Not to be outdone, Franz Antel directed two musicals: a contemporary comedy, *Ideale Frau gesucht*/Ideal Woman Sought (1952) with Wolf Albach-Retty, Gunther Philipp and his usual supporting cast, and an adaptation of an 1894 operetta by Carl Zeller, *Der Obersteiger*/The Mine Foreman. The original libretto was reworked by Antel, Gunther Philipp, Jutta Bornemann and author Friedrich Schreyvogel and replaced the romance of two fictional aristocrats with the parents of the Princess Elisabeth of Bavaria, the future Empress Elisabeth of Austria. It was clear that despite the official policy regarding the Habsburgs, they were box-office rulers. The film's wide popularity outside of Austria initiated the trend of highly fictionalized, lavishly produced imperial dramas and musicals, and this new genre known as the *Kaiserfilm* (emperor or imperial film) became the country's most popular export in its cinema history. It also fired up the competition between Marischka and Antel. But their first battle occurred with comedy: Marsichka's *Knall und Fall als Hochstapler*/Knall and Fall as Imposters (1952) with Hans Richter, Rudolf Carl and Curd Jürgens (followed in 1953 with *Knall und Fall als Detektive*/Knall and Fall as Detectives, directed by Hans Heinrich) was pitted against Antel's two neo-screwball comedies, *Der Mann in der Wanne*/The Man in the Tub (1952) and *Ein tolles Früchtchen*/A Boisterous Brat (1953). Both were outdone critically and at the box office by veteran director E. W. Emo and his *Schäm Dich, Brigitte*/Shame on You, Bridget! (1952), which brought together three of the period's best-loved comedians: Hans Moser, Heinz Rühmann and Theo Lingen.

Eduard von Borsody also took on newcomer Franz Antel and the trendy musical/*Heimatfilm*/tourist-film genre with his own *Die Wirtin von Maria Wörth*/The Innkeeper from Maria Woerth (1952) featuring Maria Andergast and Mady Rahl. The production was shot simultaneously and in the same Carinthian countryside as Hubert Marischka's *Die Rose vom Wörthersee*/The Rose of Woerthersee (West Germany 1952) and the two films continued the rivalry into release in Austria and West Germany. Von Borsody's film, which was more traditionally formulaic than Antel's work, featured what had become a near tradition in such films by the mid–1950s — the rich American who stumbles on the conventions of Austrian society.[61] Von Borsody

Discordant and disturbing images in the neorealism of Kurt Steinwender's *Wienerinnen*, 1952.

attempted to meld traditional musical icons with modern tempos in the bizarre kitsch of *Verlorene Melodie*/Lost Melody (1952), where Johann Strauss Jr. appears as a dream muse to a jazz musician. Similar to *1. April 2000*, the film attempts to define the present but sutures it to a mythic icon of Old Vienna in an effort to avoid much of the twentieth century in constructing cultural identity. For his part, Ernst Marischka also attempted a musical, *Hannerl*/Little Jane (1952), a vehicle for Johanna Matz with a solidly old-guard Wien-Film technical lineup. This remodeling of the Viennese Film as a more Hollywood-style costume musical was also supported by actor/director Hans Thimig's new Gevacolor process film entitled *Frühlingsstimmen*/Voices of Spring, with the star of the first traditional Viennese Film, Hans Jaray, who had returned from his unhappy experiences in the United States.

With Austria still languishing under four-power occupation in 1952, the national reconstruction allegory of *Hofrat Geiger* (1947) was revisited with *Abenteuer im Schloss*/Adventure in the Castle (1952), directed by Rudolf Steinböck at Rosenhügel, in which a musical revue troupe repair and convert a decaying castle into a hotel. An Austrian/German *Bergfilm* co-production, *Der Sonnblick ruft*/The Call of the Sonnblick (1952), directed by Eberhard Frowein, gave a curious mix of the mythic nature found in Fanck and the science of meteorology in a fatalistic plot regarding an old hermit weatherman, his young grandson, and the famed Austrian

Sonnblick Observatory (built in 1886 at a height of 3,100 meters). The director had been the film dramaturge for UFA during the Reich and had gained notoriety for scripting Liebeneiner's euthanasia drama *Ich klage an* (Germany 1941). Like Harald Reinl's *Nacht am Mont Blanc* (1951), this film pays homage to Arnold Fanck's seminal mountain epic, *Stürme über dem Mont Blanc* (Germany 1930). The year's noir film was *Abenteuer in Wien*/Adventure in Vienna (1952), based on Alexander Lernet-Holenia's 1933 novel *Ich war Jack Mortimer* (I Was Jack Mortimer), first filmed in Germany in 1935. It was directed by Emile Reinert and marked the return of Hollywood-exile actor Francis Lederer to Austrian film. Kurt Meisel also offered an unusually dark look at the artist milieu in the Austrian/West German co-production of *Die Todesarena*/Arena of Death (1953), shot by Austria's progressive cinematographer Elio Carniel.

The noir film and the crime drama have always been underappreciated rarities in Austrian cinema. This meant that a non–Alpine *Heimatfilm* like Kurt Steinwender's *Flucht ins Schilf*/Brutality (1953), which begins with the discovery of a corpse and focuses on gypsies in the eastern Austrian province of Burgenland, an economically depressed area, may have been considered a healthy blend of genres and neorealist style by the critics but would hardly find an audience. The once popular director- or star-driven venture also soon vanished at the box office. It was obvious at this juncture that imperial Vienna as the subject of the epic film was the answer to Austrian and German entertainment desires. Ernst Marischka felt that this topic would also be of international interest as well and a far better representative of Austrian cultural identity than the *Heimatfilm* (which was also a German genre), borrowed Italian neorealism, or the contrivances of *1. April 2000*. He began the buildup to his successful "Sissi" trilogy with *Der Feldherrnhügel*/Maneuver Charm, a comic period stage work by Austrian authors Roda Roda and Karl Rössler. Ernst Marischka also endeavored to revisit the 1930s trend of bringing recording stars to the screen and chose to portray the life of opera star Richard Tauber in *Du bist die Welt für mich*/You Mean the World to Me (1953), with one of postwar Austria's most impressive voices, Rudolf Schock. He followed this with Schock doing popular tunes in the circus epic *König der Menge*/King of the Crowds in 1954. Going in the other musical direction was the Agfacolor production of *Die Regimentstochter*/Daughter of the Regiment, based on the 1840 Gaetano Donizetti opera and directed by former UFA head Georg C. Klaren and Günther Haenel at the Rosenhügel studio. Given the international identification of Vienna as a city of opera (as well as of the cinematically overused operetta), it is surprising that more opera film was not produced for export. The Donizetti work, however, was primarily of interest because its Tyrolean setting also made it a *Heimatfilm*.[62] Unlike its heyday during the silent and early sound era, films based on opera texts had become a rarity. Two years passed before another would be attempted: Walter Kolm-Veltée's *Don Juan* (1955), an adaptation of Mozart's *Don Giovanni*, starring Cesare Danova in the title role and Josef Meinrad as Leporello. Georg Wildhagen directed what is arguably Johann Strauss Jr.'s most accomplished operetta, *Eine Nacht in Venedig*/A Night in Venice (1953), which harked back to the immense sets of the silent and early sound days with its sprawling Rosenhügel backlot recreation of the Italian city. Operetta composer Franz von Suppé also received a lavish Agfacolor biopic from Eduard von Borsody, *Hab' ich nur Deine Liebe*/The Life of Franz von Suppé (1953).

Kaiserwalzer/Emperor Waltz (1953) was Antel's luxuriant follow-up to his popular *Obersteiger* film. The imperial musical-romance-drama may have been a formula of royal clichés, but his production painstakingly recreated the historic milieu. Costumes were modeled after original period designs, furnishings were loaned out from the state's warehouse of palace interiors, and a roster of advisors was employed to oversee every period detail.[63] The film presents Rudolf Prack as Archduke Ludwig, Gunther Philipp as his adjutant, Winnie Markus as the Archduke's love interest, a schoolteacher who is also loved by her colleague, played by Hans Holt. The intentional confusion between Archduke and adjutant becomes a greater problem of misalliance, which is solved in best *deus ex machina* tradition by the Empress Elisabeth, played by Maria Holst. The film suggests the Cinderella-like possibilities of upward mobility, while simultaneously praising a benevolent absolutism that protects and promotes an order, security, and even traditional class structure. Such an elitist and undemocratic world seemed, at least in its romanticized fantasy, quite preferable to the angst of cold war occupation. The film also touts Austria's historical greatness in a period of vague neonational identity. Although the critics were less than enthusiastic, it was an audience pleaser at home and in West Germany.

Given the anxieties surrounding sovereignty and identity, the Biedermeier's ideology of introversion, personal happiness and social order, along with images of an idealized old Vienna, become as potent an escapist illusion as it had been during the Anschluss. Schönbrunn-Film saw this reborn period popularity as an opportunity to revisit a character from Wien-Film's heyday, *Die Fiakermilli*/Milli, the Coach Woman (1953), directed by Arthur Maria Rabenalt, based on the theater work by Martin Costa, and starring Gretl Schörg as the legendary nineteenth-century female folksinger. *Praterherzen*/Prater Hearts (1953) followed, based on the play *Tingeltangel* by Hans Schubert, and directed by Paul Verhoeven, which explored and romanticized the lost world of the Prater amusement park. The ultimate Biedermeier musical figure also returned in a biopic directed by Walter Kolm-Veltée, *Franz Schubert* (1953), who had hoped to repeat the success he had with his Beethoven film.

Literary-based films, particularly those from the Biedermeier folk tradition, continued to be popular, such as Leopold Hainisch's Gevacolor production of *Der Verschwender*/The Spendthrift (1953), based on the 1834 fairy tale by Ferdinand Raimund, and Georg Marischka's *Einen Jux will er sich machen*/Out for a Lark (1953), adapted from Johann Nestroy's popular 1842 comedy. There was also cinematic treatment of contemporary German author Erich Kästner's comedy *Pünktchen und Anton*/Dotty and Anton (1953). Kästner had been one of the most popular writers of the Weimar Republic and had been banned by the Nazis. His urban satires of depression-era Germany continued to have resonance in the no less absurd postwar world. *Pünktchen*, an official entry in the Venice Film Festival of 1954, was followed by an Austrian film treatment of the author's most famous work, *Drei Män-ner im Schnee*/Three Men in the Snow (1955).

But the mainstay of Austrian filmmaking in 1953 still belonged to the *Heimat-film*, albeit evolving with stylistic variations and hybrid qualities: Alfred Lehner's historical *Das letzte Aufgebot*/The Great Debt (1953) and the Cain and Abel–themed reworking of *Der Wildschutz*/The Gamekeeper (1953) joined Anton Kutter's Aus-trian/German co-production peasant drama *Hoch vom Dachstein*/From the Heights of Dachstein (1953) and a comedy based on the folk song of the same name, *Geh' mach dein Fensterl auf*/Open Your Window (1953). There was also Fritz Böttger's musical *Auf der grünen Wiese*/On the Green Meadow (1953) and Richard Häus-sler's contemporary rural drama on love and marriage, *Dein Herz ist meine Heimat*/Your Heart Is My Homeland (1953), based on a novel by Irmgard Wurmbrand and scripted by *Metropolis* co-creator Thea von Harbou. This Austrian/West German co-production had originally been planned as an Eduard von Borsody–helmed comeback film for Attila Hörbiger in 1947. But the most interesting comeback in postwar film was certainly in 1953's *Die fünf Karnickel*/Five Little Bunnies, directed by Kurt Steinwender, a small-town story created as a vehicle for Austria's first film star, silent screen siren Liane Haid. Unlike Gloria Swanson's critically acclaimed role in Billy Wilder's *Sunset Boulevard* (USA 1950), Haid's return in this unre-markable film did not garner significant attention or command a renewed career.

It was the 1954 *Heimatfilm*, *Echo der Berge*/Echo of the Mountains, known in Germany and abroad as *Der Förster vom Silberwald*/The Forester of the Silverwoods that truly brought the Austrian *Heimatfilm* to international audiences and thereby spawned many copies and semi-sequels. An Agfacolor production directed by Alfons Stummer (1924–) with exquisite nature photography by Walter Tuch, Sepp Ket-terer, Hans Gessl and Ernst Teumer, it showcases mostly new talent: Anita Gutwell, Rudolf Lenz, and Lotte Ledl. The film was an accidental hybridization between a culture film on nature conservation and a feature drama, which at first had difficulty in finding distribution but ultimately became the prototype for the tourism-pro-moting *Heimatfilm* genre into the following decade. It began as an idea by Franz Mayr-Melnhof, who in 1952 wanted to commission a short Austrian documentary for the 1954 international hunting exhibition in Düsseldorf. Since Mayr-Melnhof had hoped for theatrical distribution of this project as well, and major cinemas would not feature a short film, he decided to support the production of a feature film, which would emphasize nature conservation and concepts of protected and regulated hunting. Mayr-Melnhof insisted on color, which was still a rarity in Aus-trian film due to its expense, and wrote the first treatment for the film. He pro-moted the project as a showcase for Austria *and* as an international exhibition work, which subsequently garnered a surprisingly high financial subvention from the fed-eral government. He was given a grant of 600,000 Schillings for a project in "tourist promotion" with the proviso that the money would be repaid if the film ever showed a profit. Given its long-running financial success, *Silberwald*, unlike the official "Austria Film" *1. April 2000*, earned the Austrian state a significant return.[64] Upon completion, the film was to have been released domestically by Sascha, but one West

The start of a *Heimatfilm* trend: Anita Gutwell and Rudolf Lenz in Alfons Stummer's
Echo der Berge a.k.a. *Der Förster vom Silberwald,* 1954.

German distributor after another rejected the film as thematically simplistic and
stylistically problematic: it was deemed too much a culture film and had too little
dramatic tension. Emil E. Reinegger, president of the West German distributor
Union-Film, suggested some re-filming and re-editing by director Karl Hartl and
a change of title. The subsequent test audience in Munich cheered the film, and it
ultimately saved Union-Film from bankruptcy, which had been brought on by the
financial failure of its expensive Max Ophüls's film *Lola Montez* (France/West Germany 1955). *Silberwald* went on to receive the 1956 Bambi prize given by the West
German publication *Filmwoche* as one of the best films of the preceding year (along
with two West German films, Helmut Käutner's *Ludwig II*, with O. W. Fischer as
the doomed Bavarian king, and *Canaris*, a biopic on the Nazi intelligence director).[65] Although *Silberwald* manages to replay some *Heimatfilm* clichés, it is a surprisingly multilayered film dealing with many concepts of preservation, which
elevates it above the usual melodrama. The film's central conflict revolves around
the preservation of the natural habitats of various animals. References to neoclassical literature (Goethe, Schiller) and baroque or classical music (Bach, Mozart),
and traditional rural settings and costuming were used, in an effort to preserve the

genre — "serious art" in general — and as protest against the tendency to update the *Heimatfilm* with contemporary furnishing, costuming, and popular music.

The desire to imitate Wien-Film's production values led to a minor nostalgic wave of films that referenced the studio and German-language film of the 1930s and 1940s: Willi Forst and Paula Wessely reteamed as co-stars in a mature romantic melodrama, or as it was known in Hollywood, a "woman's film," in *Weg in die Vergangenheit*/Path to Yesterday (1954), with Wessely in a Joan Crawford–type role as a woman sacrificing herself to help her husband through financial disaster. Directed by Karl Hartl, the cast seemed a near reunion of Wien-Film stars. In addition to Wessely and Forst, there were Willy Fritsch, Maria Holst, Attila Hörbiger, Maria Eis and Josef Meinrad. Wessely also remade the 1939 Käthe Dorsch hit *Mutterliebe*/Mother Love, a film she had long admired, into *Das Licht der Liebe*/The Light of Love (1954), directed by R. A. Stemmle. The new film was an entry in both the Berlin and Locarno festivals of 1954. Hilde Krahl was also seen again in 1954 in the crime drama *Hochstaplerin der Liebe*/Swindler of Love, directed by Hans Heinz König and co-starring German wartime leads Viktor de Kowa and Viktor Staal. The Wien-Film nostalgia wave may have provided the signal that the audiences might accept serious exploration of Austria's recent past. German director Helmut Käutner's (1908–80) *Die letzte Brücke*/The Last Bridge (1954) is one of the very few films of the decade to actually deal with World War II. This action/drama concerns a German doctor (Maria Schell), who is kidnapped by Yugoslav partisans, forced to serve their wounded, and ultimately killed on a bridge battle between the two enemies. The film boldly emphasized humanitarian ideals, female equality, and the futility of war. Carl Szokoll, a figure from the Austrian resistance movement during the Anschluss, served as executive producer of the film, which was financed by industrialist/newspaper publisher Ludwig Polsterer. Unfortunately, the director's nationality suggested that the film was a West German production, and West German and Austrian critics alike praised it as a significant German film.[66] Uncommonly well distributed abroad by Columbia Pictures, it was the recipient of several prizes, including a Cannes prize for Maria Schell (1926–2005) as Best Actress. Its popularity and critical praise was not lost on producer Polsterer, who realized the time had come to deal with Nazism and the war in Austrian film, and he assembled the riskiest project of the following year, *Die letzte Akt*/The Last Act (also known as *The Last Ten Days*, 1955), a bunker-bound drama about the final days of Adolf Hitler. The last film directed by G. W. Pabst, it offers Albin Skoda in a tour-de-force performance as the Führer and Oskar Werner as the fictional Captain Wust, who attempts to block Hitler's final orders for the destruction of Germany. Based on a novel by M. A. Mussanno, the script was written by Fritz Habeck and famed antiwar author Erich Maria Remarque (*All Quiet on the Western Front*). Although the film demonizes Hitler and his inner circle, it does not deal with the deeds and guilt of his more mortal followers. Even so, Polsterer had misjudged the readiness of the Austrian public to recall the very center of Nazism. A box-office flop, it has nevertheless served as a model for several future international productions along the same theme, most notably *Hitler: The Last Ten Days* (Italy/GB 1973).

The audiences were always ready for the escapism of new musicals and imperial fantasy, and these now mostly color films rapidly escalated in scale within the
next several years. Noteworthy for their virtuosity are Johanna Matz and Paul Hörbiger in Hubert Marischka's treatment of the exotic operetta by Fred Raymond, *Die
Perle von Tokay*/The Pearl of Tokay (1954), and Winnie Markus, Rudolf Prack and
Hans Moser in Franz Antel's Agfacolor imperial romance, *Kaisermanöver*/Imperial
Maneuvers (1954). Theater legend Alexander Girardi, who had managed to make
an appearance in early Austrian silent films, was the subject of a biopic directed
(with Karl Stanzel) and acted by Karl Paryla, *Der Komödiant von Wien*/The Comedian from Vienna (1954). *Der rote Prinz*/The Red Prince (1954), by author Josef
Perkönig, which had first been filmed as a silent by Jakob and Louise Kolm in 1917,
was readapted by Hans Schott-Schöbinger in an Austrian/West German co-production. In a more contemporary vein, there was also the feature travel documentary with many star cameos, *Pepi Columbus*/Joe Columbus (1954), directed by Ernst
Häussermann and written by Carl Mertz and Helmut Qualtinger for the Film Division of the U.S. Deptartment of Public Affairs — a promotion of Austria without
the pretense of *1. April 2000* but again featuring Josef Meinrad. Additionally,
Unsterblicher Mozart/Immortal Mozart (1954), directed by Alfred Stöger, offered a
montage of staged Mozart operas featuring well-known opera stars. But it was Ernst
Marischka's fanciful tale of the young Queen Victoria's love for her future consort
Prince Albert, *Mädchenjahre einer Königin*/Maiden Years of a Queen (1954), that
would serve as the prototype for a triumph to come. Inspired by the great interest
in the 1953 coronation of Queen Elizabeth II, which was presented in Austria
through the British occupation celebrations and the documentary film *A Queen Is
Crowned* (GB 1953), Marischka cultivated Romy Schneider (Rosemarie Albach-
Retty, 1938–82) to play the young monarch. The daughter of actors Magda Schneider and Wolf Albach-Retty, and the granddaughter of Rosa Albach-Retty, she had
already appeared in two West German films prior to her lead billing in Marischka's
royal epic. Her performance opposite Adrian Hoven as Albert was an instant sensation, and Marischka knew he had found the star to rival and even overtake the
several bombastic costume epics rival director Franz Antel was planning.

The national desire that had been so reflected and refracted in cinema finally
became a reality for Austrians on May 15, 1955, as the *Staatsvertrag*, or State Treaty
was signed by the government and the four-power administration, returning Austria to full sovereignty as a neutral republic. The departure of the occupation forces
and the official start of what is known as Austria's Second Republic had, of course,
significant effect on the nation's identity, its role within Western Europe between
the two cold war military blocs, and its reconciliaation with the immediate past. It
also meant an economic adjustment from postwar reparation economy to a capitalism that no longer benefited from the spending of foreign occupation forces.
The Wien-Film concern, owned for the most part by the Creditanstalt-Bankverein,
was restored to the Austrian government, as were all Soviet USIA confiscations,
including Rosenhügel Studios. Within a year, the Wien-Film facilities in the districts of Schönbrunn, Sievering, and Grinzing, separated from the concern during

occupation, were reunited, making Wien-Film once again the largest film studio and production company in Austria. But the time for such a grand motion picture factory had passed, as it was passing in Munich (which replaced divided Berlin as West Germany's film capital), London, Paris, Rome and even Hollywood. The postwar Austrian cinema had been created by what might have been called an independent industry of contingency. It had eventually become the only industry, and the traditional film factory was no longer in tune with the technological and financial developments that had come about in the previous ten years. Such an all-encompassing corporate control was an archaic and unwieldy notion to the newer filmmakers, even as they tried to emulate Wien-Film's heyday studio style.

The Soviets had left behind a 17 million Schilling debt, from which Wien-Film would never recover. Its two in-production films of 1955 were left without financial support, and the studio had to borrow substantial funding to complete the projects. The new Austria was also able to institute the medium of television, which had been introduced in West Germany in the late 1940s. A trial broadcasting company was set up in 1955, followed by regular programming beginning in 1956. The film "boom" continued, but the popularity of television reduced the film audiences significantly over the next few years. Although Austrians retreated much later from the cinemas than those abroad, 1958 would record the largest cinema attendance since 1946, with 122 million tickets sold nationwide and 46.3 million in Vienna alone (the population of Austria was roughly 6.5 million at the time).[67] The number of moviegoers began to fall steadily as the new decade approached. A film crisis brought on by television had already been a factor in the genre and style of Hollywood productions since the early 1950s. Wide-screen and stereophonic processes were used to lure the audiences back to the cinemas, and subject matter, ranging from biblical epics to all-star color musicals, attempted to showcase the new technologies, often with a sense of overkill. Western European cinema was also forced to deal with the television threat, usually in production values and style rather than with costly technology. Costume epics returned (in Italy, Austria, and Spain), the subject matter had become more mature and frank (in Italy, France, Sweden, and West Germany), and the onset of various New Wave cinemas obliterated the traditional dominant cinema experience (in France, Italy, and Great Britain). West German cinema began to move toward sex comedies and adult dramas to win back an audience. In Austria, there was an attempt at creating a 3-D film process (by Walter Maier and Kurt Traum), but the new process found no response in a film industry where color was still costly. By 1956, however, ninety-eight theaters featured wide-screen Cinemascope projection.

Hollywood biblical epics of the era, like Cecil B. DeMille's *Samson and Delilah* (USA 1949), former *Emigrantenfilm* director Henry Koster's *The Robe* (USA 1953), DeMille's *The Ten Commandments* (USA 1956), and William Wyler's *Ben-Hur* (USA 1959), fought the cold war through typological association. American actors portrayed the good Judeo-Christian figures, while Central and Eastern European or other "exotic" actors (Yul Brynner, Hedy Lamarr, etc.) impersonated the negative figures and suggested the atheistic Soviet bloc. Secular epics, ranging from Cecil

B. DeMille's *The Greatest Show on Earth* (USA 1952) to Jean Negulesco's *How to Marry a Millionaire* (USA 1953) to Walter Lang's *There's No Business Like Show Business* (USA 1954), and the roster of extravagant Rodgers and Hammerstein and Cole Porter musicals, were no less about white American capitalist values, which reflected and set the tone for American sociopolitical identity. Mirroring the antitelevision, even anti–Communist stance of 1950s Hollywood, Austrian film reclaimed its audiences and those in West Germany and other European export targets, for a time at least, with similar bombast in the imperial costume dramas of Marischka and Antel. The Habsburg-era romances, which defined Austria through the fantasy of a highly structured social order, world prominence, and high art, were stronger influences on identity reformation in the Second Republic than the often-touted *Heimatfilm*, which also shared German roots, a connection that was, at least in terms of national representation, a closed door. Thomas Elsaesser considers these costume spectacles, "with their pageantry and melodrama, a flagrant example of postwar amnesia and the repression of history—the least promising tradition to go back to for a recovery of the past."[68] But like the illusions of American social, economic, cultural, political and even class/race superiority communicated by its attempt to please and influence (in the wake of McCarthyism) national audiences and awe the Western masses, Austrian cinema had its own green light in cinematic matters relating to national identity. *1. April 2000* had already literally held up a copy of the Moscow Declaration to the audience as permission to avoid the Nazi past. Any history immediately preceding the Anschluss was also too complicated by its politics or the suggestion of native Nazi sympathies to be essayed on the screen. And while there were social dramas that dealt with postwar reality, the setting that most suggested Austria as a distinct entity from Germany was the imperial Habsburg world. In the cinematic vocabulary of the *Kaiserfilm*, the nation was to be anchored to the "better" past, and in filmic reproduction of it. Despite the evasion of a true "coming-to-terms-with-the past," imperial nostalgia should not be seen as an unhealthy development in the forming of neonational identification in postwar Austria. Given the Second Republic's promotion of the Austrian Nation, such Habsburg-era epics did remind the population of its unique place in Central Europe, its multiculturalism, its significant contributions to Western civilization, and its particular tradition of tolerance and liberal humanism, even if it was represented by social elitism and by the operetta cliché of Viennese charm. The problems in growing Austria's reconstituted identity are not to be found in the filming of romanticized pasts but in the specific politics of the early Second Republic, which accepted neither the sociocultural threads of an immense legacy nor aimed toward a progressive future but largely chose to escape into safe provinciality.

The Wien-Film Rosenhügel Studio, once the most advanced facility in Europe, would come to symbolize the victory of television over cinema in Austria for the next two decades. Part of the complex was sold off to the Austrian national television and radio broadcasting company ORF, and between 1966 and 1988, the entire facility eventually passed to the network. But first it would be the site of the climax of Austria's cinema boom and its epic attempts to deal with the threat of television. The new shadow of West German dominance over German-language cinema began to disturb Austrian filmmakers, who were at first angered by the fact that Austrian films distributed by German companies were often redistributed without an indication that the films were of Austrian origin.[69] Austrian films were mistaken for, or simply relegated to, West German cinema, particularly in the United States. In the wake of the popular *Förster vom Silberwald* and the imperial epics, Austria had become a favorable site for West German film production for its landscapes and historical venues as well as for cheaper production costs. It seemed like the 1930s all over again: limitations on Austrian film export to West Germany increased the interest in West German co-productions, and to secure distribution and popularity in West Germany, German directors were increasingly used to helm Austrian projects. Austrian productions would even be marketed by their West German representatives as German films, as in the films by Schönbrunn-Film, ÖFA-Film and Rex-Film Vienna, all of which were represented in West Germany and internationally by Rex-Film Berlin. Moreover, the popularity of the Tyrolean landscape with German audiences led to imitation Austrian *Heimatfilms* that were produced in Austria by West German companies. It is little wonder then, given the sensitivity about the differentiation of Austria from Germany and the growing tensions in production and distribution, that, rather than the *Heimatfilm*, it was lavish Habsburg nostalgia that was promoted as the representative subject of Austrian film worldwide.

The year 1955 was ground zero for the Marischka–Antel rivalry. It was that rivalry, along with the increasing use of color and the success of Ernst Marischka's Queen Victoria epic with his new star Romy Schneider, that launched what was to become the most internationally known series of films in Austrian cinema history. *Sissi* (1955), directed by Marischka for his Erma-Film production firm, was based on the 1932 stage operetta *Sissy* by Ernst and Hubert Marischka (book) and Fritz Kreisler (music), which had starred Hans Jaray and Paula Wessely as Austrian Emperor Franz Joseph and his Bavarian princess bride, the Empress Elisabeth. The first film in the eventual trilogy had discovered a way to incorporate most of the popular film formulas in one accomplished package: it utilized the Austrian and Bavarian landscapes for *Heimatfilm* content; it was a melodramatic imperial court saga; it centered on two beloved figures in Austrian history; it recalled the elegant orchestration of the Viennese Film; and it was a stunning color production featuring exquisite palaces, impressive sets by Jüptner-Jonstorff, costume design by Leo Bei (Gerdago's rival and sometime collaborator), and new leading actors who lured the audiences away from the phenomenon of television. *Sissi* told the story of the young Emperor Franz Joseph's (Karlheinz Böhm) love for Elisabeth or "Sissi" (Romy Schneider), the sister of his intended bride (Uta Franz); their romantic courtship and marriage; and Sissi's problems with her overbearing mother-in-law (Vilma Degischer). This romantic melodrama continued in *Sissi, die junge Kaiserin/Sissi, The Young Empress* (1956), which featured much of the same cast and crew. Given the overwhelming international success of the first installment, which had been awarded the West German Bambi award as most successful foreign film of the year, the second film was entered in the Cannes Film Festival of 1957. Although it repeated the successful multiformula as the first *Sissi* film, it did not shirk from presenting the political aspects of Empress Elisabeth's biography. The sequel continues the portrayal of the empress's problems with her mother-in-law, now with regards to the raising of her daughter, and her difficulty with the strict protocol of Vienna's imperial court, which was the most traditional in Europe at the time. It also focuses on Elisabeth's support of Hungarian autonomy within the empire and on her friendship with a Hungarian political leader, Count Andrassy (Walter Reyer). The film concludes with a triumph for the empress, the crowning of the Austrian imperial couple as King and Queen of Hungary, and the creation of a dual Austro-Hungarian monarchy. The third installment, *Sissi — Schicksaljahre einer Kaiserin/Sissi —Fateful Years of an Empress* (1957), depicted a more restless Elisabeth, whose beauty, constant travel, physical fitness obsession, and artistic interests (she wrote and published poetry under a pseudonym) made her a subject for comparison with Britain's Princess Diana during the 1990s.[70] The 1957 film focuses on Elisabeth's near-love affair with Andrassy, her lung ailment and more of her travels. Franz Joseph's loneliness and his antagonistic relationship with the Austrian-resistant Italian provinces are both trivially resolved by an emotion-laden reunion of the imperial couple and their child in Venice.

The *Sissi* films made Karlheinz Böhm, the son of orchestra conductor Karl Böhm, and Romy Schneider internationally recognized as a romantic film couple and promoted Schneider as the elegant ingenue counterpoint to the sexy nymphet image of the other young European female superstar of the mid–1950s, France's Brigitte Bardot. Unfortunately, both Böhm and Schneider became so indelibly associated with these roles that their future careers were often hindered by unwise choices made in attempts to discard the *Sissi* images at all costs. Although she was voted the top star of all German-language film for the role, Romy Schneider informed the press that she was not enthusiastic about doing the third film and flatly rejected Marischka's planned fourth sequel for 1958. For the sake of variety, Marischka had cast her and her mother, Magda Schneider, as commoners in the all-star imperial musical epic, *Die Deutschmeister/The Deutschmeister* (1955), along with Paul Hörbiger as an aging Emperor Franz Joseph. The film, which seemed to be in competition not so much with Franz Antel's imperial romance factory but with Marischka's own *Sissi* films, featured compositions by Robert Stolz and costume designs by both Leo Bei and Gerdago. Romy Schneider did, however, impersonate Empress Elisabeth once more in her varied international career, as a favor for Italian director Luchino Visconti, who had helped her escape the association by casting her as a contemporary, sophisticated wife who deals with her husband's obsession with prostitutes in his segment of the episodic *Boccaccio 70* (Italy 1962). Her appearance in Visconti's operatic *Ludwig* (Italy/France/West Germany 1973) opposite the director's protégé, Austrian actor Helmut Berger, who portrays Elisabeth's troubled cousin King Ludwig II of Bavaria, allowed her a final and mature interpretation of the unhappy empress.

Marischka's imperial epics were the Austrian film industry's strongest hope at

The lavish imperial epic — historical reflections for international audiences: Karlheinz Böhm as Emperor Franz Joseph and Romy Schneider as Empress Elisabeth ("Sissi") in Ernst Marischka's *Sissi, die junge Kaiserin*, 1956.

breaking the overriding hold of Hollywood releases in Austria and in joining the international market with world-class film. For a limited time, they accomplished both goals and started a wave of well-crafted impersonators, notably Hans Schott-Schöbinger's imperial comedy *Hofjagd in Ischl*/Imperial Hunt at Ischl (1955) and Franz Antel's third entry in his *Kaiser* films (following *Kaiserwalzer*, 1953, and *Kaisermanöver*, 1954), *Kaiserball*/Imperial Ball (1956), in which love triumphs over class, even at the imperial Vienna court. The high production quality, painstaking detail and sheer visual beauty of these films gave Hollywood studio bombast true competition. Much of the Western world also seemed to find refuge from the cold war in royal romance — through the travails of Iran's Queen Soroya and Britain's Princess Margaret, and, that ultimate overlap between cinema fantasy and monarchical pomp and circumstance, the wedding of Hollywood star Grace Kelly to Prince Rainier III of Monaco. The *Sissi* export proved no one did majestic Europe like Austrian film, and it helped satisfy some of this craving for ruritanian escapism.

For Franz Antel, Habsburg nostalgia could be made even more popular with more music and the added element of cinema nostalgia. For Christmas 1955, he released a remake of the 1931 UFA operetta about the Congress of Vienna and the waltz, *Der Kongress tanzt*/The Congress Dances, in Eastmancolor and as the first Austrian wide-screen Cinemascope picture. The all-star musical spectacle, shot at Rosenhügel, presented Johanna Matz as the innocent Viennese girl who falls in love with the incognito Czar Alexander I of Russia, played by Rudolf Prack. But Antel recognized the short life span of a trend and was already branching out into serious historical drama. *Spionage*/Espionage (1955) was yet another treatment of the Colonel Redl spy scandal of World War I, this time scripted by author Alexander Lernet-Holenia and Kurt Nachmann and featuring Ewald Balser as Redl. Transferring the high-level production values of the imperial epics to a tragic look at the empire, *Spionage* was indeed one of Antel's most accomplished films and ranks as his career favorite.[71] Unlike the 1939 *Hotel Sacher*, which suggested German betrayal through Austro-Hungarian decadence, this version attempted a more accurate history to frame the fictional account of imperial Austrian officer Redl, who had been blackmailed into providing military secrets to the Russians. It functioned as a kind of antidote to the nostalgic glamour of the imperial epics, while still impersonating the genre in its opulence.

It seemed an apt decision amid so much imperial fantasy that actor/director Fritz Kortner would helm a historical drama surrounding the incident that in due course destroyed the empire and brought about the First Republic, during the year of the Second Republic's birth. *Sarajevo* (1955) (a.k.a. *Um Thron und Liebe*/For Throne and Love) explored the lives and the 1914 assassination of the heir to the Austro-Hungarian thrones, Archduke Franz Ferdinand (Ewald Balser), and his beloved wife, the morganatically wed Duchess Sophie (Luise Ullrich). But the true opponent to cinematic royalism came with *Herr Puntila und sein Knecht Matti*/Lord Puntila and His Servant Matti (1955), based on a Bertolt Brecht play and directed by the Brazilian Alberto Cavalcanti (1897–1982), who had begun his long career with the French avant-garde and had made documentaries and features in England. This Marxist attack on class structures and capitalism was not a popular draw when the film was finally released in 1960. Critically admired for its original music by Hanns Eisler, and its cool, stark quality suggesting Scandinavian cinema of the period, it has become a cult favorite among Austrian film historians and filmmakers for its progressive content and unique visual style. Brecht had, however, distanced himself from the project, eventually rejecting Cavalcanti's script and the completed film, which he felt had undermined the sociopolitical value of his characters (Curt Bois as Puntila and Heinz Engelmann as Matti) by making them fit traditional cinematic comedy types.[72]

The nostalgia for Wien-Film quality and escapism led to outright remakes with Josef von Baky's (1902–66) *Dunja*/Her Crime Was Love (1955), which featured three writers to reframe Ucicky's *Der Postmeister* (1940). It gave Karlheinz Böhm a respite from the *Sissi* films and proved to be an early success for Eva Bartok (in the role previously played by Hilde Krahl). Karl Hartl also reworked his Mozart biopic classic, *Wen die Götter lieben*/Whom the Gods Love (1942), for a new generation and in Eastmancolor. Titled simply *Mozart* (1955), (but bearing insipid renames for the English-language market such as *Put Your Hand in Mine, Dear* and *The Life and Loves of Mozart*) the film was an international hit and increased Oskar Werner's global star potential. An examination of the film vis-à-vis the earlier Hartl work and later Mozart impersonations can be found in chapter 3. There was also *Seine Tochter ist der Peter*/His Daughter Is Peter (1955), a remake of the 1936 Heinz Helbig film, directed by Gustav Fröhlich. But the major remake of the year was based on the Willi Forst classic *Bel Ami* (1955), as a French/West German/Austrian co-production directed by French director Louis Daquin in Agfacolor, with an international cast.

Since the wild success of *Der Förster vom Silberwald*, the *Heimatfilm* became a genre tried by nearly every director in style and wide span of quality. A subgenre of the *Heimatfilm*, known as the "*Silberwald* film" emerged, which imitated the original's story formula and visuals. Most notable was the ÖFA-Film production of *Die Sennerin von St. Kathrein*/The Dairy Maid of Saint Kathrein (1955), directed by German-born Herbert B. Fredersdorf (1899–1971), which starred *Silberwald* actors Rudolf Lenz and Anita Gutwell, who had both gone from unknown talents to major stars with one film. Also of interest is Anton Kutter's *Das Lied der Hohen Tauern*/The Song of Kaprun (1955), a film that revisits the technology/nature conflicts of the early *Bergfilm*. The simple plot is centered on the actual construction of a hydroelectric dam at Kaprun in the province of Salzburg. Not only did the film showcase the requisite Austrian scenery and celebrate the lives of the nature-bound, it managed to advertise Austria's modernity and technological progress as well as a refreshing counterpoint to the nostalgia of the imperial epics. Other *Heimatfilms* included the peasant comedies *Der Loibner-Bauer*/Peasant Wedding (1955), directed by Peter Baldauf; Joe Stöckel's *Die lieben Verwandten*/Beloved Relatives (1955); and the remake of the 1940 film *Krambambuli*, based on a novella by nineteenth-century author Marie von Ebner-Eschenbach. Bearing a blunt new title to leave no doubts about its genre, *Heimatland* (1955) was directed by Franz Antel, who modernized the setting, emphasized the love story over the sociocultural commentary, and added a song. There was also the fourth filming of Ludwig Anzengruber's *Der Pfarrer von Kirchfeld*, now called *Das Mädchen vom Pfarrhof*/The Girl from Pfarrhof (1955) this time directed by Alfred Lehner. The film could not use the original title because a West German film on the same material and using the Anzengruber title had been released in Austria in August of that year, one month prior to the Lehner film. Unlike the disastrous box office that usually afflicts the release of two films on the same subject in the same year, both the West German and Austrian Anzengruber treatment were successes. It was a clear demonstration of the immense popularity of material and the overwhelming demand for any sort of *Heimatfilm*.

Another film also transcended Austria's borders in a unique way. Wien-Film's *Omaru — eine afrikanische Liebesgeschichte*/Omaru — An African Love Story (1955), an Agfacolor semi-documentary directed by Alfred Quendler (1921–), written by Ernst Zwilling, and shot by Elio Carniel, featured a mostly amateur African cast. Quendler had first appeared on the scene in 1952 with his experimental music documentary *Symphonie Wien*/Symphony Vienna (1952), showcasing opera singer Wilma Lipp and several dance ensembles. But it was *Omaru* that brought him mainstream attention, and the unusual and beautifully photographed African fantasy was a surprise hit with audiences during its brief run in 1955 and at the Venice Film Festival that year. Also in 1955 Alfred Stöger filmed the stage production of Wolfgang von Goethe's drama *Götz von Berlichingen* (1955), and Walter Kolm-Veltée did the same for the staged Mozart opera *Don Juan* (1955).

Rudolf Nussgruber followed his Austrian directorial debut in 1955 with his second and final Austrian cinema film, the 1956 ski-tourist adventure, *Liebe, Schnee und Sonnenschein*/Love, Snow and Sunshine, with *Silberwald* actors Rudolf Lenz and Anita Gutwell. The title sums up its simple formula. Snow was also the topic of a feature-length documentary on the Alps by Max Zehenthofer, *Winter in dem Alpen*/Winter in the Alps (1956). But *Silberwald* continued to inspire the new Agfacolor *Heimatfilm* craze, ranging from imitations like *Försterliesl*/Ranger's Liesl (1956), directed by Herbert B. Fredersdorf and starring the *Silberwald* pair, to several peasant dramas. The expanding umbrella genre of the *Heimatfilm* also included films dealing with the countryside that were not specifically peasant themed: Helmut Weiss's *Verlobung am Wolfgangsee*/Engagement at Wolfgangsee (1956), with Wolf Albach-Retty and Maria Andergast, and Hermann Klugstadt's *Hengst Maestro Austria*/The Stallion Maestro Austria (1956). The latter altered the *Heimatfilm* formula to include a more socially sophisticated love story set between a riding teacher (Paul Klinger) and a Hungarian countess (Nadja Gray). The settings of the Lipizzaner stallion farm at Piber and the Spanish Riding School were more exotic than the usual Alpine fare and provided iconic images, which fed both the reborn Austrian cultural identity and the tourist trade. Specifically tourist-themed films, usually comedies in which urban characters find love in the country, a formula that had proven such an escapist delight to the early postwar audiences, had now also been modernized by such films as Erik Ode's all-star ski comedy *Lügen haben hübsche Beine*/Fair Legged Lies (1956); and Hubert Marischka's *Liebe, Sommer und Musik*/Love, Summer and Music (1956).

By 1956, most major and even secondary films were made in Agfacolor, which made them salable on the international market and lured the public back into the cinema and to Austrian films. Although the onset of the television era was not as widespread as in other countries — there were only 1,420 TV sets in Austria in 1955[73] — it had signaled the onset of postwar prosperity. Not quite the astonishing "economic miracle" of West Germany, which had to rebuild its entire industrial infrastructure from rubble, Austria's economy grew slowly and steadily, and with this growth came increased car ownership and the possibility of weekend trips and longer travel holidays. This was not a new phenomenon in Austria. The Third Reich had made travel vacations part of its "Strength through Joy" ideology, but it was the first time that car ownership was not confined to the wealthy. As in the United States and West Germany, the idea of such motor vacations captured the spirit of postwar freedom. In Austria, an increase in leisure time was also spent on sports and traditional cultural events (concerts, opera, theater). Rock and roll records, pop concerts, and dance halls created a youth market. And all generations discovered foreign sex symbols who overtook interest in native stars. Film was no longer needed for a virtual vacation and audiences now began to make visits to the cinema a special event, rather than a usual occurrence. The *Heimatfilm* was forced to rapidly include elements relating to these new leisure interests and began to show more exotic locals in Austria, more wealthy foreign characters (usually Americans or West Germans), more teenage romance and popular song, and more Hollywood-parodic "sex bombs" among the native country folk. The growing co-productions between Austrian and West German firms, such as Schönbrunn-Film and Rex-Film Berlin (*Försterliesl*; *Schandfleck*), Donau-Film and Melodie-Film Berlin (*Liebe, Sommer und Musik*), or Carinthia-Film and Rialto-Film Munich (*Holiday am Wörthersee*) also signaled a problematic future. Even at the height of the Austrian film production boom (the highest level was attained in 1956 with thirty-seven feature films, followed by twenty-six in 1957), the seeds for the industry's near-demise in the 1960s were being sown by an eventual subordination of Austrian cinema to West German production. Brought on by the government's lack of financial support for the Austrian film sector, the West German film industry, in its own period of crisis, nevertheless became the undisputed German-language home for cinema talent. But for the moment, the subject of an overproducing, profit-oriented Austrian film industry that had seemingly no end in sight was such a phenomenon that it even became the subject of cabaret and television humor.[74]

Event films did manage to bring the audiences back into the cinemas for a few more years. There was Marischka's lavish Agfacolor production of *Opernball*/Opera Ball (1956), based on the operetta by Richard Heuberger, and Franz Antel revisited the popular ice-revue genre with *Symphonie in Gold*/Symphony in Gold (1956), featuring Germaine Damar, Fritz Muliar, and the Vienna Ice Revue. This was the last of the novelty films to be overridingly populated by professional actors. By the 1960s, ice-revue and ski films would be utilized to showcase sports and music stars. Hans Wolf entered the operetta spectacle competition with his treatment of the Franz Lehár operetta *Wo die Lerche Singt*/Where the Lark Sings (1956), produced by Paula Wessely, who also produced the Paul Christian-Hubschmidt comedy *Liebe, die den Kopf verliert*/Love Loses Its Head (1956) and the Karl Paryla version of Carl Millöcker's operetta *Gasparone* (1956). Nineteenth-century literature was adapted to give more variation and narrative "quality" to the imperial-era films. Franz Antel directed the Anzengruber work *Der Meineidbauer*/The Perjured Peasant (1956), while Josef von Baky brought German Naturalist playwright Gerhard Hauptmann to Austrian screens with *Fuhrmann Henschel*/Waggoner Henschel (1956). Hermann Bahr's turn-of-the-century Viennese salon comedy *Das Konzert* was brought to film as a vehicle for several Bavarian comic actors and retitled *Nichts als Ärger mit der Liebe*/Nothing but Trouble with Love (1956). The shift towards West German audience tastes had begun. Rudolf Jugert (1907–79) attempted to lend some tragedy to the Habsburg-epic genre by revisiting the events at Mayerling and the doomed love affair between Crown Prince Rudolf (Rudolf Prack), the unhappily married and politically provocative son of Emperor Franz Joseph and Empress "Sissi," and his mistress, Baroness Marie Vetsera (Christiane Hörbiger) in *Kronprinz Rudolfs letzte Liebe*/Crown Prince Rudolf's Last Love (1956). The film's costumer was Charlotte Flemming (1921–93), a talented period designer whose career began just as the costume film faded from the world's screens. She worked on Willi Forst's final films in 1957 and designed her last German-language film in 1961. Moving to theater, opera, television and international cinema, she is best remembered for her designs in two films about Weimar Republic Germany: Bob Fosse's *Cabaret* (USA 1972) and Ingmar Bergman's *The Serpent's Egg* (West Germany/USA 1977).

As the interest in the epic imperial drama and musical began to wane, a new subgenre developed — the imperial military comedy — which managed to cut the sentimentality of the epics while still retaining the lavish costume spectacle and feeding the notions of Austrian cultural identity. Willi Forst led the pack with *Kaiserjäger*/The Emperor's Regiment (1956), featuring Adrian Hoven, Erika Remberg and Attila Hörbiger. But there were also two films by E. W. Emo: *K. u. K. Feldmarschall*/The Imperial and Royal Field Marshal (1956) and *Ihr Korporal*/Her Corporal (1956). Hans Quest offered *Manöverzwilling*/Maneuver Twins (1956), written by Gunther Philipp from a text by Biedermeier author Johann Nestroy. Sans the imperial uniforms, there were also a few minor star–led comedies.

Along with the height of the biggest production boom in Austrian cinema history came the end for the remnant Wien-Film/Rosenhügel Studio relationship. Although the studio had been used by other production companies and their large projects, Wien-Film could no longer keep its Rosenhügel facilities and made its farewell production with the filming of a stage presentation of Beethoven's opera *Fidelio*. Ironically, that opera had reopened the restored Vienna Opera House in 1955. The project had been planned prior to the return of the studio to the Austrian government by the Soviet Union and was therefore the last Soviet-influenced film. Wien-Film reduced its staff drastically and entered into negotiations with film and television production companies for long-term rental and even sale of various aspects of the studio, once the greatest symbol of Austria's film industry.

Alfred Solm's 1957 *Das heilige Erbe*/The Sacred Inheritance was the zenith of the *Silberwald* impersonators. The trend had now come full circle, for it was *Silberwald*'s original creator, Franz Mayr-Melnhof, who again suggested the story, this time to writers Norbert Kunze, Günther Schwab and Alfred Solm. Solm, who had been assistant director on the original *Silberwald* film, was chosen by Mayr-Melnhof to helm this production. Although Mayr-Melnhof had hoped to repeat the unique creative process of his first hunting film, *Das heilige Erbe* was no sequel in any respect. The new Eastmancolor feature was far more expensive to produce than the original. The plot was complex and offered no romantic interest, and so much footage was filmed that it was added to the cutting remnants of the original *Silberwald* film and sold to Helios-Film, which re-edited the material into a successful culture film that also made the rounds in the United States and Canada.[75] Unknown talent was also held to a minimum this time: sixteen-year-old theater student Christl Erber was cast in the lead role, but the film was populated by

Heimatfilm regulars like Sepp Rist and Eduard Köck. The nature photography was expected to outdo the original and three separate camera teams were employed to capture different seasons for over a year.[76] Although skillfully edited, these sequences did not organically work with the dramatic scenes, but the film was a measured success, and there was a critical realization that the heyday of the recent incarnation of the traditional (e.g., without elements from urban comedy, pop and teen culture or the recording industry) Austrian *Heimatfilm* was passing. *Das heilige Erbe*, like its original, however, continued to spawn imitators in West Germany.

At the same time that the *Silberwald* film was exiting as a subgenre, a contemporary replacement for the *Heimatfilm* emerged from Franz Antel. The Wachau area outside of Vienna had become a trendy weekend vacation site, and Antel was quick to use it as the background for a film. Although it still had its roots in the *Heimatfilm* subgenre of the tourist film, *Vier Mädel aus der Wachau*/Four Girls from the Wachau (1957) was constructed as a breezy, youth-oriented romp, complete with two sets of pop-singing twins. With a thin plot allowing the young women plenty of vocal performance time, an appearance by Hans Moser and Oskar Sima, and the arrival of an "American" mother of one of the twins, the film concludes with a quadruple wedding. The image of the four fresh stars on motor scooters replaced the virtual vacation that the tourist films provided in the immediate postwar era with a celebration of a mobile experience that could now be easily achieved. The Agfacolor Austrian *dolce vita* of the Wachau lifestyle, something wholly invented by Antel's films and the press, was so popular that two other films that year took place in the region. German-born *Heimatfilm* specialist Hans König (1912–2003) offered *Die Winzerin von Langenlois*/The Vintner of Langenlois (1957), an attempt to reinvent the *Heimatfilm* once again, with a rich orchestral score performed by the Vienna Philharmonic and the Vienna Boys' Choir, but without the Alpine landscape and with a more dramatically adventurous plot that underscored the difficulty of women attempting independence of thought and action in male-dominated social and economic structures. Unfortunately, it returns to cliché ideas of traditional gender roles as a solution: Herta Staal portrays a vintner's widow named Elisabeth Teky, who attempts to make a success of a failing wine business with the help of her manager (Paul Hörbiger) who suggests a marriage with a rich man. Instead, the widow loves the similarly impoverished teacher (Gunnar Möller) and adopts several children. The *deus ex machina* arrives in the form of the wine distributor Köster (Susi Nicoletti), who solves all her financial woes. Elisabeth's motherhood is presented as the appropriate female role, despite the fact that it is the intelligent and liberated Köster (a male stand-in, complete with cigar), who has resolved the crisis. The other Wachau *Heimatfilm*, an Austrian/West German coproduction directed by another German, Hans Quest, *Die Landwirtin vom Donaustrand*/On the Danube Stands an Inn (1957) was specifically intended to feed the Wachau craze that had now hit West Germany (the film premiered in Kassel) as well. With German leads, it utilizes a similar woman-succeeding-against-all-economic-odds plot and includes Austrian stars Hans Moser and Annie Rosar for Austrian flavor. As with the *Silberwald* films, the West Germans soon were creating

Trendy pop culture for new youth audiences: Franz Antel's *Vier Mädel aus der Wachau*, 1957.

their own "Austrian" films, and a wholly West German production, *Dort in der Wachau*/In the Wachau, soon followed.

Harald Reinl, the *Bergfilm* specialist who had been directing West German *Heimatfilms* and even a royal romance for most of the decade, returned to Austrian film with *Almenrausch und Edelweiß*/Alpine Roses and Edelweiss (1957), a more traditional comic Alpine *Heimatfilm* produced by the Linz-based regional film company Bergland-Film. This Eastmancolor film was aimed directly at the West German audiences (the film premiered simultaneously in several West German cities) and provided a mix of German and Austrian stars and the director's discovery, German actress Karin Dor, who would marry Reinl and rise to global visibility in the James Bond film *You Only Live Twice* (GB 1967). Franz Antel also presented his annual rural comedy, *Heimweh...dort wo die Blumen blühen*/Yearning for Home (1957), with a plot about a suicidal young woman who finds rebirth and love when she is rescued by the director of the boys' choir of St. Quirin. The film, which harked back to the "Austrian Ideology" films of the pre–Anschluss years in its celebration of the healing qualities of nature and classical music (but without the overt Catholicism of its 1930s model) starred Antel's usual troupe and the Vienna Boys' Choir. Another film utilizing the choir that year was Max Neufeld's *Das schönste Tag meines Lebens*/The Best Day of My Life (1957). Despite its Frankfurt premiere, Neufeld hoped to make a film that evoked the lingering Central European quality of Austria, in both its traditional musical setting and in its references to the 1956 Hungarian revolution, which brought many Hungarian exiles to Austria. Neufeld's discovery, Michael Ande, portrays a Hungarian refugee child who finds a new home in Vienna as one of the choir boys. The allegory of an Austrian-Hungarian *Mitteleuropa*, which is physically split by the Iron Curtain but remains culturally connected, was not lost on its large audiences. Locations of the film emphasized geographic Austria as repository of the far wider notion of the old Austrian/Central European identity and as a possible homeland for those imprisoned in the east. Two more *Heimatfilm* entries rounded off the obviously shrinking production interest in the rural film: Alfred Lehner's Austrian/Swiss co-production of *Der König von Bernina*/The King of Bernina (1957) and Hermann Kugelstadt's *Jungfraukrieg*/War of the Maidens (1957). Both were based on novels and featured a mix of Austrian and West German casting. Both also premiered in West Germany. The German direction of the Austrian film industry was no longer a suggestion; it had become a business fact. Lehner's *Bernina* was a re-visioned Austrian *Bergfilm* set in the early Napoleonic era, not the more common Biedermeier world, and in the Swiss Engadin rather than in the Austrian Alps. It reversed the usual love triangle of a woman and two men, to the more popular 1950s formula of a man caught between two amorous women. A racial aspect direct from the *Blut und Boden* ideology of the Reich also surfaces in the film's character typing, which underscores the goodness of the innocent blond woman, while the darker-skinned, more sensual woman must ultimately pay for her "sins" with death.[77]

There were only three event films in 1957 — Ernst Marischka's third *Sissi* installment, *Schicksaljahre einer Kaiserin* (1957), and two films by Willi Forst: *Die unentschuldigte Stunde*/The Unexcused Hour (1957), and his final film, suitably named *Wien, du Stadt meiner Träume*/Vienna, City of My Dreams (1957). Forst had once again reinvented his style and with it the sophisticated contemporary urban comedy that had eluded him and had been too rare in the 1950s. But the films were not the breakthroughs he had hoped for, and Forst quietly retreated into retirement. In 1966, at the nadir of Austrian film production, Austria's greatest auteur briefly explained his absence from the screen when his expertise was obviously missed the most: "Mein Stil hat Pause" (My style is taking a pause).[78] Austrian film was to have other significant swan songs in 1957. E. W. Emo, who had returned in the late 1950s to reassume his Wien-Film stature as one of Austria's leading comedy film directors, reunited Paul Hörbiger, Hans Moser and Rudolf Carl for a final time under his reign in *Ober, zahlen!*/Check Please! The Viennese urban setting was typical territory for the three comic geniuses, but there was also the added subplot of young love and the interspersion of rock and roll songs to attract a generation that had no nostalgia for the Wien-Film talents. Gustav Ucicky's dramatic folktale style was also seen again in *Die Heilige und ihr Narr*/The Saint and Her Fool, with art direction by Werner Schlichting and Isabella Ploberger, who had also worked on Forst's last film. Ploberger, the only female art director and set designer in Austrian film at the time, had begun her craft on Riefenstahl's *Tiefland* (1945–54), Forst's *Wiener Mädeln* (1949), and Curd Jürgens's *Prämien auf den Tod* (1950), and she usually worked with Schlichting. Leading man O. W. Fischer

Willi Forst (left) and Billy Wilder in Vienna, 1957.

intended to abandon German-language cinema for Hollywood in 1956 when former Austrian director Henry Koster offered him a contract, but major disagree-
ments between the two led to his replacement by David Niven in *My Man Godfrey*
(USA 1957). Universal Pictures quickly soured on him and he returned to West
German and Austrian film and television until his retirement in the 1970s.

   With the end of the imperial film in sight, Ernst Marischka, the heir to Forst
and the Viennese Film style, wrote and directed a large-scale comedy, *Sieben Jahre
Pech*/Seven Years' Bad Luck, with sets by Jüptner-Jonstorff and music by Anton Profes. Imitation of Wien-Film auteurs like Forst and Emo was now being overshad-
owed by homage to postwar directors like Marischka and Antel who had molded
the Viennese Film genre into the imperial epic. One of these "third-generation"
filmmakers was German-born Rolf Thiele (1918–94), who co-founded one of the
many West German production companies that decentralized UFA in the postwar
era and who created some of the most impressive box-office hits in the German-
speaking world during the 1950s and early 1960s, particularly with his adaptation
of Thomas Mann novels and novellas. In Austria, Thiele gathered an international
cast and directed *Skandal in Ischl*/Scandal in Ischl, a romantic comedy based on a
work by Viennese turn-of-the-century writer Hermann Bahr. The impressionistic,
imperial era work was an interesting mix of Marischka's and Antel's second wave
Viennese Film style, his own sensitivity for bringing sociocritical literature to the

screen, and a more direct manner in dealing with sex. This final aspect would be very apparent in his next film, *Das Mädchen Rosmarie*/The Girl Rosemarie (West Germany, 1958), which starred Nadja Tiller in a fictionalized story based on the experiences of a high-class call girl in Frankfurt society. Ernst Neubach (1900–68) also followed the new Marischka/Antel tradition of imperial epics and flighty comedies by spoofing them in *Der Kaiser und das Wäschermädel*/The Emperor and the Laundress (1958). But given the rising socioeconomic conditions of both Austria and West Germany, interest in retrograde fantasy had now been replaced with an audience desire for lighthearted images of contemporary family life and modern romance. Satisfying this was Helmut Weiss's family satire *Die liebe Familie*/The Dear Family (1957); the Austrian/West German co-production of Karl Boese's Theo Lingen vehicle *Vater macht Karriere*/Father Makes Headway (1957); *August der Halbstarke*/August the Hooligan (1957), directed by Hans Wolff; and another Lingen exercise, *Familie Schimek*/The Family Schimek (1957), directed by Georg Jacoby. Even the filmed theater production of the year was a comedy, albeit a classic Biedermeier work by Johann Nestroy, *Einen Jux will er sich machen*/Out for a Lark (1957).

The shift in audience tastes and the demise of the mainstay genres in the 1950s were nowhere more apparent than in the great critical attention paid a new neorealist film. Influenced no doubt by such previous experiments as Forst's *Die Sünderin* (1951), Steinwender's *Wienerinnen* (1952), and Hollywood's 1950s juvenile delinquent genres, *Unter achtzehn*/Under Eighteen (a.k.a. *Noch minderjährig*/Still a Minor, 1957) was produced by Paula Wessely-Film and starred Wessely in an uncharacteristic role as a welfare officer in a social commentary film on the plight of young women in exploitive capitalism. Directed by Georg Tressler (1917–), it introduced Vera Tschechowa as a young factory worker who lives a double life, thanks to the luxuries supplied by an older male admirer (Erik Frey). The film also looked at youth rebellion through the eyes of a troubled delinquent portrayed by Austrian ice-skating-champion-turned-actor Peter Parak. But the biggest audience draw was actress Edith Elmay, Austria's entry in the 1950s international sex symbol wars, who became known as Vienna's "Marilyn."[79] The film was technically notable for editing by Paula Dvorak (1913–) and assistant Annemarie Reisetbauer (1925–), the only female editors continually active in the postwar Austrian film industry. Dvorak began her training with Sascha-Film in 1932, Reisetbauer with Wien-Film in 1946, and both often worked together into the 1980s. Although *Unter achtzehn* did not significantly influence either a return to the Austrian social drama genre of the 1920s and 1930s, or an increased neorealist style, it did spawn several similar delinquent youth films by Tressler and director Hermann Leitner in the early 1960s.

With the film boom having peaked, television and leisure activities continuing to lure the public, and West German and American films dominating the cinemas, 1958 marked the end of the imperial epic. Most Austrian films now premiered in a major West German city, or, if the film was a prestige production, in several West German cities at once. Austria had subsequently become a secondary market for its own films, and the *Heimatfilm* struggled for fresh interpretation. Hans Schott-

Schöbinger's *Nackt wie Gott sie schuff*/Naked as on the First Day (1958), written by Johannes Mario Simmel and based on an idea by the director and folk author Perkönig, was an Austrian/West German/Italian co-production with a polyglot cast. Gustav Ucicky's *Der Priester und das Mädchen*/The Priest and the Girl (1958) features such major names as Rudolf Prack and Winnie Markus. Both were attempts at creating a serious *Heimatfilm* devoid of the comedic or trendy dilution of the genre throughout the decade. Both dealt with religious themes, and Ucicky's film even returned to the genre's traditional triangle of a woman in love with two men, one of them a priest in spiritual crisis. Alfred Lehner was inspired by and linked his film *Sag ja, Mutti*/Say Yes, Mummy (1958), subtitled *Die singenden Engel von Tirol*/The Singing Angels of Tyrol, to Ucicky's 1947 *Singende Engel*/Singing Angels and hoped, as many filmmakers did, with film production slowing, to create family films aimed at the widest possible audience. These films by Ucicky and Lehner have interesting correspondences with the late 1950s and early 1960s family pleasing formula of Walt Disney productions such as *Pollyanna* (USA 1960) and *The Parent Trap* (USA 1961),[80] wherein an innocent child manages to solve the problems of adults, usually parents in marital crisis or neglectful of their parental duties. Lehner's film and Ucicky's earlier work may well have influenced Disney, since he had long admired Austrian culture and had presented several Austrian musical biopics of the decade in dubbed and edited versions on American television. By the 1960s, Disney had set up a Vienna office with the intention of creating Austrian co-productions on the romanticized *Mitteleuropa* themes so dear to him. Only a few films were produced before Walt Disney's death in 1966 and the new studio heads abandoned the project. Among these well-crafted "imitations" of Austrian genres and styles, which utilize Austrian supporting actors and crew (usually with costumes by Leo Bei), is the story of a boy's life in the Vienna Boys' Choir in the Ucicky-esque *Almost Angels* (USA/Austria 1962), directed by Steve Previn (also recalling Max Neufeld's 1936 *Singende Jugend*) with Peter Weck, Hans Holt, and Gunther Philipp; the saga of Vienna's famed Spanish Riding School's Lipizzaner stallions at the conclusion of World War II and Soviet occupation, *The Miracle of the White Stallions* (USA/Austria 1963), directed by Arthur Hiller, with Robert Taylor, Lilli Palmer, and Curd Jürgens; and a Johann Strauss biopic, *The Waltz King* (USA/Austria 1963), directed by Steve Previn, with Brian Aherne and Senta Berger. The opportunity to bring about the long-hoped-for connection between Vienna and Hollywood film in this way was too short lived and limited in scope to have spawned any continuance.

The only other *Heimatfilm* appearances in 1958 were Hanns Deppe's *Immer die Radfahrer*/Always the Cyclists (1958) and Rudolf Jugert's *Frauensee*/Frauen Lake (1958), suggested by a novel from Austrian author Carl Zuckmayer with an interesting cast including future Broadway and Hollywood star Kurt Kasznar. Both films were of the tourist-film subgenre, now transformed into formulaic summer vacation comedies featuring several songs aimed for records and promoting Austrian venues to West Germans. Franz Antel, the inventor of this variant in the *Heimatfilm*, was not to be outdone and entered his own summer-trip comedy into the rivalry, this time with a mostly German cast in *Ooh — diese Ferien!*/Oh — These Holidays! (1958). But there were standouts even in this sea of kitschy, formulaic, personality-laden comedies. Hans Moser and Paul Hörbiger reunited one final time for Hermann Kugelstadt's Viennese-themed *Hallo Taxi*/Hello Taxi (1958), and the film, rife with dialect, could only premiere in Vienna. *Wiener Luft*/Vienna Air (1958) was a unique attempt to create an episodic trilogy featuring different directors, similar to those in vogue in Italian film. Ernst Hofbauer, Walter Kolm-Veltée, and Karl Hans Leiter helmed the three satirical looks at contemporary Vienna and managed to span the history of Austrian cinema as well. It was Hofbauer's (1925–84) first film, silent film director Leiter's (1890–1957) last, and it gave dramatic director Kolm-Veltée an opportunity to demonstrate his mid-career comedic flair.

Aside from the folk story/biopic *Sebastian Kneipp — Ein großes Leben*/Sebastian Kneipp — A Famous Life (1958), directed by Wolfgang Liebeneiner, the other popular genres of the year were the final mutations of the filmed operetta musical and the period comedy. Like most productions, they were now aimed at the West German market first and thus always ensured success with a large German cast. Paula Wessely-Film produced Hans Wolff's musical comedy *Im Prater blüh'n wieder die Bäume*/The Prater Trees Are in Bloom Again (1958), with Johanna Matz and opera singer Ljuba Welitsch. The film focused on a comic, fictionalized *Mayerling* plot involving an Austrian crown prince and his love affair with the daughter of a court counselor. Geza von Bolvary's musical comedy *Hoch klingt der Radezkymarsch*/ The Glorious Old Radetzky March (1958) is set in the imperial military world of the nineteenth century and featured a mix of mostly old and new Austrian stars. The other active veteran Viennese Film artist, Geza von Cziffra, chose to adapt the Viennese musical comedy to a contemporary setting and add new singing stars Peter Alexander and Germaine Damar in *So ein Millionär hat's schwer*/It's Difficult to Be a Millionaire (1958). Titles became more suggestive, although it would not be until the mid–1960s that Franz Antel, who offered *Liebe, Mädchen und Soldaten*/Love, Girls and Soldiers in 1958 as a vehicle for the attractive opera singer Renate Holm, would also be forthcoming with bawdy content. German-born director Rudolf Schündler's *Zauber der Montur*/The Magic of Uniforms (subtitled *Wenn Mädchen ins Manöver zieh'n*/When Girls Go on Maneuvers) (1958) proved that writer and supporting actor Gunther Philipp could carry a film and had emerged as a replacement for such old-guard talent as Hans Moser. Suitable to the demands of Austrian and most Western film audiences of the late 1950s and 1960s, Philipp represented a less verbal and more physical comedy, comparable to Hollywood's Jerry Lewis (and like Lewis, he was popular with the public but not with the critics). Although he was often self-indulgent, he could show a unique flair for irony that had evolved from his early work in Austrian cabaret and his best characterizations would sometimes be subtle enough to invite comparisons with the work of Peter Sellers.

Having been halted in his plans to launch another *Sissi* film by Romy Schneider's refusal to play Empress Elisabeth for the fourth time, Ernst Marischka turned to an operetta based on Franz Schubert's life, *Das Dreimäderlhaus*/The House of Three Maidens (1958). Karlheinz Böhm appeared as the romanticized Schubert.

Marischka's atmospheric fantasy of Biedermeier Vienna breathed life one last time into what was the most traditional-style Viennese Film of the late 1950s. It would also be Ernst Marischka's final work. The second-generation Viennese Film specialist, co-creator of the imperial epic, and director of the most successful film series in Austrian cinema history died in 1959, a few months after the December 1958 premiere of *Dreimäderlhaus* in Munich.

The sudden drop in production during the final year of what had been a decade and a half of unexpected success in Austrian filmmaking and the return of cinema identity was ominous and foreshadowed the nadir yet to come. Only three films between 1959 and 1960 can even vaguely be considered *Heimatfilms*. The first was Munich-based director Paul May's *Und ewig singen die Wälder*/The Forests Sing Forever (1959), the first of two Nordic tales produced by Alfred Stöger and his Mundus-Film company and based on novels from the 1930s by Norwegian writer Trygve Gulbranssen. Shot at Rosenhügel and in Norway with a mostly German and Scandinavian cast, the film focuses on a feud between a farmer's family and the neighboring aristocrats caused by the dueling death of the farmer's eldest son. It received the West German Bambi Award for Most Successful Foreign Film in 1961. A more atmospheric sequel of sorts, *Das Erbe von Björndal*/The Inheritance of Björndal, was directed by Gustav Ucicky in 1960. Although the popular success of these films might have been influenced by the global interest in Scandinavian cinema in the late 1950s, particularly the work of Ingmar Bergman, their content was indeed curious for the times, considering that Gulbranssen's *völkisch* themes of peasant purity and superiority and the degeneracy of an aristocratic elite had been popular in the Third Reich. Clearly the Scandinavian setting was used to mask what was in essence revised German *Blut und Boden* ideology.[81] It is little wonder that Wien-Film's *völkisch* specialist Ucicky found the material suitable for his direction. The third semi-*Heimatfilm* at decade's end was Eduard von Borsody's *Wenn die Glocken hell erklingen*/When the Bells Ring (1959), a vehicle for former child actor Michael Ande. With Italian pop singer Teddy Reno as support, it attempted to turn Ande into a teen idol with a sentimental yarn about an orphaned choirboy discovering that he has a wealthy grandfather. Hans Quest's *Zwölf Mädchen und ein Mann*/Twelve Girls and a Man (1959) abandoned the entire *Bergfilm* tradition for its star, Olympic skiing champion Toni Sailer. In addition to spotlighting Sailer's skiing talent, there was the requisite romance, a subplot about smugglers, and even a "ski ballet." The film is clearly influenced by the American pop-singer films of the era but also points toward the sexualized hero of the 1960s, such as James Bond and his imitators. And spoofing the genre before 007 appeared was the unusual accomplishment of writer Franz Marischka's directorial debut in the spy comedy *Mikosch im Geheimdienst*/Mikosch of the Secret Service (1959) with, of course, Gunther Philipp.

The decade ended with only two event films, both essentially Hollywood-style novelty entertainment: Arthur Maria Rabenalt's circus epic *Geliebte Bestie*/Dear Beast (subtitled *Männer müssen so sein*/Men Must Be That Way) (1959) and Eduard von Borsody's ice-revue extravaganza, simply called *Traumrevue*/Dream Review

(1959), with ice skaters Ewa Pawlik and Ingrid Wendel, the Vienna Ice Revue, and, for dramatic purposes, Waltraud Haas and Susi Nicoletti. Two other films attempted new roads for what had become an artistically stagnant industry. Rolf Thiele, fresh from his Thomas Mann interpretations and developing into a director of films dealing with adult themes, cast Romy Schneider as a young woman who suggests her sexy, immoral side to an American producer (Carlos Thompson) in his comedy *Die Halbzarte*/Eva (1958). The stylish film gave Schneider the opportunity for the sort of type-breaking role Audrey Hepburn had in her portrayal of a call girl in *Breakfast at Tiffany's* (USA 1961), but it was given little notice by either critics or a public that was beginning to ignore the national cinema and ultimately the medium itself. Walter Kolm-Veltée ultimately took on the betrayal of art in the financially obsessed end of the boom years in Austrian film. *Panoptikum 59* (1959), which he wrote, directed and produced with the support of the Ministry of Education, returned to the symbolism of music, but in a more experimental manner. He suggested that it was a composition for "speaker, percussion and viola d'amore," which were personified by Alexander Trojan as a repressive artistic manager, Michael Heltau as a passionate artist who attempts to battle the establishment, and Elisabeth Berzobohaty as the woman in both their lives. The approaching avant-garde attack on the commercial Austrian film and art world would receive critical attention but would be avoided by the general audiences, who had not cultivated a taste for such alternative filmmaking during the heyday of the decade's epics and comedies. It was something that West German and Hollywood cinema also had in common, despite the importation of Italian neorealism and the French New Wave. But there would be far less of any Austrian cinema before audience reception would change.

5

The Missed Wave: 1960–1979

Commercial Disintegration; Actionism;
Isolated Experimentation

The results of international cinema's loss of a substantial portion of its audience to television and other leisure activities were swiftly felt in Austria, where the collapse of the film production boom of the 1950s was compounded by lack of state film subvention and the increasing West German control of German-language productions and film distribution. The West German industry met the general crisis no better, but significant reduction there did not mean the end of commercial production as it would in Austria. West German filmmakers could also count on government film promotion subsidies that had been in effect since 1962. By then, several German releasing companies had already perished, leaving only three major firms — Bavaria, Constantin, and Gloria. Austrian co-production with West Germany had become commonplace by the late 1950s as the only way to finance and secure the earnings of a film. Austrian productions were required to pay *Kinosondersteuern* (cinema theater taxes) and the rise in production costs and star salaries made lucrative West German distribution the only hope for producers. Hence, films were created for the tastes of West German audiences and general European export, rather than in continuance of any national traditions or development of any artistic styles. In addition, many prominent Austrian filmmakers that had represented the national industry throughout the 1950s had now vanished from the screens: Both Viennese Film auteur Willi Forst and comedy director E. W. Emo had already retired. They would be joined by Eduard von Borsody and Geza von Cziffra in the mid–1960s. Paula Wessely abandoned motion pictures and found a revitalization of her career in the theater. Director Arthur Maria Rabenalt turned to television, as did actor Paul Hörbiger. Romy Schneider, one of the new Austrian stars with a major international following, moved to France in 1958 to escape her *Sissi* typecasting and turned her back on Austrian film. Writer/director Hubert Marischka died in 1959. Producer/director Alfred Stöger, who had led both Austria's Mundus and Thalia-Film companies and Schönbrunn-Film head Ernest Müller both died in 1962, followed by Viennese comic superstar Hans Moser in

178

1963, and one of the most successful directors of the postwar era, Ernst Marischka, in 1965. Just as cinema criticism/theory publications attained global popular interest through the French *Cahiers du Cinema* and the British *Sight and Sound*, Austrian journals vanished: *Mein Film* ceased publication in 1957 and Austria's "Box Office" magazine, *Paimanns Filmlisten*, founded in 1916, ended its long run in 1965.

In addition to lack of film funding, which had become the long-instituted norm in other Western European countries, the Austrian government continued to view film as something outside of the traditional artistic and cultural establishment. The film tax had gone to support cinema theaters not film, and the Ministry of Education and Culture, when it recognized cinema at all, considered only documentaries on theater and opera subjects to be of cultural or educational value. Despite the efforts of director Walter Kolm-Veltée, who chaired the film institute at Vienna's prestigious Academy of Music and Performing Arts, the growth of a new generation of Austrian filmmakers was not forthcoming in any significant way, given the lack of government funding, which made artistic or noncommercial productions a near impossibility. The development of a commercially viable "New Wave" as in other European cinemas was thus stillborn. Faced with an adapt or die prospect, only very traditional styles of the 1950s adulterated to suit West German popular demands and the internationally created generic entertainment bound for wider export survived while lack of funding and government promotion made film experimentation more marginal than anywhere on the continent. What there was failed to achieve a national audience or a critical appreciation that would launch it beyond Austria's borders. Austria's most important production legacy, Wien-Film, had shriveled into a minor releasing firm and the great Rosenhügel studio was, for a time, surviving on foreign rental and television production.

It was this largely artificial suffocation of Austrian film that allowed for the erroneous and widely spread notion that "there is no real film culture"[1] in Austria. Such a statement is wholly absurd given the importance of this art in the empire and First Republic; Austria's seeding of Berlin, London and Hollywood with film talent; Wien-Film's finely crafted subversions against the Third Reich; and the internationally recognized productions of the 1950s. But in the short memory of distributors, critics, film festivals and the world audience, Austria's apparent no-show in the international film market for almost three decades would support this negative publicity. For Austria's filmmakers at the time, the situation was a disaster. But it was certainly not the end for an industry that had been absorbed and broken before.

The imperial epics, dramas and period comedies had been left behind with the boom of the 1950s. The next genre to fade from the screens was the resilient *Heimatfilm*. Between 1960 and 1966, when the genre finally succumbed, only nine dramatic *Heimatfilms* were produced. The first of the new decade was made by the man who would provide post–1950s Austrian cinema with its only lasting connection to the postwar era, to the re-visioned traditions of the Viennese Film and the *Heimat* genres, and would in fact, be the only constant in the faltering industry for the next three decades — Franz Antel. *Glocken läuten überall*/Bells Are Ringing

(1960) was based on Julien Duvivier's *Le Petit monde de Don Camillo* (France/Italy 1951), and revisits the theme of the power of the spiritual over the earthly, in a conflict between a businessman and a priest in a small Alpine town. August Rieger directed *Der Orgelbauer von St. Marien*/The Organ Builder of St. Marien (1961), which clearly offers the traditional *Heimatfilm* collision of the religious and secular worlds, as the daughter of a baron postpones her marriage of economic convenience when she unknowingly falls in love with a monk. The financial woes of the baron's estate, which precipitate his daughter's arranged marriage, are found to be the fault of the estate manager. The baron ultimately regains respect as the "good" force of established authority. It is a sociopolitical message that clearly conflicts with the official nonpresence of the historical nobility in the Second Republic. Hans Schott-Schöbinger's *Der Pfarrer mit der Jazztrompete*/The Priest with the Jazz Trumpet (1962), an Austrian/West German co-production also explores the religious/secular conflict but is an obvious and jarring concession to the West German film market. The central figure, a jazz- and sport-loving Protestant pastor (Joachim Hansen) is a foreign body in a dramatic Austrian *Heimatfilm*, which even in its most reductive forms has always been associated with mainstream Austrian or Southern German (read: Catholic) rural culture. His modern ways attract the youth but are rejected by the small-town mayor. In order to not alienate the Austrian and Bavarian audiences, the film does include a sympathetic Catholic priest, but the film, which even suggests that several girls can spend the night in the rectory without scandal, is clearly aimed at attracting the widest possible audience, particularly the youth market, with its unconventional embodiment of the good and the safely progressive. It predicts Hollywood's attempt to satisfy a broad international market with the image of the nonconformist nun in such musicals and comedies as *The Sound of Music* (USA 1965), *The Singing Nun* (USA 1965), *The Trouble with Angels* (USA 1966), its sequel *Where Angels Go, Trouble Follows* (USA 1968), and *Change of Habit* (USA 1969).

Hermann Leitner offered a very late *Silberwald*-inspired *Heimatfilm* with *Mein Vaterhaus steht in den Bergen*/My Father's House Is in the Mountains (1960), which featured the original *Silberwald* couple Rudolf Lenz and Anita Gutwell, who were obviously not yet tired of their exploitation. The film praises the importance of those bound to the *Heimat*, in a story in which Lenz returns from a lucrative life as an agrarian expert in Canada to save his father, the manager of an estate, from dishonor and ruin. Hans Heinrich directed *Der Ruf der Wildgänse*/The Call of the Wild Geese (1961), and Paul May directed *Waldrausch*/Forest Intoxication (1962), with cinematography by Elio Carniel and art direction by Jüptner-Jonstorff. Based on a 1908 play by Ludwig Ganghofer, it offers a nature versus technology story set in that other locale of the postwar *Heimatfilm*, the hydroelectric dam. *Wilde Wasser*/Wild Waters, directed the same year by West German Rudolf Schündler, essayed the more traditional Romantic ideology of rural purity and urban decadence in the story of a farmer's son obsessed with music and women, who departs the country for a disastrous experience in the city, only to return to find happiness and love at home. Eduard von Borsody created his last serious foray into the genre with the Arnold Fanck–inspired *Bergfilm,* the tragic *Bergwind*/Mountain Wind (1964), which also suggests the division of these two worlds: Hans von Borsody portrays a veterinarian and mountain climber who retreats from life after having lost his wife in a mountain climbing accident. An exotic film actress and dancer (Alwy Becker) rescues him from his self-imposed exile, is sent away by him, returns to claim his love and perishes on the mountainside. Franz Antel offered a rare dramatic *Heimatfilm* in 1965, *Ruf der Wälder*/Call of the Forests, his second filming of the Marie von Ebner-Eschenbach novella *Krambambuli,* this time modernized to include elements of sex and crime, themes that would overtake Austrian and West German films of all genres during the decade. The final serious *Heimatfilm* of the era, Georg Tressler's production of *Der Weibsteufel*/The She-Devil (1966), was a remake as well. The film was critically lauded for its "experimental" edge and as an antidote to cliché formulas, for its employment of a solidly Austrian cast and crew, neorealistic tone, and black-and-white photography. Tressler also rejected any trendy modernization of the original Schönherr novel, aside from the contemporary costumes. The film, which was produced by Otto Dürer, one of the few surviving producers of the 1950s, showcases Maria Emo, the daughter of director E. W. Emo. Dürer had insisted she get the role over the German distributor's preference for the new Austrian "face" of the moment, Senta Berger (1941–), a talented Willi Forst discovery who had appeared in one of his final films, *Die unentschuldigte Stunde*/The Unexcused Hour (1957). After losing the Tressler picture, Berger rose to fame in West German cinema and was a stylish foreign sex symbol in mid–1960s Hollywood and international entertainment before returning to West Germany and Austria for better parts and to work as a producer. Tressler hoped to restart the genre and a form of Austrian New Wave with his film, which was subsequently shown at the 1966 Berlin and 1967 Moscow Film Festivals. Despite its quality, innovation and critical praise, it failed to influence either filmmakers or the market.

The decade began with serious attempts at continuing both the comic and musical versions of the *Heimatfilm* genre. The first was Paul Löwinger's *Dorf ohne Moral*/Village without Morals (1960), a tale about a village fool lost in the nightlife of a big city. Very popular was the semi-series (different production companies and directors) of "White Horse Inn" musicals. These were based on Ralph Benatzky's operetta *Im weißen Rössl*/At the White Horse Inn, which had been previously filmed as a German silent in 1926, an Austrian sound feature in 1935, and a West German feature in 1945 and 1952 (the latter directed by Forst). Werner Jacobs incongruously updated the imperial-era operetta to contemporary times for the 1960 version with Waltraud Haas. Character names were changed to suit modern tastes, the music was given jazz and pop tempi, yet Emperor Franz Josef, still makes an appearance here — albeit as a ghost! Recalling von Borsody's apparition of Johann Strauss Jr. in *Verlorene Melodie*/Lost Melody (1952), the suturing of contemporary Austria to the imperial myth succeeded as a cinematic reflection of national/cultural identity into the 1960s. The following year's Franz Antel entry, *Im schwarzen Rössl*/At the Black Horse Inn (1961), was not so much a sequel as an exploitation of the 1960 version to adapt and sell yet another summer vacation film. Its thin narrative plot was formulated to give screen time to popular singers Gus Backus, Lil Babs and Peter Kraus. Antel would revisit the subject one final time in *Im singenden Rössl am Königsee*/At the Singing Horse Inn (1963). It again presents Waltraud Haas as an innkeeper (one of the few female authority roles in *Heimatfilm* comedy), but this film was a mélange of themes from the original operetta and several other period works including a nineteenth-century Nestroy play. The blatant advertisement of Königsee, which is in Bavaria, helped market the film in West Germany.

The character Mariandl from the 1947 film *Der Hofrat Geiger* was also back in a remake and a sequel. Werner Jacobs's Sascha-Film production of *Mariandl* (1961) was shot by Elio Carniel and featured art direction by Jüptner-Jonstorff. Although utilizing Hans Lang's song from the original film, the remake was created to satisfy West German audiences and the popular music market. This version focused on the daughter's story and reduced the mother's romance, in order to showcase Berlin-born pop singer Conny (Cornelia) Froboess. Also updated for the 1960s was Mariandl's love interest, who is no longer just a servant but an upwardly mobile *civil servant* (Peter Weck). The original Mariandl, Waltraud Haas, returns as Mariandl's mother Marianne, and Hans Moser also briefly reappears.[2] Werner Jacobs's sequel, *Mariandls Heimkehr*/Mariandl's Return (1962), continued the story and Froboess's song machine with much of the same cast.

More traditional was the comic operetta by Max Wallner and Kurt Feltz, entitled *Saison in Salzburg*/A Season in Salzburg, brought to the screen in 1961 by director F. J. Gottlieb. Assembled with a flavoring of the imperial musicals of the 1950s, the film was scripted by Ernst Marischka, shot by Elio Carniel, and featured detailed art direction by Jüptner-Jonstorff. The film stars the two most popular film personalities of the time, Waltraud Haas and charismatic operetta and pop singer Peter Alexander, who had come to embody an update of the old "Viennese charm" for German audiences of the 1960s. The slim plot regarded the love affair between the ubiquitous innkeeper (Haas) and an unemployed actor (Alexander) who brings along several colleagues to Haas's alpine hotel.

Rolf Olsen's *Hochzeit am Neusedlersee*/Wedding at the Neusedlersee (1963) shifted the traditional Alpine *Heimatfilm* venue to Austria's Hungarian border lake resort and also dispensed with any attempt at a traditional narrative by creating what was basically a cinematic variety show featuring West German audience pleasers: Austrian pop singer/composer Udo Jürgens (Udo Jürgen Böckelmann) and attractive ingenue Mady Rahl. Curiously, the film was one of the very few that premiered in Vienna at this time. This trend was exploited by Franz Antel's *Liebesgrüße aus Tirol*/From the Tyrol with Love (a.k.a. *Hully Gully in Tirol*) (1964) and given blatantly erotic situations in Ernst Hofbauer's *Die Liebesquelle*/The Fountain of Love (1966) with Ann Smyrner, the Danish-born sex symbol in Austrian film. But the ultimate hybridization that sealed the end of the comic *Heimatfilm* was Franz Antel's absurdly trendy *00Sex am Wolfgangsee*/Double-O-Sex at the Wolfgangsee (1966), in which the James Bond phenomenon crosses over into the Austrian rural film. But while the bikini had firmly replaced the dirndl, and the film pretended to be a 007 spoof with comedian Paul Löwinger as a secret agent manqué, at its core it is little more than a typical Antel rustic comedy from the late 1950s. It is far more influenced by the "mod" updating of the bedroom farce in such films as Clive Donner's *What's New Pussycat?* (USA/France 1965) than by any spy series. Also attempting cloak-and-dagger comedy was West German television director Sammy Drechsel who helmed the Austrian/West German/French co-produced cold war comedy *Zwei Girls vom Roten Stern*/An Affair of States (1966), which takes place at a nuclear disarmament conference in Geneva, where an American "super weapon" is revealed. While the Soviets attempt to gain the device by using sex as a lure, the U.S. (Curd Jürgens) and Soviet (Lilli Palmer) delegates fall in love. But the major spy spoof of the year was the Austrian/Italian/French co-production *Gern hab' ich die Frauen gekillt*/Killer's Carnival (1966), directed by Sheldon Reynolds, Alberto Cardone, Robert Lynn, and Louis Soulanes; written by Reynolds, Vittorio Salerno and Rolf Olsen; and featuring a very non–Austrian international cast including Stewart Granger and Lex Barker. The desire to internationalize Austrian comedy also spelled the rapid loss of true national film production, since most of these films aimed at broad export reduced actual Austrian cast and crew to less than a third. Although neither Drechsel nor Reynolds could compete with the expensive global-standard spy satires such as Hollywood's "Flint" films, or the megastar James Bond spoof *Casino Royale* (GB/USA 1967), which also employed Austrian-Hollywood actor Kurt Kazsnar and utilized Billy Wilder as one of the many uncredited writers of the sprawling film, their work remains interesting examples of the brief resonance of the era's Anglo-American cinematic fads in Central Europe. Both works have lately been rediscovered as cult classics by German-language pop culture and spy movie fans.

There were also more serious crime, mystery and spy films, such as Hubert Frank's *Das Rätsel der roten Quaste*/The Puzzle of the Red Tassel (1963), Alfred Vorher's *Ein Alibi zerbricht*/An Alibi Collapses (1963), Eddy Saller's sexy *Geisel des Fleisches*/Hostage of Flesh (1965), the Austrian/Italian/Spanish co-production of Franz Josef Gottlieb's *Mister Dynamit-Morgen küßt euch der Tod*/Mr. Dynamite-Death Kisses You Tomorrow (1967), and the Austrian entries in the internationally produced *Kommissar X* series, a Bond-like serial that spanned from 1966 into the 1970s with various directors and international co-productions that picked up the trail of Agent Joe Walker, a.k.a. Kommissar X, played by Italian-American actor Tony Kendall (Luciano Stella). The two specifically Austrian-led co-productions were *Kommissar X–Drei gelbe Katzen*/Death Be Nimble, Death Be Quick (1966), directed by Rudolf Zehetgruber, and *Kommissar X: In den Klauen des goldenen Drachen*/Operation Far East (1966), directed by Frank Kramer. The 1967 entry, *Kommissar X–Drei grüne Hunde*/Death Trip, reduced the Austrian input to being one of the film's two directors (Zehetgruber and Gianfranco Parolini) and a minor role in the mostly Italian/French/Hungarian financing. Another similar series was Ernst Hofbauer's *Tim Frazer jagt den geheimnisvollen Mr. X*/Tim Frazer and the Mysterious Mr. X (1964). But the most successful "Austrian" spy film on the global market came at the peak of the craze in mid-decade: the Austrian/Italian co-production of *Wie tötet man eine Dame?*/Secret of the Yellow Monks (1966), directed by Manfred R. Köhler, featuring three actors from past and future James Bond films—Karin Dor, Adolfo Celi, and Curt Jürgens.

The romance and comedy genres (most of them partially "musicals") of the early 1960s tended to remain loyal to the models of the 1950s albeit with the addition of more physical humor. There was also an increasing, if innocuous, sexual suggestiveness, which managed to avoid the overt sexuality found in other Western European cinema. Such "adult" Austrian films have more in common with Hollywood's melodrama, teen romance/musicals, and suburban marital comedies, as their titles convey: *Meine Nichte tut das nicht*/My Niece Doesn't Do That (1960) and *Ferien mit Piroschka*/Vacation with Piroschka (1965), both by Franz Josef Gottlieb; Hermann Leitner's *Morgen beginnt das Leben*/Life Begins Tomorrow (1961); Fritz Bornemann's *Maribella, das Mädchen auf dem Titelblatt*/Maribella, the Girl on the Cover (1961); *Vor Jungfrauen wird gewarnt*/A Warning of Virgins (1961) and *Autofahrer unterwegs* (a.k.a. *Auf den Straßen einer Stadt*)/On the Streets of the City (1961), both by Otto Ambros; Erich Heindl's *Unter Wasser küßt man nicht*/No Kissing Under Water (1962); Franz Antel's *Das ist die Liebe der Matrosen*/The Loves of a Sailor (1962); *Der Musterknabe*/The Model Boy (1963), *Hilfe, meine Braut klaut*/Help, My Bride Is a Thief (1964), and *Und sowas muß um acht ins Bett*/In Bed by Eight (1965), all by Werner Jacobs; Rolf Olsen's *In Frankfurt sind die Nächte heiß*/Nights Are Hot in Frankfurt (1966); Michael Pfleghar's *Bel Ami 2000 oder: Wie verführt man einen Playboy?*/Bel Ami 2000 or, How Do You Seduce a Playboy? (1966); and Paul Löwinger's *Wiener Schnitzel* (1967).

Because the Austrian federal government refused to support filmmakers with the types of subsidies that had become the norm in other European countries, a 1961 initiative by the vice mayor of Vienna, Felix Slavik, led to the establishment of the Stadthalle productions, which would utilize Vienna's large modern city auditorium as a studio. Underwritten by the city of Vienna, this production studio was certainly unique in European film, but rather than strive for artistic excellence, the productions continued the trends that had already made Austrian film unremarkable. Its first production was the comedy *Unsere tollen Tanten*/Our Crazy Aunts (1961), the first of a trio of cross-dressing farces that included *Unsere tollen Nichten*/Our Crazy Nieces (1963) and *Unsere tollen Tanten in der Südsee*/Our Crazy Aunts in the South Seas (1964), all obviously inspired by Billy Wilder's *Some Like It Hot* (USA 1959). Rolf Olsen (1919–98), who had begun his career as an actor and screenwriter in the immediate postwar years, directed the series, which featured popular singer Udo Jürgens paired with either Barbara Frey or Vivi Bach (Vivi Bak), another Danish-born glamour girl in German-language films, and including Gunther Philipp, who also co-wrote the first installment. Geza von Cziffra cashed in on the brief cross-dressing craze with his own treatment of the famous Brandon Thomas play *Charleys Tante*/Charley's Aunt (1963) with Peter Alexander before the Olsen series ended. Other Stadthalle productions were the musical *Tanze mit mir in den Morgen*/Dance Me into the Morning (1962), directed by Peter Dörre; Werner Jacobs's *Drei Liebesbriefe aus Tirol*/Three Love Letters from the Tyrol (1962); Rudolf Zehetgruber's *Die schwarze Kobra*/The Black Cobra (1963); and two Alfred Weidenmann productions:

Broad comedy at the collapse of the commercial industry: Rolf Olsen's *Unsere tollen Nichten*, 1963.

the critically acclaimed Austrian/French/West German co-production of *Das große Liebesspiel*/And So to Bed (1963), a *La Ronde*–like romantic tale featuring Hildegard Knef, Lilli Palmer, Nadja Tiller, Charles Regnier, and Daliah Lavi among its trendy cast; and the Austrian/Italian action drama, *Schüsse im Dreivierteltakt*/Shots in 3/4 Time (1965), with a similarly diverse roster of actors aiming for global box office.

The Stadthalle Studio also produced the only two true westerns in Austrian cinema history: Rolf Olsen's *Der letzte Ritt nach Santa Cruz*/Last Ride to Santa Cruz (1964), written by Alex Berg, and shot on the Canary Islands by Karl Löb, and Olsen's *Mein Freund Shorty*/My Friend Shorty (a.k.a. *Heiß weht der Wind*/The Hot Wind Blows) (1964), co-produced with Berolina-Film Berlin. Neither could compete in quality or popularity with the Italian- and Spanish-based spaghetti westerns. There were also two *Heimatfilm* tourist comedies co-produced with West German firms: *Happy End am Attersee*/Happy End at the Attersee (1964), directed by Hans Hollmann, and *An der Donau, wenn der Wein blüht*/On the Danube, When the Wine Blooms (1965), considered one of Geza von Cziffra's least successful films.[3]

In addition to Rolf Olsen's kitsch factory at Stadthalle, the other names most frequently associated with the new "studio" were Franz Antel and Kurt Nachmann. The latter either scripted for Antel or directed his own work. The Antel/Nachmann collaboration began in 1961 with *Und du mein Schatz bleibst hier*/You My Dear, Remain Here, directed by Antel and written by Nachmann and Olsen. Nachmann soloed with the comedies *Sing, aber Spiel nicht mit mir!*/Don't Fool with Me! (1963), *Mit besten Empfehlungen*/With Best Regards (1963), and *Das haben die Mädchen gern*/What Girls Want (a.k.a. *Die lustigen Vagabunden*/The Happy Vagabonds) (1963), with Ann Smyrner, Gus Backus, Paul Hörbiger and opera singer Ljuba Welitsch. Antel utilized the venue to bring back the large Rosenhügel soundstage-type productions: the musical *Im singenden Rössl am Königsee* (1963); his all-star pop revue/romantic comedy, *Die ganze Welt ist Himmelblau*/Red Lips Are for Kissing (1964), with American "Twist" dance inventor Chubby Checker; an exotic and colorful ice-revue extravaganza, *Die große Kür*/The Great Skate (1964), co-produced with Team-Film Berlin; the dramatic *Frühstück mit dem Tod*/Breakfast with Death (1964); and the aforementioned *Liebesgrüße aus Tirol* (a.k.a. *Hully Gully in Tirol*) (1964).

The few foreign directors to utilize the Stadthalle Studio at first suggested that the undertaking might actually rise above the banality of its comedy factory with more artistic product. Director Steve Previn, who was helming Walt Disney's projects[4] in Vienna directed a Disney-like Stadthalle production with Conny Froboess, *Ist Geraldine ein Engel?*/Is Geraldine an Angel? (1963). Axel von Ambesser gave UFA's leading man of the 1930s, Willy Fritsch, a new career in fatherly roles in his *Das habe ich von Papa gelernt*/What Papa Taught Me (1964), and Wolfgang Liebeneiner returned to the Austrian screen with *Jetzt dreht die Welt sich nur um dich*/The World Revolves Around You (1964). One of the international pseudoepics of the era, *Poppies Are Also Flowers* (1966), which had the most curiously grandiose pretensions since Liebeneiner's *1. April 2000* in 1952,[5] was also a Stadthalle production. In fact, the same problems with Liebeneiner's "Austria Film"—slim plot, heavy message, overcrowded star casting—contributed to its dismal failure at the world's box offices. It had what seemed to be all the fashionable ingredients for a major international hit: based on a story by James Bond author Ian Fleming and directed by Terence Young, with music by Georges Auric, *Poppies* was commissioned by the United Nations to bring awareness to the crime of the global network of drug trafficking and abuse. The feature film, which was introduced in a documentary-style manner by Princess Grace of Monaco, told the story of United Nations agents who attempt to follow the heroin trade from Iran by injecting a shipment of opium with a radioactive compound. The trail leads them across the capitals of Europe. The film, which owed more than a little to the plot and location "bump" style of the James Bond films and to the mid–1960s trend for all-star spy spoofs, offers a roster of fashionable and veteran international actors: Senta Berger, Stephen Boyd, Yul Brynner, Angie Dickinson, Hugh Griffith, Jack Hawkins, Rita Hayworth, Trevor Howard, Trini Lopez, E. G. Marshall, Marcello Mastroianni, Anthony Quayle, Gilbert Roland, Harold Sakata, Omar Sharif, Barry Sullivan, Nadja Tiller, Marilu Tolo and Eli Wallach. Because of its heavy-handed propaganda slant, the film has not found the cult status accorded many of the international action/spy extravaganzas of the 1960s. Its *Zeitgeist* and unique collection of talents, however, have made it a sociopolitical document of an era and a statement on the folly of broad internationalization in Austrian cinema.

Despite the lack of true box-office successes, the Stadthalle company created a distribution arm in 1965 in an effort to promote this new studio abroad. But its most ambitious film was also its last, a financial disaster that had little to do with the state of the Austrian film industry but rather with the shift in audience tastes across the globe. *Der Kongress amüsiert sich*/Congress of Love (1966), a grand-scale period musical set at the 1815 Congress of Vienna, and shot in 70 mm Super Panorama, was an Austrian/West German/French co-production directed by Geza von Radvanyi and co-scripted by him with Fred Denger and Aldo von Pinelli. The expensive film re-visioned the Wien-Film musical for the international blockbuster market of the 1960s with a large cast including Curd Jürgens, Lilli Palmer and Walter Slezak. Like so many overblown musical productions of the era — *Star* (GB/USA 1968), *Hello Dolly* (USA 1968), *Goodbye Mr. Chips* (GB 1969) — it was a major flop that only succeeded in closing the Stadthalle Studio and finally killed off the imperial musical epic genre in Austrian film. But as Austrian film faded from international recognition, an American recreation of the musical *Heimatfilm*, shot in Salzburg and Hollywood, gave the world its most indelible image of the nation in Robert Wise's *The Sound of Music* (USA 1965). Wildly popular abroad, the film has either been uncritically accepted by Austrians as a vaguely positive ambassador of the nation, despite the lead characters' embodiment of the monarchist/Catholic corporate state ideology and the images of Austrian Nazism, or else they have rejected it as an example of Hollywood's kitsch co-opting of Austrian history and culture. More about this and the film's specific relationship with the New Austrian *Heimatfilm* of the 1990s will be discussed in chapter 6. The subject matter, based on the autobiography of Maria von Trapp, had already been covered by two earlier West German films by Wolfgang Liebeneiner, *Die Trapp-Familie*/The Trapp Family (1956) and *Die Trapp-Familie in Amerika*/The Trapp Family in America (1958).[6]

More modestly mounted operetta or remakes of classic Wien-Film musicals continued to have a small niche in the European market, and Austria continued to produce these best. There was Johann Strauss's *Die Fledermaus*/The Bat (1962), lavishly mounted by Geza von Cziffra with Marika Rökk, Peter Alexander, and the eighty-one-year-old Hans Moser repeating his youthful role as the drunken jailer Frosch; Franz Lehár's *Die lustige Witwe*/The Merry Widow (1962), directed by Werner Jakobs, with Peter Alexander and Karin Hübner; Ernst Marischka's *Hochzeitsnacht im Paradies*/Wedding Night in Paradise (1962), directed by Paul Martin, again with Peter Alexander and Marika Rökk; Geza von Cziffra's remake of his wartime ice-revue musical hit *Der weiße Traum* (1943) as *Kauf dir einen bunten Luftballon*/Buy Yourself a Colored Balloon (1961); von Cziffra's semi-sequel, *Ein Stern fällt vom Himmel*/A Star Falls from the Sky (1961); and Franz Antel's final attempt at the Viennese-style musical, *Das große Glück*/The Great Happiness (1967). But even this evergreen genre eventually outstayed its welcome with the audiences of the mid–1960s, which no longer accepted Belle Époque sentimentality nor cared for the costume fantasy. Even the widely popular spectacle of the Viennese ice-revue film had also finally lost its novelty. It was now a slickly packaged and safe exoticism, a "Sunday drive" with little fantasy left to it, by comparison to the consciousness-expanding palette of the decade's art.[7] Jacques Demy's *Les Parapluies de Cherbourg*/The Umbrellas of Cherbourg (France 1964) signaled that French New Wave, contemporary popular music and pre-psychedelic set design concepts might save the musical genre, but even this refreshing jazz opera was a dead end as was the iconoclastic Vietnam era antiwar farce presented in World War I guise, *Oh, What a Lovely War* (GB 1969). The sole survivor was the pop/rock variety film, ranging from Hollywood vehicles for singer Elvis Presley to The Beatles' *A Hard Day's Night* (GB 1964) and its (partially filmed in Austria) follow-up, *Help!* (GB 1965). But these works were limited to the immediate popularity of its stars and quickly dated by the rush of the decade's fads and trends. Franz Antel had understood and exploited the quick entertainment value of this genre since the mid–1950s. He was now in competition with Rolf Olsen, who attempted nearly every genre and film fad the decade had to offer.

There was one final wave of traditional comedy film led by Geza von Cziffra, with *Kriminaltango*/Crime Tango (1960), *Gauner in Uniform*/Scoundrel in Uniform (1960), two of the *Graf Bobby*/Count Bobby adventures (which will be discussed later), *Junge Leute brauchen Liebe*/The Young Need Love (1961) and *An der Donau wenn der Wein blüt*/On the Danube when the Wine Blooms (1964). The titles accurately suggest their nostalgic content. Georg Marischka and Eduard von Borsody attempted the genre and style briefly, while Arthur Maria Rabenalt applied such "old-fashioned" filmmaking style to several genres: a remake of sorts of the 1940 UFA variety film based on the popular wartime German radio program *Das große Wunschkonzert*/The Great Request Concert (1960), this time with such international stars as Carlos Thompson, Linda Christian, and Edmund Purdom. His noir *Mann im Schatten*/Man in the Shadows (1961), shot by Elio Carniel, introduced rotund cabaret actor Helmut Qualtinger, who became known for his biting caricatures of bourgeois ignorance and xenophobia. Axel von Ambesser and Wolfgang Liebeneiner had attempted to recapture the 1950s with light marriage comedies filmed at the Stadthalle studio for a variety of companies, but like the *Heimatfilm*, the traditional Austrian romantic film, regardless of its genre, could not be resuscitated. It had been surpassed by international co-productions and their exotic, polyglot quality, such as *Liebesspiele im Schnee*/Love Games in the Snow (1966), an Austrian/USA/Czechoslovakian film, directed by Curt Siodmak, and Rudolf Zehetgruber's *Frauen, die durch die Hölle gehen*/Women Who Go Through Hell (1967), an Austrian/Spanish/Liechtenstein/Italian co-production with Anne Baxter and Maria Perschy. The few West German– and Swedish-inspired sex comedies or dramas that outdid the suggestiveness of Antel's playful yarns were Paul Milan's *Das Mädchen mit dem Mini*/The Girl in the Miniskirt (1965), Hubert Frank's *Das Mädchen mit dem sex-ten Sinn*/The Girl with the Sex-th Sense (1966), Walter Häuselmayer's *Verbotenes Begehren* (a.k.a. *Die nackte Haut*)/The Naked Skin (1966), Frits Frons's *Via Erotica* (1967) and *Männer in den besten Jahren erzählen Sexgeschichten*/

Sex Stories (1967). These offered the adult content unavailable on television. Pure variety films like *Schlagerrevue '62*/Hit Parade '62 (1961), directed by Thomas Engel, also drew in more youth audiences.

Only German-born director Alfred Weidenmann (1916–2000) managed, with some critical and popular success, to briefly re–Austrianize international co-productions along the lines of the sophisticated Willi Forst films. His *Julia, du bist zauberhaft*/Adorable Julia (1962), based on W. Somerset Maugham's short story "Theater," scripted by Guy Bolton and Pascal Jardin and featuring a stylish French/Austrian cast, including Lilli Palmer, Charles Boyer, Jean Sorel, and Charles Regnier, in a film about a young man's love for an "older woman," was one of the few Austrian films of the period to be well distributed internationally and to attract American audiences. In 1965, Weidenmann joined Rolf Thiele and Axel von Ambesser in an episodic film (which had become popular in Italy and France), *Das Liebeskarussell*/The Carousel of Love (1965). This solidly Austrian production paired many of the big European names of the era into four stories: Gert Fröbe, a well-known German actor who became a quasi-superstar that same year in *Goldfinger* (1965) with France's most popular ingenue, Catherine Deneuve; Curd Jürgens with Nadja Tiller; German comedian Heinz Rühmann with Johanna von Koczian; Peter Alexander with the Swedish star of Fellini's *La dolce vita* (Italy 1960), Anita Ekberg. The failure of this formula led Wiedenmann to return to more traditional filmmaking with *Maigret und seiner größter Fall*/Maigret and His Greatest Case (1966), an Austrian/Italian/French co-production with Heinz Rühmann as Georges Simenon's famed detective. The unexpected casting of Rühmann, known for his gentle foolishness in the role of the serious Maigret, attracted comparisons with the earlier French and British incarnations and ultimately did not help the film's reception or Rühmann's career.[8] Franz Antel combined the mystery genre with screwball comedy in *Ohne Krimi geht die Mimi nie ins Bett*/Mimi Loves Mysteries (1962). He also attempted a crime adventure in ....*und ewig knallen die Räuber*/ The Robbers Always Shoot (1962) with Karin Dor before anticipating psychedelic cinema by writing and producing a bizarre romp directed by Domenico Paolella, *Maskenball bei Scotland Yard*/A Costume Ball at Scotland Yard (1963). This black-and-white pseudonarrative about an inventor of a device that can interrupt any televised broadcast is a series of linked sketches that owed more to the slapdash Italian exploitation comedies of the time than to any Austrian cinema comedy traditions. The film's structure, its polyglot cast, and its association of television culture with mind control gave it a vague role in the development of the transnational episodic counterculture satires of the mid– and late 1960s, but the plot itself is largely incomprehensible.

More successful, however, than any imported genres were two long-running comedy serials: the *Graf Bobby* (Count Bobby) films of Geza von Cziffra and the *Wirtin* (female innkeeper) films of Franz Antel. Not comparable to these directors' period films of the 1950s in any aspect of production, both series functioned through a form of cinematic nostalgia, offering a suggestion of such bygone lavish costume entertainment and lacing it with the physical and sexual comedy of the era. Von

Cziffra's Count Bobby, a charming but often bumbling Viennese aristocrat played by Peter Alexander, managed to cover the period's criminal, adventure and spy spoof interests in *Die Abenteuer des Grafen Bobby*/The Adventures of Count Bobby (1961), *Das süße Leben des Grafen Bobby*/The Sweet Life of Count Bobby (1962), and Paul Martin's *Graf Bobby, der Schrecken des Wilden Westens*/Count Bobby, The Terror of the Wild West (1966), with Yugoslavia standing in for the American West.

Franz Antel's comedies now amounted to a mocking of his own imperial epics but the franchise secured him box-office domination into the next decade. Set in the Napoleonic era, they were silly, suggestive costume romps with elements of the *Heimatfilm,* the tourist-film subgenre, and the French bedroom farce. Shot in West Germany, the series involved the misadventures at an inn and was launched with *Susanne— Die Wirtin an der Lahn*/The Sweet Sins of Sexy Susan (1967), an Austrian/Italian/Hungarian co-production with Terry Torday, Mike Marshall and Pascal Petit. This low-budget comedy outpaced even the hip Anglo-American spy spoofs at the Austrian and West German box office, and Antel issued a sequel the next year with *Frau Wirtin hat auch einen Grafen*/Hostess Has a Count (1968), with a basic lineup that would run through the series, but this time oddly including American actor Jeffrey Hunter. The films continued through the 1970s, under Antel's idea of a more internationally viable French *nom de cinema* "Francois Legrand," when his releasing company felt that the market had been saturated with Antel product.[9] Ever more suggestive titles and contrived plots followed: *Frau Wirtin hat auch eine Nichte*/House of Pleasure (1969), *Frau Wirtin bläst auch gern Trompete*/Sexy Susan Knows How! (1970), *Frau Wirtin treibt es jetzt noch toller*/Hostess Exceeds All Bounds (1970) and *Frau Wirtin's tolle Töchterlein*/The Hostess's Wild Daughter, a.k.a. Knickers Ahoy (1973). Antel defends these films by insisting that he always strove to give the audiences what they desired.[10] Their financial success in the wake of wide critical rejection bears this out. Antel's product had also ensured that some aspects of the moribund Austrian film industry continued to work.

There were a few notable dramas during the early 1960s, but these had become a rarity. Rolf Thiele's cinematic treatment of Franz Wedekind's controversial turn-of-the-century drama about sexual obsession and manipulation, *Lulu* (1962) with Nadja Tiller as the femme fatale began the decade. By the release of *Der Lügner und die Nonne*/The Deceiver and the Nun (1967), Thiele had established himself in German-language film as *the* dramatic director of sexual themes. Edwin Zbonek scripted and filmed Theodor Csokor's play on the collapse of the Austro-Hungarian empire, *3. November 1918*, in 1965. One of the few films in the 1960s to deal with the imperial past, it was a startlingly intimate and neorealistic antidote to the grand imperial costume epics in its portrayal of the divergences of the multicultural empire as represented by a group of soldiers in a convalescent home at the end of the Great War. Zbonek (1928–), a young Austrian filmmaker of the times who seemed to span what became the wide cleft between the dying Austrian commercial cinema and the isolated avant-garde filmmaking, also worked in West Germany and wrote film criticism. Among his other West German films, he had documented the Greek resistance movement in World War II in *Am Galgen hängt* *die Liebe/*Twenty Brave Men (1960). In Austrian film, he followed the Csokor play with the lensing of a more traditional Austrian stage comedy, Johann Nestroy's folk piece *Lumpazivagabundus/*Lumpaci, The Vagabond (1965), a fitting vehicle for Helmut Qualtinger's Moser-like talents. John Olden directed a television production that went on to cinemas on the then still taboo subject of Austria's brief civil war and the introduction of Chancellor Dollfuss's authoritarian corporate state in 1933-34. The ironically named film *An der schönen blauen Donau/*On the Beautiful Blue Danube (1965) starred Attila Hörbiger and Lotte Lang. Finally, Werner Jacobs attempted to outdo Walt Disney with a neorealist-tinged version of *Heidi* (1965).

The filming of theater-based productions, mostly by Neue Thalia-Film, was the only filmmaking that received any true state recognition, and these preserved many legendary performances of the 1960s. Although they were more than recorded stage presentations — the attempt was to create "filmed theater" on special sets designed for the film — they cannot be considered a healthy development in Austrian cinema because they inhibited the promotion of new styles and original film writing. Alfred Stöger offered two final stage documents to his impressive résumé before his death in 1962: the Vienna Burgtheater's version of Friedrich Schiller's *Don Carlos* (1960), with Ewald Balser and Fred Liewehr, and the Salzburg Festival production of Ferdinand Raimund's *Der Bauer als Millionär/*The Peasant as Millionaire (1961), with Josef Meinrad, Käthe Gold and Paula Wessely. Kurt Meisel filmed the Burgtheater's production of Raimund's *Der Verschwender/*The Spendthrift (1964), and Günther Anders preserved yet another Burgtheater production of a Raimund folk comedy, *Der Alpenkönig und der Menschenfeind/*The Alpine King and the Misanthrope (1965), with a rare coupling of the Hörbiger brothers, Attila and Paul. Anders also captured a performance of Reinhard Raffalt's *Der Nachfolger/*The Successor (1964), a contemporary work that delved into the problems of the Catholic Church during the election of a new pope. Gottfried Reinhardt (1913–94), the West German/Hollywood producer son of Austrian stage director and founder of the Salzburg Festival Max Reinhardt, put the Salzburg Festival production of Hugo von Hofmannsthal's *Jedermann/*Everyman (1961) on film, featuring landmark performances again by Josef Meinrad, Käthe Gold and Paula Wessely. Opera was also given this type of simple stage-to-screen transference in Georg Tressler's Technicolor German and English versions of Otto Nicolai's *Die lustige Weiber von Windsor/*The Merry Wives of Windsor (1965).

Franz Kafka was the subject of a documentary in 1964, entitled *Die Welt des Herrn K/*The World of Mr. K., but the most notable literary material brought to film in the era is certainly Axel Corti's *Kaiser Joseph und die Bahnwärterstochter/*Emperor Joseph and the Stationmaster's Daughter (1963). The film is based on a play by one of the final exponents of turn-of-the-century Viennese literary impressionism, Fritz von Herzmanovsky-Orlando, as interpreted by Hans Holt, Inge Konradi and Hans Moser. It was Moser's final film, and the first major work for Paris-born Austrian film director Axel Corti (1933–93), who would be a significant, if too brief, presence in combining experimentalism and commercialism in the lead-in to New Austrian Film during the 1980s. On the lighter side, Wolfgang Liebeneiner also updated the antimilitary satire surrounding the reticent character of Prague dog-catcher Schwejk with Peter Alexander, Rudolf Prack and Susi Nicoletti in *Schwejks Flegeljahre*/Schwejk's Awkward Years (1964).

Goswin Dörfler who reported on Austrian cinema for the influential British annual *International Film Guide* officially declared the Austrian film industry dead in 1968:

> Last year we reported that "Austrian film production and cinema attendances are in a state of crisis." As far as 1968 is concerned, this crisis has been resolved — the patient having died peacefully.... In practice there is no more national film production. The Austrian cinema has reached its year zero, thus giving the hope for a new start. Both the state and private enterprise have given serious thought to this, and there are vehement discussions at various levels for the reconstruction of the home industry. The king is dead; long live the king![11]

By 1966, only eighteen Austrian films (half were co-productions) were made and by 1967, the amount had fallen to twelve; the majority (and the "best" as Dörfler insisted) were co-productions. By 1967, fourteen cinema theaters had closed in Vienna. Attendance had fallen drastically: from 65.8 million in 1966 to 57.6 million in 1967.[12] The paucity of Austrian cinema art had also compromised a major film festival, the Viennale, which had been founded as the Vienna Film Festival in 1961. Its 1968 theme of "Humorous Cinema" had to be abandoned due to the lack of material and the festival instead managed to convey the disaster of Austrian production and lack of audience by scraping the bottom of the barrel with "Films That Failed to Reach Us." Hungarian and Soviet films were presented in the series to make up for the lack of not only Austrian film but the obvious disinterest by Western European releasing companies to contribute anything to the failing Austrian market. Even the remaining "art" houses had abandoned Austrian cinema for foreign avant-garde film. But the Austrian government continued to resist the concept of support for film production and distribution.

Only seven nominally "Austrian" films made it to the screens in 1968 and six of these were international co-productions: Truck Branss's Austrian/West German documentation of the Margot Fonteyn–Rudolf Nureyev *Swan Lake* ballet staged at the Vienna State Opera; Antel's *Frau Wirtin hat auch einen Grafen* and another Austrian/West German comedy, *Otto ist auf Frauen scharf*/Otto Gets Women (both as "Francois Legrand"); Hubert Frank's Austrian/West German thriller *Die Funkstreife Gottes*/God's Police Patrol; Italian director Osvaldo Civirani's Austrian/Italian costume epic *Lucrezia*; and Eddy Saller's Austrian/West German/French erotic thriller *Schamlos*/Shameless. The film, which deals with the underworld execution of the "shameless" daughter of a crime boss, who sends a gay actor (Udo Kier) to uncover the plot, results in a nihilistic destruction of all concerned. Film historians Elisabeth Büttner and Christian Dewald consider the film to be a sly melding of the various audience interests during the nadir of Austrian commercial filmmaking: "fast images for the [film] business of sex and crime with Austrian potency — an attack on order as a cinematic motivation for a parade of the demimonde."[13] More than ten years after the death of the imperial epic, and while Austrian filmmakers were attempting to break from the Agfacolor/Gevacolor nostalgia with more critical examinations of the past, the British, French, and Americans came to Vienna to create a blockbuster version of this Austrian genre with MGM's *Mayerling* (France/GB 1968), directed by Terence Young. The lavish examination of the love affair and apparent suicides of Crown Prince Rudolf and his mistress Baroness Marie Vetsera was more politically framed than previous versions, particularly as it mirrored the contemporary era in scenes of student revolts and the "generation gap" in the Habsburg dynasty. Filmed on location throughout Vienna, the imperial costume drama was solidly un–Austrian in its cast.

The only true Austrian film of 1968 was one made for television, an ORF production with the regional West-Film (Bregenz) company, and only later entered European cinemas. But *Moos auf den Steinen*/Moss on the Stones was without doubt the most remarkable and memorable Austrian film of the decade. Based on the 1956 novel by Austrian author Gerhard Fritsch, the film features Erika Pluhar, Heinz Trixner, Fritz Muliar, Louis Ries, and Wilfred Zeller-Zellenberg, who have all indelibly become associated with this pioneering work. In the midst of the worst crisis in Austria's film history, young filmmaker Georg Lhotsky (1937–) offered a work that not only embraced and successfully adapted French New Wave stylistics but also provided a brilliant allegory for Austria's sociocultural problems as a small republic haunted by the memory of a once powerful empire. The film projected the very qualities of what would resurrect Austrian filmmaking late in the next decade: a culturally localized topic, regional on-location photography, mild experimentation, Austrian cast and crew, and a low budget funded by private means and co-production with television. Shot in black and white and color by Walter Kindler, Lhotsky's film interprets the *Mitteleuropean* meditations of novelist Gerhard Fritsch with great poignancy. In eastern Austria, where the phantom presence of the former crown lands of the empire are still to be felt, the collision of the past and the present, tradition and pragmatism, monarchy and republic are acted out in microcosm by the old aristocrat whose baroque castle is overrun by visitors who intend to refurbish it as a cultural center. Recalling the nostalgia of the 1950s imperial epics, the film plays between the past and present, the memories of the old baron and his daughter Jutta, the enthusiastic plans of Jutta's fiancé, Mehlmann, and his friend, the writer Petrik. As Jutta leads Mehlmann through the rooms of the castle and the family's past, the romantic ritual of imperial life is evoked, but Jutta also offers her memories of the execution of two deserters hiding at the castle in the final days of World War II. As they don the antique clothing of her family and joyously romp across the grounds, the temporal boundaries seem to disappear. The baron parallels this escapism by writing a novel about Austria's past, "Moos auf den Steinen," where the characters "love the moss that grows on the crumbling walls of the Danube Monarchy, the soft pillows of transitoriness on stones that are no longer Austria."[14] The bittersweet masquerade in a lost identity must, however, come to an end: the baron casts the pages of his novel into the wind, and when the costumed lovers

The collision of the imperial past and the cold war present: Heinz Trixner led by Erika Pluhar in Georg Lhotsky's *Moos auf den Steinen*, 1968.

reach the end of the estate, they see the barbed wire and machine-gun turrets of the Iron Curtain. Mehlmann ultimately retreats from his modernization plans and allows the castle to find its slow, elegant death. The moss remains on the stones.

While it suggests the capitalist exploitation of a romanticized imperial past in the Second Republic, Lhotsky's work also is a metafilmic commentary on the 1950s imperial epic films, in which the audience desired to "costume" themselves in a mythic past for a few hours in a fantasy of identity, which must then be abandoned for cold war reality. Most important, however, is the exposure of this nostalgia as a symptom of Austria's lingering identity crisis. Literary historian Reinhard Urbach finds that for author Fritsch "preserving traditions also means to mourn their passing. Such an interest in the Austrian past is not about a desire for collapse, or decadence, or cynicism towards a present, which could not preserve the past and had no strength for a new beginning. Rather it is about the sadness for the loss of continuity and about preservation and renewal."[15] Lhotsky's film was not the only 1960s attempt at delivering an Austrian New Wave, but it was the most commercial approach. Also attempting to reach a wider audience with an artistic/critical film, director Leo Tichat examined the plight of urban youth in his *Die Verwundbaren*/The Vulnerable (1966). Artists Sepp Jahn and Edith Hirsch also wrote, directed, and shot several films in an intimate cinematic style reminiscent of the

French New Wave, *Momento Mori* (1963) and *Reflexion/*Reflection (1970) among them, but for the most part Austrian experimentation in film remained obscure and of little influence on what was left of mainstream cinema or cinema audiences. This was certainly due to problematic reception, but the lack of government film subsidy and promotion of film as a national art was most responsible for stifling the Austrian avant-garde in an era when most other European countries celebrated revolutions in their national cinemas.

Although Austria had no equivalent of an organized movement to dispel poor commercial product, as was announced by young West German cinema artists in their Oberhausen Manifesto of 1962, there were several schools of experimentation and avant-garde filmmaking. Unfortunately, these developments were shunned by the failing mainstream industry. The surviving Austrian film publication *Film und Kino Zeitung* (Film and Cinema News) did not even report on the West German Oberhausen event but eventually offered a backhanded explanation for the overall avoidance of what was happening in critical and artistic film outside of Austria. It blatantly admitted that the rising cost of filmmaking and the lack of box-office success in a shrinking Austrian market made feature experimentation prohibitive.[16] Discussion of such trends was obviously deemed useless and unnecessary.

The first appearance of Austria's avant-garde cinema had actually come on the heels of the Italian neorealism and before the French New Wave. The early 1950s saw the creation of the Vienna Art Club where noncommercial filmmakers found a home. Wolfgang Kudranofsky, Kurt Steinwender, Ferry Radax, Gerhard Rühm, and others assembled a loose-knit alternative film movement, which was launched by the 1951 creation of Kudranofsky and Steinwender's filmic translation of Edgar Allan Poe's poem *Der Rabe/*The Raven. Other literary subjects became the subject of alternative filmmaking, notably Herbert Vesely's Kafka montage, *Und die Kinder spielen so gern Soldaten/*And the Children Like to Play Soldiers (1951), and a film based on Trakl's expressionist poetry, *An diesen Abenden/*On These Evenings (1952). Soon, artistic interpretations of short literary works were replaced by original scripts on a similar theme that ran through the French New Wave — the personal interpretation of social alienation. Vesely's *Nicht mehr Fliehen/*Flee No More (1955) and Edwin Zbonek's *Erschießungsbefehl/*Execution Order (1962) managed to marry avant-garde techniques with a still semicommercial narrative form. Ferry Radax, Peter Kubelka and Konrad Bayer led the avant-garde into the 1960s and joined together to create *Mosaik im Vertrauen/*Mosaic of Trust (1955), while Jörg Ortner offered *Eine Fuge/*A Fuge (1959) as "aggressive melancholy against a city." [17] Radax (1932–), who was one of the few filmmakers who managed to acquire a subvention from the Ministry of Education for an experimental work, took advantage of this unique occurrence by making several versions of his abstract *Sonnehalt!/*Stop Sun! between 1959 and 1962 with Ingrid Schuppan, Alberto Jolly and Konrad Bayer. Film historian Walter Fritz has compared Bayer, an avant-garde literary figure who worked on several film projects and committed suicide in 1964, to French New Waver Jean-Luc Godard, for his radical style and overt sociopolitical commentary.

Over one hundred films were created between the early 1950s and 1968 by the members of the Art Club movement by such artists as Peter Weibel, Kurt Kren, Valie Export, Marc Adrian, Ernst Schmidt Jr., Peter Kubelka, Otmar Bauer, Hans Scheugel, Günter Brus, and Gottfried Schlemmer. Yet for all their startling new visions and even new performance art tactics in the showing of these films, the lack of government and media industry sponsorship disallowed any showcasing as was available in West Germany, where theaters and television attempted to offer at least a taste of such alternative creations. Filmmaker Erik Frey (1947–) has come to represent the other side of the avant-garde experience. Unlike members of the Art Club movement who have tended to remain outside the mainstream throughout their creative lives, Frey moved uniquely into the establishment. Holding a doctorate in analytical psychology, his experiences in the French New Wave working with actor Jean Vilar in Paris in 1966 led to the creation of his own experimental films and garnered him recognition by the Underground Festival in Cannes in 1967. Since 1968, he has worked as cinematographer, writer or director on approximately five hundred films, most of them documentaries for ORF. Today his Vienna-based Frey-Film is regarded as one of Austria's major educational film production companies.

Another factor that made Austrian alternative filmmaking less accessible to the audiences than their other European counterparts was its radical style. Firmly grounded in trends outside cinema, it began with abstract art and moved only very slowly toward film narrative rather than move from narrative film to a more abstract interpretation, as other New Wave movements tended to do. The intellectual/artistic core of this film movement that totally opposed dominant or commercial motion pictures (rather than influence them or replace them, as was the case in France, Italy and to some extent, England), found its ideology in modern painting and the Austrian performance art known as Viennese Actionism.[18] Its radicalism, as Thomas Elsaesser succinctly notes,

> was quite different from that of other European "young" cinemas and New Waves of the 1960s. Austrian experimental cinema divides into an abstract-formalist wing (Kubelka and Radax) and a politically interventionist grouping around Kurt Kren, Günther Brus and Otto Mühl, who came out of the "fluxus" movement and "happening" aesthetics, scandalizing the public with provocative, often pornographic and scatological body-centered action pieces.[19]

The iconoclastic aim was to angrily protest against what was seen as calcified, even fascistic, sociopolitics and a retrograde cultural elitism of the nation. Since avant-garde Austrian film owed more to such fringe forces as Andy Warhol and Yoko Ono than to any mainstreamed European New Wave narrative styles, there was little popular interest by the national or international audiences, which had already abandoned interest in Austrian product. As with the anti-establishment performance pieces, Actionist film aimed at local allusion rather than universal message. Through its visceral references to ecstasy, wounding, pain and death, Actionism could, in fact, trace its visual art to the Baroque, which presented the metaphysical through the extremes of the physical.

Ultimately, it was conservative censorship that won the day and several proponents of Viennese Actionism immigrated to West Germany to avoid prosecution in Austria and to set up an "alternative Austrian government in exile."[20] In response, film artists Kren, Weibel, Schmidt, Scheugl, Schlemmer and Export formed the Austrian Filmmakers Cooperative in 1968. It managed to promote and distribute the alternative films of its members and even broke through the export barrier that had made Austrian film experimentation a very limited internal presentation. The influential West German publication *Film* named Hans Scheugl's *ZZZ Hamburg Special* (1968), which consisted of thread being pulled through a projector, as one of the ten best films of 1967–68 along with Godard's *Week-end* (France 1967) and Arthur Penn's *Bonnie and Clyde* (USA 1967). Scheugl commented: "In this way the viewer is forced to think about whether the thread is really on film or whether it is really running through the projector. Thus an important requirement of intermedia is fulfilled: the creative input of the projectionist."[21]

Peter Weibel and Valie Export had also obliterated the axiom that "film requires celluloid" or even a screen with their theory of "expanded cinema," which professed to move illusion cinema to *material* cinema by creating what they called "Instant Film":

> Film was brought back once again to its value as a medium, liberated from any linguistic character which it had taken on in the course of its development. The formal arrangement of the elements of film, whereby elements are exchanged or replaced by others — for example, electric light by fire, celluloid by reality, a beam of light by rockets — had an effect which was artistically liberating and yielded a wealth of new possibilities, such as film installations and the film-environment. In the production of the film medium, celluloid is only one aspect that could (also) be deleted. Instead of the projected image, the film strip itself can become a site for expanding the medium and, consequently, if the celluloid becomes a filmic image as material rather than through projection, a transparent PVC-foil, held before one's eyes, can supply the desired image, since if the user projects his own image of the world onto the foil, he sees the world in accordance with his own image.[22]

Beyond these metafilmic experiments, Kurt Kren's abstract *Schatzi* (1968), which presented shock images in rapid positive/negative manipulation, gained cult attention, and Peter Kubelka, who had become the curator of the Austrian Film Museum in Vienna upon its founding in 1964, moved toward seminarrative style in *Unsere Afrikareise/Our Africa Trip* (1966). Ferry Radax moved even more so in this direction with *Testament* (1968), a political satire depicting Vienna run by a mad dictator and in the midst of a revolution led by the literati. James, the apolitical hero, attempts to topple the dictator, but the results are as contradictory as the global antiwar and youth revolts of 1968. Otto Mühl remained loyal to the Actionist ideology and form and took part in a presentation by several Actionist artists and filmmakers including Oswald Wiener, Günter Brus and Peter Weibel at the University of Vienna on June 7, 1968. Their "Kunst und Revolution" (Art and

Political protest and cinematic experiment: Ferry Radax's *Testament*, 1968.

Revolution) included a "lecture" that featured excrementation, vomiting, and masturbation. It resulted in arrests, psychological examinations, and jail sentences for the artists. Günter Brus later commented that aside from Austria, only Franco's Spain and the Eastern Bloc had such negative attitudes toward progressive art. Mühl went on to film *Sodoma* (1969) and *Der geile Wotan*/The Lascivious Wotan (1970), which blended sex acts and body-oriented performance art in anarchic/abstract non-narratives. The most internationally recognizable exponent of this alternative filmmaking is Valie Export (Waltraut Höllinger, 1940–), a photographer and performance and video artist who successfully made the transition from the "expanded cinema" experiments and abstract shorts of the mid–1960s to narrative feature films in the late 1970s and beyond, as one of the inspirations to New Austrian Film. Working with her partner Peter Weibel, she created *Tapp und Tast Kino*/Touch Cinema (1968), which she called the "first real woman's film." This performance art action consisted of inviting the viewer to insert their hands into the box strapped to Export's chest. It was intended to transcend male-dominated cinema by a female material destruction of cinematic illusion. Export maintained that

> Tactile reception counteracts the fraud of voyeurism. In state-sanctioned cinema, they sit in the dark and see how two people make it with each other, and they themselves are not seen. In *Tapp und Tast Kino*, social prescriptions are no longer

obeyed; the intimate sphere of what the state permits is forced open into public space. Since the consumer can be anyone — child, man, woman — it is an unveiled intrusion into the taboo of homosexuality; the morality of state prescriptions, the state, family, property, is exploded. For as long as the citizen remains satisfied with a reproduced copy of sexual freedom, the state will be spared a sexual revolution.[23]

She continued to "redefine the audience-performer relationship and to extend cinematic conventions"[24] in other film "happenings" such as *Cutting* (1967–68) and *Der Kuß/*The Kiss (1968), which explored the value of the female body in a patriarchal society. Her twelve-minute film *Mann&Frau&Animal/*Man&Woman&Animal (1973) returned to her Actionist roots, and it features among other visuals the artist filming her menstruation in a visceral examination of gender and the "artistic nature of blood." Experimental filmmaker Friederike Petzold took this voyeurism to its ultimate step with *Toilette* (1979). In 1977, Export offered her first feature film, *Unsichtbare Gegner/*Invisible Adversaries, written by Peter Weibel, which was not only a cohesive narrative but showed that humor and wit could also exist in a film about female identity, social representation and the environment. Export called the film a "feminist science fiction film" that managed to be both visually and ideologically progressive and entertaining. A tabloid newspaper, *Die Kronen Zeitung*, launched a campaign against the film, labeling it "perverse trash" and condemning the rare government subvention it received for supporting its "call to anarchy." Although Export's work was selected by a jury for the 1978 Austrian State Prize in the arts, Fred Sinowatz, the Minister of Education and Culture, refused to award Export and gave no prize that year. She followed this scandal with *Menschenfrauen/*Human Women (1979) and later with a widely seen traditional narrative film, *Die Praxis der Liebe/*The Practice of Love (1984), a leading feminist work to be discussed in the following chapter.

Despite the shock value of Viennese Actionism and the few alternative films that received significant attention inside and outside Austria, the mainstream film industry continued its nadir into the new decade of the 1970s. Even more bleak than the previous year in which the Austrian film industry was declared dead, 1969 offered only four commercial films: two by Franz Antel — a "Wirtin" series entry, *Frau Wirtin hat auch eine Nichte*, and a sex comedy, *Liebe durch die Hintertür* (a.k.a. *Nacke-Di, Nacke-Du, Nacke-Dei*)/Wild, Willing and Sexy; Rolf Thiele's pale attempt at a sex comedy, *Komm nach Wien, ich zeig dir was!/*Come to Vienna, I'll Show You Something!; and *Neurotica*, a three-episode film written and directed by Helmut Pfandler. Except for Pfandler's somewhat alternative entry, the films were all multinational co-productions. The only critical success was Peter Beauvais's Austrian/West German television film of Arthur Schnitzler's *Das weite Land/*The Distant Land with O. W. Fischer and Ruth Leuwerik, which was given belated theatrical distribution in 1973.

Wien-Film, which still owned most of the Rosenhügel Studio complex and surrounding property, sold off land in a desperate move to finance a return to

Feminism and the gaze: Valie Export's *Unsichtbare Gegner*, 1977.

production in 1970. Several ambitious films were announced, including a costume epic with Vanessa Redgrave and Franco Nero, features directed by John Oppenheimer and Wolfgang Leibeneiner, and a dramatic vehicle for Paula Wessely. None of these projects were realized. The coup de grâce was the decision by the organization of Austrian film journalists, "The Golden Pen," not to give an award for the best film of 1969 due to "lack of interest on the part of the Society's members."[25] Instead of the ambitious Wien-Film program, only two "Wirtin" comedies by Antel and two alternative features appeared in 1970: the Jahn/Hirsch *Reflexion* and Greek-born Antonis Lepeniotis's (1932–) *Alkeste — Die Bedeutung Protektion zu haben*/The Meaning of Protection (1970), produced by the Viennese companies of Edos-Film and Schubert-Film. The director, who attempted a blend of French New Wave stylistics, neorealism and traditional formalism, placed the ancient drama into contemporary garb to reflect on the power abuse of the state. Lepeniotis had worked as an assistant to Michael Curtiz and Elia Kazan in Hollywood and with Geza von Bolvary and Geza von Cziffra in Vienna and subsequently emerged as a short documentary filmmaker for Austrian television in the 1960s. His 1974 film *Das Manifest*/The Manifesto continued the style and theme of his debut, in an examination of the makings of a resistance movement against a dictatorship.

Although the Socialist majority government and its pragmatic Chancellor Bruno Kreisky promised a law to encourage film production and promotion in 1970, committees, party demands, and official procrastination delayed any implementation of support until the end of the decade. The city of Vienna again attempted to support film production while there was still something to be saved and upstaged the national government in its creation of a film promotion law in 1977. That same year, the national government shelved its planned law, and offered only the "laughable"[26] sum of about $1,500,000 as an annual subsidy for the entire national industry. In the meantime, Austrian television had only strengthened its hold on audiences.

On New Year's Day 1969, Austria's national network ORF began color broadcast, and as Goswin Dörfler reported, the accessibility of great entertainment and art was on the small screen: "Why bother to go to the cinema, when every week one can view in the comfort of one's own home (and in color too) a cross-section of all the major films (including famous classics like *Battleship Potemkin* and *Metropolis*, and premieres of works such as Wajda's *Pilate and Others* and Saura's *The Garden of Delights*)?"[27] While Austrian cinema foundered, Austrian television presentations developed into one of the best sources of filmed entertainment on the continent. As the audiences stayed away from the ever-decreasing number of cinema venues, registered television owners in Austria increased at a rapid rate.[28] After having lost its large Gartenbau cinema (the second largest in Vienna), which was demolished to make room for a computer center, and given the paucity of material, the Viennale Film Festival no longer even attempted to offer a theme and resorted to selecting national and international works wholly on the basis of merit. An association known as *Der gute Film* (The Good Film), which recalled the publication of the 1930s, and had offered an Austrian film series and awards since 1956, began to show works by foreign directors. The Austrian Film Archive managed to mount several well-attended retrospectives, ranging from G. W. Pabst to Hans Moser, suggesting that while the commercial industry languished and the avantgarde marginalized itself Austria was nevertheless a nation of film fans: one that might again be made aware of its significant role in the development of the motion picture. The decade of the 1970s bore this basic fact out. As the government stalled on film support and commercial product was only to be found in a few multinational co-productions, a new generation of filmmakers arrived on the scene to reinvent the national narrative cinema with privately raised funding, vastly downsized productions, and unknown talent. Despite all odds against it, the embryonic New Austrian Film was being formed.

Remnants of the commercial film modes of the 1960s maintained a presence throughout the 1970s, but as the Actionists returned to performance art or evolved into narrative filmmakers, and the internationally co-produced sex comedy or thriller receded, the only commercial director of the 1960s to outlast the 1970s would be Franz Antel. His bedroom farces, exploitation films and broad musical comedy style continued to generate box office at home and abroad with actors Terry Torday, Waltraud Haas, Paul Hörbiger and Gunther Philipp, and later with more polyglot casts. Again, the titles tell all: *Mein Vater, der Affe und ich*/My Father, the Ape and I (1971); *Einer spinnt immer*/Someone Is Always Crazy (1971); *Ausser Rand und Band am Wolfgangsee*/Cutting Loose at the Wolfgangsee (1972); *Sie nannten ihn Krambambuli*/They Called Him Krambambuli (1972); *Die lustigen vier von der*

Tankstelle/The Merry Four from the Gas Station (1972); *Frau Wirtins tolle Töchter-lein*/The Hostess's Crazy Daughter (1973); *Das Wandern ist Herrn Müllers Lust*/Mr. Müller Likes to Hike (1973); *Wenn die Mädchen zum Manöver Blasen*/When the Girls Trumpet for Maneuvers (1974); and *Der kleine Schwarze mit dem roten Hut*/Johnny Chitarra (1975). Antel's adaptability, production savvy and factory tactics are astounding, but by the late 1970s, even he had abandoned the low-budget, regionally aimed entertainment to make better use of his international style in potential global blockbusters. In 1977, he directed Tony Curtis, Marisa Berenson and Hugh Griffith in the Austrian/West German/French/Italian co-production of *Casanova & Co.* (1977), followed by *Ab Morgen sind wir Reich und Ehrlich*/As of Tomorrow (1977), an Austrian/West German co-production with Arthur Kennedy, Carroll Baker and Curd Jürgens, but neither was a critical success nor succeeded in spotlighting Antel to a larger international audience. He ended the 1970s and his exploitation phase with a film that summed up all the comedy, tourist films, and sex trends in cinema that Antel had succeeded in melding during the last two decades: *Love-Hotel in Tirol*/Love Hotel in the Tyrol (1978). It was obvious to all, including the director himself, that his recent work had offered Austrian cinema little beyond faltering box-office earnings and that his talents were being squandered and his reputation destroyed. Antel retreated from the industry for several years until he reemerged in 1981 with a film that gave him the critical praise he had not had since the imperial epics of the 1950s. With *Der Bockerer*/Bockerer, which will be discussed in the following chapter, Antel had once again reinvented himself and his style — and reclaimed his status as Austria's longest-running filmmaker.

Several other directors continued their well-tested sexploitation genre of the 1960s in forgettable films of the 1970s. Frits Frons, the Austrian exponent of the West German sex film, offered *Perfekt in allen Stellungen*/Perfect in All Positions (1971) and the pseudodocumentary of *Hurenreport-Sexvariation blutjunger Mäd-chen*/Report on Prostitution (1972). Eddy Saller directed *Liebe durch die Autotür*/Love through the Car Door (1972), *Geile Nichten*/Wanton Nieces (1978), and the French *Emmanuelle*-like *Monique-Mein heißer Schoß*/Monique (1978). Walter Vogel wrote and directed a more avant-garde–edged sex film entitled *Mäander-Erotik ohne Worte*/Eroticism without Words (1971); German director Rolf Thiele, who had long since abandoned both Thomas Mann and serious adult themes, offered *Undine 74* (1974); and Georg Tressler (as "Hans Georg Keil") entered the erotic comedy scene with the soft-core yarns *Ach jodel mir noch einen*/2069: A Sex Odyssey (1974) and *Die kleine mit dem süßen Po*/Sweet Derriere (1975).

But the sexploitation film had exhausted even its quick box-office return potential by the mid-decade. Remaining art house cinemas began to attract small audiences curious to see a variety of modest new works, which had grown from individual attempts at overthrowing the failed commercial genres without group manifesto or general artistic ideology and which moved beyond the limitations of Actionism. New directors or those new to Austrian film created these semidocumentaries, montages, intimate narratives, and socially critical dramatic or tragicomic tales. Many of these films were solidly Austrian productions, usually financed by several small companies or with such formerly important firms as Sascha-Film or Wien-Film and frequently with the participation of ORF. Among these new filmmakers attracting early art house audiences was Jörg A. Eggers, who directed *Der letzte Werkelmann*/The Last Werkelmann (1972) and *Ich will leben*/I Want to Live (1976), which dealt with the experiences of the parents of a severely injured child. Despite the lack of serious interest in creating a film fund or promoting filmmakers and their attempt to resurrect a national cinema in the postcommercial era, Eggers's film was presented by the Austrian government as the national entry for the Foreign Language Film nominations leading to the 1976 Oscars. Other films would be "honored" in this way, although their poverty-level creation and distribution owed nothing to official support. Czech director Vojtech Jasny had tried to inspire a commercial "New Wave" in Austrian film during the mid–1960s with his Austrian/Czechoslovakian film *Pfeifen, Betten, Turteltauben*/The Pipes (1966) and returned in 1976 with *Fluchtversuch*/Escape Attempt, which examined the life of the child of a Yugoslavian guest worker who longs for home. Georg Lhotsky, who predicted New Austrian Film in 1968 with his artistic meditation on national identity and his particular production mode in *Moos auf den Steinen*, directed only one more film, the 1977 *Schatten und Licht*/Shadows and Light. Götz Hagmüller, an activist for government film funding support, directed the semidocumentary feature *Die denkwürdige Wallfahrt des Kaisers Kanga Mussa von Mali nach Mekka*/The Thoughtful Journey of Emperor Kanga Mussa from Mali to Mecca (1977), which was shot by Dietmar Graf in Africa and featured African actors, music by George Zamfir and narration by Attila Hörbiger. Alfred Ninaus's *Lauf Hase, lauf!*/Run Rabbit, Run! (1979) told the story of a thirteen-year-old boy who flounders on the fringes of society as a thief but who ultimately decides to change his life. The ability of these independently produced works to attract audiences in limited screenings demonstrated that the sociocritical narrative form had come to the fore after nearly two decades of failed traditional entertainment genres and isolated experimentation. Montage and art films continued to develop beyond the pure shock effects of the Actionists: the avant-garde film couple of Sepp Jahn and Edith Hirsch directed, wrote and produced *Protokoll einer Montage*/Protocol of a Montage (1974) and Ernst Schmidt Jr. wrote, shot, directed and produced *Wienfilm 1896–1976*/Vienna Film 1896–1976 (1977), a surrealistic and culturally critical montage of documentary and artistic images of Vienna, featuring artists Peter Weibel, Joe Berger and Arnulf Rainer. Similarly, Alfred Kaiser created all aspects of his Austrian historical montage, *Kaiserschnitt— Eine Operette*/Caesarian–An Operetta (1978), as did Peter Dressler for his experimental semidocumentary *Sonderfahrt*/Extra Trip (1978). The early 1970s had also marked the return of more traditional documentaries on culture and music, such as Hans Conrad Fischer's *Ludwig van Beethoven* (1970) and *Das Leben Anton Bruckners*/The Life of Anton Bruckner (1974); Alfons Stummer's *Europa—Leuchtfeuer der Welt*/Europe— Beacon to the World (1970); Alfons Benesch's *Traumreise über die Alpen*/Dream Journey across the Alps (1971); and Walter J. Zupan's *Vorarlberg—Land der Alpen*/Vorarlberg— Land of the Alps (1973). Titus Leber (1951–), however, blended experimental visuals and the narrative to interpret classical music in Gustav Mahler's *Kindertotenleider*/Songs for Dead Children (1976) and *Fremd bin ich eingezogen*/I Was a Stranger When I Moved In (1978) with August Schuschnigg portraying the young Franz Schubert. The AFI Los Angeles–trained director's 1981 music-themed dramatic short *Anima-Symphonie Phantastique* became the first Austrian film in thirty years to be named an official selection for that year's Cannes Film Festival.

Narratives that would influence the direction of early New Austrian Film in the 1980s are found in Toronto-born director John Cook's (1935–) *Langsamer Sommer*/Slow Summer (1976) and his breakthrough work *Schwitzkasten*/Sweat Box (1978), a realistic examination of the life of the working-class Hermann Juranek (Hermann Holub), alienated from society, work, family and self, who ultimately finds a skeptical hope and love in the person of Vera (Christa Schubert). From his first film in Austria the short, *Ich schaff's einfach nimmer*/I'll Never Make It (1972), which looked at the pathos in the everyday life of a boxer, Cook has followed a Godard-like exploration of the urban neurosis and claustrophobia born of the demand for order and conformity in Austria's conservative society. *Schwitzkasten* is directed in a low-key, almost meditative, style but offers a powerful message on the alienation of those on the lower rungs of a supposed "upwardly mobile" consumerist society.[29] Wim Wenders (1945–), one of the leading figures of New German Cinema, known for *Der amerikanische Freund*/The American Friend (West Germany 1977), *Paris, Texas* (West Germany 1984), and the poetic postmodern fantasy of angels and the German experience, *Der Himmel über Berlin*/Wings of Desire (West Germany 1987), began his mainstream career with two feature films: *Summer in the City* (West Germany 1970), made while Wenders was still a film school student, and the Austrian *Die Angst des Tormanns beim Elfmeter*/The Goalie's Anxiety at the Penalty Kick (1971). The latter film was co-scripted by the director and Austrian author Peter Handke. Austrian-born international actor Maximilian Schell (1930–) moved behind the camera in what became one of the first examples of this new phase in Austrian filmmaking that attained a measure of global attention. His *Geschichten aus dem Wienerwald*/Tales from the Vienna Woods (1979) with Birgit Doll, Hanno Pöschl, and Helmut Qualtinger was based on the 1930 Ödön von Horváth play and scripted by Christopher Hampton. Although the title suggests a Viennese Film or an imperial epic named after the Johann Strauss Jr. waltz, Schell's film examines the tattered social fabric of interwar Austria, which as a small republic is beset by political polarization and economic crisis and locates its identity in nostalgia for empire or in looming Nazism. *Geschichten* specifically focuses on the world of the Viennese petit bourgeoisie during the 1930s. The dull bleakness and the brutality of relationships, particularly the objectification and abuse of women, make Horváth's play and Schell's film drama, which many criticized had ventured too far from the original in its cinematic approach, universal statements on outmoded gender roles and relationships and the roots of fascism in the reactionary values of the financially imperiled lower middle class. Despite the sociopolitical criticism of the 1930s in Schell's film, the 1934–38 Austrofascist state was still a taboo subject in popular Austrian discourse as was the Austrian role in the Third Reich. Another examination of fascist roots in working-class milieu was Wilhelm Pellert's *Jesus von Ottakring*/Jesus of the Ottakring District (1976). This modern passion play, which received critical acclaim in Austria and was viewed by many as a welcome commercial direction of the artistic New Wave, was co-scripted by Pellert and Helmut Korherr and features Hilde Sochor, Peter Hey, and Rudolf Prack, the romantic leading man of the 1950s.

Prack's appearance was not the only image from the past in the reemergence of artistic and critical Austrian film. Several names reminded the audiences of their images and talents, often for one final time: Helmut Pfandler's romance *Abenteuer eines Sommers*/A Summer's Adventure (1974), written by Veit Heidruschka and Kurt Nachmann, lensed by Elio Carniel, features Marthe Harell and Fred Liewehr; Ottokar Runze's version of Alexander Lernet-Holenia's bittersweet novel on the collapse of the Austro-Hungarian empire and the birth of the small Austrian republic as seen by an Austrian officer torn between duty and love, *Die Standarte*/The Standard (1977), features UFA diva Lil Dagover; and Vojtech Jasny's *Die Rückkehr*/The Return (1977) features Attila Hörbiger and Trude Marlen. There was also a very brief attempt at revisiting "quality" commercial international co-production or Austrian production with international casts aimed at showcasing Austria as a film location. Two films from 1975 began this short-lived trend: Gerd Oswald's *Bis zur bitteren Neige*/To the Bitter End, a Wien-Film/Roxy-Film (Munich) co-production, and Cyril Frankel's thriller *Vollmacht zum Mord*/Permission to Kill, a Wien-Film/Warner Brothers co-production shot by Freddie Young and Sepp Riff. This was followed by the more artistic *Die Wildente*/The Wild Duck (1977), a Sascha-Film/Solaris (Munich) co-production written and directed by Hans W. Geissendorfer and Helmut Pfandler's *Tod im November*/Death in November (1978), a co-production of three Austrian firms. There were also two ambitious attempts to utilize Vienna's historical sites and technical talents for international "blockbusters" in 1978. Ken Annakin directed Beau Bridges, Sylvia Kristel and Ursula Andress in the historical adventure of *Das Geheimnis der eisernen Maske*/The Secret of the Iron Mask, and Broadway director Harold Prince, who had only rarely ventured behind the camera, helmed a film version of his successful Stephen Sondheim Broadway musical *A Little Night Music*. Based on the Ingmar Bergman film *Sommarnattens leende*/Smiles of a Summer Night (Sweden 1955), and offering Elizabeth Taylor, Len Cariou, and Diana Rigg, the film relocated the musical's setting from turn-of-the-century Sweden to imperial Vienna, making the film perhaps more of a comment on the lost art of the Viennese operetta film than the material warranted. Despite the waltz score and impressive art direction, the setting seemed contrived, and the existentialist questions of choice, fate and love alienated rather than won over international audiences who no longer had a taste for the genre. Shot at the Rosenhügel studio, the production was to have reactivated Wien-Film and its facilities as a draw for Hollywood and European co-production. Wien-Film had become Sascha-Wien-Film when the large West German Kirch Group media concern had purchased the films of both companies for a mere 500,000 DM. The hopes of expanding Sascha-Wien-Film were dashed with the box-office failures of

Maske and *A Little Night Music*, and it subsequently closed its new Los Angeles office. Much of Wien-Film's legacy also appeared to have been lost, and upon Kirch's purchase of the company's stock, there were only ten films available. Most of the negatives of the other films had been taken by the Soviets as they ended their occupation in 1955. Not until 1994, when Ulrich N. Schulenburg and Herbert Schmitt of the Vienna's Thomas Sessler publishing house purchased Wien-Film, was there an active attempt at reclaiming this lost legacy from post–Soviet Russian film archives.

The most positive development of the late 1970s had been the introduction of several new filmmakers who would help create the early New Austrian Film of the 1980s and influence the movement into its stride in the 1990s. Axel Corti (1933–93), who had made only one previous Austrian film in 1963, returned with *Der Fall Jäger-stätter*/The Case of Jägerstätter (1972), which was written by Hellmut Andics and co-produced by Vienna's Neue Thalia-Film and ORF. The film explores the plight of Franz Jägerstätter, who refused to be drafted into the army of the Third Reich. Confronted with various representatives of the National Socialist state, the church, family and friends, he concludes that a Christian cannot be a National Socialist and he is imprisoned for his crime. Corti concludes the film by positing the choice of conscience versus duty in several contemporary interviews. The film was a rare first attempt at exploring Austria in the Reich and questioned the still rather undisputed importance of order above individualism in post–1960s Austrian society. Corti fol-lowed this groundbreaking film with *Totstellen*/Dead Places in 1975, with the par-ticipation of author Michael Scharang and Xaver Schwarzenberger. The film, an Austrian/West German co-production, secured Corti's place as one of the most impressive new Austrian filmmakers not only at home but abroad. The realistic look at the doomed economic and social constraints of the construction worker son of self-sacrificing farmers as he attempts to make a life for his girlfriend and their unborn child attacked the idyllic agrarian world of the *Heimatfilm*. A six-part series on Austrian television, *Alpensaga* (1976–80), did this with even greater sweep by focusing on life in a small rural Austrian village between 1899 and 1945. Written by Wilhelm Pevny and critical "folk" playwright Peter Turrini and directed by Dieter Berner, the controversial series was less cathartic in dealing with Nazism than the later West German *Heimat* series (1984) by Edgar Reitz. Another television series re-visioning the concept of the *Heimatfilm* was *Das Dorf an der Grenze*/The Town on the Border (1979–83; 1992), which looked at a bilingual village on the Aus-trian/Slovenian border from 1918 to the 1990s. The series was written by Thomas Pluch and directed by Fritz Lehner and Peter Patzak. But actual attempts to cre-ate a new *Heimatfilm* in cinema, with critical takes on rural life, Catholicism and the Nazi past, did not truly emerge until the late 1980s.

Director Peter Patzak (1945–) aimed at establishing a politically critical direc-tion in early New Austrian Film and was first popularly known as the creator of a hit detective television series, *Kottan ermittelt*/Kottan Investigates (1976–84), which often satirized sociopolitical and cultural clichés. Despite his interest in generating controversial examinations of political corruption and latent fascism, his films tend

The socially critical "local" film: Axel Corti's *Totstellen*, 1975.

toward a more cosmopolitan and commercial style than most of the new Austrian directors. British actress Rita Tushingham appeared in his first film, *Situation* (1973), which he followed with *Parapsycho-Spektrum der Angst*/Parapsycho (a.k.a. *PSI*, 1975), an Austrian/West German thriller written for Marisa Mell and Mathieu Carrière. But it was Patzak's 1979 *Kassbach–Ein Portrait*/Kassbach–A Portrait, written by the director with Helmut Zenker, that gained him true critical attention. Here actor Walter Kohut portrays Karl Kassbach, a petit bourgeois man who feels threatened by foreigners and deals with the issue in a violent manner. The film dissects Kassbach's family life and his relationship with society. Kassbach's creation of an organization for "Peace, Security and Order" underscores what the director sees as the xenophobia of an urban underclass, victimized by consumerism and idealized cultural nostalgia. Another director attacking social and political stagnation in Austria during the 1970s is Iranian-born Mansur Madavi (1943–), whose films like *Die glücklichen Minuten des Georg Hauser*/The Happy Minutes of Georg Hauser (1974), *Notausgang*/Emergency Exit (1976), and *Die blinde Eule*/The Blind Owl (1979) deal with the possibilities and limitations of freedom and individuality in contemporary society.

Cable television was introduced in 1979, and with the proliferation of home video recorders and films on video there was a sense that this new media might well succeed in closing Austria's remaining cinema theaters. But post–1960s filmmakers succeeded in attracting a younger generation whose parents had abandoned cinema during the decline of commercial product and in the period of Actionism and marginalized experimentation. Unlike the directors of the New German Cinema's *Autorenfilm* during the 1970s and 1980s who saw themselves in the tradition of the French *cinema d'auteurs* in their all-controlling combination of writer, director and producer, Austrian multitasking, while also a rejection of commercial cinema conventions, was driven by poverty and necessity. While New German Cinema was made possible by generous government funding and promotion, and West German critics helped elevate the movement as artistically and culturally important, Austria's early film revival was mostly heralded by word of mouth and the perseverance of its creators. A growing interest in the new narrative style, in critical subject matter, and in local production indicated the path for Austrian filmmakers into the following decade and kept the theaters open.

6

New Austrian Film: 1980-2000

*Limited Government Support; Resurgent
National Audience; International Recognition*

National financial support for film development, when it finally came, seemed to take filmmakers by surprise. It had been hoped for since the immediate postwar era and vaguely considered by various governments since the 1950s. It had been challenged in the 1960s by Vienna's municipal film support and had ultimately become something of a bad joke among filmmakers, who eventually created the basis of New Austrian Film without it. It finally arrived in 1980, not so much because its time had come or was in fact long overdue but because the government's lack of film support was an embarrassment to a country with such a high standard of living and which was awaking from its neutralist sleep into a Western Europe moving toward nominal unity. On a more political level, it was the direct result of a bribery scandal suffered by the ruling Socialist Party, which was defused by quick actions and concessions by Chancellor Kreisky. On November 25, 1980, film support was passed into federal law as the Filmförderungsgesetz (Film Promotion Act), which provided that filmmakers raising at least 20 percent of funding for their project could compete for national funding. Additionally, the application, original script, and prints of the completed film would be archived, to demonstrate the importance of the medium and its new history. Government support favored first-time filmmakers and innovative works and strongly embraced the practice that had made a great deal of recent product a reality — co-production with Austria's national television network, ORF.

The debut funding in 1981 was greeted with the kind of criticism that usually follows anything that has taken too long in arriving. The support was swiftly deemed too little or too late or both. It seemed awkward, even specious at first — the concession of a rushed decision, which had been decades in the making. While some of the federal provinces provided small subsidies for regional filmmaking, Vienna had offered solid film support since 1977, in the form of its now well-known and internationally utilized Wiener Filmförderungsfonds or WFF (Viennese Film Promotion Fund). This source had become a recognized and trusted source for serious

filmmakers, while the new federal fund was initially plagued with demands by those
who simply wanted to exploit its offerings for profit. The vagaries of the new law
were worked out in the first year and more than twenty-eight million Schillings
were given to filmmakers between the inception of the law in 1981 and October
1982.[1] Goswin Dörfler, reporting for the *International Film Guide*, considered that
several areas of the legislation had been budgeted far too low, "such as the concept
encouragement with 1%, marketing 5% and professional training 1%. The share
for short films is not to exceed 10%. Which means there will be more than 80%
left for the production of feature films. Doubtless it is the feature film which represents the film culture of a people or country."[2] The Ministry of Education, Science and Culture also instituted a sum of an additional thirty million Schillings
for short and experimental films and to aid film institutions, such as the Austrian
Film Archive. Moreover, ORF agreed to make about twenty million Schillings
available for co-production. Yet the image of Austria as a "non-film nation," founded
in the commercial disaster of the 1960s, continued to influence international opin-
ion, despite the emergence of New Austrian Film and the very tardy government
support:

> Annually a total of around eighty million Schillings will be available for Austria's
> film development — for this small, in filmic terms unimportant country by all
> standards a handsome sum, higher than the allocated funds for literature and the
> visual arts but still distinctly less than what the upkeep of theatrical stages, espe-
> cially the Vienna State Opera and the Burg Theatre, cost![3]

The new possibilities of federal funding boosted the film industry somewhat,
allowing for the entry of new talent, a few larger production budgets, and for minor
promotion outside of Austria, but the innovation in the art had already developed
without any government-led campaign. Audiences, too, had learned to again show
an interest in the national cinema. Despite the introduction of cable television in
1979, much of this new awareness of homegrown filmmaking was due to the
increased role of ORF and the often made-for-television film. Works receiving little or no distribution were able to find an audience via television broadcast. The
continued recession of Austrian cinema theaters was halted through the multiplex-
ing of former large theaters, and the alternative art house theaters that had sprung
up in Austria in the 1970s to show experimental work continued to attract a small
progressive or cult film audience. By the 1980s, these art houses expanded their programs to offer limited release-films from Austria and foreign films that did not play
in mainstream theaters or on ORF. Many of these art houses organized a distribution arm to promote alternative work. It was clear that a new generation of film
audience had arrived, which expected local accessibility to world film and had a
healthy curiosity for the national cinema. Even corporate aspects of the industry,
which had faded in the failure of international co-productions and exploitation
films of the mid–1960s, returned with an initiative that had long since been considered an impossibility. Two business-based prizes were created by the industry in

1983: the "Golden Ticket," awarded to any film with a minimum of 300,000 visitors in eighteen months, and the "Austrian Film Prize," which was given to the film that stimulated the largest box office of any given year.

Eight Austrian feature films were produced in 1980, followed by thirteen in 1981, ten in 1982, thirteen in 1983 and fourteen in 1984. Production would hover at this number for the decade, the healthiest amounts since the early 1960s. On an artistic level, it is easy to see a transformation in Austrian cinema. While the director or cast would usually convey the genre or subgenre of most feature films of the 1960s and 1970s, this was now no longer possible. Austrian filmmakers actively dispensed with cliché in title, casting, or execution. Feature films at the start of this new era were also aimed toward the commercial market. Franz Novotny (1949–), who had been active in film since the experiments of the 1960s, offered *Exit— Nur keine Panik*/Exit — Don't Panic! (1980) as his first major feature film. It is best described as a socially critical tragicomic action hybrid about a lower-middle-class crook attempting to come by his dreams in any way possible. But in his actual life, which is inundated by bizarre characters from the fringes of Viennese society, he only manages to fail brilliantly. The film features the colorful cast of Eddie Constantine, Hanno Pöschl, playwright Peter Turrini, and filmmakers Paulus Manker and Peter Weibel, and it became one of the first true box-office successes of early New Austrian Film. Novotny gained national attention with his controversial television film *Staatsoperette*/State Operetta (1977), which satirizes Austria's embattled history from 1927 to 1938. Difficulty with ORF financing due to the subject matter was only the tip of the iceberg, and the project made Novotny's film the cause célèbre of the broadcast season from the outset. Accused of radical leftist manipulation of historical facts and creating insulting, even pornographic, depictions of government and religious leaders from the First Republic even before completion of the film, the long-postponed showing resulted in viewer protests, opened the state-owned ORF network to political scandal, and saturated the press. It ultimately received only mild critical interest, which focused above all on the musical score by Otto M. Zykan.[4] The debacle, however, helped bring Novotny's sociopolitical filmmaking to the large screen, and he followed the success of his first feature film with another television film based on Elfriede Jelinek's novel *Die Ausgesperrten*/The Excluded (1982), an examination of the psychological wreckage of a postwar Austrian family and the murderous rampage brought on by a son's existentialist crisis. Marxist author Jelinek considers her novel to be "about the seeds of anarchy ... individual, not its political counterpart — as we can observe the process in a secondary school in Vienna ... the story is based on a true incident: an eighteen-year-old schoolboy reacted to reading Albert Camus' *L'Etranger* by stealing his father's revolver and shooting his entire family."[5] In addition to its psychological underpinnings, the film can be considered as part of the coming-to-terms-with-the-past subgenre; it does so prismatically by examining the "fascistic" nature of the bourgeoisie in a capitalist/consumerist environment. Into the next decade, Novotny also wrote and directed the grunge road picture *Coconuts* (1985) and the coolly received sequel to his first film, entitled *Exit II — Verklärte Nacht*/Exit

II — Transfigured Night (1995). Film historian Claus Philipp finds Novotny had so sanitized the original provocations in the sequel as to make them into the sort of clichés the original film sought to break. He draws a comparison with the conflicting styles of American director Peter Bogdanovich's neorealist *The Last Picture Show* (USA 1971) and its self-conscious, commercially oriented sequel, *Texasville* (USA 1990) and suggests that Novotny's problem is that of most artistically aimed international directors, who, in the wake of a unique and provocative creation, ultimately turn its elements into formulaic structures in later films.[6]

Other films indicated the nascent New Austrian Film's transformation of, or total break from, traditional genres. Herbert Vesely's *Exzess und Bestrafung — Egon Schiele*/Egon Schiele — Excesses (1980), about the famed Viennese expressionist painter, was a reinvention of the traditional Austrian biopic in a collection of biographical sketches written by Vesely and Leo Tichat and set to music by Brian Eno, Anton von Webern and Felix Mendelssohn. Valie Export's feminist feature, co-scripted by Peter Weibel, *Menschenfrauen*/Human Women (1980) examines four women who rebel against male domination in their lives. The film had a strong social psychological and existentialist tone that was echoed in Gerhard Kleindel's *Neon* (1980), about a young man's attempt to free himself from social isolation, and in Robert Polak's *Johnny Unser*/Our Johnny (1980), a psychodrama about the collapse of a tidy marriage and household due to the addition of a cat.

It was 1981, however, that is considered the pivotal year in the arrival of New Austrian Film. The most fascinating event of the year was the comeback, or better said, reinvention of veteran director Franz Antel, whose career as one of the top directors of Austrian imperial epics, musicals and light comedies was replaced by his kitsch factory of slick sex comedies in the 1960s and 1970s. His new film *Der Bockerer*/Bockerer (1981), scripted by Kurt Nachmann from a play by Ulrich Becher and Peter Preses, was nothing anyone had expected from the entertainment and exploitation mogul, but it reminded critics and national audiences of the significant cinematic contribution of Antel's early films. The tragicomic saga of a Viennese butcher Karl Bockerer (Karl Merkatz) and his family during the Reich was the coming of age of the heretofore largely avoided topic of Austrian Nazism, as the film managed to be both profound and entertaining. An antihero picaro figure who resists and underscores the absurdities of the era, Bockerer witnesses the forced emigration of a Jewish friend, the death of a Social Democratic friend at Dachau, and the loss of his son, who joins the SA (Storm Troopers) and is eventually sent to be killed in the battle of Stalingrad when he resists the advances of a homosexual SS officer. This subplot of decadent sexual politics in Nazism seems particularly influenced by Italian cinema, specifically Rossellini's neorealist *Roma citta aperta*/Rome Open City (Italy 1945) and the neodecadent Italian films of the 1970s beginning with Luchino Visconti's operatic Nazi melodrama, *The Damned* (Italy/West Germany 1969). The son's love affair with the daughter of an aristocrat essays the strong class divisions in Austria at the time, although the potential problems of this unequal pairing and the subsequent child are resolved with relatively little social disruption. Despite all, Bockerer refuses to yield either his

Approaching the Nazi past in early New Austrian Film: Karl Merkatz and George Schuchter in Franz Antel's *Der Bockerer*, 1981.

individuality or humanity to the Austrian Nazis or the German occupation. In addition to performances by Merkatz, Alfred Böhm, Ida Krottendorf and Klaus Jürgen Wussow, the film also recalled the Wien-Film era with cameos by such classic cinema actors as Hans Holt, Marte Harell and Gustav Knuth. This Austrian/West German co-production signaled the return of a more "international" creation of Austrian film, but this new mode of cooperation, often between Austria and West Germany or France, was not the overwhelming polyglot prospect of the 1960s nor were these films made to appeal to a broad multinational audience. Such modest co-production was generally loyal to national trends in location, style and content. Antel's film did make use of support from both the Film Promotion Act and the Vienna Film Fund, and it earned back far more than its subvention when it became a measured box-office success in Austria and in West Germany. It was presented at the 1981 Moscow Film Festival (where it received the Best Actor Prize for Merkatz), at Cannes, and at the film festivals of San Remo and Prague. Antel's comeback with *Bockerer* brought together the lavishly filmed historical epics and the politically critical alternative cinema into a hybrid that recalled the social dramas of the 1930s. It displayed the world-class filmmaking traditions of Austria in an intelligent and self-examining drama that is analogous to the elegantly produced British films of the 1980s and 1990s that undertook a critical look at Victorian, Edwardian and 1930s England while it also satisfied world audiences with pleasing drama and fine production values.

Antel offered two sequels into the next decade: *Der Bockerer II: Österreich ist Frei*/The Bockerer II: Austria Is Free (1996) and *Der Bockerer III: Die Brücke von Andau*/The Bockerer III: The Bridge at Andau (2000), which followed Merkatz's butcher into the Allied occupation of the postwar era and the Hungarian revolution of 1956 with the same jaundiced tragicomic eye as the original. Although the more subtle sociopolitical critiques of Austria after the Reich did not have the same effect on audiences and critics as the first installment, they nevertheless served the mainstreaming of New Austrian Film. Antel had reinvented himself and Austrian film genres yet again and had cinematically anticipated the national discourse on Austria's role in Nazism during the 1986 presidential election campaign of former U.N. secretary general Kurt Waldheim. Waldheim's international renown had made him a conservative hope for the position, but apparent amnesia regarding his whereabouts during the Reich as a junior Wehrmacht officer had been manipulated by the "investigative" media and then by opposing political forces into possible association with Nazi war crimes. The international criticism of the Austrian presidential election had the opposite effect, and citizens angered at what amounted to an external interference in Austria's internal political affairs swept Waldheim to victory. Although eventually found innocent of any direct involvement, his omissions regarding his service record had a lingering taint, and he remained a pariah on the international stage. Although what has become known as the "Waldheim era" is understood by many to be the impetus for a long-needed national Austrian self-examination regarding the Anschluss and Nazism, it did not inspire a new historical drama trend in film. Rather, the examination of the past through fascist metaphors found in the petit bourgeoisie and the working-class experience of contemporary Austria dominated the films of the 1980s and 1990s.

Antel's cinematic rebirth allowed him to return once more to the imperial spectacle in 1987 with an Austrian/West German/French co-production about the "waltz king," *Johann Strauss — Der König ohne Krone*/Johann Strauss — A King without a Crown, which was scripted by Austrian-American cultural historian Frederic Morton among others. Beautifully photographed by veteran cinematographer Hanns Matula on location in Vienna and at the East Berlin DEFA studio (the former UFA facility), the film was populated by American television and international performers. Antel proved he could still do this sort of entertainment better than anyone, but it was the wrong time to do it and the film did not evolve into the blockbuster he had hoped for. It received no attention in the United States, where Antel had hoped it would gain him a Hollywood connection and the American audiences that he had long sought as another Billy Wilder. This comparison was not totally unfounded. Wilder also saw similarities in some of their work and in response to Austrian press suggestions he return to Austria at some point, Wilder reportedly once commented, "Why should I come to Vienna? You already have Antel."[7] The

Strauss film was a financial disaster for the director, who had invested a significant amount of his own money in the project.[8] Despite its production values, the reasons for the dire failure of this film is clear: Austrian film now had a critical quality and a new topical focus, which Antel had helped foster with *Bockerer*, and pseudo-imperial epics set to waltz music were not what audiences desired from the "Alpine Republic" in flux.

The second work of the new decade that moved New Austrian Film into some mainstream success with national audiences was *Der Schüler Gerber*/The Student Gerber (1980), directed by Wolfgang Glück from a novel by Austrian author Friedrich Torberg and written for the screen by Torberg, Glück and Werner Schneyder. Glück (1929–), a nephew of the Golden Age Austrian-Hollywood leading man Paul Henreid, had been prolifically active in West German television, film and stage direction since the 1950s and had adapted several Austrian literary works for television but it was *Gerber* that brought him to the forefront. The film, originally co-produced for television by three new companies — Satel-Film, Arabella-Film and the Munich-based Almaro-Film — was later released theatrically. Xaver Schwarzenberger, who was to launch his directorial career in 1983, served as *Gerber*'s cinematographer and the period film featured the most widely known New Austrian Film actor of the 1990s, Gabriel Barylli (1957–), as a graduating student who is faced with unhappy love, a dying father, and the despotic, even sadistic attitude of his mathematics professor. Gerber's story ends on a bleakly ironic note, as he despairingly commits suicide to escape certain failure, unaware that he has passed his exit examination. Although the original novel was published in 1930 (revised in 1954) as a criticism of the lingering academic traditions of the Old Order in the First Republic, the film treatment shifts the parable to an examination of the seeds of fascism. *Gerber* represents the return to "traditional" quality (linear narrative, studio-type production values) and topics (war, romance, family melodrama) in Austrian filmmaking that, along with such later commercial successes as Xaver Schwarzenberger's *Donauwalzer*/Danube Waltz (1984) and Axel Corti's *Welcome in Vienna* (1985), are influenced by the mainstream family viewing style of ORF's television films. Despite *Gerber*'s break with the clichés of the interwar "monarchistic Austrian spirit" in favor of a critical view of the petit bourgeoisie as the *Austrian Film News* would declare, Arno Russegger points to the calculation of its coming-of-age/school drama and Glück's aesthetization of historical imagery.[9] The other style, which historian Gottfried Schlemmer calls "das Unreine" (the unclean), influenced by John Cook's *Schwitzkasten*/Sweat Box (1978), Peter Patzak's *Kassbach* (1979), and the films of Franz Novotny, rejects the television influence and finds its fractured narrative inspiration in experimentalism, neorealism and Actionist documentary. By the 1990s, films by Valie Export, Paulus Manker, Wolfgang Murnberger, Christian Berger, Wolfram Paulus and Michael Haneke would display a more mainstreamed version of this avant-gardism, which could co-exist in cinemas with Austrian films that were more "traditional" or influenced (usually co-financed and often bound for ORF broadcast) by the television aesthetic.[10]

Glück's second Torberg feature adaptation, *38: Auch das war Wien*/38: Vienna

Before the Fall (1987), again produced by the Satel-Film and Alamaro-Film companies, became the most successful work of his career and scored a triumph for the
early phase of New Austrian Film. Set in the year of the Anschluss, the film takes
on Austrofascism and Nazism, as seen through the experiences of an "Aryan" actress
(Sunnyi Melles) and her fiancé, a Jewish journalist (Tobias Engel). The doomed
relationship, which is smothered by the not-so-subtle sociopolitical change in Austria in the weeks prior to Hitler's entry, is a valiant attempt at broaching a difficult
subject in an accessible cinematic manner, despite some Austrian critics labeling it
as "anti-fascist kitsch."[11] But national and international audience reception was
positive and the film was nominated for the Best Foreign Language Film Oscar of
1987 and received the Austrian Film Prize. Glück, who was subsequently named
to the Academy of Motion Picture Arts and Sciences' Oscar Selection Committee
(with the encouragement of Austrian-Hollywood legends Billy Wilder and Fred Zinnemann[12]), headed the Film Academy at Vienna's University of Music and Performing Arts (formerly known as the Academy of Music and Performing Arts) until
his retirement in 2003.

The reemergence of another director, one who had settled in Los Angeles in
1969, recalled the Austrian diaspora in Hollywood. Romanian-born Robert Dornhelm (1947–) had directed nearly one hundred documentary projects for ORF
between 1967 and 1976 and had earned (with Earle Mack) an Oscar nomination
for the 1976 ballet documentary narrated by Princess Grace of Monaco, *Children
of Theater Street*. He received no credit for his script work on the planned Dino de
Laurentis biopic entitled *Wallenberg: A Hero's Story*, which was purchased by the
American NBC television network and reworked into a two-part miniseries following the collapse of the original project. Similarly, his unfinished 1980 comedy
Rearranged included Princess Grace in an acting role but was shelved after her death
in 1982. Dornhelm's 1981 docudrama *She Dances Alone* about Vienna-born dancer
Kyra Nijinsky, the daughter of ballet legend Nijinsky, finally brought him to elu-
sive international attention as a promising "new" filmmaker. His *Echo Park* (1985),
produced by the short-lived Sascha-Wien-Film company, a low-budget film relating the intertwined lives in the multicultural and bohemian Echo Park area of Los
Angeles, became an unexpected critical success and cult film in the United States.
The Malibu resident followed this with an Austrian film, *Requiem für Dominic/
Requiem for Dominic* (1990), based on the true story of the innocent Romanian
who was falsely accused of being the "Butcher of Timisoara." Dornhelm balanced
his vacillating reputation as an international director of entertainment films and as
a more esoteric Austrian filmmaker with *A Further Gesture*, an IRA assassination
thriller shot in Ireland and New York (1997), and *Der Unfisch/The Unfish* (1997),
a magic realist tale about a small village, a stuffed whale, and the chaos brought
about by the whale's power to grant wishes. In 1999, Dornhelm created *The Venice
Project*, a postmodern pastiche that is at once an Austrian film and an international
art documentary with a fictional narrative and art direction by architect Frank
Gehry. Shot in the Italian city with Lauren Bacall, Dennis Hopper, Stockard Chan-
ning, Anna Galiena, Linus Roache, Dean Stockwell, Hector Babenco and Parker

Posey, the film's reflection on Italian art from the seventeenth century to the present is framed by a party given by Countess Camilla Volta, who invites three hundred guests to her palazzo on the Grand Canal to celebrate the final art biennale of the millennium.

Peter Patzak, who influenced the cinematic path of the 1970s, emerged during the 1980s as one of Austria's most well-known film directors. Although he has not been able to match the audience challenges and critical successes of his early works, he has become a kind of New Wave Franz Antel, with his prolific product and widely varied styles. His film, *Den Tüchtigen gehört die Welt*/The Upper Crust (1981), an Austrian/U.S. co-production, was followed by a roster of films often using international casts: *Strawanzer* (1983); *Tiger-Frühling in Wien*/Spring in Vienna (1984); the Wagner film *Wahnfried (Richard und Cosima)* (1986); *Lex Minister* (1990); the biopic of the assassin of Archduke Francis Ferdinand and his wife at Sarajevo in 1914, *Gavre Princip-Himmel unter Steinen*/Gavre Princip-Heaven under Stones (1990); *Rochade* (1992); and the Antel-esque sex farce *Es lebe die Liebe, der Pabst und das Puff*/Long Live Love, the Pope and the Bordello (1993). He turned to television features in 1994, with a specific focus on themes of greed and murder. His hostage drama *Gefangen im Jemen*/Captured in Yemen (1999) suggests a return to a more political position.

Niki List (1956–), one of contemporary Austria's most audience-pleasing directors, began his cinematic reign in 1982, following a spate of short films, television and press photography work. He appeared as an actor in Peter Schreiner's experimental documentary *Grelles Licht*/Harsh Light in 1982 and that same year wrote and directed his first feature, *Malaria* (1982), a social satire that explored the customers of the fictional but trendy Viennese "Café Malaria." His re-vision of the traditional Austrian society comedy earned wide critical and popular appreciation and the work received both the German Max Ophüls Prize in 1983 and the Austrian Film Prize in 1984. The continued lack of a professional atmosphere in Austrian film financing, however, was evident with this film, as the difficult process of launching it was ultimately capped by press accusations regarding mismanagement and debt, although the film played well in Austria and abroad.[13] He continued his unique focus on the individual in mass society with a moving documentary about a boy with Down Syndrome in *Mama lustig...?*/Mama happy...? (1984) and its sequel, *Muss denken*/Gotta Think (1992). But it was his 1986 *Müllers Büro*/Mueller's Office that fulfilled the promise of wider popular interest he had garnered with his first film. Despite mixed critical reaction, the film was such a commercial draw that its actors — Christian Schmidt, Andreas Vitasek and Barbara Rudnik — have been associated with their roles ever since. The film established an all-time Second Republic box-office record and received both the Austrian Film Prize and the Golden Ticket Award. This blend of film noir, musical comedy, and parody deals with a seedy detective and his best friend who search for a missing man at the behest of a mysterious woman. The job places them into a maze of increasingly nihilistic intrigues. Although played for camp, the audiences seemed to find List's send-up of the detective and musical genres a refreshing change from the more serious works

Hollywood redux: Niki List's *Müllers Büro*, 1986.

of New Austrian Film. Indeed, the work is almost completely constructed with references to Hollywood Golden Age film and the West German and Austrian pop musicals of the 1950s and 1960s. Filled with Raymond Chandler intertexts and allusions to Michael Curtiz's *Casablanca* (USA 1942) and *To Have and Have Not* (USA 1944), it is also a heavily stylized film that mixes 1980s clothing designs with iconic elements from the 1950s (a Wurlitzer jukebox, petticoats, rubber plants), the 1930s (gangster suits and machine guns), and suggestions of 1920s art deco (its title design). Aimed at the era's youth market, it satisfied the period's Western audience desire for parody (such as the 1980s films by American directors/writers Jim Abrahams and David and Jerry Zucker), self-referential retro-musicals (*Grease*, USA 1978), and vulgar provocation and eroticism (the American *Porky* series). Ultimately, film historian Isabella Reicher mourns the success of this film, which she believes is little more than a collection of recycled stylistic elements and an attempt to adapt the worst of trendy international commerciality for Austria. Although one might certainly consider the film to be a hollow stylistic pastiche worthy of Frederic Jameson's theoretical postmodern nostalgia film of the 1980s, it is not an example of post-classic cinema, which is defined by new genre, technical, production and marketing structures. *Müllers Büro* hardly distanced itself from classic cinema, merely overloaded its codes and added some experimental cinematographic elements. Its marketing style also borrows from standard post–1960s Anglo-American practice, with end credit nods to various consumer product firms.[14] List has been more critically and less popularly successful with *Sternberg-Shooting Star* (1988), the morbid black comedy *Ach, Boris*/Oh, Boris (1990), and *Der Schatten des Schreibers*/The Shadow of the Writer (1995). But his early hits have given him a level of audience identification akin to the fan base that directors had prior to the 1960s, and it seems that when his name is brought up, filmgoers easily dismiss the more recent work and inevitably recall *Müllers Büro*. He has also continued to develop his nostalgic film style with some virtuosity: his 1998 *Helden in Tirol*/Heroes in the Tyrol proved to be a very original parody of the *Heimatfilm*, while *Nick Knatterton* (2000), the German co-production he directed with Marcus O. Rosenmüller, unabashedly borrows from Mike Myers's *Austin Powers: International Man of Mystery* (USA 1997) by reawakening the legendary 1950s German detective from his deep freeze to battle super villain Virginia Peng.

The growing sensibilities and appreciation of New Austrian Film, as well as the increasing possibilities of funding, made the early to mid–1980s an unusually fertile period that offered significant first features from new or returning directors. Mansur Mahdavi (a.k.a. Madavi) began his career with obscure psychodramas in the 1970s and developed the genre into the 1980s. In 1999, he wrote, directed, shot, edited and produced the Spanish-language film *With Closed Eyes*. Tone Fink, who had co-written and co-directed *Johnny unser*/Our Johnny with Robert Polak in 1980, directed his own scripts, *Narrohut* in 1982 and *Katijubato* in 1986. Walter Bannert returned in 1982 as the socially critical director of *Die Erben*/The Inheritors, the internationally acclaimed film about two sixteen-year-old boys who are caught up in neo–Nazism, and *Herzklopfen*/Heartbeats in 1984. *Alpensaga* creator Dieter Berner, who had made a splash with his second film *Der richtige Mann*/The Right Man in 1981, which reexamined the often-told parable of a lonely old man who refuses to give up his apartment. Leopold Huber's first feature *Hirnbrennen*/Brainstorm (1982) evoked elements of the Austrian *Heimatfilm* genre in its critical look at the problematic and ritualistic life of a farm town. Similarly, Ernst Josef Lauscher wrote and directed *Zeitgenossen*/Contemporaries for Wega-Film in 1983, created two television movies, but waited nearly a decade for his next feature, *Das tätowierte Herz*/The Tattooed Heart (1991). He returned to the small screen with a social comedy that pushes the conventional misalliance theme to the blatant extreme: *Ich liebe eine Hure*/I'm in Love with a Whore (1999).

Vienna-born Lukas Stepanik (1950–) directed his first feature, *Kieselsteine*/Pebbles, for Arabella-Film in 1982. A late entry to the subgenre of European films on the theme of relationships between former Nazi victims and "Aryans," which has ranged from the early Marxist considerations of *Die Mörder sind unter uns*/The Murderers Are Among Us (Germany 1946) to Liliana Cavani's still controversial *Il Portiere di notte*/The Night Porter (Italy 1974), Stepanik's film deals with a Jewish woman and a gentile man whose relationship is doomed by the memories of the past. Largely a television feature director, he returned to the big screen in 1988 with *Unter Freunden*/Among Friends and in 1999 with *Professor Niedlich*, a rare children's film. Andreas Gruber directed *Drinnen und Draußen*/Inside and Out in 1983 and followed this in 1994 with *Hasenjagd*/Rabbit Hunt, an Austrian/German/Luxembourg co-production. Alfred Ninaus, who directed *Seifenblasen*/Soap Bubbles in 1984, also returned in the 1990s with two very different films: *Der Bienenkönig*/The King Bee (1990), a children's ecological detective film, and *Abenteuer eines Traumes*/ Adventure of a Dream (1996), a documentary about twenty-year-old Valentin Nita and his flight from Romania to Austria after Ceausescu's fall. The film follows Nita's problematic education and social integration in Austria. Milan Dor, the son of Hungarian writer Milo Dor, entered Austrian film with *Malambo* in 1984. The feature, which follows a boy's fascination with legendary escape artist Houdini, may have been forgettable, but its new production company, Dor-Film, developed into a major force in bringing Austrian film to the international screens in the mid–1990s. Andreas Riedler (1962–), born in Innsbruck and trained at the UCLA film school, made several shorts and a documentary before his feature film debut with *Früstück zu dritt*/Breakfast for Three in 1988. He returned in the 1990s with *Die neue Generation*/The New Generation (1998), a drama of interrelated stories of heterosexual nightlife and the spread of HIV taking place in Vienna on World AIDS Day in 1996.

One of the few filmmakers from the experimental scene of the 1960s still active in the 1980s and 1990s was Michael Pilz (1943–). He first reemerged in 1982 with the three-year project *Himmel und Erde*/Heaven and Earth (1979–82), a five-hour, two-part documentary about the lives of the remote mountain villagers of Sankt Anna in Austria's Styria province. Pilz defines his film as "capturing the light of things and breaking it by projection onto the screen." Influenced by Jean-Luc Godard's distancing effects as well as by Austrian impressionism, Pilz divides his collection of images in *Himmel und Erde* with statements on his philosophy of being and cinema: "the only thing we can describe are external representations. The external may change, the actual being remains."[15] His lengthy assemblage of life in the town of Sankt Anna is intended to allow time to evolve the subjects naturally and give the audience a glimpse into the complexities of the transitory nature of things. In 1996 he released *Was übersetzt ist noch nicht angekommen*/Streetwise, an experimental documentary about the misadventures of a tour of New York in a taxi.

This period also brought a relatively significant number of women into film direction, eventually giving New Austrian Film a reputation for being one of the most female-driven cinemas in Europe. Greek-born director Penelope Georgiou began her self-produced run with *Petunia* in 1981, which she wrote and directed and performed in along with performance artist and feminist filmmaker Valie Export. She also wrote, directed, starred in and produced *Tonis+Eleni* (1983), *Apostolis* (1986) and *Hans* (1991). Journalist Heide Pils (1939–), a television documentary and feature director since the late 1970s, offered *Lieber reich und glücklich*/It's Better to Be Rich and Happy (1996). Kitty Kino's (Kitty Gschöpf, 1948–) first feature film, a comedy about a woman infiltrating the male world of billiards called *Karambolage*/Collision (1983), generated controversy for its feminist aspects. Kino has continued to direct sporadically, with *Die Nachtmeerfahrt*/The Night Sea Journey (1986), and a specifically Austrian take on the self-important young upper-class milieu so dear to American filmmaker Whit Stillman in, *Wahre Liebe*/True Love (1990), which Jack Kindred called "a stylish comic investigation of sexual confusion among smart-set yuppies in Vienna."[16] It was produced by one of the most active new companies, Wega-Film, led by Veit Heidruschka, who was responsible for Niki List's emergence. Kino moved into the mainstream as a television series director and in 1996 directed the television feature *Das Geständnis*/The Confession, about a retired doctor who is confronted by his own past when he witnesses an attack by right-wing extremists. Wega-Film's rival, the more mainstream-oriented company Satel-Film, produced the first feature by Susanne Zanke, *Die Skorpionfrau*/The Scorpion Woman in 1989. Here, a middle-aged female judge has an affair with a young law student, which destroys her relationship with her partner and her son and influences her work during a trial of a woman accused of seducing and abusing a fifteen-year-old boy. Zanke followed this with television features shot in Germany and Austria, which continue her focus on the difficult lives of women, such as *Ein Schloss für Rita*/A Castle for Rita (1997), an update of the late 1940s and 1950s female innkeeper films, about a woman competing with big business in the hopes of converting an abandoned castle into a day-care center; and *Vergewaltigt— das Ende einer Liebe*/Raped — The End of a Love (1998), which deals with rape within marriage. Käthe Kratz offered her first film in 1976, but it was the television specials on women's lives entitled *Lebenslinien*/Lifelines (1983–86), which she wrote and directed, that brought her to the fore. A cinema film written by sociocritical Austrian "folk" playwright Peter Turrini was next, *Atemnot*/Breathing Need (1984), followed by *Marlene— Der amerikanischer Traum*/Marlene — The American Dream in 1987 and *Das zehnte Jahr*/The Tenth Year in 1995, which attempted a revision of the woman's picture genre. Maria Knilli (1959–), born in Graz and educated at the Munich Film School, has been a writer and a film editor since 1980. Beginning as a cinema feature director with *Lieber Karl*/Dear Karl in 1984, she has maintained her socially critical stance as a television feature director and documentarian in the 1990s. Vienna-born Maria W. Arlamovsky (1965–), a former short filmmaker, made her feature directing debut in 1996 with *Seltsame Unruhe*/Restless Solitude, which looks at an alienated group of young people who avoid integration into mainstream society.

The creator of *Toilette* (1979), the confrontational video of female physical self-exploration, Friederike Petzold (1945–), offered more artistic experimentation in 1980 with her *Radio Free Utopia*, a completely private broadcast station installed at Vienna's Museum of Modern Art. In 1983, she returned to the motion picture medium with a film she wrote, directed and appears in, and which was lensed by Elfi Mikesch, *Canale Grande*/Grand Canal. Rather than couch her feminist visions in audience-pleasing co-productions with ORF, Petzold remained provocative and produced her next films under the blatant banner of her own No Budget-Filmproduktion company. *Eines Tages*/One Day (1986) was written, directed, and shot (with Thomas Meissner) by Petzold, who also appears in the film along with Marianne Sägebrecht, known for her role as the abandoned German wife in Percy Adlon's *Bagdad Cafe* (West Germany/USA 1988). Petzold's next film, *Das geheime*

Labyrinth des Horrors/The Secret Labyrinth of Horror (a.k.a. *Allein gegen die Würs-tel*/Alone against the Sausages) (1989), was also written, directed, and shot by Pet-zold and features avant-garde actors Mimi Mimosa and Toni Tortura. Maria Lassnig (1919–), a professor of painting at Vienna's College of Applied Art and the founder of Austria's school for film animation, and Sofia-born painter and performance artist Mara Mattuschka (1951–), a former student of Lassnig, have created notable experimental films, such as Lassnig's *Maria Lassnig Kantate*/Maria Lassnig Cantata (1992) and Mattuschka's short experimental films *Kuglknopf*/Bullet Button (1985), *Parasympatica* (1986), *Pascal-Gödel* (1986), *Kaiserschnitt*/Cesarean Section (1987), *Die vollkommene Bedeutungslosigkeit der Frau für die Musikgeschichte*/The Utter Insignificance of Women in the History of Music (1987), the animated feature *Der Einzug des Rokoko ins Inselreich der Huzzis*/The Advent of Rococo on the Island of the Huzzis (1989), the experimental live action/animation film *Loading Ludwig* (1989), *S.O.S. Extra Terrestria* (1993), and a decidedly non–Disney version of *Beauty and the Beast* (1993). Most of these films feature Mattuschka as her "star" alter ego Mimi Minus. A former student of mathematics, ethnology and linguistics, Mat-tuschka borrows aspects from Viennese Actionism in her portrayals of ritualistic abuse of the body, from abstract painters such as Francis Bacon, from Andy Warhol's parodic underground "star" creations, and from the often morbid animation tradi-tion of Eastern Europe.

Ruth Beckermann (1952–) began her impressive documentary run in 1983 with *Wien retour*/Vienna Return, which she co-directed with Josef Aichholzer. The film approaches the First Republic, Austrofascism, and Nazism through the recol-lections of Communist and Jewish writer and historian Franz West. Her own Jew-ish identity is explored in *Die papierene Brücke*/The Paper Bridge (1987) as Beckermann, the daughter of an Austro-Hungarian Jewish family, journeys to Czer-nowitz in Bukovina (now in Ukraine) to trace her father's idealized recollections of his life there. Beckermann's reasons for the documentary are both personal and theoretical: "What I had in mind was not only to trace the few clues to my family history but also to find out how the proven and the narrated historical narrative strands would blend in with my own experiences and emotions."[17] *Nach Jerusalem*/Towards Jerusalem (1990), a mosaic of diverse landscapes and ethnic images that examines "what happened to the dream of a Jewish homeland,"[18] completes her tril-ogy on Jewish identity. Conflating memory and representation, Beckermann often explores commonplace locations that do not in themselves display a past in order to re-imprint them with both personal and historical events. Reassigning the past onto the present, *Jenseits des Krieges*/East of War (1996) uncovers atrocities com-mitted by the German Wehrmacht or army (previously attributed only to the SS) on the eastern front. In an even more prismatic vision of her own journey as woman and artist, *Ein flüchtiger Zug nach dem Orient*/A Fast Train to the Orient (1999) attempts to take space out of time to free it for memory. Fascinated by the jour-neys and significant writing talents of Empress Elisabeth and her iconization as "Sissi" in Austrian popular culture and film, Beckermann suggests an unseen Elis-abeth on a train, fleeing the constraints of the Vienna court as she so often did.

Contemporary images of Cairo are accompanied by voiceover readings from her diaries. While giving the audience a unique example of the female flaneur, the juxtaposition of the past and the present in this way dispels the romanticized clichés surrounding the images of Elisabeth and Egypt and questions the continued nature of repression by undermining the twentieth century with the nineteenth century, and vice versa.[19] In a similar vein, Elizabeth T. Spira (1942–), who was born in Glasgow of Austrian Jewish parents escaping the Anschluss, is a director of television documentaries and reports on "absolutely normal people" in order to catch "a — sometimes unwanted — glimpse of the Austrian soul."[20] Andrea Wessely (1962–) is another television-based filmmaker who explores news and human-interest stories with an artistic twist. Associated with ORF since 1980, she has also concentrated on national and international celebrity portraits. Margareta Heinrich (1951–94) directed an impressive documentary on the sociopolitical turmoil in Nicaragua: *Der Traum des Sandino*/Sandino's Dream (1981). She moved to television features with a treatment of *Ihr glücklichen Augen*/Oh, Happy Eyes (1992), a short story by protofeminist Austrian author Ingeborg Bachmann (1926–70), wherein a woman's myopia becomes symbolic for her shortsightedness in love and life. But the most impressive filming of Bachmann to date is of her most well-known novel, *Malina*, about a woman struggling for her identity between two distinct male love interests. Directed by the German-born Werner Schroeter (1945–) this 1991 Austrian/German co-production was scripted by Elfriede Jelinek, shot by Elfi Mikesch, and features an international cast including Isabelle Huppert. *Malina* was voted best film at the German Film Awards and the Bavarian Film Prizes in 1991.

Karin Brandauer and Valie Export represent the opposite directions of female focus and style in film during this period. Karin Brandauer (1946–92), the wife of stage and screen actor Klaus Maria Brandauer, began her career on television with documentaries and literary adaptations. She remained a television director for the most part, contributing greatly to the reputation of ORF productions, and her dramas were often screened as theatrical features abroad. Her telepics on Arthur Schnitzler, *Der Weg ins Freie*/The Way Outside (1982), and on Peter Rosegger, *Erdsegen*/Earth Blessings (1986), brought wide attention to her elegant style and her adaptation of *Heimatfilm* form and style. Her docudrama about a village suffering through a mining strike in 1930, *Einstweilen wird es Mittag oder, Die Arbeitslosen von Marienthal*/Meanwhile It Is Noon or, The Unemployed of Marienthal (1988), was praised for its sensitive study of the effects of rural unemployment. Brandauer was one of the few contemporary filmmakers who offered intellectually and emotionally satisfying period pieces, meticulous in historical detail, such as her work on Tyrolean playwright Felix Mitterer in *Verkaufte Heimat*/Bartered Homeland (1989), which observes "the role of women in traditional communities confronted with industrialization and social change."[21] She completed two episodes of what became a four-part miniseries about the 1939 referendum on Austria's truncated South Tyrol province[22] and its lingering postwar effects (*Brennende Lieb'*/Burning Love and *Leb' wohl du mein Südtirol*/Farewell, My South Tyrol). After her death, stage, opera and television director Gernot Friedel (1941–) directed the postwar episodes of this miniseries (*Feuernacht*/Fire Night and *Komplott*/Plot) in 1994, which centered on the movement for South Tyrolean autonomy within Italy and the irredentist movement of the early 1960s in which South Tyrolean activists dynamited power pylons to protest Italian rule. *Sidonie* (1990), Brandauer's treatment of the novel by Erich Hackl, focused on the plight of a gypsy girl who is taken from her "Aryan" foster parents by the Nazi regime and placed into a concentration camp.

Following Valie Export's provocative performance art and experimental shorts of the 1960s, she had scored critical appreciation with her first feature, *Unsichtbare Gegner*/Invisible Adversaries (1978), the "feminist science fiction" film about female identity, now considered one of the few important films of that decade. In a loosely structured tribute to Hollywood's alien invasion films of the 1950s, Anna, a photographer and video artist, comes to the shocking conclusion that her alienation from an icy and technocratic lover, Peter, who "mistrusts humanistic discourse" and from male-dominated society as a whole is the result of a body-snatching invasion of aliens from the planet Hyksos. She considers everything from simple squabbles to major wars as examples of the alien aggression, and the rejection of her reasoning by both her lover and a psychiatrist only increases her panic, as it underscores the monolithic and oppressive power of "male definitions of objective reality." The unyielding male codes of communication silence Anna, and she subsequently retreats to the creation of photographs, videos and sound tapes that record her anxieties, frustrations, and longings. Her evidence on the invasion from Hyksos is resisted or dismissed by the surface values set by the men in her life and in society. "The real and the image of the real, blurs as their relationships shift, split and converge," notes Export, who also critiques "the interaction of technologies and gender."[23] With a similar theme, even character constellation, her political thriller frame *Die Praxis der Liebe*/The Practice of Love (1985) helped Export find breakthrough reception outside Austria. Managing to win over mainstream audience desire for suspense entertainment without compromising her ideology and style, particularly regarding the visual exploration of the female body, Export's *Praxis* takes on the professional and personal "glass ceilings" of a female television reporter. Caught in faltering relationships with an emotionally unstable psychiatrist and a suspected arms dealer, Export's female archetype (Adelheid Arndt) comes to realize the undemocratic aspects of the press and the government as well as her repression as a woman in society and vis-à-vis her sexual relationships.

Measured international co-production began to transcend the negative film-by-committee image it had earned in the 1960s and became a viable if limited alternative to ORF partnership by the mid–1980s. This time around films were directorially driven, such as Swiss director Luc Bondy's 1987 version of Arthur Schnitzler's *Das weite Land*/The Far Land, and Peter Ily Huemer's Austrian/American film, *Kiss Daddy Good Night*, with Uma Thurman, but once again, the potential of building on two historically interrelated national cinemas was not realized. With New Austrian Film's interest in referencing classic cinema and exposing the repressive constructs of dystopic society, the "Krimi," or criminal thriller, a rare genre in Austrian cinema, has been approached by directors Michael Schottenberg in *Caracas* (1989) and Max Linder in *Stille Wasser*/Still Waters (1996), both attempting to bring the popularity of television detective shows like Peter Patzak's *Kottan ermittelt*/Kottan Investigates to the large screen. Thomas Roth (1965–) has made documentary and television films since 1992 but has gained a reputation as a Hitchcock-style director with such mainstream television and cinema dramas as the Cinemascope *Kaliber Deluxe*/Calibre Deluxe (1999) and *Der Millenniumsmörder*/The Millennium Murderer (1999).

Documentary and docudrama remained the strongest representations of Austrian cinema outside the country during the 1980s. Albert Quendler's *Erinnerungen*/Remembrances of OK (1986) was regarded as a "truly great and fascinating commemorative film about [the artist] Oskar Kokoschka"[24] and won first prize at the Premiere Biennale Internationale du Film sur l'Art in 1987. Wolfgang Lesowsky, who had directed in the 1970s, offered the kind of musical docudrama/fantasia Austrian cinema had always done so well with and which became associated with British cinema since the late 1970s, mainly through the work of director Ken Russell. Lesowsky's *Sterben werd' ich, um zu leben — Gustav Mahler*/I Will Die to Live — Gustav Mahler (1987) signaled the return of the high art biopic that had long been abandoned by filmmakers but with a new sensibility and frankness that made them iconoclastic. Also notable is the first attempt to explore a controversial chapter in Austrian cinema history with Robert Quitta's *Die Stadt ohne Juden*/The City without Jews (1987), a documentary feature on Hugo Bettauer's novel, and H. K. Breslauer's 1924 film. Michael Kreihsl's film of Mozart's opera *Idomeneo* (1989) was screened at the Berlinale in 1990. It was a well-received throwback to the quality opera films Austria had produced with regularity throughout the 1950s. Tyrolean-born Theodor Eisner (1956–) continued the cultural documentary form with several short films such as *Eine Reise zu Verdi*/A Journey to Verdi (1995), *Conours Geza Anda* (1997), and feature-length films on both conductor Franz Welser-Möst (1997) and composer Benjamin Britten's *War Requiem — Ein Filmepos*/War Requiem — A Film Epic (1998).

As Austrian film both past and present slowly found its way back into the consciousness of the country's audiences and onto the screens of a few film festivals, its international icons had dwindled since the end of Hollywood's studio system. While the Austrian film industry languished in the 1960s and 1970s, Austrian-born actors Oskar Werner, Romy Schneider, Senta Berger, Kurt Kasznar, Paul Henreid, Oskar Homolka, Vanessa Brown, Leon Askin, and Austrian-by-choice Curd Jürgens continued to populate American cinema and television as well as international co-productions. Even director/producer Otto Preminger reinvented himself as a minor pop icon by appearing in film cameos and as "Mr. Freeze," a villain on the late 1960s American *Batman* television series, later impersonated by fellow Austrian Arnold Schwarzenegger in the film *Batman and Robin* (USA 1997). By the 1980s, however, most of the Austrians from Hollywood's Golden Age had retired from film or had died, and the generation of the 1960s had returned to more serious theater and television work in Europe. Austria seemed to be represented in English-language film solely by classically trained actor and theater director Klaus Maria

Brandauer (1943–). While attaining stardom for his critically praised performances as tormented, power-hungry victims in Hungarian director István Szabó's trilogy on Central European fascism —*Mephisto* (Hungary/West Germany 1981), *Colonel Redl* (Hungary/Austria/West Germany 1985) and *Hanussen* (Hungary/Austria/West Germany 1988)— he also appeared in several important international productions: the non-series James Bond film *Never Say Never Again* (USA/GB 1983), where he is the nemesis to Sean Connery's last performance as 007; *Out of Africa* (USA 1985) opposite Meryl Streep, for which he received an Academy Award nomination for Best Actor in a Supporting Role; with Faye Dunaway in *Burning Secret* (GB/West Germany 1988), a film based on Austrian author Stefan Zweig's novel; and again with Sean Connery in *Russia House* (USA 1990). He reemerged briefly for American audiences in the cable television film *Introducing Dorothy Dandridge* (1999), where he interpreted the late Otto Preminger's professional and romantic relationship with the African-American Hollywood star of the 1950s. With Brandauer favoring more satisfying work as actor and director in European film and theater, the mantle of vaguely representing Austria in English-language film fell to Arnold Schwarzenegger (1947–). A former bodybuilder, his successes in big-budget American action/adventure films, marriage into the Kennedy dynasty, and stint as restaurateur and physical fitness guru has made him a wealthy popular culture icon on the scale of a Golden Age superstar. Ironically, comic imitation of his specific Austrian accent and of his physical superstructure, which some cultural analysts consider a signifier of postmodernity, has also made his international audiences more aware of a contemporary Austria. Although Schwarzenegger has been honored by Austria for promotion of his homeland, he has also distanced himself from it in the world press, particularly in the service of his American social and political ambitions, which resulted in his election as California governor in a controversial recall campaign of 2003. But despite his pop-icon image as an "Austrian" superstar, he has no actual relationship with Austrian cinema.

While there is no immediately visible caesura in Austrian cinema during and following the collapse of communism in Eastern Europe between 1989 and 1991, as multiculturalism or the refugee experience had always been aspects of New Austrian Film (along with xenophobia, spousal and family abuse, class conflict, social alienation and sexual/gender-role topics), the start of the 1990s did mark wider interest in this national cinema outside the country and the German-speaking world. A new sense of tradition had been created in the past two decades of poverty/auteur filmmaking, as Austrian filmmakers had made do and had done well with what there was. A growing presence at international film festivals and international critical interest in the work of these new filmmakers had also helped to dispel the debacle of the 1960s and the resulting notion that Austria had no cinema culture. Even without the knowledge of Austria's long and influential film tradition, emerging talents would overturn this perception.

Like Karin Brandauer, Axel Corti's career as an internationally recognized Austrian filmmaker was cut short by early death. The Paris-born director originally worked in Austrian radio and theater before moving to television in the 1960s. Like

Brandauer, Corti favored period pieces and literary adaptations and was influenced by Willi Forst's Viennese Film style and the social dramas of the 1930s. But unlike the rural focus of Brandauer, Corti tended toward urban themes. As the last director to work with Hans Moser in the film based on Fritz von Herzmanovsky-Orlando's play *Kaiser Joseph und die Bahnwärterstochter*/Emperor Joseph and the Signalman's Daughter, 1963), his connection with the Austrian cinema's heyday made him the New Wave incarnation of the pre–1960s Austrian film mogul for many. This was due to the very Austrian subject matter of his films, his attention to production values, which gives his work an elegant studiolike quality, and the international commerciality of his films. His talent paid off with a critical enthusiasm and popular reputation that was almost unknown for Austrian filmmakers of his time. He seemed to be at the very core of Austrian socioculture for a period, since in addition to his well-known films he was also the host of a weekly radio program that examined topical issues. Most of his television films for ORF were released theatrically abroad, such as *Herrenjahre*/Master Years (1983), based on Gernot Wolfgruber's existential novel about the bleak world of a young carpenter, and *Eine blaßblaue Frauenschrift*/A Pale Blue Woman's Handwriting (1994), based on the short story by Franz Werfel, examining the private impact of Nazism through the love affair between a conflict-avoiding Austrian civil servant and a young Jewish woman. But it was his trilogy *Wohin und Zurück*/Where To and Back (1982–85) for ORF, which follows a Jewish emigrant who escapes the Anschluss, finds an incongruent life in New York, and returns to Austria in 1945 as a U.S. soldier, that brought Corti brief global acclaim. His notability also managed to put Austria back into popular international cinematic discourse for a short time, as different segments of *Wohin und Zurück* were screened in European theaters and on various American public television network affiliates. All three films are masterworks of character study and tragicomedy, dealing with recent historical themes usually avoided by the Austrian popular media. As Wolfgang Glück would discover with his 1986 film *38*, this taboo period seems to provide untapped Austrian subject matter that attracts not only national audiences but also international fascination. The final entry in the trilogy *Welcome in Vienna* (1986), written by Georg Stefan Troller from his own experiences, garnered the greatest attention as a theatrical release. Concluding the saga of Freddy Wolff, as portrayed by Gabriel Barylli, Corti offers a mosaic of impressions and occurrences, which evoke a sense of both detachment and belonging as Wolff deals with the American lack of comprehension regarding his plight and Austria's socioculture. He is confronted by the broken lives of a surviving concentration camp inmate and a former guard, a disillusioned Communist, an ambivalent young actress (inspired by Alida Valli's character in *The Third Man*) and others who try to reconnect with old identities or adapt to the devastation of the new. Wolff discovers that the denazification process is a pragmatic illusion, adjusted to satisfy immediate U.S. occupation designs, and the American respect for his cultural identity is only tolerated because he is in an American uniform. Ultimately, Wolff realizes that although he can no longer be an Austrian, he is not comfortable as an American. Having decided to return to the United States, he abruptly jumps out of the truck that leaves the city in the final shot of the film. Georg Stefan Troller recalls that upon his return to Germany as an American officer he never considered thoughts of revenge, not even at Dachau where he felt "monstrous surprise." His *Heimat* no longer existed for him; Germany had been changed more by the Hitler years then he had been by his own emigration.[25] Evoking aspects of the Austrian identity crisis in the twentieth century, the film also presents a pessimistic commentary on the formation of the early Second Republic and its avoidance of the Nazi past.[26]

Possibly because of the impressive response to *Welcome in Vienna*, Corti's next work was an overproduced semiblockbuster, which was destined to fail because it gave the audiences, who had come to know Corti only through his single attempt at neorealism, nothing recognizable. But Corti actually preferred period drama to the style and topic of *Welcome in Vienna*. *The King's Whore*, a seventeenth-century melodrama penned by American scriptwriter Frederic Raphael (*Darling*, 1965; *Two for the Road*, 1967; *Eyes Wide Shut*, 1999) was an Austrian/French/Italian/British co-production made specifically for international cinema release. It displays the bombast of the lavish but unremarkable transnational costume epics that killed off the genre in Austrian cinema in the 1960s and subsequently flopped at the box office. Corti's final project, however, which was completed after his death by the cinematographer Gernot Roll, marked a return to solid ORF production and Austrian subject matter with a three-part miniseries that was shown in theaters abroad. *Der Radetzkymarsch*/The Radetzky March (1993) was based on Joseph Roth's novel about the collapse of the Austro-Hungarian empire as seen through two generations of an aristocratic family. Roth's novel is considered one of the masterworks of the imperial demise/World War I genre of interwar Austrian literature, and Corti's impeccably detailed production, with Max von Sydow, Charlotte Rampling, and Tilman Günther remained true to Roth's visions and the poignancy of the saga. Unlike the misfire of *The King's Whore*, this film expertly blended the visual pleasure of the 1950s imperial epic with the author's historical criticism and the human tragedy that so pervades *Welcome in Vienna*. Had he lived, it is probable that Corti might have launched a revitalization of the historical drama in Austrian cinema, analogous to the critical nostalgia of Britain's Merchant-Ivory productions.

Radetzkymarsch was produced by Satel-Film and headed by Michael von Wolkenstein, one of the more traditional movers and shakers of Austria's reborn film industry, who packages international co-productions with solid Austrian content or setting. He has excelled with period films and literary adaptations, among them Wolfgang Glück's *38*; Maximilian Schell's *Geschichten aus dem Wienerwald*/Tales from the Vienna Woods; the adaptation of another Joseph Roth novel, *Hotel Savoy* (1995); *Opernball*/Opera Ball (1998), Josef Haslinger's popular novel about a neo–Nazi terrorist gassing of Vienna's opera ball and its subsequent effects on democracy in Austria; and the Thomas Mann novella *Mario und der Zauberer*/Mario and the Magician (1994), which marked actor Klaus Maria Brandauer's segue into film direction. Brandauer appears in his film as a famous but ugly magician who humiliates a working-class Italian boy during a performance and suffers his revenge. Mann had written this parable about fascism in Italy, the apathy of the upper classes, and the resistance qualities of the working class as a warning to pre–Hitler Germany. The film captures both the atmosphere of the period and the universality of the story. Less popular, though equally impressive, was the first directorial turn by actor Helmut Berger (1949–), not to be confused with the more prominent Austrian-born actor of the same name (1944–), who rose to international stardom as Italian director Luchino Visconti's protégé in such films as *The Damned* (Italy/West Germany 1970), *Ludwig* (Italy/West Germany 1972) and *Conversation Piece* (Italy 1974), and in De Sica's *Garden of the Finzi-Continis* (Italy 1970). Berger directed, co-wrote and appears in the black comedy *Nie im Leben*/Never in Life (1991), which was honored with the Max Ophüls Award, but he has found no lasting career as a film director and has subsequently returned to television acting and directing.

Having been the favorite cinematographer to the most recognizable master of New German Cinema, Rainer Werner Fassbinder (1945–82), as well as to Axel Corti, may have given Vienna-born Xaver Schwarzenberger (1946–) an impressive artistic genealogy, but his camerawork for four episodes of ORF's *Alpensaga* series (1976–80) earned him his own creative status. Noted for his tribute to the lighting and camera style of the wartime UFA productions in Fassbinder's *Lili Marleen* (West Germany 1980), of Austrian-Hollywood director Josef von Sternberg in Fassbinder's miniseries *Berlin Alexanderplatz* (West Germany 1980), and the Hollywood women's picture in Fassbinder's *Lola* (West Germany 1981), Schwarzenberger's relationship with Austrian cinema began with his camera work for Wolfgang Glück's *Der Schüler Gerber*/The Student Gerber in 1981. His debut as a director came with *Der stille Ozean*/The Quiet Ocean (1983), based on the novel by Gerhard Roth. The film explores the existentialist crisis of a traumatized physician who retreats to a small town after having caused a death and was remarkable for its disturbing mise-en-scène, its unusual camera movement, and its stark black-and-white photography. But it was Schwarzenberger's next film that brought him swift recognition as a mainstream director. *Donauwalzer*/Danube Waltz (1984), written by Ulli Schwarzenberger, showcases Christiane Hörbiger (1938–), one of the three actor daughters of Attila Hörbiger and Paula Wessely, in Axel Corti's complex story about relationships that are made and broken by the Iron Curtain: an Austrian woman, Judith (Hörbiger) and her Hungarian lover Taddek plan to escape Hungary during the uprising in 1956 with the help of an Austrian press photographer. Judith escapes but Taddek is left behind and disappears. Fifteen years later, Taddek appears in Vienna. Judith has long since married the photographer but Taddek reminds her of their lost relationship and their promises. Once again, Schwarzenberger references historic cinema with this bittersweet romantic saga intended as a tribute to director Willi Forst. Thomas Kuchenbuch believes it to be a pastiche of genres, overloaded with elements from the *Vergangenheitsbewältigung* film, the *Heimatfilm*, the socially critical film, the Hollywood woman's picture, and the feminist emancipation film. There are also suggestions of a visual style reminiscent of the early films of Pabst and Wiene, as well as from Italian neorealism. Additionally, the film has an anecdotal narrative structure recalling Schlöndorff's *Die Blechtrommel*/The Tin Drum (West Germany/France 1978), quotes from Fred Zinnemann's *From Here to Eternity* (USA 1953) and has similarities to Richard Brooks's *Cat on a Hot Tin Roof* (USA 1958), particularly in the framing and blocking of Christiane Hörbiger.[27] The film can also be read as an allegory on Austria's distanced relationship with its former imperial partner, Hungary, in the way Fassbinder's *Die Ehe der Maria Braun*/The Marriage of Maria Braun (West Germany 1979) suggests the history of a divided Germany and the dangerous projections of reunification.

The films *Gewitter im Mai*/Storm in May (1987) and *Souterrain* (1989) followed *Donauwalzer* with somewhat less critical and popular interest, but in 1993, Schwarzenberger's unique retro-referenced style and quirky storytelling came together again in another success, *Tafelspitz*/Boiled Beef, a contemporary version of the 1949 Paul Hörbiger/Hans Moser vehicle *Hofrat Geiger*, which moves the story beyond Vienna to New York and seasons it with the irony Schwarzenberger showed in *Donauwalzer*. Gabriel Barylli, Corti's discovery and Schwarzenberger's star, also moved behind the camera in the 1990s, directing several theatrical features on the theme of self-realization brought about by love.

By the 1990s, the notion of a multicultural Austrian cinema became a much wider concept than that of Central European identity and culture. One of the significant Austrian filmmakers of the final decade of the twentieth century is Tehran-born Houchang Allahyari (1941–), an Iranian who studied psychiatry and neurology in Austria for many years until he turned, self-taught, to filmmaking. His work focuses on the experiences of the social outsider, which the director can no doubt relate to as a foreigner in Austria and as a behavioral scientist. Of note are his debut films *Pasolini inszeniert seinen Tod*/Pasolini Directs His Death (1985) and *Borderline-Schuldig?*/Borderline-Guilty? (1988), the latter being the story of a young pianist accused of murdering his teacher and who slowly comes to believe the accusation due to guilt feelings, ultimately retreating into a fantasy world. Allahyari was praised for his promise in a backhanded swipe against the still financially struggling Austrian film industry by the *International Film Guide*, which noted his "incredible sensitivity" and "admirable ability": "If international cinema gave him the chance to prove himself in a large production with proficient colleagues at his side, a new talent might be born."[28] In 1991, he attempted comedy with *I Love Vienna*, which features a mostly Iranian cast and the final screen appearance of Austrian star Marisa Mell. In an unusually optimistic film for the director, it looks at the xenophobia brought on by increased Eastern European and Middle Eastern emigration during the 1990s as seen through the eyes of an Iranian teacher of German who, fearing the political situation in Iran, attempts to move his family to Vienna. *Höhenangst*/Fear of Heights, from 1994, includes veteran Hollywood character actor Leon Askin, who returned to Austria in the 1990s, in the story of one man's urban alienation and subsequent repression in a village community where he flees for safety and freedom. After several television films, Allahyari moved again to the large screen with *Black Flamingos* in 1998, which takes on the very Austrian sociocultural notion of *Schein und Sein* (image and reality) and recalls the darkly surreal dystopia found in the films of American director David Lynch: a reporter writing a story about the deceased mayor of a small Austrian village who discovers that nothing in the mayor's biography adds up and that the ideal of small-town life is a façade that hides grotesque truths. *Geboren in Absurdistan*/Born in Absurdistan (1999) returned Allahyari to his culture-clash focus in a film about the accidental mix-up of an Austrian baby and a Turkish baby in a Vienna hospital, and the subsequent journey of the Austrian parents to a small Turkish town to correct the error. Racism is explored from an almost taboo emotional aspect in this anxiety-ridden "dramedy."

Examining alienation and relationships from inside rather than from Allahyari's "outside" is the central characteristic of Wolfram Paulus's (1947–) work. Paulus is another director who began in the late 1980s and picked up momentum in the 1990s. He has brought a new cinematic image to his native Salzburg and its surroundings, which had become the cliché in the trivial *Heimatfilm* variants of pre-1970s Austrian cinema. His mountain story *Heidenlöcher*/The Gorge (1986) is an example of Andre Bazin's theory of reconstructing reality in cinema through selectivity and simplicity in perfect practice. Filmed in a stark black-and-white mode, his frames are stylized and create a near-abstract pattern of images. Borrowing from the French New Wave, Paulus favors diagetic sounds with little music scoring. Like the seemingly unrelated cinematic images Paulus often sets together, the story of the farmer Santner, an army deserter in 1943 who hides from the Gestapo in a cave and visits his wife at night, suggests the wide consequences that even the most secret or isolated act can foster. The neighboring farmer Dürlinger also helps feed the hidden Santner, but Dürlinger's berating of his son Ruap, who has been rejected for armed service and envies the men in uniform, leads to disaster. Ruap's vengeful exposure of Santner's hiding place ultimately results in the execution of both Santner and Ruap. Santner's wife and Dürlinger are arrested, but a Polish prisoner-of-war farmworker is able to use this situation to escape. Influenced by Robert Bresson, Paulus rejects the creation or "invention" of cinematic reality. Respecting and reflecting the rhythm and ritual of life in the rural world he films, he uses his camera to "reassemble" the milieu. Paulus's camera also seeks accentuations and distance: a cup of tea, an injured hand, a slice of bread, or a particular window holds more interest for him than the details of the plot. The director considers this a method for allowing the viewer the freedom of exploring and associating the events of the film individually without the constraints of a strongly manipulated narrative construct. He utilizes only a few professional actors; most of his casts are made up of amateurs or local inhabitants.[29] With *Zug um Zug*/Bit by Bit (1994), Paulus revisits the Nazi era with the story of a farmer who joins the National Socialist Party to save his farm from financial ruin.

Also spearheading the growing move toward regional productions is Christian Berger (1945–), who has worked in film since 1968. His first feature, *Raffl* (1984), is a *Heimatfilm* redux set in the French-occupied Tyrol during the Napoleonic Wars, which he wrote and directed for Innsbruck's TTV-Film company. He has since turned to documentaries such as the 1997 *Ethnische Idyllen* —

Skizzen aus einem Nachkriegsland — Kroatien 1995/96/97/Ethnic Idylls — Sketches from a Postwar Country — Croatia 1995/96/97. Film writer Gustav Ernst classes Berger with Paulus as among the new Austrian filmmakers who have attempted to radicalize dominant cinema modes rather than create isolated experiments that tend to alienate audiences.[30] Like Paulus, Berger concentrates on the mountain milieu and is continually refashioning the *Heimatfilm* genre. Another exponent of the new Austrian *Heimatfilm* is Wolfgang Murnberger (1960–), whose origin is urban Wiener Neustadt rather than rural Austria. His *Himmel oder Hölle*/Heaven or Earth (1990), produced by Vienna's University of Music and Performing Arts, approaches an impressionistic cinema from the subjective point of view of the central character rather than from the "objectivity" of the director's camera as in Pilz or Paulus. The film offers the experiences of a young boy in the Burgenland province town of Wiesen, where escapism through cinema, playing "cowboys and Indians," sexual exploration, and, ultimately, acts of aggression and cruelty relieve the banality of his surroundings. It picked up third prize in the "Young Cinema" section of the 1991 Tokyo Film Festival. His *Ich gelobe*/I Vow (1994) visits similar alienation in a story that follows the life of a soldier living in provincial barracks. Translating his own experiences and dreams, Murnberger's surreal quality is strongly influenced by Buñuel.[31] While magical realism has been an important interwar and postwar movement in Austrian literature and painting, surrealism had never taken root in Austrian arts or cinema. But like the elements of the French New Wave that were adapted for New Austrian Film, French-based cinematic surrealism eventually filtered into Austrian film imagery by the late 1980s. Beyond Murnberger, Paulus Manker (1958–) has also made surrealism part of his cinematic style. Another second-generation performing artist, Manker first appeared as director with *Schmutz*/Dirt (1985), an allegory on the obsessive outsider and the banal roots of totalitarianism. The title refers to the character Joseph Schmutz (but also to the German word for dirt), a security guard who is obsessed with duty and cleanliness. He refuses to relinquish a position given to him temporarily and continues to serve the concept of order, literally to his death. Manker also played the title role in his next film, which again explores the self-destructive order mania behind fascism, *Weiningers Nacht*/Weininger's Last Stand (1990), an adaptation of the play by Joshua Sobol, and featuring Manker's mother, Hilde Sochor. Manker gives full reign to his surreal visions in this fantasia on the last night of philosopher Otto Weininger (1880–1903), which has been compared to the best work of British director Ken Russell.[32] Weininger was a Jewish anti–Semite and misogynist whose book *Sex and Character* developed a psychological theory of the sexes founded on Sigmund Freud's consideration of human bisexuality. He was accused of plagiarism by Freud and subsequently committed suicide in the room in which Beethoven had died. Influential in early twentieth-century philosophical thought, his self-reflexive anti–Semitism was also used by the National Socialists to justify their racism. Manker's tour-de-force performance of unbridled passion and self-destructive mania interwoven with surreal representations of Weininger's ideas has made this a cult classic abroad. He applied his surrealistic biopic style on cultural muse and composer

Alma Mahler-Werfel in *Alma — A Show Biz ans Ende*/Alma (1997) in a television miniseries.

Ignoring stylistic trends, Reinhard Schwabenitzky (1947–) creates a neorealist cinema that contemplates the everyday lives of the working class. Tending toward comedy, Schwabenitzky's greatest successes have been two television series, *Ein echter Wiener geht nicht unter*/A True Viennese Never Gives Up (1975–77) and *Kaisermühlen-Blues*/The Kaisermuehlen Blues (1992–93). His comic theatrical films have been less caricaturish and include a bittersweet comedy about an inheritance swindle, *Ilona und Kurti*/Ilona and Kurti (1991); *Verlassen Sie bitte Ihren Mann*/Please Leave Your Husband (1993) with Elfi Eschke (Schwabenitzky's wife); and *Ein fast perfekter Seitensprung*/A Nearly Perfect Affair (1995). *Hannah* (1996), also with Eschke and scripted by Schwabenitzky and Susanne M. Ayoub, proved that the director could transcend both comedy and television style. The title character, a dynamic corporate executive (Eschke), accepts a job at a toy company and is immediately attracted to the junior manager. Discovering that the company's dolls conceal a secret, her life is threatened and the film lurches into a political thriller dealing with the popular topics of Austrian cinema of the 1980s and 1990s: xenophobia, urban violence, and neo–Nazism. Newspaper critics Claus Philipp of *Der Standard* and Stefan Grisseman of *Die Presse* labeled the film as crude and historically problematic: a cliché attack on right-wing radicalism framed by cheap eroticism and voyeurism and as the type of film traditionally overfinanced by the government. Schwabenitzky retaliated by rejecting such "Kulturfaschismus" (cultural fascism) and appealed to the government not to pay attention to calls for cutting financial support of films that have a chance to appeal to large audiences in Austria and abroad.[33] The argument eventually focused on the role of the Austrian critic in influencing the type of film that is funded and made, to the detriment of more popular films aimed at an international public. Schwabenitzky refused to alter his popular angle and returned to a continuation of a television series and to cinema comedy with *Eine fast perfekte Scheidung*/An Almost Perfect Divorce (1997). The films had become a popular Austrian franchise by the time *Eine fast perfekte Hochzeit*/An Almost Perfect Wedding arrived in 1999.

From a more recent generation comes the Viennese Götz Spielmann (1961–), who is seemingly at home in many styles and genres including farce, re-visioned *Heimatfilm*, romance, and character-driven work in his films. *Der Nachbar*/The Neighbor (1992) offers another allegory on the rage and neofascism lurking just below the calm bourgeois surface in this story of a polite elderly gentleman who becomes capable of murder when a young Czech mother whom he loves from afar is encouraged by her boyfriend to work in a brothel. After a few television features, Spielmann returned to cinema with the feature he co-wrote with Maria Scheibelhofer, *Die Fremde*/The Stranger (1999), which continued his look at the dystopic aspects of modern urban life, combined with a subtle commentary on the xenophobic atmosphere in Austria of the 1990s, in an odd love story between Mercedes (Goya Toledo), a Mexican drug dealer in Vienna, and Harry (Harry Prinz), a passive Viennese taxi driver. The film also features Nina Proll, Simon Schwarz and

Fritz Karl, new film actors who would be among those dominating Austrian cinema in the next decade. The director notes that the film

> grew out of fragments taken from everyday life, which were pieced together to form a complete story. The key image, which provided the inspiration, was that of a woman from South America sitting in a public-housing apartment, listening to a song in her native tongue, thinking of nothing more than going home.... After hearing so much talk about foreigners, there was suddenly this image of a woman longing for her home country. I wanted to know how she got there and why she wants to leave.[34]

With its heady mix of character study, social critique, aspects of the thriller and even screwball comedy, *Die Fremde* has become the director's most successful film internationally, appearing at over twenty-two film festivals between 2000 and 2001.

Although New Austrian Film had come into its own by the 1990s, it was still "long on talent but short on cash,"[35] and production was mostly dependent on the subsidy financing from the federal government, the AFF (Federal Film Board) and ORF. Private funding did not materialize in the 1990s as had been hoped, and films had to find 30 percent of their budgets from other sources in order to qualify for AFF support. With only about $4.3 million available from the AFF and $2.25 million from ORF (in return for broadcast rights) in 1989, or far less than a single average major American feature, "small" films continued to be the norm and large-scale productions were still required to look for international cooperation and talent. In 1990, Austria became a member of the European Union's "Low Budget Film Project" within the EFDO (European Film Distribution Office), which helped facilitate both EU co-production and distribution of Austrian film. In 1992, centralization attempted to put a recognizable face on the government relationship with filmmakers. The Austrian Film Fund was renamed the Austrian Film Institute and relocated, along with the Austrian Film Commission, the Vienna Film Fund, the Viennale, and the organization of Austria's screenwriters, ARGE Drehbuch, into a user-friendly "Filmhaus."[36] Much of this, as well as subsequent amendments to the national Film Promotion Act, was intended to bring Austria into line for European Union membership in 1995. This came, of course, not without controversy, since any change brought hope for producers who desired a stronger commercial industry but also fears for filmmakers who felt art and experimentation would be lost to the new business-aimed interests.

There were also positive signs by the last decade of the century that Austria had indeed become a nation concerned with its own cinematic legacy. The historic Rosenhügel studio, which had been bought up by ORF and was used primarily for television production or rented out for international productions since the 1970s, was to have been demolished in 1990 to make way for a shopping center. The complex had failed to become a center for international television production in the 1980s, and Damiano Damiani's *Il Treno/ Der Zug/*The Train, a 1987 Austrian/Italian/French/West German series about Imperial Germany's deliverance of Lenin from Swiss exile to Russia in 1917 in order to foment revolution, had been the studio's only major client after Franz Antel's *Der Bockerer* in 1981. The studio was subsequently abandoned by ORF and then sold but was literally rescued from the wrecking ball by ORF head Teddy Podgorski, who bought it back from the construction firm that was to demolish it. Given the very modest Austrian film industry outside of ORF co-productions and with the new accessibility of more inexpensive alternatives to Western European studios after the fall of Communism in Prague, Bratislava and Budapest, Rosenhügel would have to become a unique site to earn its keep beyond being an empty museum of soundstages. Kurt J. Mrkwicka (1937–), head of the MR-Film and MR-TV-Film companies, saw the opportunity to revitalize Vienna's greatest film relic with Vienna's most popular cultural icon, Johann Strauss, in a twelve-part television series, *The Strauss Dynasty,* to be directed by American miniseries specialist Marvin Chomsky (*Roots*; *Holocaust*). The 1991 series, which called for lavish sets and costumes in the tradition of Wien-Film and the imperial epics of the 1950s, featured a primarily British, American and Austrian cast along with 130 supporting players and almost 7,000 extras. Mrkwicka's production worked financial and publicity magic on the reputation of Rosenhügel as a viable new European filmmaking venue. Along with producers Andreas Kamm and Walter Hirscher, Mrkwicka rejected the museum route for the studio and with the support of Vienna's mayor Helmut Zilk, Federal Minister for Education, Science and Culture Rudolf Scholten, and the ORF, a new company was born. Utilizing funds contributed by both the federal government and the city of Vienna, the revitalization of the studio began in July 1994. Renamed the Filmstadt Wien (Film City Vienna) it opened its six soundstages, new technical labs, and several business offices to world filmmakers on November 2, 1995, in a gala for over 3,000 international film and media industry guests during which Maximilian Schell was honored with Austria's new Billy Wilder Prize. Mrkwicka's gamble paid off before the actual completion of the studio's renovation. As early as 1994, Austrian and foreign film companies arranged to rent the facility, followed by television commercial and music video productions, and corporations who scheduled large events there. Finally, in a bit of symbolism that heralded a new respect for the film industry and Austrian film tradition, both the Vienna Film Ball as well as the new Romy Awards (the audience popularity award named after Romy Schneider) were both held at the revitalized Filmstadt Wien complex.

Marvin Chomsky's experience with the studio and its Viennese support proved to be so positive that his following miniseries *Catherine the Great*, a German/Austrian co-production, was also made there in 1994, demonstrating that Filmstadt Wien not only could support monumental sets (which it had done since the great epics of the silent era) and was on the cutting edge technically but was as financially welcoming as Prague's Barrandov studio, its main rival before the similar reconstruction of the former UFA/DEFA Babelsberg studio outside Berlin. Ultimately, the traditional Berlin-Vienna-Prague "golden triangle" of Central European film studios reemerged along with the untapped possibility of cooperation. The Mickey Rourke production, *Love in Paris* (USA/GB/France 1997) discovered that for its purposes at least, the Filmstadt Wien was far more accommodating than the usual facilities for Hollywood-European co-productions in Paris, and Franz Antel subsequently shot his first sequel to *Der Bockerer* there, with large-scale set constructions recreating postwar Vienna. Urs Egger had brought the difficult prospect of recreating one of Vienna's most famous sites and events to the studio. For his television film treatment of Josef Haslinger's novel on neo–Nazi terrorism and its aftermath, *Opernball*/Opera Ball (1998), the interior and exterior of Vienna's famed opera house, including the large urban square that surrounds it (one of the grandest in the city) was built in several soundstages and populated by extras that approached the amount used for *The Strauss Dynasty*.

But what of Austrian film from the audience point of view? By the late 1980s there had been some interest in rediscovering Austrian film history, thanks in part to the restoration activities of the Austrian Film Archives, later renamed the Film-archiv Austria (Film Archive Austria). The 1987 "Austrian Film Days" in Wels pre-sented a retrospective of films by Sascha Kolowrat, who had been labeled the "Film Count" seemingly for foreign consumption and with a nod to Austria's love/hate relationship to its imperial past. There was also an event screening of Kertesz's epic *Sodom und Gomorrah* (1922), which consisted of roughly half of the film, painstak-ingly reconstructed after years of searching for the lost work, as well as a glowing new print of Ucicky's *Café Elektric* (1927) where both Willi Forst and Marlene Dietrich would create the cinematic personas they perfected in later films. The Film Archive's exhibition "80 Years of Austrian Film: 1908–88" found sufficient popular interest to continue with presentations throughout the 1990s along the model of the British Film Institute. The Austrian Film Museum, which was cre-ated in 1964 by Peter Konlechner and experimental filmmaker Peter Kubelka, fea-tures international dominant and avant-garde cinema in its retrospectives. Its collection of over ten thousand films and its large research library has prompted the German news magazine *Der Spiegel* to label it "one of Europe's most versatile cinematheques."[37] The noncompetitive Viennale expanded with international offerings and received critical praise throughout the 1980s and 1990s for its retro-spectives and extensive auteur coverage. Nearly shut down in the 1970s due to lack of interest by both filmmakers and the public, it has found a new generation of filmgoers and has become viable as an international venue, not only for its focus on film history but for showcasing new filmmakers as well. The opening day of the festival in 1989 attracted a record twenty-five thousand viewers.[38] In 1993 it coop-erated with Synema, an academic/popular organization founded in 1984 that fea-tures seminars and lectures, in an impressive program titled "Departure into Uncertainty," which focused on the large Austrian film talent that emigrated prior to 1945. In addition to the aforementioned Austrian Film Days in the town of Wels, which has been run by the Österreichisches Film Büro (Austrian Film Office) since its establishment in 1983, the Graz-based Diagonale concentrates on Austrian cin-ema and has evolved into one of the nation's major artistic events. But perhaps the most effective organization promoting Austrian film is the Austrian Film Com-mission (AFC), which was originally set up as part of the Film Institute. This unit assists filmmakers with marketing and festival entry, records Austrian film data and publishes an elegantly produced annual catalogue and website in German, English and French, offering details and stills of the year's theatrical and television films. Supplementing the commission's work is the private nonprofit organization Sixpack Film, which was founded by Brigitta Burger-Utzer, Lisl Ponger, Peter Tscherkassky, Martin Arnold and Alexander Horwath in 1991 for the purpose of packaging and marketing short and experimental film for distribution at Austrian and foreign venues and in international film festivals.

Despite the growing popular interest in film, only 345 cinema screens were functional in 1988, a decline from 495 in 1981. The closing of large houses, the construction of uncomfortable small, multiplex-style theaters, and the long wait for first-run features in rural communities had subverted box-office health despite the rise in production. Two theater chains have long dominated Austria's cinema landscape: the oldest is Kiba, created by the Social Democratic Vienna city council in 1926 for the purpose of promoting political propaganda. Today it is wholly commercial and majority-owned by the Vienna municipality. It also runs the Stadtkino, established in 1981 by the city as an outlet for alternative and noncommercial film. The other chain, Constantin, a subsidiary of Germany's large Neue Constantin production/distribution powerhouse, is known for its more modern theaters. The Kiba theaters are often more profitable since they own the larger houses that are desired by American feature distributors. Small private exhibitors also exist in provincial cities, but given the near monopoly by Constantin, they have little chance in obtaining first-run prints. To combat this, the Austrian Cinema Theater Association launched a program similar to one in Germany, by which public subsidies would allow first-run prints to be made available to small exhibitors. The outdated taxes on movie tickets levied by many provincial communities have also cut into small theater survivability. This led to the founding in 1993 of the Ring of Independent Theater Owners, which hoped to battle dominance by Constantin and become the "third power" on the Austrian cinema market.[39] Nevertheless, in a spirit of cooperation reminiscent of the Rosenhügel revitalization, Constantin and Kiba launched a cooperative venture in 1991 to create a joint multiplex in northern Vienna, and to renovate the large old Apollo theater into a film center with seven screens and 1,400 seats as a flagship house for first-run blockbusters. The privately developed nine-screen UCI multiplex (2,200 seats) opened in 1994 but was a disappointment in attracting audiences. As Susanna Pyrker noted in 1994, "Austrian movie theaters have gained in quality but lost in number."[40] There were twelve less cinemas in Austria in 1993 than in the previous year. Given the UCI Center failure, the new Constantin/Kiba association planned on modernizing and enlarging older theaters rather than building more multiplexes. But the Ring of Independent Theater Owners created a miniboom with their own multiplex construction in the provincial capitals of Linz, St. Pölten, Graz, and Innsbruck. With more planned for these cities and for Vienna, the Austrian cinema theater seating capacity should increase by as much as 20 percent.[41] Additionally, Vienna also offers one of the world's largest IMAX theaters, which has added to audience interest and growth.

Responding to international media coverage of film ranging from stories on cable news networks like CNN and BBC, to celebrity and fashion tie-ins on MTV, the new generation of filmgoers continued to make American films the strongest box-office draws in Austria. But by the end of the 1990s, some Austrian features, while never in the top ten, managed to attract relatively impressive numbers among Austrian and German audiences. Austria's film market is dominated by six major distributors — Columbia Tristar, UIP (distributing Universal, Paramount and MGM product), Buena Vista, Warner Brothers, Constantin Film and Centfox — that account for more than "90 percent of box-office take" with Buena Vista in the lead.[42] The remaining 10 percent is split by ten independent distributors, such as the German and Austrian Filmladen, Polyfilm and Stadtkino. The mid–1990s demonstrated a significant increase in ticket sales from the previous period of decline. It would have to grow substantially to match the high point of 18 million tickets in the early 1980s, but by 1996, there were 12.3 million visits to the cinema and 13.7 million admissions in 1997. While growth was apparent, it was still among the lowest numbers in Europe.

A new generation of filmmakers specializing in postmodern hybrid-genre work emerged in the 1990s alongside those that had continuing or sporadic careers since the 1970s. Nikolaus Leytner (1957–) directs films that examine the social outsider or misfit such as *Schwarzfahrer*/Fare Dodger (1996), about a drop-out student who passes himself off as a train ticket inspector to extract money from fare dodgers, and *Drei Herren*/Three Gentlemen (1998), a comedy/drama about three mental patients accidentally involved in the search for their own disappearance. *Drei Herren* features Karl Merkatz, Karl Markovics and Ottfried Fischer, a trio of Austria's best male character leads in a film that suggests the spirit of the legendary Hörbiger/Moser partnerships. Florian Flicker, (1965–) whose first feature film had been in 1989, wrote and directed 1993's utopian fantasy *Halbe Welt*/Half World and returned with *Suzie Washington* (1997), about a teacher from Eastern Europe who aims for the United States but is arrested in Vienna for falsified documents. Escaping the police, she takes on the title name as she attempts to find a new identity. Flicker moved from victimless crime to unrelenting tension and violence in *Der Überfall*/The Hold-up (2000), which presents a bloody power struggle between three men during a robbery in a small tailor's shop in Vienna. The film became one of the new crop demanding attention at several European film festivals and was awarded at Locarno in 2000. Leopold Lummerstorfer (1968–) directed, wrote and produced the documentaries *Rosa Heimat— Eine Landillusion*/Rosy Homeland — A Land Illusion (1990), *Tage mit Josef*/Days with Josef (directed with Herbert Papek) (1993) and, along with Victor Jaschke, Kenan Kilic and Hannelore Thiefenthaler, the experimental, *Halb Wien*/Half Vienna (1995). In 2000, he made his feature film debut with *Gelbe Kirschen*/White Cherries, which looks at a love affair between an Austrian country boy and a rural Czech girl, that is plagued by urban expectations and immigration policies. The most unique of the crop is the communally written and directed film by Angela Hans Scheirl, Ursula Pürrer and Dietmar Schipek entitled, *Rote Ohren fetzen durch Asche*/Through Ashes (1992). Intended to counter to the growing commercialization of New Austrian Film, it was shot on Super 8 and manipulated in its 16 mm transfer. The partially animated film set in the year 2700 is a rich hybrid of horror, science fiction, action and underground cartoon/anime film genres and deals with mutated humans, burned-out cities, and crablike creatures that live in cellars. The work of Buñuel, Dali, and Maya Deren all appear to have had strong influence in the film's trancelike montage aesthetics.[43]

By the end of the decade and century, New Austrian Film had proven its staying power and had begun to interest cineastes, critics and the film festival crowd. The new genres and themes of this phase reveal the still uneasy concept of Austrian identity along with the new sociopolitical impulses that had come to film following the nadir of the 1960s and the fall of Communism in Europe at the end of the 1980s. The feminist or critical women's film grew into a major genre via the social movements of the 1960s and the experiments of female directors in the 1970s. The immigrant film, developed from the xenophobia and political discussions brought on by Eastern European and other immigration, grew as an important film topic while populist politician Jörg Haider of the right-wing Freedom Party (FPÖ) utilized an anti-immigration platform throughout the 1980s and 1990s. His early comments suggested an admiration for the Third Reich and set his controversial image, despite apologies and clarifications. With his party (but not Haider) joining the conservative People's Party in coalition after the federal election of 1999, the European Union subsequently instituted sanctions against Austria for its "undemocratic" and "xenophobic" political forces, which were then lifted in September 2000. The European Union was criticized by the non–EU Central and Eastern Europeans for this French, Belgian and German-led reaction against a non–NATO state (a similar political constellation followed in Italy, a NATO state, without any action by the EU), which in retrospect appears to have been a backhanded warning to ascendant nationalist parties in the countries that led the protest. The EU boycott caused significant rifts in Austria's friendly relationships with France and Germany, to the point where pundits declared that the country's only true friends in Europe were its former imperial partners to the east. A stronger sense of *Mitteleuropa* might have arisen from this experience, but it was in the best interest of Chancellor Wolfgang Schüssel, and ultimately the nation, to demonstrate a return to EU business as usual and as quickly as possible. There was, however, a significant protest movement within the country during the first year of the coalition — not just by the political Left, but by those opposing Haider's comments regarding Nazism and those who understood Austria to be a nation based on multiculturalism. The vocal Austrian arts community continued to slam the perceived antiliberal political bent of the coalition, particularly the reduction of arts funding and the shuttering and reorganization of Austria's cultural venues abroad, from the autonomous Austrian Cultural Institutes to more solidly Foreign Ministry–controlled Austrian Cultural Forums.

Three genres actually survived the experimentalism and commercial film industry collapse of the 1960s to reemerge at the end of the century: the cinematic treatment of the folk play; the social-critical drama, which had been transformed by the experience of Nazism, and now tended toward allegorical or psychological explorations; and the cabaret-inspired comedy film. Martin Schweighofer, the managing director of the Austrian Film Commission, sees the return to this latter genre as a unique and very commercial aspect of New Austrian Film:

> The pressure to succeed with commercial films and to appeal to a large audience has resulted in the so-called cabaret films. The idea behind this strategy is quite simple. In Vienna and in other cities we have a very active comedy scene. Films based on these stage productions would thus have a ready cabaret audience. It all started with *Indien* (India), a popular cabaret program. Paul Harather, its director, made a film out of the play; in the cast he included the two lead actors. *Indien* was very successful, and of course the minute you have something successful, you consider possible spin-offs.... There is a bonus though: the further we get away from home, the more exotic we seem.... In general, one could say that if humor depends too much on play of words then it doesn't translate very well. And how does Austrian humor compare with German? I'm not too fond of German humor and I cannot very much relate to it. I think Austrian humor, if it's good, is that much more elegant, it's playful and a bit more tongue in cheek.[44]

Paul Harather's (1965–) *Indien*/India (1993), written by Harather, Josef Hader and Alfred Dorfer, was a box-office success in Austria, Germany and other European venues in 1994. Essentially a road picture on the misadventures of two "odd couple" inspectors of the catering trade, the cabaret-style material eventually gives way to a more universal tragicomedy, as the men's friendship grows and one discovers he has terminal cancer. Harather returned to the cinemas with a feature shot in Germany, *Weihnachtsfieber*/Christmas Fever (1997), which reworked the "odd couple" aspect of *Indien* as a romantic comedy about a television moderator and a traveling salesman who have opposing views on the one thing that connects them — Christmas. Harather, who briefly moved to German television production, returned to Austrian screens in 2000 with *Die Gottesanbeterin*/The Praying Mantis, based on the true story of "Black Widow" Elfriede Blauensteiner, a housewife who financed her race-track addiction by marrying and subsequently poisoning several men. The material is given a satirical treatment by screenwriters Susanne Freund, Gerda Edelewiss, Grossmann, and Harather. Two actors known for their sinister-edged performances, Udo Kier and Jan Niklas, were brought on to support lead Christiane Hörbiger, whose elegantly perverse performance as Trixi Jancik, plays off her media image and her continuing role as a small-town attorney in the highly popular television series *Julia*, as much as it interprets the persona of the notorious Blauensteiner. Screened at no less than eight film festivals between 2000 and 2001, the film demonstrated that New Austrian Film is capable of more than art house fare. Unfortunately, it could not crack the international distribution prejudice against Austrian entertainment films lingering from decades of nonpresence on the global market.

The new *Heimatfilm*, with its interest in critical and alternative views of rural and mountain life, revitalized a genre that had died of formulaic and broad comedy exhaustion in the 1960s. Brought back with two dramatic ORF series (*Alpensaga*

A tragicomedy of urban alienation: Josef Hader and Alfred Dorfer in Paul Harather's
Indien, 1993.

and *Das Dorf an der Grenze*) and by Christian Berger's *Raffl* (1984), Wolfram Paulus's
Heidenlöcher (1985), and Niki List's *Helden in Tirol* (1998), a surreal parody of a
lost village where the codes of the *Heimatfilm* still hold sway, the new version of
the Austrian cinema staple rejected the idyllic notions of country life and subverted
clichés by locating problems of Austrian society and recent history in the milieu.
Stefan Ruzowitzky's (1961–) *Die Siebtelbauern*/The Inheritors (a.k.a. The One-Sev-
enth Farmers, 1998) is a perfect case in point. While cinematographer Peter von
Haller captures Austria's Mühlviertel region in both misty grandeur and jewel-like
tones, suggesting that the beauty of nature is the one constant in the long and varied tradition of the Austrian *Heimatfilm*, art director Isi Wimmer and costume
designer Nicole Fischmaller offer a sense of earthiness that has little in common
with studio fantasies. Placing the action into the impoverishment, political instability and national identity trauma of the Austrian First Republic, Ruzowitzky
underscores the difficult life of the farm-worker and the unyielding traditions of
the landed farmers who behave with aristocratic privilege and capitalist manipulation to maintain their control. Ruzowitzky's film is also a hybrid, sharing its plot
structure with the mystery or crime film. It recalls the Austrian social dramas of
the 1920s and 1930s, which focused on the plight of the working classes, as well as
displaying the new neorealism. Nevertheless, the director clearly locates his reinvention of the genre in a symbolic rather than time-specific reality. The production company calls the film an *Alpenwestern* (Alpine western) and reviewers have

Stylized cynicism: Christiane Hörbiger in Paul Harather's *Die Gottesanbeterin*, 2001.

additionally labelled it a *Heimatwestern*, due to the film's concentration on land own-ership.[45] But this does not mean that *Die Siebtelbauern* is at the forefront of some new genre. Rather, the notion of such a seemingly exotic work only underscores the accomplished publicity machine at Dor-Film, which has obviously discovered that, with regards to international promotion, Hollywood-style hype still works. A reading of the film as sociopolitical allegory reveals Ruzowitzky's critical com-mentary on the strife of the First Republic and on the ideology of Austrofascism, which supported social and cultural tradition with repression. Additionally, exam-ination of the director's specific approach to the genre's aesthetics, conventions, and religious connotations indicates how the *Heimatfilm* can also have a progressive and more universal message.

The film's action is framed by the narration of a supporting character, Severin (Lars Rudolph): After Hillinger, a landowning farmer, is found murdered, his seven farmworkers (of different ages and levels of education) discover they have inherited the farm. The community of wealthy farmers immediately rejects this situation as untenable on the basis of tradition and class and conspires with the farm's foreman (Tilo Prückner) to purchase the farm from the workers. When the workers refuse to sell and eject the foreman, the local farmers, led by Danninger (Ulrich Wild-gruber), attempt to destroy the farm by violence. Led by the unwed mother Emmy (Sophie Rois) and the naïve but promiscuous Lukas (Simon Schwarz), the work-ers-turned-landowning-farmers organize and create a successful communal enter-prise. Rosalind (Elisabeth Orth), an old worker who has returned, confesses to Hillinger's murder. It is later revealed that Lukas is the son of Rosalind and Hillinger.

She had been sent away because workers could not marry or have children and had left her son in the care of her best friend, the Alte Nane (Julia Gschnitzer), to be raised as a foundling. During a violent raid on the farm by Danninger's group, Lukas kills the foreman. He is subsequently hidden, but after visiting his mother in jail, he is killed during a lynching in which Severin is tortured and Emmy is raped. Severin, Emmy and her son abandon the farm for America at the same time that Danninger is found murdered — as the audience learns — by Severin to avenge Lukas's death.

Clearly, the murdered Hillinger and the inheritance of his land by the workers suggest the collapse of the monarchy and the establishment of an embattled parliamentary democracy. Unlike the traditional *Heimatfilm*, which would praise the farmers' tradition and the church into which they often parade, here the poorly dressed and vulgar workers are the "heroes." The narrative reveals them as honest if uneducated, trustworthy if foolish, and very industrious. By comparison, the farmers are foul mouthed, hypocritical, and abusive. Reinforcing a hierarchy of privilege and class distinction, which obviously runs counter to reality, they lay down their reactionary law immediately: no worker can be a landed farmer. Despite their inheritance, their burgeoning success in running the farm and their rights as landowners and individuals, the new farmers are denied control over their own lives and participation in the running of the town. Violence breeds violence, and although the new farmers are ultimately exiled, they have toppled both the foreman and Danninger. The murders, mob justice, and a social cannibalism, resulting from the farmers' attempt to uphold tradition and class distinction, has ruined the community.

Ruzowitzky's *Die Siebtelbauern* is also an addendum, even a corrective, to one famous American attempt at recreating the Austrian *Heimatfilm*, *The Sound of Music* (USA 1965). This film is without doubt the most popular cinematic image of Austria and Austrians in the world. It should, however, be understood for the allegorical dyad it offers of the aristocratic former imperial naval officer Captain von Trapp and the postulant nun Maria. Together these characters represent the sociopolitical direction of the Austrofascist corporate state: political conservatism, Alpine *völkisch* culture, latent monarchism, and a class-distinct society based in the Catholic social ideology of Othmar Spann. Although the film depicts only Austrian Nazis, and so undercuts any suggestion that Nazism was only brought by the German Anschluss, it does not offer any corresponding allegory dealing with the repressed Left and the working class (the only two representatives, a messenger and a butler, are National Socialists). Second Republic Austria, which has officially avoided dealing with the Dollfuss/Schuschnigg era even more than with the Nazi period, would certainly not find *The Sound of Music*'s Austria to be an allegory that could provide representation of the nation today. Yet its 1965 characterizations of both Austrian Nazis and anti–Nazis have suggested a victim/abuser Austria beyond the total victimization interpretation of the Moscow Declaration that has held sway in the country until the 1990s.[46]

Ruzowitzky may not have set out to create an anti–*Sound of Music*, but an intertext with Robert Wise's one-sided interwar Austrian allegory is easy to locate. The very famous opening shot of Maria (Julie Andrews) running up the green hills of the Untersberg is paralleled several times in Ruzowitzky's film by the farm-workers. Certainly, this is an Austrian *Heimatfilm* convention Wise borrowed in the first place. But if we examine Ruzowitzky's obvious reference to old *Heimatfilm* and its Hollywood translation, the director's reinvention of the genre by shifting the ideological meanings behind traditional cinematic vocabulary becomes apparent. The ascent of the farmworkers (symbolic also of their social climb) on the hillside relates to their daily work in taming and harvesting nature. By comparison, a traditional *Heimatfilm* tended to use this hill-climbing and meadow-wandering convention as a suggestion of liberation in nature. It represented an escape from the rules and troubles of society and often functioned as a prelude to a love scene. Wise's *Sound of Music* not only appropriates this convention as an indication of social release (in this case Maria's escape from the constraints of the abbey) but as a Romantic transcendence in which Maria finds song, self-realization and, ultimately, the divine spirit in nature. At the conclusion of the film, the von Trapp family adds a political frame to Maria's epiphany as they climb the hill and the mountains beyond to escape Nazism. Ruzowitzky's rational/realist concept of this climb into nature is, however, devoid of any notions of Romantic liberation: the workers are simply in their toiling element and do not "escape" into nature. It can be placed on the opposite end of the spectrum from the metaphysical/political connotations found in Hollywood's translation of the traditional *Heimatfilm*.

Ruzowitzky's background as a student of history and his approach in filtering the past through the present also suggest that such shifts in meaning are aimed at creating a conscious allegory regarding Austrian history. While he does not attempt to reenact specific junctures in the sociopolitical history of the Austrian First Republic and the corporate state, the subtext of the film's conflict development seems based in the flow of real events: the end of the monarchy and the declaration of a parliamentary republic; economic inflation and depression followed by some promise of stability; growing tensions between the paramilitary forces of the Left and Right; the Justice Palace Fire of 1927[47]; the creation of the clerico-authoritarian corporate regime; the suppression of the Left[48]; and the murder of Chancellor Dollfuss in a failed coup attempt by Austrian Nazis in 1934.

Ruzowitzky also deflates the Habsburg myth in this representation: the murdered Hillinger was not a benevolent patriarchal figure, rather he is recalled by Severin as distant, stingy and mean, having had a single occasion of sentimentality (drunk, he asked his workers to sing for him and gave them each a coin); this creates an aura of ambiguity around his memory. The shock of absolutism's end leaves the workers numb and mute. So conditioned to work without question or even conversation, Severin has taken to talking to a cow. The silent workers, now heirs to the farm, sit at their table unable even to eat, since the master's plate at his separate table remains empty. The hierarchy and self-definition of the group continues through their relationship with the "monarch" even after he is gone: Ruzowitzky's camera offers Hillinger's phantom point of view, which lingers on the empty plate before it focuses on the worker's table beyond. The Alte Nane, believing she is no longer responsible to any man in the house, finds no reason to suffer for lack of a "monarch." She helps herself to the soup, but the others, conditioned by hierarchy and authority, await the leader manqué, the foreman, who sits at the head of their table and insists they now respect his orders in the name of tradition. He will decide when the table can begin their meal and who will do the gender-oriented duties: Lukas and Severin will mend the fence; Emmy will wash his clothes, etc. But the young and intelligent Emmy also quickly dispenses with patriarchal rules, bringing her illegitimate child to live with her at the farm, despite the rule that workers may not have children or a family that might distract them from their work.

Severin informs us that the wealthy farmers have already laid claim to Hillinger's farm, because without a natural heir, the Church would obtain it. This reveals the thin façade of the community's church-bound "loyalty" and their actual capitalistic motives. Hillinger, however, has left a will that deeds the farm to his workers. Again, there is no myth of a benevolent monarch here; it is clear from the will's offensive language and personal insults that Hillinger has done this to spite the community and to cause a rift among the workers who he believes would fight each other for the property. The conflict is instantaneous for members of the landed elite, who reject the possibility of a worker ever owning land and rising to the status of a farmer. The foreman, who betrays his own class by currying favor from his superiors, arranges the farm to be sold for petty profit and a sense of minor authority.

Once again, we return to the worker's table via the icon of the dead "monarch's" point of view. His empty plate, now covered with flies, continues to hold symbolic power. As they plan what each will buy with their share of the farm, Emmy suddenly insists she will not sell and is immediately pitted against the foreman. Her self-determination suggests a manifesto of liberation, as the other workers soon chant along with her. When the foreman responds with violence, the previously passive Lukas throws him off the farm.

The collision of the old and the new occurs for the first time at the gathering of the community for Sunday Mass. Led by Danninger, the farmers and their long-skirted wives appear uniformed in their country costume. Disrupting this sea of black are the workers, led by Emmy in a red sweater and short skirt, and Lukas in a light-colored jacket. The clothing colors suggest those used to represent the Austrian political ideology of the era: black for the Christian-Social Party and the ideologies of the Catholic-based Right; red for the Socialists and the other Marxist parties of the Left. The visual clash of color introduces the verbal conflict. Danninger openly condemns the workers' ownership of the farm because it is against "God's law." Emmy ridicules this and insists on her social ascendancy by leading the workers to the front pews of the church and singing loudly, to the chagrin of the farmers' wives.

As the workers explore their dead master's room and view his encased artifacts as if they were staring at the imperial crown jewels in the national treasury, they take turns jumping on the bed and imagining their ownership of his belongings. When Lukas blurts out that he and Severin might now sleep here, Emmy immediately bars a continuation of the past. The *Casa d'Austria*[49] must remain vacant; its objects of power and wealth will belong to all and yet to no one. The Alte Nane refuses to even visit the room, because of its association with patriarchal abuse: to keep the "foundling" Lukas, she was summoned to the master's bed twice a week, until she began to eat garlic to ward him off.[50]

For Ruzowitzky's microcosmic First Republic Austria there can, of course, be no replacement of the monarch. Leftist insistence of an "empty monarch's seat" clashed with the goal of restoration by legitimist conservatives throughout the era, even with the imperial nostalgia that transcended party politics in literature, film and popular culture. As the Anschluss nears in Wise's *Sound of Music*, Captain von Trapp mourns the loss of this phantom imperial Austria, a "world that is slowly fading away." It is Maria, as representation of the Catholic social values and the idealized peasantry that transforms the captain into a more pragmatic man in the face of Nazism. In Ruzowitzky's *Siebtelbauern*, the brutal and repressive landowning farmers represent this reactionary Austria. They are the Austrofascist aspect of the corporate state, which has been suggested by leftist historians as having been the preparation for Hitler rather than as the bulwark against him. Indeed, the foreman, who willingly sells out the workers for profit and a patronizing pseudoacceptance by the farmers, sports a moustache that ambiguously references both traditional style (the ends have turned gray) and Hitler's (a dark center patch). It is an unavoidable emblem suggesting the evolution of fascism from faded absolutism and petit bourgeois values.[51]

The difficult adjustment by the new farmers to a democratic rule of the land mirrors the social discord of the gender-role shifts and cultural quakes of the First Republic. Lukas informs his co-farmers that the farmer does not work on Sunday; he simply rests and drinks his coffee. But Emmy insists she is also a farmer and refuses to serve the men. The Alte Nane completely ignores Lukas's nonwork order by hushing him and clearing the table. For her, even a benevolent law given by a man is now one law too many. Lukas brings Hillinger's phonograph and a record of Italian opera out of the forbidden bedroom into the barn. Despite their lack of education, which leaves them at a loss to understand what the music is (Lukas wrongly informs them it is "American"), they enjoy it and dance with each other, as high art is passed from the elite to the masses.[52] Lisbeth's pregnancy by the member of a traveling circus advances the antitraditionalism and female self-realization on the farm, which also inspires neighboring farmworkers into change: an old worker demands payment long owed her by her farmer, a couple marries despite farmer protest, and two female workers depart from the countryside to work in a factory when their farmer refuses them proper wages. Finally, even Emmy and Lukas discover they must adjust their physical relationship to meet their new self-realizations. Emmy rejects having her usual casual sex with Lukas because now there is the possibility of a life with goals. The social and sexual revolt comes about through physical violence rather than intellectual discourse: they quarrel, Lukas slaps her, but she slaps him back. And the little stable boy, who all thought was mute, begins to speak. The formerly silent masses have not only found their rights but their often clashing voices as well.

The relative success of the farm is threatened by the 12,000 Schillings they must pay out to the three departed workers. But continuous hard work (the men take a job at a foundry during the day and continue to work the farm at night), Emmy's shrewd financial planning, and a jeweled broach that suddenly appears among Lukas's belongings, raises the money ahead of schedule. Through this process, a desire to reach for symbols of the bourgeoisie begins to appear. Lukas asks Severin to teach him to read and write in order to change his social identity. Lisbeth and Liesl, carried away by the thought of their first profit from the harvest, buy an elegant lady's hat, which Ruzowitzky captures with the same front-of-frame dominance as he previously did with Hillinger's empty plate. The parallelism indicates that bourgeois upward mobility based in money and self-promotion has now replaced calcified social stratification and birthright elitism.

The new farmers' rejection of a continuation of the traditional patriarchal hierarchy (Emmy becomes the de facto leader of the commune) is met first with verbal abuse then with physical violence from the traditional farmers, escalating in the town's "civil war." As the traditional farmers plan their attack to end this new liberalism, the story behind Rosalind's murder of Hillinger emerges from two sources—the Alte Nane and Danninger. Raped by Hillinger as a young worker, Rosalind reported him to the police, but Hillinger claimed she had stolen a broach. She subsequently disappeared but was found and served fifteen years in prison. For Danninger, she is yet another "whore." For the Alte Nane, her killing of Hillinger and the return of the broach to Lukas have served justice.

Ruzowitzky's camera ultimately replaces the "monarch's" empty plate and the ritual of the modest worker's meal with representations of a democratic era: a photograph of the successful *Siebtelbauern* is now followed by a feast of dancing, eating and drinking. The past has been supplanted by a new social concept, but it is still rejected by Danninger and his group. Understanding herself to be a farmer equal to all others, Emmy counters Danninger's and the foreman's vulgar insults with her own, but when Danninger attempts to hit her, Lukas stops him and reminds him of his own vaunted traditions.

The Danninger-led arson attack on the new farmers, in which the barn is burned and Lukas kills the foreman in self-defense, sets a secularized Christ theme in motion. This contrivance acts to ironically underscore Danninger and his group's hypocritical façade of godliness—his misused Catholicism-as-social ideology. Emmy cradles the wounded, sobbing Lukas in her arms, reminiscent of a pietà tableau, and Severin's narration takes on the suggestion of a biblical tale, as the Alte Nane hides Lukas in the caves where his mother hid to give birth to him before she was arrested. Lukas was born on the Catholic holiday of *Maria Lichtmess* and has thus been known as Lukas Lichtmess ever since. Severin explains that when Lisbeth and Liesl subsequently left the farm there was a rumor that Lisbeth named her son Lukas. He also relates that since Lukas's martyrdom, more boys in the valley than Lukas could have ever fathered have been given his name. Moreover, Danninger's promise of money for anyone who can capture Lukas, and the appearance of vagabonds and day workers who would take on the dishonorable task, recalls the

The new *Heimatfilm* and historical allegory: Stefan Ruzowitzky's *Die Siebtelbauren*, 1998.

biblical Judas. Aspects of the original Christian myth are shifted to reflect a progressive realism: Lukas is the innocent (albeit not sexually) and good martyr, Rosalind is the virgin raped by her lord-master to become the vengeful mother of the martyr, Emmy is the "fallen woman" who teaches Lukas about individuality and self-respect, and Severin, who has been shown the joy of life by Lukas, in turn teaches him the Word(s). Lukas and Severin had earlier "baptized" each other in the mud of the farm as they celebrated their newly found social roles.

The religious references continue with the Danninger-led lynch mob that comes to the farm to capture Lukas after he is seen visiting his mother in jail. Severin is crucified on a cartwheel, Emmy is beaten and raped, and Lukas is killed. Severin relates how Lukas was to be buried in secret and that no church bells rang, but that the workers from the valley came to his funeral and no livestock were fed that day. The final exodus of the remaining new farmers (past a respectful crowd of workers) evokes the Austrian exiles from 1934 to 1938, but Severin's murder of Danninger undercuts any reactionary victory and suggests the ultimate destruction of Austrofascism.

It is important to examine Emmy and Rosalind vis-à-vis the faceless image of women among the traditional farmers. These wives and daughters, dressed in traditional costumes, have no involvement in the running of the town, are only seen attending church, and only heard mindlessly echoing the politics of their men. The sociopolitical dysfunction of Weimar Germany and First Republic Austria has often been located in the collapse of traditional gender roles. It has been noted that this was a world of the "old man" and the "new woman." Danninger's hatred of Emmy transcends her social class and attacks her emancipation: her unwed motherhood, her lack of a dominant male partner, her rejection of traditional clothing, and her dominance if not actual leadership of the new farmers. She offers her body to Danninger to save Lukas, because she understands that this is the only way Danninger can understand her. Danninger later admits that she is not a whore and has her own principles, which makes her far more dangerous to his obviously corrupted patriarchal rule.

Rosalind is a remnant of an older era, a traditional worker who was forced to have sex with Hillinger and subsequently forfeits her child. She returns to kill him only when she learns she is dying. Although she makes no claim on Lukas, telling him that he is Hillinger's son as well, she dies bitter and repressed. Lukas's murder extinguishes Hillinger's bloodline, and within the leftist allegory — the actual heir (the peasantry and working classes) to the inheritance of the farm — or the postimperial nation. The farmers who kill him are but elitist usurpers, representing outmoded order and abusive tradition but have, according to Ruzowitzky's allegory, no overriding rights to the house of Austria. The *Siebtelbauern* farm is ultimately left to the Alte Nane and the stable boy — representations of a troubled past and an undefined future, but of no distinct present.

As the self-examination of the Austrian twentieth century has become a more common topic in national discourse, so filmmakers increasingly approach formerly taboo eras and show audiences that Austria not only has cinematic traditions that can be rediscovered but that explorations of recent history can also bring a sense of universality. But why are *historically* based images of social, gender and political conflict now so potent and popular? Rupert Koppold may have provided an answer in his review of Ruzowitzky's film: "It has become too complicated to show the mechanisms of contemporary society. At least too complicated to capture them in such palatable images as this film can."[53] Experiencing the illusion of a lost world is one of the basic pleasures found in the voyeurism of cinema. It is telling that the Austrian discourse on the Anschluss, arriving decades after the postwar era, and the nation's recent return to international film prominence both relate a critical reviewing of the past through the concept of a "safe" distance. Perhaps just to show that he could do a highly commercial film as well, Stefan Ruzowitzky's following picture, *Anatomie*/Anatomy (Germany 2000), is a very Hollywood-style thriller, a star vehicle for Franka Potente, who plays a medical student whose inquiries regarding the corpse on her dissecting table place her in peril.

Much of the accessibility of *Siebtelbauern*, particularly to the English-speaking world, is due to its production company Dor-Film and its lead producers Danny Krausz and Kurt Stocker. The pair has been responsible for producing films that have not lost their critical edge yet manage to be commercial as well, and which are packaged to the appeal of the foreign film market. Krausz also has managed to make Austrian film a player in major large-budget successes abroad with István Szabó's *Sonnenschein*/Sunshine (Hungary/Germany/Austria 1999), the saga of an Austro-Hungarian Jewish family's experience under the monarchy, Nazism and Communism, with Ralph Fiennes in a triple role as grandfather, father and son, and in German director Joseph Vilsmaier's *Comedian Harmonists* (1998), the critical

and popular success about the 1930s German a capella singing group, whose international Beatlemania-like fame was destroyed by the racial laws of the Third Reich.
Vilsmaier had previously scored critical interest with his Austrian/German co-production (including Dor-Film) of *Schlafes Bruder*/Sleep's Brother (1995).

Among the promising directors produced by Dor-Film to have found not only
an audience but also an interesting style in the latter 1990s is Michael Glawogger
(1959–). A former student of the San Francisco Art Institute and the film academy at Vienna's University of Music and Performing Arts, he began his film career
in 1980 with a series of avant-garde shorts and with work as a cameraman and
scriptwriter. In 1989, he collaborated with Ulrich Seidl (1952–) on the documentary *Krieg in Wien*/War in Vienna and directed his first feature in 1995, *Die Ameisenstraße*/Street of Ants. The film borrows from the genres of the folk play and the
social drama but transforms the elements of both into a claustrophobic Kafkaesque
tale with a strong sense of the surreal. Robert Acker compares Glawogger's telling
of the strange inhabitants of a Viennese apartment house and their eviction by the
new landlord to the work of David Cronenberg, Peter Greenaway, David Lynch
and Luis Buñuel.[54] In addition to the colorful characters, the film employs a folk
play character constellation (identifiable types that allow the audience a critical
stance) and social drama framework (class inequality and conflict) in re-visioning
Austrian cinema themes but also ruptures the traditional narrative with an irrational use of stylistic conventions:

> The film uses an authoritative voice-over narrator, who is somewhat paradoxically
> one of the protagonists privy to a wide range of information and [who] also pro-
> vides an orientation and interpretation of events, twisted though it might be....
> Each shot is crammed full of authentic artifacts to create the illusion of docu-
> mentary accuracy [and] the film is interrupted three times with intermediate titles
> to give the birth and death dates of deceased apartment dwellers.[55]

The overriding obsession of the characters is their relationship to time and
death, which seem to turn the inhabitants inward, away from the threat of an outside interruption of their orderly existence, even to the point of avoiding their
neighbors. The renovation of the apartment house into condominiums is rejected
by most of the inhabitants and they are reduced to paralysis by the emotional and
physical destruction of their world, while the new owners scurry about like the ants
of the title. Critic Robert Acker reads this grotesque, pessimistic comedy as a statement on the multivalent, centerless structure of postmodern society, perhaps even
meant as a microcosm of the European Union. Another interpretation might suggest that the film is an allegory on Austria's relationship with Nazism. Like the
building, lingering guilt is "covered over," while the inhabitants are unable to deal
with the past or the future in the hollowness of their environment. As one character relates, "We didn't know how to interpret the signs. Right from the beginning
nobody paid any attention to the wiles of everyday reality."[56]

Die Ameisenstraße did not, however, alienate the government, which submitted it as the national entry for Oscar nomination in the category of Best Foreign

Language Film. It subsequently was awarded the Austrian Film Prize in 1995 and the Saarland Film Festival Prize for Best German Language Debut. The following year Glawogger offered *Kino im Kopf/*Cinema in the Head (1996), which he not only wrote and directed but shot as well. Glawogger's earlier film partner Ulrich Seidl, who served as casting director on *Ameisenstraße*, has since become one of Austria's noted documentarians with *Good News* (1990), which observes the lives of the foreign newspaper sellers in Vienna, and *Tierische Liebe/*Animal Love (1995), which focuses on the often bizarre relationships lonely or antisocial Austrians have with their pets. Rejected for television showing by ORF and by some cinemas as well, the provocative film created a sensation at European festival screenings. Glawogger followed this with a 1998 documentary on the survival of members of the under-class in Bombay, Mexico City, Moscow and New York in *Megacities* and the 1999 documentary on the Austrian national soccer team at the World Cup finals in France, *Frankreich, wir kommen/*France, Here We Come.

Stockholm-born Harald Sicheritz (1958–), who came from television, is one of the other exponents of the successful transfer of cabaret theater to feature film with his first hit, *Muttertag/*Mother's Day (1993). Borrowing from the social drama's focus on the problems of the family unit as symbol for sociopolitical discord, the film also returns to the Austrian screwball comedy with its rapid-fire wisecracking dialogue and the disintegration of order as the Neugebauer family's plans for a Mother's Day celebration go awry due to revelations of the husband's (Roland Düringer, who also co-wrote the script) infidelity, the wife's (Andrea Händler) kleptomania, the son's peculiarities, the grandfather's malicious nature, and several unexpected interruptions. Along with Harather's *Indien* and Schwabenitzky's *Ein echter Wiener geht nicht unter*, it was one of the bona fide box-office successes of 1993–94 and demonstrated that contemporary social comedy about the average Austrian had the attention of the nation. Sicheritz returned to the family-under-duress theme in *Hinterholz 8* (1998), a Dor-Film produced by Danny Krausz and Kurt Stocker, about a Viennese couple and their difficult attempt to save money in order to escape their cramped apartment for a rundown farmhouse. With an atten-dance score of 600,655, it surpasses the 1986 *Müllers Büro* (439,000), which brought Austrians back into the cinemas in the early years of New Austrian Film, the 1995 *Schlafes Bruder* (305,700), and the 1993 *Indien* (221,000) as Austrian box-office champion. The 1999 feature *Wanted* looks at another type of "escape" from the urban world: distraught by an unsuccessful operation, a physician turns his back on reality for life in a psychiatric hospital, where he can fantasize a life in the Wild West. When a former schoolmate, now a priest, is called in to help, he is convinced by the patient to join in the fantasy.

With public discourse taking on the long-avoided past and the world taking on Austria's political present, Austrian films at the end of the decade and century were often comedy-dramas focusing on the deconstruction of the status quo or the idealized image, on the exploration of the concept of the relativity of truth, or on the reinvention of self and surroundings. Michael Kreihsl (1958–), a cameraman on Manker's controversial 1986 *Schmutz/*Dirt, made his promising directorial debut with the opera film *Idomeneo* (1989) and secured interest in his work with *Charms Zwischenfälle*/Charms's Incidents (1996), a surreal look at the life of Russian writer Daniil Charms. In 1999, he directed Ulrich Tukur as a sociopathic restorer of old-master paintings who loathes capitalism and destroys advertising in *Heimkehr der Jäger*/Return of the Hunters (1999). It is an interesting extension of the director's own persona, since, in addition to his filmmaking and his former studies in art and archaeology, he is an art restorer. The film offers a metaphor on the self-destructive nature of reactionary impulses in contemporary society. Shorts filmmaker Christian Frosch (1966–) made his feature debut in 1997 with a tragicomic thriller, *Die totale Therapie*/Total Therapy, featuring Blixa Bargeld and Sophie Rois. When a charismatic self-awareness guru is murdered during a retreat at an isolated country estate, chaos sets in among the followers. It is clear to the audience that one of the clients has finally been liberated from her fears and allergies and can bury both her former life and her therapist. A wry look at New Age religion and pop psychology, the film metaphorically attacks political populism and cultism in Austria. Based on letters by Franz Kafka, Frosch wrote and directed an intimate look at the writer (Lars Rudolf) and his difficult love affair with Felice Bauer (Ursula Ofner) in *K.aF.ka-Fragment* (2000). Andreas Prochaska (1964–), an editor on Michael Haneke's *Funny Games*, has become a director who specializes in the absurdities of crime and the justice system: on the large screen with Christine Nöstlinger's novel *Die drei Posträuber*/The Three Postal Robbers (1998) and on television with a story about the "perfect" murder, *High Society* (1999). After work in commercials and documentary films, Michael Bindlechner (1957–) offered his first feature, *In Heaven* (1998), a look at a young man having to make an impossible choice between the two different paths of two new friends. Salzburg-born Bernhard Semmelrock (1973–) offered a quirky first feature, *Wolken über dem Paradies*/Clouds over Paradise (1998), which moves from whimsy and comedy to anxiety and despair as Konrad, a meek bank employee, lost in bizarre daydreams in an effort to escape his drab life, falls for Maria, a woman who he knows will change his life. Edgar Honetschläger (1963–), an Austrian filmmaker based in Tokyo, directed *Milk* (1997), which takes on four urban nomads and their adventures in the Japanese capital. He continued his exploration of Japanese socioculture through the eyes of a young Japanese woman in *L&R* (2000). The films respond to the ardent fascination Japanese tourists have with Austria and its imperial culture by providing Austrians with a more realistic view of the Japanese experience. Stephan Wagner's (1968–) *Kubanisch rauchen*/Smoking Cuban Style (1998) features a love triangle, ultimately a quadrangle, which comes between two men who own an antique shop. Peter Payer's (1964–) *Untersuchung an Mädeln*/Girls Under Investigation (1998) follows the story behind two young hitchhiking women wrongly accused of murdering a cattleman. Foreign directors and international co-productions, although with a distinct Austrian "center" (cast and crew, location), made up a portion of the nation's film output between 1997 and 1999. Among them, Dutch author, screenwriter and director Frouke Fokkema (1952–) has directed several Austrian/Dutch co-productions and is revisiting the brief film relationship the two countries enjoyed prior to the

Anschluss. In 1999, she offered her most "Austrian" film, *Der Umweg/*The Detour, an unusual blend of fiction and reality that looks at the obsession of a young Dutch woman with controversial Austrian writer Thomas Bernhard.

Without doubt, the three most internationally significant Austrian filmmakers recognized for their stylistic impact at the end of the decade were Michael Haneke, Barbara Albert and experimentalist Peter Tscherkassky. Haneke, whose work has stimulated international cinema discourse on the level not seen since directors of the French New Wave or of New German Cinema, was born in Munich in 1942 and studied psychology, philosophy and drama at the University of Vienna. Originally a television editor, he has worked as a freelance screenwriter and stage director in Austria since 1970. Also finding the inevitable employment in Austrian television, Haneke offered bleak films on the experience of social isolation or on dysfunctional relationships in a style influenced by Robert Bresson: *After Liverpool* (1974); *Lemminge/*Lemmings (1979); the adaptation of Peter Rossei's novel *Wer war Edgar Allen?/*Who Was Edgar Allen? (1984); and *Nachruf für ein Mörder/*Obituary for a Murderer (1991). His breakthrough as a filmmaker came with his very first feature, *Der Siebte Kontinent/*The Seventh Continent in 1989, which along with his two later films, *Benny's Video* (1992) and *71 Fragmente einer Chronologie des Zufalls/*71 Fragments of a Chronology of Chance (1994) form a trilogy on the social alienation and narcissism nurtured by the age of video and computers. His sparse, even cold, directorial style serves to portray what he suggests is Austria's "emotional glaciation."[57] Firmly couched in psychology and the social drama genre tradition, which he then deconstructs and subverts, Haneke's revelation of the pain that lurks beneath the daily life of the bourgeoisie and the horrors it may spawn was shockingly evident with *Kontinent,* wherein the director with the distance of icy logic follows a family as it prepares and commits mass suicide — its journey to the "seventh continent." This devastating parable was selected as Austria's entry for the Best Foreign Language Film Oscar and remains a controversial film. Like his previous film, *Benny's Video* takes on the isolation of contemporary life, this time through the mind-numbing effects of video games, which have become the obsession of the young son of a wealthy family. Having lost touch with reality, he plots and performs the murder of a young girl. The depiction of the murder in all its gruesome, premeditated detail was attacked for exploiting the violence the film supposedly deplores, but the film was generally praised by Austrian and European critics and was awarded the European Film Academy's Felix Award for Best Film. Concluding the trilogy, and the savvy international promotion by producer Veit Heidruschka and his Wega-Film company, *71 Fragmente* also gained acclaim and received a Golden Hugo Award. More than any other film, it is Haneke's "manifesto" on postmodern filmmaking. Unlike the previous family-focused disaster brought by consumerism, *71 Fragmente* examines the entire hierarchy of society. Haneke suggests that the film is not populated by characters but by surface representations of the "fears, desires, and fantasies of the spectators" and that he preferred not to offer "realism" but aimed toward creating a paradigmatic model. As for Wolfram Paulus, only the fragment can suggest reality, and Haneke believes his role is to provide a simple construct by which the audience can interpret meaning and integrate the story into their individual value and belief systems. The film must not come to an artificial "end" but should continue in audience reception:

> In short, a film as such does not exist, it comes to exist only in the minds of the spectators. A film's essential feature, its criterion of quality, should be its ability to become the productive center of an interactive process.... I attempt to provide an alternative to the totalizing productions that are typical of the entertainment cinema of American provenance.[58]

Haneke's theoretical influence beyond Bresson is clear: the fragmentary, subjective concept of Viennese impressionism, the distancing effects of Brechtian theater, and, finally, the rejection of the false totality of art that Walter Benjamin saw as a strong contribution to the aesthetic/political aim of fascism. Haneke also regards "interesting" or "beautiful" films to be "banality," the result of the advertising aesthetic and a detriment to the precision of image. His films have less explicit violence than an average detective story, Haneke claims, but it is the confrontation with self-deception that makes them seem more violent than other films. Haneke's 1997 film *Funny Games* would prove his point. Although showing no explicit violence, this deconstruction of the traditional thriller in which a couple and their young son arrive at their lakeside vacation home and are subsequently met by two well-mannered but bored young men who slowly menace the family and ultimately kill them offers no safety net for the audience. Unlike the resolution of mainstream dominant cinema, no order is restored, no reason is plumbed, and the viewer is left to contemplate the relationship between the media and escalating social violence. *Funny Games* has been regarded as a film that spearheaded the wider festival interest in Austrian cinema during the late 1990s, especially after it became the first Austrian feature in competition at Cannes since the 1960s. It was subsequently sold to more than thirty countries, an "unprecedented figure for an Austrian feature in recent times."[59]

Haneke's most widely seen and controversial films, however, demonstrate his postmodern transnational hybridity as a German-born filmmaker in Austria who utilizes French casts. This also evokes the unique multiculturalism of pre–Anschluss independent Austrian cinema. Both *Code Inconnu/Code Unknown* (1999) and *Die Klavierspielerin/The Piano Teacher* (2001) convey that Haneke is a Eurodirector whose obsessions expand the self-critical Austrian visions of Nobel Prize winning author Elfriede Jelinek and comment on the entire post–Soviet European sociocultural environment with its collision of humanist unification and exclusionary nationalisms. In the very "European" film (in French and other languages) of *Code Inconnu/Code Unknown* (1999), a simple frame — a passerby drops a wadded paper into a beggar's hand — ties together several stories that deal with the complex and often impenetrable "codes" that make or break human relationships in a world of growing uniformity and alienation. Haneke's claustrophobic camera with its long takes and his cut-to-black scene punctuations emphasizes the silent despair, sense

The thriller deconstructed: Michael Haneke's, *Funny Games*, 1997.

of displacement and aggressive nature that seethe just below the surface of everything and everybody. Indeed, the many silences in this film vibrate with tension; the attempts at communication always miss, whether between friends, lovers or families. There is Anne (Juliette Binoche) and her problematic relationship with her photographer lover Georges (Thierry Nouvic) who is covering the war in Bosnia; the boy (Alexander Hamidi) in conflict with his demanding father; the black teacher (Ona Lu Yenke) arrested for defending the dignity of a beggar (Luminita Gheorghiu), a despairing Romanian immigrant. Although Haneke agreed that the film takes on xenophobia, he avoids, as with all his films, any specific ideological bent: "this is not a political, rather a humanistic, moralistic question. Xenophobia is a mixture of stupidity and fear. The only thing one can do to battle it is to attempt to enlighten people a bit and expose those on the other side, who would use it for their own gain."[60] Haneke subverts what he sees as the lie of a benevolent contemporary European multiculture by intercutting Georges' photographs of brutal victimization and murder in Bosnia.

As the most recognizable star in a cast of "normal" people, Binoche can only play an actress, a metafilmic comment on the audience relationship with its cinema icons. He also places a film within the film, the only segment of *Code Inconnu* that features conventional camera work and editing. While the sexy Anne flirts with a handsome man in a high-rise building's pool, a small boy climbs the wall that surrounds the rooftop area. The imminent disaster is "resolved" only when the audience discovers they have been watching rushes from Anne's film. The film within the film has provided the accessible and trivial mix of emotion expected from

Hollywood film: attractive people, sexual titillation, danger, resolution and emotional catharsis. Anne's actual life is far more complex and ambiguous. Having been threatened by Arab boys on the Metro, she has come away from the experience somewhat more wary, perhaps more racist, and she ultimately shuts out her "foreign" lover. The violence simmers just under the surface, erupting and subsiding; the codes are ever shifting. As the film begins with a deaf child acting out an emotional situation in front of other deaf children who to her growing frustration and sadness cannot guess what she is doing, so it ends with the child now recoiling — symbolizing the noncommunicability of human anguish. *Code Inconnu* attracted major attention at Cannes in 2000 as well as in the United States, and Anthony Lane, writing in *The New Yorker,* praised the director's technical and narrative prowess: "Haneke cuts back and forth from one to the next with such skill, and with so little superfluous detail, that the effect is oddly bracing [editing is by Karin Hartusch and Nadine Muse]; his is not the portentous alienation of Antonioni, but the hard, topical distillation of ethnic strife — not of a Europe deep in thought, but of a Europe under fire."[61] He also sees it as an "antidote to *Scream* [an American film of the hybrid teen flick/slasher/horror genre] — to that whole sniggering franchise, which was dedicated to the decivilising nostrum that fear is a sick joke and death no more than the convenient tool of a genre…it may take an unpopular or recalcitrant artist to remind us just how unreadable, if not unreachable we can sometimes be."[62]

After his television adaptation of Kafka's *Das Schloss*/The Castle (1996), *Die Klavierspielerin*/The Piano Teacher (2001) is Haneke's second novel adaptation and the first for the large screen. Calling the Jelinek text a "chamber piece for three people"[63] he builds the film around the talents of Isabelle Huppert, as tortured piano virtuoso Erika Kohut, a proper and demanding Viennese music professor who enjoys attention and respect, while tolerating a cruel mother (Annie Giradot), and finding release through abuse, voyeurism, and sadomasochistic sexual fantasies. When a charming student (Benoît Magimel) enters her life and attempts a relationship with her, she insists on controlling their sexual encounters to the point that it becomes an abusive power play. Ultimately she reveals her bondage desires and rejects his declaration of love. Frustrated and unable to find the nurturing, even tender, sexual relationship he seeks with her, the student beats and abandons her. She plans on stabbing him with a kitchen knife during a public recital but turns the weapon on herself and flees the concert hall into the night. Like *Code Inconnu,* the film teases the audience to expect narrative conventionality. The beautiful piano music elevates the film and Huppert's image into the realm of high art, which is then obliterated by the reality of her incongruent and claustrophobically presented sadomasochism for which there is no resolution or trivial salvation. Haneke's brisk cutting between moments of elegant piano recitals, troubled academic relationships, violent personal arguments, self-abuse, voyeurism and sexual acts takes on an almost musical pattern of theme and variation, or a psychological mosaic of public persona and private truths that collide and overlap. Although sex and sexuality is at the core of the film, it is unerotic and disturbing for its obvious joylessness and mechanical quality. Also like the violence in *Code Inconnu,* which

Extremes of the human experience or a metaphor for national dysfunction? Benoît Magimel and Isabelle Huppert in Michael Haneke's *Die Klavierspielerin*, 2001.

remains implicit, the sex scenes in *Klavierspielerin* are shot so that actions are obscured and the film has no nudity except during Erika's genital self-mutilation and her beating. While it is obvious that Jelinek's character is a metaphor for what she considers to be the sadomasochistic, even fascistic, impulses in contemporary Austrian society — self-denial, incongruous ideals of high-art and culture, unbending social etiquette and role playing, resentment and finally self-abuse/punishment — Hanke denies that he has created any symbolism at all. Speaking before an audience at the Los Angeles premiere, Haneke insisted that he is fascinated with the "extremes" of human experience in society and did not set out to create any political statements.[64] He rejects trendy style, form and analysis in an almost Kubrickian manner and has criticized Lars von Trier's Dogma cinema, which rebels against Hollywood-based emphasis on high technology with a neo–French New Wave minimalist manifesto: "For me, Dogma is a contradiction of freedom. As soon as I am forced to do something according to a recipe, I have lost my freedom.... I want to set my own limits, not have them be set by a colleague. Dogma is a very clever publicity idea, to draw attention to one's work."[65] Haneke is equally resistant toward the new trend of international co-production, which he believes may work for large-scale historic epics but not for other films. For the director, such multinationalism leads to synthetic films that have little relationship to specific locations or cultural qualities. Yet his own productions are often transnational, and he avoids the issue of whether he is an Austrian filmmaker or if he is making films about Austria:

In discussions I then always say, the films provoke you so much, whether in France, in America or elsewhere, because you obviously know from your own experience what they are getting at. In other words, my films don't specifically target Austria, they have to do with the entire advanced industrialized world.... My films are made for our industrialized West, for our affluent society, that's where they belong and that's where they should be seen.[66]

Although critics are hardly of one mind regarding the director's provocative images, he has created a personal cinematic ideology, which is far more profound than the various international trends of shock cinema. After decades of scant film festival participation, the fact that *Die Klavierspielerin* appeared in official competition at the 2001 Cannes Film Festival was sensation enough for Austrian cinema. Its awards for the director and actors Isabelle Huppert and Benoît Magimel stunned Austria and suggested to some that a "spell" had finally been broken. The film subsequently swept the European Film Academy Awards.

Another Austrian filmmaker caught the eye of Cannes that year: Jessica Hausner (1972–), a student of both Haneke and Wolfgang Glück and a promising director of short films, screened her feature debut, *Lovely Rita* (2000) and caused major discussion about her visions of the teenage outsider. Unlike Haneke, and perhaps for financial reasons, Hausner tends to adhere to the minimalist dictates of the Dogma movement. As critic Roman Scheiber, reporter on the Austrian film scene for *Variety's International Film Guide* notes, the director is a "good example of how young Austrian filmmakers can make rapid progress — if they get enough money to put their visions on screen."[67] At a reception at Vienna's city hall celebrating Haneke, Hausner and producer Veit Heidruschka, the cinema-friendly City Councilor for the Arts Andreas Mailath-Pokorny responded by referring to "these historic days at Cannes"[68] and appealed to the Austrian media, particularly to the ORF, to maintain its financial partnership with the impoverished film sector (*Die Klavierspielerin* had been financed in part by the television network). Haneke, receiving a golden city hall statuette in recognition for his successes, was far more blunt as he spoke of the "catastrophic financial situation" of the Austrian film industry and expressed concern for his filmmaking colleagues who did not have the French support he enjoys.[69] But controversy swirled around the internationally recognized Haneke work in, of all places, Vienna. The director refused to have *Die Klavierspielerin* (or any of his previous work) screen at the Viennale film festival because of his long-standing feud with festival director Hans Hurch over what Haneke considered Hurch's mean-spirited attitude toward filmmakers and their work during his days as a critic. Hurch had apparently attempted to screen *Code Inconnu* the previous year; after he was unable to get a print of the film from the director, he commented that he was relieved, because he thought the film to be so bad. Hurch defends his stance as part of his ideology as a film festival director and as part of a defense of Austrian cinema quality. Haneke maintained that a festival director has no right to impose his own questionable criteria on films and that the hypercritical attitude is part of the inferiority complex of a country that has no film tradition and therefore no reputation of quality. Thus, everything produced must automatically be discounted. This attitude has also caused Austrian film to remain unpopular at home to the point that government cuts are "applauded." And regarding these cuts, Haneke maintains that in France the public would join in the protest against such film policy. The fact that a director of Haneke's stature, who helped bring Austrian cinema back into the international theaters, would insist that he may have to make his future films outside of Austria because of the lack of financing is a sad irony that ought to embarrass the Austrian government. Haneke's notion, however, that Hurch's difficult ways stem from a lack of Austrian film tradition, should equally embarrass the filmmaker, whose obvious lack of knowledge (or selective memory) regarding Austrian cinema history makes him appear less the "Austrian" filmmaker and more the foreign filmmaker, who believes he has imported a sense of "quality" with his work.

Goran Rebic (1968–), whose personal experiences in Serbia have influenced his several short films, emerged with his feature *Jugofilm* (1997) and a documentary *The Punishment* (1999), about the inhabitants of Yugoslavia's capital, Belgrade, from the period of NATO bombardment to the millennium celebrations. The film, which enters the lives of a wide variety of citizens from different professions, questions the concept of collective guilt and collective punishment, a subject quite topical in Austria given the recent popular discourse on its own war past. The film strives to show an image of Yugoslavia that is more human and differentiated than news reports have presented. Rebic sees himself as a protagonist in the film: "It was important for me to have a face as well. The film is a journey, a quest, with me." Rather than remain behind the camera, Rebic breaks the unwritten rule regarding documentary film and appears on camera with his production team. He considers this a more transparent form of filmmaking, one that is able to suggest that there are many realities.[70] *The Punishment* received the Grand Prize at the Diagonale, the festival for Austrian films. Very ambitious, more mainstream, but less successful was Australian film and opera director Bruce Beresford's Austrian/British/German co-production of *Bride of the Wind* (2001), the story of composer and muse Alma Schindler (Sarah Wynter) and her relationships with her three husbands — composer/conductor Gustav Mahler (Jonathan Price), Bauhaus architect Walter Gropius, and novelist Franz Werfel — and two artist lovers, Gustav Klimt and Oskar Kokoschka. Shot on location in Vienna, sumptuously designed by Herbert Pinter and costumed by Shuna Harwood, the film strives for a neofeminist quality in its examination of the subject's artistic repression, but its too-studied impersonations of legendary figures ultimately make for a beautiful but aloof docudrama.

It was at the 1999 Venice Film Festival, where no Austrian film had competed in decades, that the new era was truly brought to the fore by critics praising the work of emerging filmmaker Barbara Albert (1970–). After several short films and a documentary, Albert created two feature films in 1998. *Alles Bunt und Wunderbar*/Slidin'-Shrill, Bright World was co-written and directed with former journalist-turned-screenwriter Reinhard Jud (1959–) and Michael Grimm (1962–). The film is an intertwined trilogy focusing on the counterculture of the teenage world, which foreshadowed her breakthrough, *Nordrand*/North Side; a.k.a. City Skirts (1999), and also dealt with a topic that most fascinates Albert — the loss of innocence. Written by Albert with cinematography by Christine Maier, *Nordrand* focuses on two women (Nina Proll and Edita Malovcic) whose lives attract other young people of different ethnic and sociocultural backgrounds: a Romanian immigrant, a Bosnian refugee and an Austrian who has just completed his military service. Seeking self-realization, emotional support, and concerned with bringing children into this world, they live in a housing project on Vienna's north side, and flounder between memories of war in Yugoslavia, temporary jobs, and unwanted pregnancies until they finally drift apart. Albert sets inserts from television news, flashbacks, symbolic montages and spaces of hybridity and impermanence (bars, discos, underground passages, shopping areas, streets) against long takes dealing with the characters' desire for stability and control, but no harmony is found or projected.[71] In a more authentic manner than Haneke's French-based "Austrian" cinema, Albert populates her films with the ethnicities that make up Vienna and have always been a part of the city and the culture. That Vienna is once again a hub for polyglot Central Europe seems quite natural here, but it also underscores the curious xenophobia and the attempt at creating an impossible homogeneous Austrian national identity that has emerged in the last decade of the twentieth century since the fall of the Bloc system. Yet it is precisely this movement across Central/Eastern Europe that has allowed Vienna to reassert itself as a major influential cultural site in Europe beyond its impressive museumlike qualities.

Albert, who had won laurels for her short film work and who co-founded the COOP 99 production company, was greeted with wide critical acclaim for this "small" film, which also generated significant box office and garnered the Marcello Mastroianni Prize for Best Newcomer for Nina Proll. Rumors abounded that American festivals and the Oscars ignored her film because of fallout from the EU boycott and a lingering Hollywood protest against Jörg Haider. The quick success everywhere else did not, however, launch Albert into the rapid production of new work: "I am not a director who considers the shoot the most creative aspect of the production process. I am always expending a great deal of energy. I first have to feel relaxed enough to think about what I want to say in my next story."[72]

Following Albert's sensation and offering a similar film context was Ulrich Seidl's *Hundstage*/Dog Days (2001), which won the Grand Jury Prize at the 2001 Venice Festival. Seidl is primarily known for his quirky documentaries *Good News* (1990), *Tierische Liebe*/Animal Love (1995), and *Der Busenfreund*/The Bosom Buddy (1997), about a forty-year-old teacher who lives with his mother and abandons his job to concentrate on his sexual fantasies about actress Senta Berger. Seidl's *Hundstage*, which features only two professional actors in a production populated by semiprofessionals and amateurs, presents six interrelated episodes taking place during a late summer weekend. Lurking just beneath the façades of peaceful and tidy suburban life are often grotesque vignettes of desire, loneliness, criminality, and brutality. Unlike the dark kitsch-decadent visions of American director David Lynch, whose work is comparable in theme, Seidl's imagery, as recorded by Wolfgang

Thaler's astringent camera work, gives this dystopia an arid and engineered quality that makes its disciplined order seem all the more inorganic. While the film articulates contemporary Austrian social anxieties, it is also universal in its exploration of middle-class alienation: "The audience is forced to take part in this world. People are confronted with themselves," comments Seidl about his film, which reportedly even stunned Michael Haneke.[73] *Hundstage* was made over a three-year period to capture the appropriate atmosphere of the season.

Because of the continued problems in funding large features and the legacy of the Actionist art of the 1960s and 1970s, Austria has continued to have an inordinately large share of filmmakers who specialize in the short experimental format. Some, like Valie Export, span the genres as "media artists." Other formerly important names in short or experimental filmmaking have moved on to the classroom lectern, returned to their visual art roots or entered mainstream television production. Vienna-born Peter Tscherkassky (1958–), who teaches filmmaking at the Academies of Applied Arts in Vienna and Linz, however, and has had several decades of presence on the national and international experimental scene, continues to create strictly within his noncommercial genre and yet maintains celebrity status. His career began in the late 1970s, not as an Actionist but as a Super 8 documentarian of performance art. His film *Aderlass*/Blood Letting (1981), for example, captures the self-abusive performance of Armin Schmickl Sebastiano in manic, jittery editing that not only conveys the shock and confusion of the act but also reorders the artist's monologue and harangues until they too have been cut and tortured into an ugly poetry. Super 8 continues to have a specific quality of mainstream subversion for the filmmaker, although he has now moved on to 16 mm and even 35 mm Cinemascope. Although he appreciates the ease of digital video, Tscherkassky continues to work with celluloid, since his specific editing manipulations can only be done to individual frames. He also wants his work, whether shot or found and manipulated, to evoke the quality and look of traditional "film" as a statement of the aesthetics and ideology of the medium.[74]

Frustrating the viewer's voyeuristic desire is at the heart of Tscherkassky's work from the 1980s. In the seventeen-minute Super 8 film *Tabula Rasa*, which manipulates shots of a woman undressing herself, he renders Lacanian theory as film:

> [The theory] considers the screen as a mirror, wherein the viewer is under the impression that he himself is creating the film through identification with his own (inherent voyeuristic) act of watching. In fact there are specific conditions, which make this way of looking at film possible. *Tabula Rasa* accounts for these preconditions, swinging from the figurative to the abstract, which as a visual irritation does not allow itself to be understood as one's own creation as a viewer.[75]

Although the film continuously teases the viewer with an object of desire, it also obscures and even blocks the gaze. Tscherkassky here underscores and rejects the relationship between the commercial filmmaker and audience reception, demolishing calculated/expected visual satisfaction. Although no longer stylistically transferring the Actionist's violent confrontation of the traditional "art lover's" expectations to film, Tscherkassky's more subtle play with the imagined reality of film can be seen as a response to the cliché and sexist narrative aspects in commercial Austrian cinema prior to the 1970s. Through such popular genres as the imperial epic, the *Heimatfilm*, and the operetta/musical, the reductive postwar concepts of history and national identity became synonymous with visual pleasure and clearly aided in the creation of the mythologies of the Second Republic.

Tscherkassky's found cinema has been among the most important influences in recent European experimental filmmaking and has even returned the concept of manipulating fragmented narratives to American avant gardists, who have forgotten that the method had a brief run in the underground cinema of San Francisco and New York during the early 1960s. Among his astonishing pieces is *Happy-End* (1996) in which Tscherkassky edits celebratory moments of several New Year's toasts between a middle-aged couple only to reveal joyless alcoholism, the rigidity of the husband, and the ultimate despair of the wife. His "Cinemascope Trilogy" takes on dominant cinema modes and audience expectations. *L'Arrivée* (1998), a tribute to Lumière Brothers, consists of a short scene cut from Terence Young's 1968 imperial epic *Mayerling*,[76] where, like Haneke, he reduces the conventions of danger, sexual/aesthetic attraction (between the characters and for the audience gazing at a sumptuously presented Catherine Deneuve) and resolution/catharsis to just over two minutes, in which he not only underscores such formalism but hijacks it through editing and film manipulation: the approaching train bringing Deneuve into the station and into the arms of her lover nearly skips out of the sprockets and collides with itself before the heroine emerges unscathed. Tscherkassky comments that his short displays the construct behind all dominant cinema, or how "an anonymous American housewife … [described] Hollywood's version of life: 'getting into trouble and out of it again.'"[77] The filmmaker goes one step further with *Outer Space* (1999), by cutting and reprocessing a scene from *The Entity* (USA 1981), a Hollywood horror film with Barbara Hershey. Her confrontation of an unseen force in a dark house becomes a startling commentary on the very nature of the conveyance of fear in motion pictures, as the film material itself appears to be pursuing Hershey, collapsing in on her, torturing her with a soundtrack gone haywire, and with the very nature of the damaged film itself. What remains after the meta-cinematic storm is Hershey's tense but unyielding face, staring at multiple reflected/recut images of herself and at the audience. It is a wry reference to Jean Seberg's realization of an "audience" in the final shot of Godard's *Breathless* (France 1960), the French New Wave film that so startlingly explored the human need to construct filmic realities and identities to survive the chaos of life. In Tscherkassky's *Outer Space*, however, Hershey's survival of both the internal and external filmic threat tells us there is no escape, even into cinema. Most interesting is the feminist message that slips though Hershey's gaze. As a female within a horror film, a Hollywood star acting out the traditional heroine-in-peril fantasy of the original male writer (Frank De Felitta) and director (Sidney J. Furie), and subjected to the additional terrors created by Tscherkassky, her expression seems to breathlessly indict the true cinematic horror — the convention of female abuse for audience enjoyment.

Following Tscherkassky's lead is Martin Arnold (1959–), who was a student of psychology and history before turning to cinema in 1988. His experimental found-film shorts such as *Pièce Touchée* (1989) have attracted wide attention, but it is his manipulation of scenes from a Judy Garland/Mickey Rooney film, *Alone. Life Wastes Andy Hardy* (1998), which deconstructs the codes of Hollywood film musicals into Freudian subtext, that has become a cult classic in Europe and the United States. Two years earlier, Martin Arnold and Peter Tscherkassky joined other major experimentalists, Gustav Deutsch, Hiebler/Ertl, Thomas Keip, Mara Mattuschka, Lisl Ponger, and Friedrich Rücker, in a joint project, *Eine Geschichte der Bilder — acht Found Footage Filme aus Österreich*/A History of Images — Eight Found Footage Films from Austria. Experimental animation has had little representation in Austrian cinema and has been left to the traditional experts in Hungary, the Czech Republic and Poland. But that neglected genre also began to emerge in Austria in the 1990s through the work of Hubert Sielecki (1946–) and Lisi Frischengruber (1963–).

Like Michael Haneke, a German-born filmmaker who finds a European vision working in Austria, so Hubert Sauper (1966–), born in Kitzbühel, finds an international cinematic vision living in France. Having lived in Italy, England, and the United States, and trained in Vienna and Paris, Sauper has appeared as an actor in several short films and in features. His work as film writer and director began in the fictional short format, which garnered him the Max Ophüls Prize for *Blasi* (1989), but he soon turned to reality-based subjects and has since become known as one of Europe's most provocative documentary filmmakers. His television film *On the Road with Emil* (1993) established Sauper internationally, and his full-length documentaries, *Kisangani Diary* (1998) and *Seule Avec Nos Histoires/Alone with Our Stories* (2001), have been awarded a total of twelve international film prizes and have screened on television in thirty countries. *Kisangani Diary*, which essays the plight of the eighty thousand starving and brutalized Hutu refugees who fled to Zaire in 1997 following Tutsi reprisals in Rwanda, is unrelenting in its attempt to show the depths of human misery and contemporary genocide, as well as the ignorance and apathy of the world in the face of such inhumanity. Although well known throughout Europe and Asia, the film has suffered from the same lack of attention as its subject in the United States. With the interview mosaic of *Alone with Our Stories,* Sauper takes on domestic violence across the sociocultural spectrum in France. But he returns to Africa in *Darwin's Nightmare* (2004), which explores the consequences of the introduction of the Nile perch into Lake Victoria in the 1960s. This large predatory fish eventually eradicated most of the lake's native species and multiplied so quickly that the area was transformed into an immense fishing, filleting and transport center during the following decades. The result has moved far beyond ecological damage and provides a cautionary tale on globalization: international politicians rationalize the industry without interest in human cost; the Russians trade armaments to be used in African civil wars for their fish cargo; an AIDS epidemic rages as workers spend their few earnings on women who flood the area to work as prostitutes; homeless children are exploited and abused by the industry;

and as tons of fish are flown daily to Europe, unabated famine creates a black market for decayed and discarded fish among the Tanzanian population. Shot mostly in undercover situations over a period of six months, Sauper's film was presented with several major awards including the special Europa Cinemas Label Jury Award at the 2004 Venice Film Festival.

Diego Donnhofer (1961–) has moved from third-world documentaries such as *Eritrea* (1992), *Schwarzafrika*/Black Africa (1994) and *Paradise Is Elsewhere* (1997) to a feature drama, *Die Jungfrau*/The Virgin (1998), which funnels his experiences about the abuse of a people into the metaphor of a picaro figure, a handsome young man who is used by lovers, drug dealers, and sexual predators but manages to maintain his "purity" and the intense love of his sister. Another filmmaker who moves more frequently between documentaries and features is Vienna-born and Düsseldorf-based Peter Kern (1949–), who is also a stage and film actor. Kern focuses on sexual identity and social reception in the documentaries *Sex, Lear and Schroeter* (1990); *Knutschen, Kuscheln, Jubilieren*/Kiss, Cuddle and Celebrate (1998), about the lives of five elderly gay men whose lives center on a local bar; and *Suche nach Leben*/A Search for Life (1999), in which Kern follows a dying friend as he revisits the exotic stations of his life. Egon Humer (1954–), born in Wels, has directed and produced a variety of documentaries since the mid–1980s, among them *Reise nach Brody*/Journey to Brody (1993), *Emigration, N.Y.* (1995) and *Leon Askin-(Über)leben und Schauspiel. Private Anmerkungen*/Leon Askin-Living, Surviving and Acting. Private Observations. A veteran of over seventy films in Europe and the United States, character actor Askin (1907–2005) was among the many Austrian artists who fled to Hollywood in the wake of the Anschluss while his parents became victims of the Holocaust. A stage actor in his homeland and a comedy support in many American films including Billy Wilder's 1961 cold war farce, *One, Two, Three,* he gained popular recognition on American television as a blustery Nazi general in *Hogan's Heroes,* the American television comedy series of the 1960s. Humer captures the eighty-nine-year-old actor who returned to Vienna in 1994 as he interacts with other residents of a Jewish retirement home, as he conducts his career from a wheelchair, and as he reflects on his work, identity, and reputation as a "Hollywood star" in Austria.

Karin Berger (1953–) is a political scientist and ethnologist as well as a filmmaker and has published several books including *Women and National Socialism.* Her film and video work also displays her sociopolitical and feminist bent beginning in 1984 with *Tränen statt Gewehre—Anni Haider Erzählt*/Tears Instead of Weapons—Anni Haider Narrates and her 1985 *Küchengespräche mit Rebellinnen*/Kitchen Talk with Revolutionaries (co-directed with Elizabeth Holzinger, Charlotte Podgornik and Lisabeth Trallori). Her 1998 documentary *Ceija Stojka* is a portrait of the difficult life of the Roma author, painter and singer and focuses on the Austrian and post–Soviet Central European relationship with the "gypsy," or, more accurately, the Roma and Sinti cultures. Also focused on the effects of a changing environment on concepts of personal identity is writer/musician Harald Friedl (1958–), who is noted for his strong almost abstract compositions and sense of irony. His 1996 *Ein Leben in diesem Jahrhundert—Wilhelm Kaufmann*/A Life in

This Century — Wilhelm Kaufmann follows the life of the Salzburg painter who has lived in Austria, Canada and Africa, and whose nonartistic experiences range from work with Albert Schweitzer to the co-founding of the Salzburg Green Party. Friedl's *Land ohne Eigenschaften*/Land without Qualities (2000) is named after Robert Menasse's essay on contemporary Austrian identity, which recalls the title of Robert Musil's sprawling and unfinished novel on the collapse of the Austro-Hungarian monarchy, *Mann ohne Eigenschaften* (Man without Qualities) (1930–43). It records the reflections of noted writers (including Menasse) in a fragmented mosaic that attempts to define the complex and contradictory nature of Austria. An open-ended talking-head documentary intercut with banal images of the Austrian landscape and teenagers presenting their patriotic poetry, Friedl's work appears to be an uncomfortable litany against almost every aspect of Austrian life until one realizes that the writers tend to portray the traits they criticize and benefit from, even enjoy, the surroundings they disparage. His *Africa Representa* (2003) departs Austria and examines the displacement of indigenous and traditional society through European influences in central Tanzania.

The resurgence of national interest in Austrian cinema and its new reception abroad also brought with it other aspects related to film appreciation and study that had long been missing. The respected if sporadically published journal from Graz, *Blimp*, which concentrates on international film history and theory was joined at the turn of the century by several internet sites and three high-quality cineaste/trade publications: *Celluloid*, *RAY Kinomagazin*, and the more technically oriented *Media Biz*. Beyond the established Film Academy at Vienna's University of Music and Performing Arts, the new Filmschule Wien (Film School Vienna), created and headed by Arno Aschauer, offers more practical programs of instruction and working relationships with film schools and production companies outside of Austria and the German-speaking world.

There were other notable first appearances and returns in the final years of the twentieth century, which demonstrated that the burgeoning international interest in Austrian cinema was not just a trend or a short-lived phenomenon but that Austrian filmmakers had found their focus, relocated traditions, attracted an audience, and had a measure of box-office success, despite continuing financial difficulties. The debuts tended not to be as experimental and controversial as they had been during the previous two decades but aimed toward the mainstream. There is also a definite desire to connect with the younger audience at home. Salzburg-born Michael Pfeifenberger (1965–) has made short films since 1991. His first feature in 1999, *Erntedank*/Thanksgivin', scripted by producer Stephan Demmelbauer, is a tragicomic character study on the collision of two social misfits, a murder suspect and a toilet janitor. Johannes Fabrick (1958–), who scored major attention with the television film/series *Bernhardiner und Katz* (1996), moved to television and cinema features with the "misfit daughter/perfect mother" theme of *Beastie Girl* (1998) and the stillborn baby drama of *Morgen geht die Sonne wieder auf*/Wild Mourning (1999). Fritz Lehner (1948–), a well-known television writer/director since the 1970s, moved to feature films with *Jedermanns Fest*/Everyman's Feast (1997), an

Austrian/German co-production (from Veit Heidruschka and German director Volker Schlöndorff) with Klaus Maria Brandauer, Juliette Greco, and Otto Tausig, about a middle-aged fashion designer and publicity showman suddenly confronting the possibility of death. Although Brandauer gives an impressive performance as the doomed artist who strikes a deal with Death not to take him until after the climax of his career — a fashion show staged on the roof of Vienna's opera house — the three-hour film's premiere was delayed for six years and was trounced on by the critics as pretentious and boring. Its subsequent Grand Prize at the Diagonale gave Austria more of the scandal and sensation the public is said to desire and more of the contradictions Austrian film has always maintained: the award presentation was interrupted by protests, not from the audience, but by one of the jury members and by the festival directors themselves.[78] The surviving co-founder of Vienna's first postwar film studio, Belvedere Film, Elfi von Dassanowsky, resurrected the firm's name for her Los Angeles–based production company in 1999. She has since executive produced both an award-winning dramatic short on the discovery of the cure for Childbed Fever in Vienna in 1849, *Semmelweis* (USA/Austria 2001), which was directed and partially shot in Vienna by New York filmmaker Jim Berry and a digitally shot independent spy comedy feature, *Wilson Chance* (USA 2005), written and directed by Jeffrey Bunzendahl. Michael Riebl, director of the very successful *Kommissar Rex* television series about a police dog, turned to the traditional love triangle in his feature/television film, *Liebe versetzt Berge*/Love Can Move Mountains (1999). Like Michael Haneke, who visualizes Austria through French performers and language, stage director Kurt Palm (1955–) brought novelist Flann O'Brien's fantasy of old Ireland, *In Schwimmen-Zwei-Vögel*/At Swim-Two-Birds (1997) to the screen in a German-language, Austrian-shot feature in which the filmmaker applied his talents with literary adaptations to a new medium. Suitably, it was screened at the 1998 Dublin Film Festival to a fascinated audience.

German-born shorts filmmaker Sandra Nettelbeck (1966–), who studied film at San Francisco State University, arrived on the Austrian feature front in 2000 with her Austrian/German/Swiss co-production of *Martha*, a bittersweet comedy about a woman who has replaced all aspects of her life with a passion for cooking. When she suddenly becomes the guardian of her dead sister's seven-year-old daughter, who refuses to eat, and the restaurant where she works hires a second chef, she is confronted with having a child and a possible lover. Documentarian Markus Heltschl (1952–), from Innsbruck, directed an unusual improvisational film, *Am Rande der Arena*/As Ever (2000), in which his two actors, Tatjana Alexander and Lois Weinberger, meet and spend time together in Lisbon. They wander and converse aimlessly, visit the suburbs, the working-class districts, and the dying rural edges of the city. Ultimately, although there is mutual attraction, the couple abandons the possible relationship. The film was shot without a complete script and with the reality of the actors' lives and the Lisbon surroundings becoming the improvised "fiction" of the film. As the director puts it, "a rudimentary story took shape during the editing process — one could say that the screenplay was written on the cutting table."[79] Salzburg-born Virgil Widrich (1967–) a multimedia artist and shorts filmmaker, entered feature films with *Heller als der Mond*/Brighter than the Moon in 2000, which he co-wrote with Enrico Jakob and produced and directed. The comedy-drama is about an unemployed Italian man in Vienna who becomes involved with the discarded fiancée of a bank robber's Romanian driver, who has smuggled her over the border. They decide to pull their own job by breaking into a bank through a Chinese restaurant. The plot fails, of course, but it leads to further misadventures, love and the capturing of the true criminals. Similar in theme and tone to Woody Allen's *Small Time Crooks* (USA 2000), the film shows regional film interest in its financing (along with the Vienna Film Fund) by the city and province of Salzburg and is also notable for including veteran German actor Horst Buchholz in one of his final film appearances.

Mirjam Unger (1970–), a student of Axel Corti, emerged from short films with her feature *Ternitz Tennessee* (2000). The film takes on the fanciful and generally outmoded European notion of escaping a small town for a Hollywood-style happy ending in America. It suggests the universality of late twentieth-century popular culture and parodies the Hollywood road movie, romantic adventure films and the female "buddy movie." Unger claims her influence in the creation of her postmodern, television-based "fantasy in pink" that "plays out in a world that doesn't exist in reality" is American underground-turned-camp director John Waters's *Cry Baby* (USA 1990).[80] Betty (Sonja Romei), a dog groomer, and her friend Lilly (Nina Proll), a car mechanic who drives a red Mustang and longs for Pamela Anderson–sized silicone breast implants, set their sights on a television host/Elvis impersonator and an African-American stagehand and former rodeo performer from Memphis, respectively, as their love-tickets out of Ternitz. Supporting Unger's and cinematographer Jürgen Jürges's swirling kitsch-pop vision is a tongue-in-cheek soundtrack by film composers Christof Kurzmann and Fritz Ostermayer, well-known avant-garde/electronic musicians. Gabriele Neudecker's (1965–) *Freaky* (2001), a short film about longing, loss, and the concept of home, portrays a fifteen-year old Austrian girl who recalls her friendship with a Russian girl, Natalja, who suddenly disappears. It became a surprise hit at several film festivals. Two shorts, *Null Defizit*/Zero Deficit (2001), directed by Ruth Mader (1974–), and the sensitive teenage romance *Mein Stern*/Be My Star (2001), directed by German-born Valeska Grisebach (1968–), both produced by the Film Academy at Vienna's University of Music and Performing Arts, have had nearly immediate interest at international film festivals. The quick jump from student to director to national film representative, with the film school cutting out the need for a commercial producer is an amazing turnaround for a country that just two decades previously had no significant training venues in the medium and had few young talents that could make films for a national, not to speak of an international, audience.

At the 2001 European Film Awards, Stephen Gaydos of *Variety* announced that "the Austrians are enjoying perhaps the greatest flowering of cinematic talent in seventy years."[81] While it is a welcome thing to have international cineastes recognize New Austrian Film and its significant growth, the history of Austria's substantial and influential film industry is still obscured by a lack of information outside of the country. Gaydos might well cut his seven barren Austrian decades by more than half.

7

Austrian Film in the
Twenty-first Century

Smashing Façades and Shifting Identities

Two unrelated events signaled a poetic caesura in Austrian cinema at its second turn of the century: Liane Haid, Austria's first film star, died in Switzerland at age 105, and Barbara Albert's film *Nordrand* emerged as the festival and box-office sensation Austria had not experienced since the postwar era, fulfilling what Susan Ladika writing in *The Hollywood Reporter* in 1997 had suggested when she remarked that Austrian film "is ready to take on an international profile."[1] Haid's death in 2000 at such an advanced age served to remind Austrians and cineastes abroad that Austria had had a long film tradition, that it had once been at the forefront of European cinema, and that it had somehow lost its cultural connection with that past. Even in death Haid, like the major star she had been, briefly refocused the nation's attention away from politics and the economy and onto the world of lost glamour and fantasy. For a nation conditioned to paying tributes to the passing of opera stars, orchestra conductors and theater actors, the sudden reflections on Haid's demise seemed almost apologetically fascinated with the subject, as if some treasure, negligently and long misplaced, had suddenly reappeared. Indeed, one can safely surmise that most of those reporting her passing had previously never heard of her. There was also a bittersweet tone to the television reportage, which sought to remind Austrian audiences that this too was part of the cultural landscape of the nation and had deserved far more attention. A pioneer of such magnitude would not have been so forgotten in France, Italy, Germany or the United States. As Austria paused to consider who Liane Haid had been, what she had contributed to the art of Austrian film, and why she fled Austria in 1942 to settle in Switzerland, the world was learning anew that Austria was indeed a "film nation." The death in 2002 of veteran Hollywood writer/director Billy Wilder also had a similar effect on the collective film memory of the nation, although Wilder, born in the town of Sucha in imperial Austro-Poland, had been a journalist and minor scriptwriter in Vienna and never directed a film there. It was enough that as a globally known and celebrated film legend, he was an Austrian, especially in view of fresh political blows to Austria's international reputation. Wilder had been very vocal about his rejection of recent Austrian politics but nevertheless accepted honors from the federal government (as well as from Germany and France) shortly before his death. And it was at his death that American film critics and journalists who hailed him as one of cinema's greats, rediscovered on several tangential levels, the once significant Austrian population in Hollywood. It seemed almost a Freudian slip that Wilder obituaries in the English-language press would repeatedly make Vienna his birthplace.

But even prior to Wilder's demise, Austrians, buoyed by the sudden fascination of the world with its New Film, decided that there was an important cinema history to be known and (re)presented, and that people would come to pay tribute to not only operatic and theatrical greats but to film giants as well. In 2001, the Vienna Theater Museum mounted one of its most successful exhibitions on Austrian-by-choice Curd Jürgens. Although his stage work seemed to be the excuse for the showing, his films were a major part of the exhibition, and the museum chastised Austria's film institutions for having allowed his substantial memorabilia collection to escape to German archives, where Marlene Dietrich's artifacts have been such an attractive draw. But it was the 2001 exhibition at the usually high art venue of the Historical Museum of the City of Vienna that indicated a new attitude toward Austrian film history with their *Alles Lei(n)wand: Franz Antel und der österreichische Film* (the play on words is roughly translated as "All [on Loan] for the Screen"). Presentation of the veteran director/producer as a major contributor to Austrian and international cinema art was a major volley against the amnesia that has for so long discounted the national cinema. Perhaps more than any other director, Antel represents the phoenixlike experience of Austrian cinema since the postwar era. His lush imperial epics and pre–1960s musicals, comedies and dramas are undeniable classics. His frivolous titillations of the 1960s kept a fatally ill cinema alive at a time when there was no other production to speak of, and his international co-productions of the 1970s and 1980s brought international talent to Vienna, employing Austrian artists, technicians and studio facilities in a manner even Hollywood had abandoned. In addition to the German-language actors he brought to stardom, he also helped launch the careers of directors Peter Sämann and István Szabó. His *Bockerer* films have been an important part of the New Austrian Film trend to deal critically with the nation's recent past — in the commercially entertaining way that had always been central to the director's reputation. As one of the oldest active directors in the world at age ninety, Antel directed the fourth installment of his *Bockerer* saga, *Der neue Bockerer — Prager Frühling*/The New Bockerer — Prague Spring, in 2003. The film finds the now aging Viennese butcher, so deftly played by Karl Merkatz, involved in the Czechoslovakian uprisings of 1968. The title and the introduction of a younger generation of Bockerer's family belies the announcement that this would be the final installment in what has become a series on the trauma of Central Europe in the mid- and late twentieth century.

The Film Archive Austria paid official tribute to the rebirth of Austrian cinema in July 2003, with its new program/magazine publication *Filmarchiv*. The first issue, aptly named "Sonnenaufgang" (Dawn), presented essays on current Austrian film and listed the rich offerings of the archive's summer showings at the restored Imperial Cinema in the center of the city or on the open air screen and in the large cinema tent adjacent to the archive's complex in the Augarten park. On the occasion of the sixty-fifth anniversary of the Anschluss in March 2003, the Film Archive Austria offered a retrospective that utilized film to aid in Austria's more recent coming to terms with the past. "Kino vor dem KZ" (Cinema before the Concentration Camps) paid tribute to over fifty actors, directors, producers, writers, and composers that perished in the Holocaust. Among them are many influential figures from Austrian film of the 1920s and 1930s: Kurt Gerron, Otto Wallburg, Fritz Grünbaum, Ida Jenbach, Rudolf Meinert, Robert Dorsey, Paul Morgan, Joachim Gottschalk, Alfred Deutsch-German, Siegfried Lembach and Max Ehrlich. With ORF's purchase of the Wien-Film library and the rights to all aspects of the historical production company in 2003, a major portion of Austria's film history, long lost and only recently rediscovered and restored, will be ensured preservation as well as national and international broadcast.

In the space of a few short years, the work of the Film Archive Austria has elevated old Austrian films into something far more valuable than the filler it had been on morning television. Similarly, the presentations of the Austrian Film Museum, which in 2002 found new direction under the former co-director of the Viennale, Alexander Horwath,[2] proved that the showcasing of even obscure film figures have become newsworthy public events. *Tribute to Sascha*, a book by the other former Viennale co-director Michael Omasta, published by the Synema Society for Film and Media, and an Austrian Film Museum retrospective recognized the pioneering work of Austrian-American cinematographer, editor and film critic Sascha Hammid (Alexander Hackenschmied 1907–), who was instrumental in the development of IMAX. Hammid began his experimental cinema work in Prague in the 1930s and assisted his wife, avant-garde filmmaker Maya Deren, in the creation of her milestone experimental film, *Meshes of the Afternoon* (USA 1943). He directed documentaries for the U.S. Office of War Information, and subsequent film projects with Francis Thompson for the United Nations led to the technical concepts that have become the IMAX system. Although praised for his progressive camera work by John Ford, William Wyler and Jean Renoir, cinema verité exponent D. A. Pennebaker and cinematographer Douglas Slocombe, Hammid and his work remained unexplored in American film scholarship, and it proved to be a rare triumph for Austrian historians to reclaim a pioneer of such stature. In cinematic concert with the book and retrospective, filmmaker Martina Kudlacek (1965–) offered her portrait, *In the Mirror of Maya Deren* (2001), followed by a documentary on Hammid in New York entitled, *Aimless Walk* (2002). Vienna now hosts the most advanced IMAX theater in Europe, which continuously screens the first IMAX film produced in Austria, *Majestic White Horses* (about the Lipizzaner Stallions at Vienna's Spanish Riding School).

A modest upswing in cinemas (201), screens (564) and seats (104,314) has continued since the first year of the new century. Austrian releases have also found a steady average of eighteen or nineteen films a year, with the extremes being twenty-three in 1999 and twelve in 2001. Although the top ten films in 2001 were all American blockbusters and comedies, a surprise hit, *Der Schuh des Manitu*/Manitou's Shoe (Germany 2001), a "trash-comedy"[3] parody of the very popular nineteenth-century Karl May western novels was on the list. The recent Austrian films *Hinterholz 8, Komm, süßer Tod, Hundstage* and *Schlafes Bruder* have also generated significant box office. Moreover, Austria's emergence at A-level international film festivals allowed Martin Schweighofer, director of the Austrian Film Commission, to declare something that would have been unpredictable even five years earlier: "Without doubt, Austria is among the most successful film countries in 2001."[4]

A circle had indeed closed when Barbara Albert's *Nordrand* became the first Austrian production in decades invited to screen in competition at the Venice Film Festival in 1999. Perhaps even more so than Haneke's pan–European work, Albert's film represents the first wave of Austria's solid return to the international film community. It also demonstrates the major role of women in this cinematic resurrection. Like the legendary actress Liane Haid and pioneering writer/director/studio founder Louise Kolm-Fleck, who propelled Austrian cinema to its first international interest and acclaim, Barbara Albert, along with Mirjam Unger, Jessica Hausner, Ruth Mader, Gabriele Neudecker and Sandra Nettelbeck, now represents a "new" cinema, or better — a new start in an old and influential one. With the European Union's overreactive boycott of Austria in response to its 1999 elections rapidly placed into the past, commentary about the "change" in Austria had taken on a completely different meaning by 2002. The innovative Museum Quarter in Vienna, consisting of a splendid restoration/conversion of the imperial stables by Baroque master architect Johann Fischer von Erlach and several provocatively designed new buildings, has been hailed as among the largest sites devoted to art exhibition in the world. Its focus on modern and contemporary painting, sculpture, dance, performance, poetry, film and children's art has inspired the world press to repeatedly dispel the image of Vienna as a well-preserved but inert beauty.

In evaluating the innovative design of the new Austrian Cultural Forum building in New York by Austrian-American architect Raimund Abraham, *The New York Times'* architecture critic Herbert Muschamp labeled it "a gift of Vienna that skips the Schlag." Fascinated by the fact that something was "going on" here, Muschamp offered his own explanation: "Since the end of the Cold War, it has become increasingly clear that Vienna, past and present, has a pivotal role to play in developing a new cosmopolitan outlook."[5] Christoph Thun-Hohenstein, the film- and art-promoting director of the Forum, has managed to connect with the postmodernism that is currently evolving in Austria just below the hackneyed tourist image. Film, of course, is a major aspect of this new artistic energy, and it is telling that recent Austrian films have captured the postmodernist imagination internationally, often disturbingly so, and with it have stimulated a new critical sympathy toward their country of origin. For with the opening of Eastern Europe, the return of Vienna as a hub of Central European culture, and the emergence of controversial regional and federal politics, there is much here for artistic reflection and transformation.

There is also veiled critique in the praise of Austria's newly strengthened artistic presence in the United States, as in the statement by Leon Botstein, music director of the American Symphony Orchestra, who finds discord between Thun-Hohenstein's avant gardist, even cultural revolutionary, interests and recent Austrian national politics: "A nation shouldn't be confused with its government."[6] Laura Heon, curator of a show on new Viennese art at MASS MoCA (Museum of Contemporary Art) in North Adams, Massachusetts, considers that "for the first time in seventy-five years, artists from Eastern Europe are coming to Vienna for art school. There is this flourishing scene now after 100 years of languishing."[7] Well meaning but exaggerated in terms of time, the commentary, like the many others that greeted Austria's reemergence in the American and global art and film scene, suggests a nation that has too long tolerated a lack of its own international promotion, particularly in the visual and media arts. It also implies a slight shift in the concept of Austrian national identity. Not a homogeneous culture, but a mélange that grew from an empire colonizing itself eastward (as the United States, its only true mirror, colonized itself westward), its reduction to a small country with a superpower history would be traumatic enough for any nation. But given its antagonistic relationship with the larger and more powerful Germany in the twentieth century, and the disconnection from its other ethnocultural roots in Eastern Europe during the cold war, Austria's slippery national identity and role embraced neutralist escapism and artificial sociocultural reinvention. The new Europe has allowed for the return of polyglotism, multiculturalism, and even controversial politics to Austria. This flux inspires and drives the Austrian visual, and no other art can bring the postmodern "crisis of reason" and Austrian cultural multivalence to the masses as film does.

The most provocative work dealing with the culture was New Austrian Film's assessment of the center-rightist government formed in 1999, which it for the most part opposed (primarily the Haider-associated FPÖ or Freedom Party), and which had not supported Austria's film emergence financially. *Zur Lage*/Situation Report (2001) from Lotus-Film, a joint documentary from Barbara Albert, Michael Glawogger, Ulrich Seidl and Michael Sturminger, critically explores the prevailing political and social atmosphere under Austria's neoconservative coalition government. Following the experimental short form, the documentary (short and feature length) remains the mainstay of Austrian cinema. Originally, this was the easiest launch for a new filmmaker given the limited subsidies available. But even with the reemergence of the more commercial Austrian feature film, the documentary has not shown any sign of abdicating its primacy and has in fact become an expected starting point for new talent and a comfortable genre for established filmmakers who find a great deal to capture in a rapidly changing Austria and Central Europe. Since the late 1990s, Austrian experimental film and documentary often cross into a hybrid that subverts the authority of the non-narrative film and mainstreams the abstract visions of edgy cinematic exploration. Borrowing from literary theory, this might be called New Historicist cinema, as it emphasizes personal history/mythology over preconceived or "official" concepts as a form of more tangible reality or perceived truths. Even so, formal properties are far stronger than narrative structure and the result is contemplative, atemporal and open ended. Reflecting the metamorphosis of Austria's self-image, its new interest in historical reexamination and its geopolitical shifts, found footage, found events, and random imagery deconstruct preconceived or static identity into a collage of reference-less filmic vocabulary that ruptures the idea of any central ideology other than its own immediate imprint. Seminal to this style is both Nicholas Geyrhalter's (1972–) nearly five-hour *Elsewhere* (1998), which offers interviews with people living in difficult environments across the world and Michael Glawogger's *Megacities* (1998), which in its "world spanning collection of slum and slaughterhouse images, functions as a *Koyaanisqatsi* of squalor."[8] Unlike the international shock semidocumentary genre that began with *Mondo Cane* (Italy 1962) and focuses on unrelated sequences of the unusually lurid, morbid and grotesque, Glawogger's film disturbs the viewer by simply framing the ugliness of banality without an overriding ideological or moral point, as Ulrich Seidl does with his coolly detached narrative feature, *Hundstage*/Dog Days (2001). Seidl's filming of six Austrian Catholics sharing their thoughts and problems through prayer for his *Jesus, Du weißt*/Jesus, You Know (2003) allowed the monologues to stand on their own and gave no closure, but it is Gustav Deutsch's *Film ist. 7–12*/Film is. 7–12 (2002) that functions as a sort of manifesto for the hybrid style:

> Deutsch's compilation of footage from cinema's earliest decades sets decaying, hand tinted images of ancient modernity against droning, staticky electronic soundscapes by Christian Fennesz and Martin Siewert. The result is a hypnotic drift of relentless disjunctions: lions invade the sitting room of mauve decade aristocrats; a decapitated, haloed saint recovers her severed head; a black-coated apparition rises from a time-scratched sea.[9]

The very title of the work suggests an excerpt from a multichaptered documentary on cinema, but the work itself questions the very idea of interpretive objectivity. Deutsch organizes the widely varied material into an Aristotelian dramatic structure so that the audience desire to connect even random images into a satisfying narrative is blatantly achieved in all its obvious and repetitive artificiality. The result of his metafilmic experiment is the realization that film, film history, or even the "film" of history is the subjective fictionalization of fiction. The documentary can offer nothing but multivalent images that have no authority beyond their application to personal mythology.

More traditional documentary is the genre for the actor Maximilian Schell's long-awaited return to the director's chair. In his first theatrical film since the acclaimed success of *Marlene* in 1984, Schell looks at the life and career of his sister, Maria Schell, in *Meine Schwester Maria*/My Sister Maria (2001), an Epo-Film produced by Dieter Pochlatko. Georg Misch looks at the roots of another artist's life — Andy Warhol — as he explores the Slovakian town of Warhol's family in *I Am from Nowhere* (2002). On a more infamous level, one of Adolf Hitler's private secretaries,

Suburbia unmasked: Ulrich Seidl's *Hundstage*, 2001.

Traudl Junge, steps in front of the DigiBeta video lens of André Heller and Othmar Schmiderer in their documentary, *Im toten Winkel, Hitler's Sekretärin*/Blind Spot: Hitler's Secretary (2001). Unforgiving of her own naïveté and ignorance, she relates her experiences in a minimalist film that borrows from the experimental documentary by dispelling with the subjective influences of supporting historical footage and concentrating solely on Junge's "talking head." *Bunica* (2002), directed by Elke Groen and Ina Ivanceanu, looks at Romania's Nicolae Ceausescu, another brutal dictator, and the changing society of Bucharest since his demise. Lukas Stepanik and Robert Schindel offer *Gebürtig*/Born (2001), an Austrian/German/Polish co-production from Niki List and Cult Film about the sons and daughters of the Holocaust — its victims and its perpetrators. In *Atlantic Drift* (2001), French director Michel Daëron essays the experiences of two thousand Jewish war refugees aboard the ship *Atlantic*, which drifted for three months hoping to reach Palestine, but with the prevailing anti–Semitism outside of Germany after the war found only sickness, hunger, death and ultimate deportation to Mauritius. Another documentary about displacement is *Das ist alles*/That Is All (2001) by South Tyrolean Tizza Covi and Vienna-born Rainer Frimmel, which looks at the lives today of those who were forcibly resettled into and out of the Soviet-annexed East Prussia in the 1950s.

Encouraged by international interest and critical acclaim, it is obvious that Austrian filmmakers are now aiming at wider popular reception and are tailoring some films to capture an English-speaking audience. While this is not a detrimental development in principal considering the long Vienna–Hollywood connection, the failure of painfully diluted "Austrian" co-productions of the 1960s should also serve as a warning. The most potentially commercial feature film of 2002 was an Austrian/German co-production from Dor-Film, Stefan Ruzowitzky's *All the Queen's Men*. The English-language comedy-drama written by David Schneider and set in 1944 Berlin, relates the fictionalized story of four Allied soldiers disguised as women who attempt to steal the German Enigma coding machine. Although immediately bringing to mind the transvestite humor of Billy Wilder's *Some Like it Hot* (USA 1959) and the Rolf Olsen/Günther Philipp *Tolle Tante* series of the early 1960s, Ruzowitzky deftly uses the wartime setting to seriously question concepts of manliness and heroism. The film's international cast should have moved the film beyond festivals into wide release, but poor foreign distribution hampered by corporate fears surrounding the still "untested" reputation of Austrian commercial film killed off its potential. It may yet join Ruzowitzky's 1998 *Die Siebtelbauern*/The Inheritors as one of the few Austrian films to become a relatively popular English-language video/DVD rental. Another Dor-Film production that was poised to repeat the box-office success of Harald Sicheritz's *Hinterholz 8* is the director's comedy *Poppitz* (2002), a quirky turn on the typical disastrous family vacation theme. But it is Kurt Mrkwicka and his MR-Film that produced the director's 2003 very Austrian but still exportable comedy *MA 2412: Die Staatsdiener*/The Civil Servants. Based on Roland Düringer's sitcom of the same name, the film, co-written by Alfred Dorfer, Düringer and Sicheritz, explores the nearly eternal presence of the fictional "Vienna Magistrate Department for Christmas Decorations" and its civil servants in prehistory, on Noah's Ark, during the Roman Empire, the Congress of Vienna, the post–World War II era, and in the 1980s. Rather than creating a feature-length television episode, the director and writers decided to explore the very nature of civil service and the static values it creates. Moreover, this "historical" journey also parodies Austrian cinema's varied visions of history: the imperial Rome sequence is laden with pretentious dialogue and plays in overdecorated silent-era backlot sets; the Vienna Congress episode recreates the lavish and romantic imperial epics of the 1950s; the scenes set in the postwar years utilize poor film stock and have bad sound quality. Reinhard Schwabenitzky followed his series of *Eine fast perfekte* .../An Almost Perfect ... commercial comedies with another look at romantic relationships, *She, Me & Her* (2001), a Star-Film production with an international cast. Produced by the director and co-written with Fred Schiller, the film offers yet another twist on both an old Hollywood theme and the topical Austrian subject of reinvention and re-vision, as a singer and dancer assumes the identity of a more famous twin sister and makes a success of it. Sicheritz and Schwabenitzky are now both considered to be at the forefront of the Austrian comic film. After several television films, Wolfgang Murnberger returned to cinema with one of Austria's big box-office hits of 2001, *Komm, süßer Tod*/Come, Sweet Death, with popular actors Josef Hader, Simon Schwarz and Nina Proll. The film, best described as a tragicomic Austrian take on Martin Scorsese's more monotone *Bringing Out the Dead* (USA 1999), looks at the cutthroat and illegal methods of competition between ambulance services in Vienna. Moving into mainstream recognition on the basis of her short films, Valeska Grisebach emerged as a feature director in 2001 with *Nicole*, a teenage love story in the last phase of young life where "everything seems possible"[10] and responsibilities of adulthood wait just around the corner.

Michael Haneke again directed French actress Isabelle Huppert *(Die Klavier-spielerin*/The Piano Teacher) in the Austrian/French *Wolfzeit*/Time of the Wolves (2003), a film noted for its unusually dark cinematography, which revisits the family under siege theme of his breakthrough *Funny Games* by way of Jean-Luc Godard's apocalyptic 1967 classic *Week-End*. In this alternative disaster film, a middle-class family flees an unspecified catastrophe to the safety of their country home, only to wander hopelessly through a predatory landscape caused by the collapse of traditional order. Another society-in-crisis film that symbolically responded to the upheaval in Austrian politics is Franz Novotny's *Yu* (2002), a film based on material by Bernhard Seiters and written by Novotny and Michael Grimm. The film looks at three thirty-something friends whose joyride to Trieste in a Porsche is transformed by the sudden violence of growing civil unrest.

Also relating to the change in Austrian politics and its image at home and abroad are the themes of ethnic and psychological self-realization, which pervade the films of several new feature director/writers: Gerhard Fillei and Joachim Krenn's *The Orange Paper* (2002), the story of a man on the run for most of his life and the brief revelation of love; Markus Heitschl crosses film noir and French New Wave cinematic elements in *Der gläserne Blick*/Dead Man's Memories (2002), a thriller filmed in Lisbon, about a mysterious woman captured on a video camera found in a murder victim's car; Chinese director Hu Mei looks at the difficult romance of an Austrian woman (Nina Proll) and a Chinese student (Wang Zhi-weng) in 1930s Vienna in *Am anderen Ende der Brücke*/At the Other End of the Bridge (2002). Many of these films are almost completely populated by specifically ethnic casts, such as Tehran-born AliReza Ghanie's parable about artistic creation, *Windspiel*/Wind Play (2001), in which Austrian writer H. C. Artmann appears as an old poet mentor to a young man searching for identity in an Iranian community. Caspar Pfaundler's *Lost and Found* (2001) was shot in Taipei utilizing a mostly Chinese cast, and Istanbul-born Kenan Kilic offers an all-Turkish cast in the drama of a group of legal and illegal immigrants who frequent a Viennese bar in *Nachtreise*/Journey by Night (2002). A standout among these is *Mein Russland*/My Russia (2002), the first feature film by shorts director and former physician Barbara Gräftner. Basing the story on her own family's experience with her brother's marriage to a Ukrainian, she presents a divorced middle-aged Viennese woman who resists her son's marriage to a Russian girl. Gräftner's tragicomedy arises from the bringing together of what she sees are the pragmatic, even metaphysical, Russians and prejudicial, goal-oriented Austrians. While Gräftner looks forward to "greeting old neighbors again," in the eastern expansion of the New Europe, she is very pessimistic about what she considers to be a Western economic imperialism that might well destroy "the Slavic soul."[11] The film, considered by many as the first true Dogma feature from Austria, garnered the 2002 Max Ophüls Prize. In the wake of the film's success, Gräftner formed her own production company, Bonus-Film. Also dealing with Eastern Europe is Andrea Maria Dusl's feature film debut *Blue Moon* (2002), a mystery/romance that moves from Vienna to Slovenia to the Black Sea in its tale about a money courier caught between his fascination for a missing woman and her mysterious sister in Ukraine. Goran Rebic, who has focused on Eastern European subjects in his previous films, abandons his rough-edged documentary style with *Donau*/Danube (2003), an elegiac fable that connects Vienna with the East. Rebic traces the final trip of a rusty Austrian freighter, its grizzled captain, and its vivid *Ship of Fools*–like collection of passengers down the river to the Black Sea.

There has also been a revival of the existentialistic Austrian character drama, such as the Dor-Film production of *Nogo* (2001), a cinematic triptych by experimental filmmakers Sabine Hiebler and Gerhard Ertl about three diverse couples who arrive at a distant gas station. Peter Gersina's *Vienna* (2001) focuses on three social outsiders who find friendship and even success. Bernhard Weirather's *Ikarus* (2002) examines the life of a woman who dares to return to the village she once left for a disappointing stay in the city, and Tajikistani-born Bakhtiar Khudojnazarov meditates on the power of memory in the construction of personal (and symbolically national) identity with *Leo* (2003), where a young security guard's sleepwalking accident removes the past but allows a future.

With short films as the proven testing ground for the new generation of Austrian filmmakers, undoubtedly many of the new short filmmakers of this period will surface as feature filmmakers later in the decade. Emerging from a now almost typical creative arc beginning with early Super 8 experimentation and requisite study with Peter Kubelka to sound/color 16 mm short films and promising international attention is Thomas Draschan (1967–). His seven-minute pastiche of brief excerpts from international kitsch films and television programs of the 1960s and 1970s edited into a "narrative," *Encounter in Space* (2003), at once imitates and lampoons traditional cinema structures. Like Gustav Deutsch, Draschan sutures found cinematic conventions but without the explicit suggestion of a pseudodocumentary. With its snippets from Hollywood B-movies, Japanese and British sci-fi, Disney cartoons, Austrian historical drama, and Euro sex films, *Encounter* underscores the ideologies of entertainment film and the expectations of the pop-culture audience. The effect is evocative of the kaleidoscopic color and vocabulary of Anglo-American psychedelic cinema of the mid– to late 1960s, but the "narrative" suggests a postmodern sense of futility to the adventure/spy/psychodrama formulas it emulates:

> *Encounter in Space* tells the story of a man and his alter egos…. He has to undertake several adventures, fight his enemies, also alter egos of his personality. A promising sexual act is interrupted by eye surgery and the promise of introducing the man to his real self. The promise turns out to be false and the protagonist continues to search for sexual adventures, which seem to be the only alternative.[12]

Virgil Widrich, whose surreal comic short on image reproduction gone mad, *Copy Shop* (2001), was Oscar nominated, recycles scenes from Westerns, action films, melodramas and animation in a similar manner to achieve a different parody of formulaic cinema narratives in his *Fast Film* (2003).

A parliamentary session on the future of Austrian film was called in July 2002,

with noted producers, directors, critics and actors presenting views regarding government financing and promotion of film. This was a major political advance for
the Austrian film industry, which, despite the increase of its global importance faces
a decrease of its already poverty-level financing at home. The center-right national
government of the People's Party (ÖVP) and the Freedom Party (FPÖ) coalition
that came to power in 1999 and collapsed due to the Freedom Party's internal strife
was returned to coalition after national elections in November 2002 and long-
winded negotiations in early 2003. The previous coalition cut state funding, particularly in the film sector, by 37 percent between 2000 and 2001.[13] The government
nonetheless referred to the session as the realization of their "responsibility" to the
Austrian film industry in hopes of initiating a "new era" in Austrian film production.[14] But just as Austrian State Secretary for Media Franz Morak praised the
reemergence of Austrian film, funding was cut. The Green Party demanded that
Vienna support the organization and called for reform in film funding and in screening policies, announcing they would present a "first-aid" initiative to parliament.
For their part in opening significant doors for better funding, co-production and
preparation for the industry's involvement with incoming EU member nations, the
Association of Austrian Film Producers (AAFP) announced they would join the Ger-
man-based producers' alliance, Film20. Although quickly attacked as a step toward
the absorption of Austrian film by German interests reminiscent of the early 1930s,
the Film20 group assured Austrian critics that there was also a Swiss component to
the organization, and Austrian membership would make it a wide German *language* cartel.

Andreas Mailath-Pokorny, Vienna's Social Democratic City Councilor for Arts
and Culture, responded to the industry's criticism regarding budget cuts with an
initiative that demanded national funding be raised to the level of other European
nations, tax incentives be created to stimulate private investment, and a stronger
collaboration between federal and regional funding structures be instituted. The
Vienna municipal government has continued to be the strongest supporter of all
aspects of New Austrian Film, particularly in funding and expanding the possibilities of film education. An example is the 235,000 Euros granted the Filmschule
Wien for the introduction of innovative degree programs in lighting design, production coordination and dubbing, previously unavailable in Vienna. Regional film
industry has also shown interest in the future of New Austrian Film, at least symbolically: Cine Culture Carinthia, the film promotion organization in the province
of Carinthia, announced its "Young Movie Carinthia" initiative, which would ear-
mark a modest 1 percent of its overall film promotion budget for limited productions by artists under the age of twenty-eight. For his part, State Secretary Morak
announced the federal government would offer up to ten film scholarships per year
(for a total of 95,000 Euros) beginning in 2003, to promote young filmmakers and
provide "fresh impetus for the Austrian film industry."[15]

One of the most controversial films shot in 2002 and continuing to resonate
beyond 2003 is *Haider lebt—1. April 2021*/Haider Lives—April 1, 2021, privately
financed and directed by Vienna-born Peter Kern (1949–), an actor who has also

been a documentary and short-film director in Germany. The satire reframes the postwar *1. April 2000* appeal for Austrian sovereignty while it attacks both Jörg Haider and the U.S. relationship with Iraq. Although obviously quickly and cheaply made, the film's imaginative iconoclasticism has made it a modest cult hit: after twenty years of Haider's rule, Austria has been placed on the roster of outlaw states and has been invaded by U.S. troops. Johnny Bush, the fictional son of the former U.S. president, now controls occupied Austria, where all freedom of expression is banned, Viennese dialect is forbidden, and the dollar has replaced the Euro. A German television reporter (August Diehl) searches the enervated landscape to find the missing Haider and comes across several absurdly aging remnants of the contemporary Austrian political scene. In a sharp parody of Oskar Werner's discovery of the "book people" in a world that forbids books in François Truffaut's *Fahrenheit 451* (GB 1966), Diehl finds notable writers and cinema figures Peter Turrini, Marlene Streeruwitz and Helmut Berger wandering through the Vienna Woods, reciting forbidden Austrian literature and keeping dialect alive. In a reference to *The Third Man*, Diehl arranges for Haider's funeral, but the former politician reappears to ferment a disastrous ending. Detaching the director's obvious stand on American involvement in the Middle East and focusing on the intertext with *1. April 2000*, the film's depiction of a withering of individual freedoms and indigenous culture for an ideological "liberation" through foreign occupation comments on a national experience Austrians have only rarely approached in cinema. The ease in which it is now presented in the medium corresponds with the more recent national discourse on Austria's role in Nazism and on its postwar occupation, but it also suggests the New Austrian Film's ability to reach a relatively large audience with controversial sociopolitical viewpoints. Kern's film also encouraged the renewed notion of private investment productions. The modes of American independent film production and the continued limitations of government support have given rise (or rebirth of Austrian modes of the 1970s) to the very untraditional European idea of a self-produced low-budget feature film. Christian Mehofer's debut film, *Die Hoffnung*/The Hope (2003), will certainly test the viability of the concept. Inspired by a Kurt Tucholsky poem, the film deals with two Hitler Youths who are trapped in a cellar with a hidden Jewish girl during the final days of the war. This complex and moving character study about propaganda, independent thought, and human relations was rejected by several production companies, which found Mehofer's name "too small" for a story that would be so "expensive and large" to mount.[16] Refusing to abandon the project, the director and his cinematographer Alexander Boboschewski raised a small budget of about 13,000 Euros and managed to hire a full production team and thirty-five actors, including one star name, Fritz von Friedl, who was so taken by the enthusiasm of the production that he took on the role of the Nazi officer. Production chief Genny Masterman located an army practice range that approximated what might normally have been expensive sets representing a bombed-out city. The film was completed in eighteen days in August 2002.

Among the familiar names from the period leading to New Austrian Film is Titus Leber, who has expanded the reach of the Austrian diaspora cinema to Thailand, where he has created the script for the fantasy film *Nakee* (Thailand 2004) and has spent two years developing the filmic treatment of Richard Wagner's opera on the Holy Grail, *Parsifal*. Although this project continues the popular Austrian genre of the opera film, its concept is as fresh and provocative a take on an old standard as the new *Heimatfilm* has been. Leber's *Parsifal* is to be shot in Angkor Wat and will be presented from a "Buddhist perspective." Following several years creating interactive media in Vienna and Paris, Leber moved to Thailand to create an interactive project on the teachings of Buddha in 1999. True to the elastic notion of film in the postmodern era, Leber considers these projects to be a part of his cinematic work. But the director finds himself distanced from the current generation of New Austrian Film artists, not only by location and age but by what he sees is the continuing "provincialism" of the national film industry. His departure from Austria was precipitated by the "disgraceful" manner of the government's relationship with the industry in the 1980s. He has found little change in his own current dealings with the official film offices and mourns a country whose attitude toward its resurgent cinema is so "pitiful" that it "forces its artists into exile."[17]

While many of the world's major film festivals and awards had already featured New Austrian Film by 2003, the American Academy Awards continued to ignore Austrian productions in their foreign-language film category. At Cannes, Michael Haneke's *Wolfzeit*/Time of the Wolf received the best audience reaction in a festival that was considered by many international critics as one of the poorest in recent memory. It was presented outside of competition, however, because two of its performers, Isabelle Huppert and Patrice Chéreau, served on the awards jury. Joining Haneke's work was Ruth Mader's debut feature *Struggle* (2003), Virgil Widrich's experimental short *Fast Film* (2003), and two ORF co-produced films, *Im Anfang war der Blick*/At the Beginning There Was the Gaze (2003), an experimental film utilizing 1,800 postcards to explore the realities and fantasies of the Austrian landscape created by Luxemburg-born Viennese graffiti artist Bady Minck (1959–), and the French/Austrian rural film noir *Pas de repos pour les braves*/No Rest for the Brave (2003) by Alain Guiraudie. Minck took the opportunity of her sudden press visibility to remind Austria how unsatisfactory its film fund is despite recent promises: "Luxemburg has a higher promotional budget than Austria, with a population that is forty times less."[18]

Like Ulrich Seidl (*Hundstage*), both Sabine Derflinger and Ruth Mader rupture the façade of an orderly or satisfying life in their feature debuts. Derflinger began with dramatic shorts and then turned to documentary shorts, with *Achtung Staatsgrenze*/Attention, State-Frontier (directed with Bernhard Pötscher, 1995–96) about illegal aliens and others awaiting deportation in Austrian jails, and *The Rounder Girls* (also directed with Pötscher, 1999), on the soul and gospel singing group. She moved into feature film with her breakthrough *Vollgas*/In High Gear (2001), where behind the images of beauty and relaxation at an Austrian winter resort an overworked and frustrated single mother's unhappiness leads to self-destructive alcoholism and one-night stands. Her young daughter's love provides the only possibility of salvation. Ruth Mader's feature (scripted with Barbara Albert and Martin Leidenfrost) *Struggle* follows the lives of very different characters: a Pole (Aleksandra Justa) who has moved to Austria to work in a turkey processing plant, as a berry picker, and as a cleaning woman, in order to better provide for her young daughter, and a wealthy, divorced Austrian who seeks diversion from his unfulfilling life with sex and sadomasochism. Ultimately, their lives are altered when they meet in a swingers' club. Abandoning a classical narrative for the sake of an "anti-dramatic" exploration of the dehumanization and alienation of various work environments, the intersecting stories also relate the collision of two classes and geopolitical worlds: the woman represents the impoverished yet hopeful Eastern Europe; the man embodies a hollow consumerist and "emotionally bankrupted" West. Mader flatly dismisses the Cannes critics who compare her film style to Haneke, Seidl or a mix of both. Unlike their male gaze, which is disturbingly voyeuristic and often dialogue-laden, Mader and the other women of New Austrian Film such as Albert or Hausner utilize a more neutral, distant camera and leave much to the imagination. Since much of what she desires to show "cannot even be conveyed with words," dialogue is noticeably scarce in her work. Mader also rails against television, which in its rapid and expedient product orientation has "ruined" actors for the thoughtful, detailed work of motion pictures.[19] But the representation of Eastern Europe as exploited woman and the association of Western European malaise with recreational sex is not a gender-specific interpretation. Michael Sturminger's (1963–) feature film debut *Hurensohn/*The Whore's Son (2004), based on the novel by Austrian author Gabriel Loidolt and co-written by Michael Glawogger, visits similar territory and generates a comparable mood of resignation. Unlike Mader's film, Sturminger's imagery is stylized and his narrative is more traditionally structured. For the most part, dialogue propels this story of the sixteen-year-old son of an immigrant Yugoslavian family who discovers that his mother has worked as a prostitute for the many years they have been in Vienna. Increasingly alienated from his aunt and uncle who find solace in Catholicism and the past, and from his peers who know the truth, Ozren (Stanislav Lisnic) desperately attempts to reconnect with his mother (Chulpan Khamatova). But he is left behind, as is the rest of his family, by his mother's refusal to abandon her successful exploitation in capitalism. Ozren's crisis of idealism, love, and identity suggests Barbara Gräftner's apprehensions about an economic imperialism that is injurious to the emerging Eastern Europe.

With the exception of Haneke's film, the Austrian films represented at Cannes in 2003 were all produced by Amour Fou, a new company directed by Alexander Dumreicher-Ivanceanu (1971–) and Gabriele Kranzelbinder (1968–) whose willingness to initiate petitions against the actions of the government and the media (including ORF's decision to remove experimental work from their programming) have made them highly visible in cultural politics. With a name evoking the French New Wave, their firm's standards distill the very direction of the mature New Austrian Film: "Amour Fou produces films ... which transcend borders aesthetically, in content, or technologically. Films that ignore the demarcation line between cinematic genre and category. And films which reflect upon and question the past and present, the possibilities and the future of society and cinema."[20] The headlining of Austrian feature projects at international festivals, so unthinkable just a few years earlier, now generate expectation as has Barbara Albert's *Böse Zellen*/Free Radicals (2003), an Austrian/German/Swiss co-production under her Coop99 banner, which received its world premiere at the Locarno Film Festival in October 2003. Albert's film breaks the same illusions of control Gräftner rails against in *Mein Russland* and Mader discounts in *Struggle*. In *Böse Zellen*, Albert again shows her virtuosity in working with ensemble casts and within the topic of contemporary alienation, this time in a more philosophical film created around the idea of the "butterfly effect." Her film begins with a plane crash in the Gulf of Mexico, whose sole survivor, Manu (Kathrin Resetarits), is later killed in an automobile accident. Manu becomes the hub of several parallel stories involving her troubled surviving family and friends and their haunting symbol of the irony and unpredictability of life as they fight off abuse and loneliness. A pastiche of the coming-of-age, thriller, and erotic film genres, the film hovers disturbingly between existentialist choice and the incomprehensibility of fatalism.

Götz Spielmann's *Antares* (2004), the festival hit of the following year, also ties an episodic drama about three couples who reside in the same housing complex and eventually cross paths to a cosmic notion: the title refers to the brightest star in Scorpio, the astrological sign of sexuality, passion and power. But unlike Albert's philosophical approach, Spielmann's overlapping story lines are incidental and his sexually frank and open-ended examination of seduction, jealousy, deceit, and domestic violence recalls far more the desolation of Seidl's *Hundstage*.

American critic Ed Halter believes there is a specific New Austrian Film style and feel, at least among female directors, which is crystallized in Albert's work: "quiet, cool, and subjective, [these films] achieve a detached, contemplative air so rarely attempted by overcompensating American cinema, communicating a bittersweet beauty through the simple evocation of interior life."[21] Jessica Hausner has clearly moved into that stylized direction with her second feature, *Hotel* (2004), in which a young woman (Franziska Weisz), working as a receptionist in a luxury mountain resort hotel, stumbles upon the mysterious circumstances of her predecessor's disappearance. She is pulled into a maze of secrets and false conclusions until her own identity and possible fate begins to replicate that of the victim. Although referencing the crime thriller, Hausner avoids formula and concentrates on more Hitchcockian themes of perception, the interpretation of reality, and the fear of the unknown. Unlike the almost documentary feel of *Lovely Rita*, the anxiety and paranoia of *Hotel* is aided by a more distant "smooth and noble"[22] look, which enforces the façade of beauty, control and safety.

Whether directly, symbolically or allegorically, filmmakers by the mid-decade have reacted to the shifting identity values of the nation by exposing and rejecting artificial representations, particularly with regards to national image and social construction. Their attack focuses on what Slavoj Žižek considers the

> contemporary redefinition of politics as the art of expert administration, that is, as politics without politics, up to today's tolerant liberal multiculturalism as an

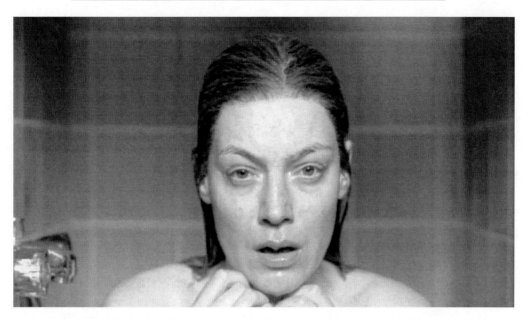

Breaking the illusion of control: Barbara Albert's *Böse Zellen*, 2003.

experience of the Other deprived of its Otherness (the idealized Other who dances fascinating dances and has an ecologically sound holistic approach to reality, while practices like wife beating remain out of sight...)" Virtual Reality simply generalizes this procedure of offering a product deprived of its substance....[23]

It appears to be the goal of most, if not all, Austrian filmmakers of the era to put the substance, no matter how discordant or unpleasant, back into the "product." The touting of Austria's multicultural legacy and the promotion of the nation as a reborn hub of an EU *Mitteleuropa*, are countered by images vacillating between xenophobia and self-hate, and representations of broad economic/social success are tempered by individual reaction ranging from latent dissatisfaction to despair. Poised against virtualization and the postmodern "anxiety of perceiving oneself as nonexistent,"[24] the new socially critical film has quickly become the genre generally associated with current Austrian cinema. But this type of filmmaking is not as new as it appears to be. It represents a resurfaced continuity of Austrian film and themes regarding national identity, national representation, and sociopolitical/gender-role–related dissension that were present at the very start of the national cinema.

Vienna has finally "outpaced even Berlin in terms of cinema seats per capita,"[25] due to the multiplex boom and the revitalization of several abandoned theaters as art houses or programmatic cinemas. Despite the cuts in film funding, audiences flock to festivals and retrospectives, inspiring innovations like St. Pölten's Cinema Paradiso, which is not only aimed at presenting art-house screenings (complete with an additional bistro screening room and a café) but provides multimedia spaces for readings and cabaret, musical, and small theatrical performances. The Hollywood onslaught continues to captivate a large portion of the ticket buyers (if not the critics), as it does for most of Europe, but the success of New Austrian Film and the return of audiences to the cinema should not be measured by mega box-office earnings but by the enthusiasm and visibility greeting the art in national discourse. This was tested throughout 2003, ignited by State Secretary Morak's replacement of the Graz-based Diagonale Film Festival's leadership with Miroljub Vuckovic, ex-program director of the Belgrade International Film Festival, and Tillmann Fuchs, former head of Austria's first private television network, ATV. The sudden shift of the festival's mission from a showcase of Austrian film to a cash prize–awarding platform encouraging television-linked films and Southeastern European production was greeted with anger by most Austrian filmmakers who suspected that the restructuring of the festival without the input of the industry was an attempt to override demands for increased federal film funding. Morak claimed that planned incentives and a "media fund" to stimulate private investment needed further discussion and that funding policies would be effected by Euro regulations. By shifting the Diagonale's emphasis to television co-production, a new television film promotional fund could be utilized and the government might more distinctly monitor subsequent product. Morak ignored the Amour Fou company–led petition to reinstate the former directors and abandon the new program, pleading with the industry to let Vuckovic and Fuchs do their work. Filmmakers in Austria and abroad considered this to be the worst example yet of any Austrian government's disregard of the national film industry. By autumn of 2003, opposition political parties demanded Morak's team quit, and an alternative protest Diagonale (based on the original Diagonale) had been formed by Ruth Beckermann, Ulrich Seidl and Barbara Albert. A boycott of the new Diagonale was underway, which suggested that there would be no festival at all in 2004. But with over two hundred films entered into the protest festival, and statements of solidarity arriving from festivals in Bordeaux, Hamburg, Karlovy Vary, Leipzig, Oberhausen, Pesaro, Stuttgart and Rotterdam, the host city, Graz announced that it would not support the new Diagonale and would only fund the original festival. Morak admitted defeat, the directors of his new Diagonale resigned and the original Diagonale concept was reinstated. At the April 2004 Vienna session of Eurimages, the Council of Europe's film promotion program, Morak articulated the importance of film production and distribution to the expansion of the European Union and the creation of a European identity: "The independent producer is the central figure in the European film industry. A producer-friendly attitude must therefore be the basic principle of any European film politics."[26] Created by the failure of traditional modes, by the long reinvention of production and distribution, and by audience cultivation, the realities of Austria's present film industry might ultimately become a useful paradigm for other (re)emerging cinemas.

By 2005, the federal government could point to positive developments in its relationship with film culture of the nation. The opening of the Central Film Archives building at Laxenburg near Vienna to house over 70,000 films and to function as one of the three national sites for restoration and documentation of Austria's cinematographic heritage was presented as part of Morak's comprehensive attention to film art and industry. An amendment to the Film Promotion Act was also undertaken to establish a national Film Advisory Board, which would represent all interest groups, and would be responsible for drafting film policy recommendations.

The massing of Austrian filmmakers, actors and technicians as a politically engaged front would have been considered unlikely — the proverbial cinematic fantasy — only a few years before. To actually wrest national focus from the other arts, and in doing so gain international visibility, popular respect and the defeat of government policy, provides the most impressive harbinger that Austria has indeed rediscovered itself as a film nation. It is clear that this new era in Austrian film has been in the making for some time, developing through artistic/theoretic concerns rather than for commercial interests, from the impecunious experiments of the 1970s to current global interest and even influence. Much of this journey is also based in the development of the Austrian nation during the past decades, as its socio-culture wrestles with identity and its geopolitical role. A most important factor, however, for film as for national identity is the new desire to look back to the traditions, innovations, and talents that Austrian cinema has had and has given of so generously to other cinemas.

Chapter Notes

Preface

1. Frederic Morton, *Thunder at Twilight: Vienna 1913–1914* (New York: Scribner, 1989).
2. Frieda Grafe, "Wiener Beiträge zu einer wahren Geschichte des Kinos," in *Aufbruch ins Ungewisse. Österreichische Filmschaffende in der Emigration vor 1945* (Vienna: Wespennest, 1993) 227–44.
3. Peter Bondanella, *Italian Cinema: From Neorealism to the Present*, 3rd ed. (New York: Continuum, 2003) xi.

Chapter 1

1. Elisabeth Büttner and Christian Dewald, *Das tägliche Brennen. Eine Geschichte des österreichischen Films von den Anfängen bis 1945* (Salzburg: Residenz, 2002) 22.
2. Büttner and Dewald, *Brennen* 24.
3. Büttner and Dewald, *Brennen* 26–33.
4. Walter Fritz, *Im Kino erlebe ich die Welt. 100 Jahre Kino und Film in Österreich* (Vienna: Brandstätter, 1997) 12.
5. Walter Fritz, *Geschichte des österreichischen Films* (Vienna: Bergland, 1969) 28.
6. Markus Nepf, "Die ersten Filmpioniere in Österreich. Die Aufbauarbeit von Anton Kolm. Louise Veltée/Kolm/Fleck und Jakob Fleck bis zu Beginn des Ersten Weltkriegs," in *Elektrische Schatten: Beiträge zur österreichischen Stummfilmgeschichte* (Vienna: Filmarchiv Austria, 1999) 12.
7. Walter Fritz, *Kino in Österreich 1896–1930. Der Stummfilm* (Vienna: Österreichische Bundesverlag, 1981) 22.
8. Nepf 13.
9. The bourgeois tragedy may have existed in various guises prior to G. E. Lessing's 1775 play *Miss Sara Sampson*, but this Enlightenment writer developed the German-language theater genre to its influential perfection. The genre consists of variations on the theme of the lower-class maiden who is loved and abandoned by an upper-class suitor. Abandonment may be intentional or unintentional, the suitor may return (usually too late to halt the tragedy) and there may be an illegitimate child involved, but the subsequent destruction of the female's reputation often ends in her death or suicide. A powerful and progressive critique on class conflict and gender roles in the eighteenth and nineteenth centuries, the genre lasted into the early twentieth century when it began to lose its edge due to changes in European social and gender role construction following World War I.
10. Fritz, *Im Kino* 24–25.
11. Nepf 11.
12. Fritz, *Im Kino* 25–26.
13. Fritz, *Im Kino* 25.
14. Fritz, *Im Kino* 27.
15. Bioskop (Germany), Le Lion (France), Kineto Ltd. (U.K.), American Wild West Film Manufacturing Co. (USA), and Pasquali & Co (Italy). Nepf 18.
16. Nepf 19.
17. Nepf 19.
18. Nepf indicates that Hiller gained fame as composer for several later Asta Nielsen films. 19–20.
19. *Mitteilungen der Österreichisch-Ungarische Kino-Filmindustrie* 30 (October 1911) 4.
20. See Robert von Dassanowsky, "Male Sites/ Female Visions: Four Female Austrian Film Pioneers," *Modern Austrian Literature*, vol. 32, no. 1 (1999): 126–40.
21. Walter Kolm-Veltée, personal interview, Vienna, June 1997.
22. Alexander Lernet-Holenia, "Aristocracy and Society in Austria," trans. Thomas Ring-

mayr, *Southern Humanities Review*, Winter (2000): 1.

23. Nepf 21. Translation by Robert von Dassanowsky.

24. Interview with Walter Kolm-Veltée.

25. Nepf 27.

26. Fritz, *Im Kino* 31.

27. Walter Panofsky, *Die Geburt des Film* (Würzburg: Triltsch, 1944) 71.

28. Nepf 29.

29. Günter Krenn, "Der Bewegte Mensch — Sascha Kolowrat," in *Elektrische Schatten: Beiträge zur österreichischen Stummfilmgeschichte* (Vienna: Filmarchiv Austria, 1999) 38. Translation by Robert von Dassanowsky.

30. Krenn 40.

31. Following Johann Strauss Jr.'s "Golden Age," the period from 1900 to the end of World War I is usually considered the Silver Age of Viennese operetta. It is represented by the second wave of the genre's masters, such as Franz Lehár, Oskar Straus and Robert Stolz.

32. Fritz, *Im Kino* 45. Translation by Robert von Dassanowsky.

33. In a letter dated Vienna, May 5, 1913, and labeled "highly confidential," Prince Montenuovo, the director of Imperial Court Protocol and Affairs responds to the First Imperial Chamberlain, Prince August Lobkowitz, regarding Kolowrat's request to film the emperor and members of the imperial family for a "patriotic film" that would be shown in theaters with the agreement of political representatives. He conveys the emperor's inaction on this request, adding that the Emperor "does not wish that a film be made for such purposes." Translation by Robert von Dassanowsky. From the private collection of the author.

34. Ingrid Maria Hübl, "Sascha Kolowrat. Ein Beitrag zur Geschichte der österreichischen Kinematographie," dissertation, University of Vienna, 1951, 81.

35. Krenn 41.

36. See Büttner and Dewald, *Brennen* 237.

37. Krenn 42. Translation by Robert von Dassanowsky.

38. Krenn 42.

39. Produced by Riport-Film, Budapest.

40. Known as the "Sixtus Affair," negotiations were secretly begun through Empress Zita's brother, Prince Sixtus of Bourbon-Parma, who was in the French armed forces. The attempt failed and was fanned into a public embarrassment for the imperial couple by the French government. It resulted in subjugation of the Austro-Hungarian war effort by the German emperor and his generals. See Tamara Griesser-Pecar, *Die Mission Sixtus. Österreichs Friedensversuch im Ersten Weltkrieg* (Vienna: Amalthea, 1988). The heroic attempt, hardly mentioned in international accounts of World War I, gained popular attention in the 1990s by its fictionalization in George Lucas's television series *The Young Indiana Jones Chronicles*.

41. See Klaus Kreimeier, *The UFA Story: A History of Germany's Greatest Film Company 1918–1945,* trans. Robert and Rita Kimber (New York: Hill and Wang, 1996).

42. The opera, which depicts a gypsy dancer caught between the control of a sadistic aristocrat and the love of an innocent shepherd, can well be understood as a political statement against capitalism and authoritarianism. It was remade by Leni Riefenstahl as her final film during the Third Reich and the opera by d'Albert had been a popular one in communist Eastern European opera houses. Although the Kolm/Fleck team created pro–Habsburg propaganda films, *Tiefland* must have been a calculated choice for production based on the atmosphere of war fatigue, nationalism and the growing resentment of the class system in the collapsing empire. For information on Riefenstahl's use of the material see my article, " 'Wherever you may run, you cannot escape him': Leni Riefenstahl's Self-Reflection and Romantic Transcendence of Nazism in *Tiefland,*" *Camera Obscura* 35 (1995): 107–29.

43. Fritz, *Im Kino* 84.

44. Fritz, *Im Kino* 80.

45. Krenn 42.

46. Gyöngyi Balogh, "Die Anfänge zweier internationaler Filmkarrieren: Mihály Kertész und Sandor Korda," in *Elektrische Schatten: Beiträge zur österreichischen Stummfilmgeschichte* (Vienna: Filmarchiv Austria, 1999) 83. Translation by Robert von Dassanowsky.

47. Fritz, *Im Kino* 96.

48. Balogh 86.

49. Balogh 88.

50. Fritz, *Im Kino* 106.

51. See Walter Fritz and Gerhard Tötschinger, *Maskerade: Kostüme des österreichischen Films. Ein Mythos.* (Vienna: Kremayr & Scheriau, 1993) 89.

52. Judith Beniston, "Vienna Meets Tyrol: Austrian Peasant Plays 1900–45," Continuities and Discontinuities in the Austrian Twentieth Century: International Conference of the Centre for Austrian Studies at the Universities of Aberdeen and Edinburgh, University of Edinburgh, Edinburgh, 6 April 2003.

53. Fritz, *Im Kino* 137.

54. See Murray G. Hall, "Hugo Bettauer," in *Elektrische Schatten: Beiträge zur österreichischen Stummfilmgeschichte,* (Vienna: Filmarchiv Austria, 1999) 149–68.

55. Fritz, *Im Kino* 111–12.

56. Walter Kolm-Veltée quoted by Gabrielle Hansch and Gerlinde Waz, *Filmpionierinnen in Deutschland. Ein Beitrag zur Filmgeschichtsschriebung,* Berlin, 1998. Unpublished.

57. Steiner, *Film Book* 15.

58. Fritz, *Im Kino* 136.

59. Christian Strasser documents the secondary film industry in that city in his *The Sound of Klein-Hollywood. Filmproduktion in Salzburg — Salzburg im Film* (Vienna: Österr. Kunst- und Kulturverlag, Wien 1993).

60. Fritz, *Im Kino* 134.

Chapter 2

1. Armin Loacker, *Anschluss im 3/4-Takt: Filmproduktion und Filmpolitik in Österreich 1930–1938* (Trier: WVT Wissenschaftlicher Verlag, 1999) 2.

2. Fritz, *Im Kino* 143.

3. Fritz, *Im Kino* 146.

4. Nancy Scholar, "Leontine Sagan," in *Sexual Stratagems*, ed. Patricia Erens (New York: Horizon, 1979) 219.

5. Dassanowsky, "Male Sights/Female Visions" 120–31.

6. See Büttner and Dewald, *Brennen* 114–21.

7. Steiner, *Film Book* 25.

8. For information on this important costume designer who has few personal facts in print, see Fritz and Tötschinger, *Maskerade.*

9. Fritz, *Im Kino* 151.

10. Fritz, *Im Kino* 151. Translation by Robert von Dassanowsky.

11. Fritz in Steiner 26. Translation by Gertraud Steiner.

12. Loaker, *Anschluss* 93–95.

13. The Vienna *Justizpalastbrand* of 1927 was as shattering to the Austrian First Republic as the 1933 Reichstag fire was to Germany. It was started by a mob protesting the acquittal of rightist Frontkämpfer militia members who wounded and killed several leftist Schutzbund followers as they marched in a peaceful parade. The revolt was brutally crushed by the government. Strikes, protests and more partisan violence followed as a latent civil war atmosphere loomed into 1928.

14. Loaker, *Anschluss* 31.

15. Loaker, *Anschluss* 36.

16. Loaker, *Anschluss* 36.

17. Armin Loaker and Martin Prucha, "Die Unabhängige deutschsprachige Filmproduktion in Österreich, Ungarn und der Tschechoslowakei," in *Unerwünschtes Kino: Der deutschsprachige Emigrantenfilm 1934–1937,* eds. Armin Loacker and Martin Prucha (Vienna: Filmarchiv Austria, 2000) 57.

18. Loaker, *Anschluss* 142.

19. Loaker, *Anschluss* 144.

20. Loaker, *Anschluss* 150–51. Translation by Robert von Dassanowsky.

21. Linda Schulte-Sasse in *Entertaining the Third Reich: Illusions of Wholeness in Nazi Cinema* (Durham, NC: Duke University Press, 1996) considers the 1943 German *Titanic* a potent example of Nazi propaganda since it "ascribes responsibility for the shipwreck to British capitalists playing the stock market" (247). She fails to mention, however, that production was halted at one point and that, due to subject matter, the film did not receive its premiere in German-speaking Europe until 1949. By 1950, the Allies had forbidden the showing of *Titanic* in West Germany because of the film's anti-British slant. Klaus Kreimeier in *The UFA Story* reports that during the filming of this *Titanic* the director, Herbert Selpin, had been denounced for making insulting comments about the Wehrmacht, which he would not recant. He was subsequently expelled from the Reich Film Guild and arrested. Selpin reportedly committed suicide in his prison cell in August 1942 (327–28). The film was completed by Werner Klingler "whom the National Socialists had [then also] forced out of work" (369). Thomas Kramer and Martin Prucha claim that the topic of a sea disaster was considered too psychologically disturbing for the homefront during the war and therefore the film remained relatively unseen *Film im Lauf der Zeit: 100 Jahre Kino in Deutschland, Österreich und der Schweiz* (Vienna: Ueberreuter, [1994] 147). In fact, Propaganda Minister Goebbels forbade the showing of the film within Germany because he considered the scenes of mass panic unsuitable for German audiences. The film subsequently premiered in occupied Paris in 1943. Ironically, despite its anti–British propaganda, *Titanic's* special effect scenes were used without credit in the 1958 British film *A Night to Remember.*

22. *Filmemigration aus Nazideutschland,* dir. Günter Peter Straschek, WDR, West Germany 1975.

23. Loaker, *Anschluss* 168.

24. Loaker and Prucha 28.

25. Loaker and Prucha 29.

26. Loaker and Prucha 94.

27. Joe Pasternak quoted in Loaker and Prucha, 94. See also Joe Pasternak, *Easy the Hard Way: The Autobiography of Joe Pasternak as told to David Chandler* (New York: J. P. Putnam's Sons, 1956).

28. Loaker and Prucha 94.

29. Rudolf Ulrich, *Österreicher in Hollywood* (Vienna: Filmarchiv Austria, 2004) 246–47.

30. Bondanella, *Italian Cinema* 132–33.

31. Paul Schrader, "Notes on Film Noir," in *Film Noir Reader*, eds. Alain Silver and James Ursini (New York: Limelight, 2003) 55.

32. Loaker and Prucha 94–97.

33. Loaker and Prucha 156.

34. Steiner, *Film Book* 30.

35. Loaker and Prucha, 152.

36. Loaker, *Anschluss* 191.

37. Loaker, *Anschluss* 191. Translation by Robert von Dassanowsky.

38. Loaker reports that American film representation, which had been down by 6 percent in 1936, had fallen to 39 percent the following year, with German film up by 36.6 percent. *Anschluss* 197.

39. See Guoqiang Teng, "Fluchtpunkt Shanghai. Louise und Jakob Fleck in China 1939–1946," *Filmexil* 4 (1994): 50–58; Paul Rosdy, "Emigration und Film," *Zwischenwelt. Zeitschrift für Kultur des Exils und des Wiederstands* 2 August (2001): 61–65.

40. Gertraud Steiner, *Traumfabrik Rosenhügel* (Vienna: Compress, 1997) 35–37. Translation by Robert von Dassanowsky.

Chapter 3

1. Steiner, *Rosenhügel* 37.

2. Fritz, *Im Kino* 179. Translation by Robert von Dassanowsky.

3. Steiner, *Rosenhügel* 40.

4. Steiner, *Rosenhügel* 44.

5. The star-system hierarchy was based not only on the changing tastes of the audiences, but on concrete Wien-Film contract salaries: Forst, Hartl and Ucicky are reported to have earned 80,000 RM per feature, Emo and Marischka 35,000 RM and Thimig 25,000 RM. Competing with the directors was the fee for actor Paul Hörbiger who earned a base salary of 150,000 RM, and composer Willy Schmidt-Gentner whose top fee was 40,000 RM for *Wiener Mädeln*. Hans Moser was contracted for 2,000 RM per *day* compared to a more mortal talent, such as actress Inge Konradi, who earned 150 RM per day. See Steiner, *Film Book* 35.

6. Fritz, *Im Kino* 185.

7. Büttner and Dewald, *Brennen* 328.

8. Büttner and Dewald, *Brennen* 209.

9. Fritz, *Im Kino* 197. Goebbels had asked the German masses if they were prepared to sacrifice all for a "total war" in 1943.

10. Steiner, *Film Book* 35.

11. Steiner, *Rosenhügel* 45.

12. Sabine Hake, *Popular Cinema of the Third Reich* (Austin: University of Texas Press, 2001) 159.

13. Steiner, *Rosenhügel* 56.

14. The fire caused by a backstage gas lamp during an evening performance on December 12, 1881, killed over 386 people (exact figures are unknown). Panic broke out as the stage curtain exploded into flames and the theater lighting was extinguished. Most of the audience in the balcony could not reach the exits in time to save themselves. Moreover, the doors opened inward and were blocked by the crowds. The nominal procedures to guard against such a fire were apparently not implemented and a fire brigade was not called until more than ten minutes after the start of the blaze. The disaster led to a trial accusing theater director Franz Jauner and others of criminal negligence. Vienna's mayor, Julius von Newald, admitted originally covering up the incompetence of the theater personnel and subsequently resigned. The Ringtheater tragedy was ultimately responsible for increased safety regulations for theaters in Austria-Hungary and later throughout Europe and led to the general use of a metal curtain to prevent stage fires from spreading. See Felix Czeike, *Historisches Lexikon Wien, Band 4* (Vienna: Kremayr & Scheriau, 1995) 679.

15. Hake 163.

16. Steiner quoting Jürgens from his interview in the 1971 Austrian television broadcast of *Filmgeschichten aus Österreich*, created by film historian Walter Fritz. Translation by Gertraud Steiner. *Film Book* 39.

17. Schulte-Sasse.

18. Kramer and Prucha, 168.

19. Friedrich Heer, *Der Kampf um die österreichische Identität* (Vienna: Böhlaus Nachf., 1981) 423.

20. Fritz, *Im Kino* 209.

21. See Gertraud Steiner, "Besides, ich bin Österreicherin: Elfi von Dassanowsky, eine Wienerin in Hollywood," *Wiener Zeitung*, Freitag, 2 August 1996, 14, and Hyde Flippo, "Interview with an Austrian Film Pioneer and Cultural Activist, Elfi von Dassanowsky," *The German-Hollywood Connection*, online 1988. See also my article, "Male Sites/Female Visions.

22. Schulte-Sasse 150.

23. Jochen Schmidt, *Die Geschichte des Genie-Gedankens in der deutschen Literatur, Philosophie und Politik 1750–1945*, 2 vols. (Darmstadt: Wissenschaftliche Buchgesellschaft, 1985) 2:202.

24. Schulte-Sasse 167.

25. Schulte-Sasse 150.

26. Schulte-Sasse 162.

27. Kramer and Prucha 155.

28. Steiner, *Film Book*, 33.

29. Schulte-Sasse 149–50.

30. Theodor Adorno, *Ästhetische Theorie, Gesammelte Schriften*, 7 vols. (Frankfurt: Suhrkamp, 1970) 7:255–56.

31. Büttner and Dewald, 385. Translation by Robert von Dassanowsky.

32. Fritz, *Im Kino* 201.

33. Steiner, *Film Book* 37.

34. Steiner, *Rosenhügel* 41.

35. Excerpted from "Rundschreiben und Verordnung an den Filmschaffenden der Wien-Film 1941–1944."

36. Fritz, *Im Kino* 201.

37. Fritz, *Im Kino* 188. Translation by Robert von Dassanowsky.

38. See Walter Fritz, ed., *Der Wiener Film im Dritten Reich* (Vienna: Österreichische Gesellschaft für Filmwissenschaft, Kommunikations- und Medienforschung, 1988) 36.

39. *Traumfabrik: Abschied von den Sieveringer Filmateliers*. Interview with Axel Eggebrecht. Südwestfunk Baden Baden, 1989.

40. Günther Berger, *Bürgermeister Dr. Karl Lueger und seine Beziehungen zur Kunst* (Frankfurt: Peter Lang, 1998) 98.

41. She normally commanded about 60,000 RM per annum on her Wien-Film contract. See Steiner, *Rosenhügel* 41 and *Film Book* 35.

42. Steiner, *Film Book* 40.

43. Wien-Film-Band, 6 October/November 1941.

44. The publication of the autobiographies of Marika Rökk and Kristina Söderbaum in the 1990s, which deal with their exile from cinema in the postwar era, has not escaped hefty German criticism. See "Unendliche Geschichte," *Der Spiegel* 43 (1993): 29, 60.

45. Renata Berg-Pan, *Leni Riefenstahl* (Boston: Twayne, 1980) 164.

46. David Stewart Hull, *Film in the Third Reich* (New York: Simon and Schuster, 1973) 174.

47. See Carl Zuckmayer, in *Geheimreport*, eds. Gunther Nickel and Johann Schrön (Göttingen: Wallstein, 2002).

48. Helma Sanders-Brahms, "Tyrannenmord: *Tiefland* von Leni Riefenstahl," in *Das Dunkle zwischen den Bildern: Essays, Porträts, Kritiken,* ed. Norbert Grob (Frankfurt: Verlag der Autoren, 1992) 245. Translation by Robert von Dassanowsky.

49. See chapter 2 and Loacker, *Anschluss* 220–21.

50. Riefenstahl, *Memoiren* 354. Austrian director/producer Max Reinhardt once considered Riefenstahl for the part of the Amazon queen in his own stage production of *Penthesilea*. See Stephen Schiff, "Leni's Olympia," *Vanity Fair*, September 1992: 251–96.

51. Trude Dreihann-Holenia (Trude Lechle), personal interview, Kleinrötz, Austria, June 1998.

52. Fritz, *Im Kino* 208.

53. *Das Kleine Volksblatt*, 18 August 1945.

Chapter 4

1. Hubert Klocker, "Gesture and the Object, Liberation as *Aktion*: A European Component of Performance Art," in *Out of Actions: Between Performance and the Object, 1949–1979*, ed. Paul Schimmel (Los Angeles: The Museum of Contemporary Art/Thames and Hudson, 1998).

2. Fritz, *Im Kino* 211.

3. See *Kleines Lexikon des österreichischen Films*, eds. Ludwig Gesek et al. (Vienna: Filmkunst, 1959).

4. See *Mein Film* 8, 14 December (1945) and 9/10, 12 December (1945).

5. Viktor Matejka, *Was ist österreichische Kultur?* (Vienna: Stadt Wien, 1945) 3. Translation by Robert von Dassanowsky.

6. Fritz, *Im Kino* 211–12.

7. Steiner, *Rosenhügel* 62. Translation by Robert von Dassanowsky.

8. Geza von Cziffra, *Kauf dir einen bunten Luftballon: Erinnerungen an Götter und Halbgötter* (Munich: Herbig, 1990) 337.

9. Gertraud Steiner, *Die Heimat-Macher: Kino in Österreich 1946–1966* (Vienna: Verlag für Gesellschaftskritik, 1987) 5. Translation by Robert von Dassanowsky.

10. Thomas Elsaesser notes that émigré directors Fritz Lang, Douglas Sirk, Billy Wilder, William Dieterle, Robert Siodmak and Frank Wisbar "found to their surprise that the West German film industry in the 1950s seemed to consist of nothing but white-washed former Nazis" who had "developed a 'siege mentality.'" *New German Cinema: A History* (New Brunswick, NJ: Rutgers University Press, 1989) 14.

11. Steiner, *Heimat-Macher* 56.

12. Fritz, *Im Kino* 212.

13. Steiner, *Heimat-Macher* 57.

14. Elsaesser, *New German Cinema* 273.

15. The *Holocaust* miniseries was received with overwhelming emotional response. It was not only a success in terms of viewers, but it also "provoked a truly emotional outburst ... which constituted a veritable event in the history of the relationship between German television and its public." The miniseries also sparked national discussion on the ethics of turning "national shame into melodrama and thriller." Elsaesser, *New German Cinema* 271.

16. Fritz, *Im Kino* 214.

17. Steiner, *Heimat-Macher* 49.

18. In Wien-Film's *Liebe ist Zollfrei* (1941) and UFA's *Die goldene Stadt* (1942).

19. The address is Bauernmarkt 24. A plaque recalling the founding of Austria's first postwar studio has marked the site since 1999.

20. Marielies Füringk, "Besuch in Wiens kleinstem Film-Atelier," *Mein Film* 10, 7 March 1947.

21. John Walker, *Haliwell's Who's Who in the Movies, 15th Ed.* (New York: HarperResource, 2003) 472.

22. Fritz, *Im Kino* 214–15.

23. *Mein Film* 23, 6 June 1947, 8.

24. Steiner, *Heimat-Macher* 70.

25. Maria Steiner, *Paula Wessely: Die verdrängten Jahre* (Vienna: Verlag für Gesellschaftskritik, 1996).

26. Maria Steiner in Elisabeth Büttner and Christian Dewald, *Anschluß an Morgen: Eine Geschichte des österreichischen Films von 1945 bis zur Gegenwart* (Salzburg: Residenz, 1997) 151–52.

27. Gottfried Schlemmer in Büttner and Dewald, *Anschluß* 151–52.

28. See Robert Dassanowsky, *Phantom Empires: The Novels of Alexander Lernet-Holenia and the Question of Postimperial Austrian Identity* (Riverside, CA: Ariadne, 1996).

29. Fritz, *Im Kino* 218.

30. Fritz, *Im Kino* 219.

31. See Eric Rentschler, ed., *G. W. Pabst: An Extraterritorial Cinema* (New Brunswick, NJ: Rutgers University Press, 1990) and Schulte-Sasse.

32. Steiner, *Rosenhügel* 66.

33. "Sensationelle Filmaufführung mit Tyrone Power. *Zehn Jahre Später*— Ein großes Erlebnis," *Tiroler Nachrichten*, n.d. 1948.

34. Trude Dreihann-Holenia (Trude Lechle), personal interview, Kleinrötz, Austria, June 1998.

35. Fritz, *Im Kino* 221.

36. *Filmkunst* No. 1 (1949).

37. Elfi von Dassanowsky, "Märchen vom Glück am Bauernmarkt — Erinnerungen an die Belvedere-Filme und das Aufbruchstadium im österreichischen Nachkriegskino." *Wiener Zeitung*, September 10–11, 1999, Extra. 3–4.

38. Chaplin's various approaches in creating "silent pictures with sound" such as the successful *Modern Times* (1936), his underappreciated *A King in New York* (1957), and the disastrous *A Countess from Hong Kong* (1967), particularly come to mind here.

39. Emmerich Hanus was apparently a monarchist who preferred a Habsburg restoration. Elfi von Dassanowsky, personal interview, Los Angeles, July 2002.

40. Elfi von Dassanowsky, interview.

41. Steiner, *Heimat-Macher* 92.

42. Steiner, *Heimat-Macher* 97.

43. *Wien und "Der dritte Mann." Zur Österreich-Premiere von Carol Reed's Film im Wiener Apollo-Kino am 10. März 1950* (Vienna: Austrian Feature Service/Bundespressedienst, 2000).

44. Despite such Nazi-era portrayals as in *Once Upon a Honeymoon* (1942), postwar Hollywood continued to present Vienna in the traditional imperial setting. Even Billy Wilder, who in 1946 offered a dark comedy about Nazi sympathizers (Marlene Dietrich) the black market and U.S. occupation in Berlin against the black-and-white images of a decimated city in *A Foreign Affair*, could not approach Vienna in the same light. The following year he directed *The Emperor Waltz*, a Technicolor backlot Bing Crosby musical comedy recreating Vienna at its imperial height in a romantic story about a phonograph salesman, a countess, their dogs and a dotty but wise Emperor Franz Joseph.

45. H. J. Gottschalk, *100 Years of Cinema in Austria — A Historical Profile* (Fachverband der Lichtspieltheater und Audiovisionsveranstalter Austria, 2000). Online.

46. Steiner, *Heimat-Macher*, 107–8. Eric Rentschler gives a detailed exegesis on the *Bergfilm* in "Mountains and Modernity: Relocating the *Bergfilm*," *New German Critique* 51 (1990): 137–61.

47. Steiner, *Heimat-Macher* 122.

48. *Die Furche*, No. 17, 29 April (1981): 15.

49. Hans Veigl, "Hinter den Spiegeln: österreichische Identität. Zwischen Möglichkeits- und Wirklichkeitssinn. Bemerkung zur Konstituierung nationalen Selbstgefühls," in *1. April 2000*, eds. Ernst Kieninger et al. (Vienna: Filmarchiv Austria, 2000) 277.

50. Barbara Femuth-Kronreif, "Der 'Österreich-Film.' Die Realisierung einer Idee," in *1.*

April 2000, eds. Ernst Kieninger et al. (Vienna: Filmarchiv Austria, 2000) 43.

51. Femuth-Kronreif 44–47.

52. Armin Loacker, "Das offizielle Österreich dreht einen Film. Ein Resümee zum Staatsfilm, *1.April 2000*," in *1. April 2000*, eds. Ernst Kieninger et al. (Vienna: Filmarchiv Austria, 2000) 351.

53. Loacker, *1. April 2000* 345–46.

54. Loacker, *1. April 2000* 347.

55. Michael Palm, "Die Geburt der Nation aus dem Geiste der Operette. Musikalische Rhetorik am 1. April 2000," in *1. April 2000*, eds. Ernst Kieninger et al. (Vienna: Filmarchiv Austria, 2000) 133–47.

56. Palm 144–45.

57. The *New York Times*, the *New York Journal* and the *New York Post* all greeted the film with negative reviews. The United Nations and American critics regarded the film's futuristic stand-in, the WPC and its death rays, as an affront. Scandinavian countries were more positive in reception, but the specter of Austria's role in the Nazi occupation of these countries would surface in critical reaction to Austria's demand for an end to its Allied occupation. The Dutch press particularly attacked the film's avoidance of recent history as well as its role in the Nazi occupation of Europe: while it sympathized with the Austrian desire for independence, it resented its audiences being subjected to what was essentially an internal Austrian political problem. See Beate Hochholdinger-Reiterer, "Politik getarnt als Aprilscherz. Zur Rezeption des Österreich-Films *1. April 2000*," *1. April 2000*, eds. Ernst Kieninger et al. (Vienna: Filmarchiv Austria, 2000) 93–96.

58. Beate Hochholdinger-Reiterer 97.

59. Beate Hochholdinger-Reiterer 103.

60. Fritz, *Im Kino* 237.

61. Steiner, *Heimat-Macher* 124.

62. Steiner, *Heimat-Macher* 133.

63. Steiner, *Heimat-Macher* 140.

64. Steiner, *Film Book* 65.

65. Alfred Lehr, the film's production manager and now a film historian recalls the creation of the film in a 1981 interview by Gertraud Steiner in *Heimat-Macher* 160–64.

66. Kramer and Prucha, 201.

67. Fritz, *Im Kino* 245.

68. Elsaesser, *New German Cinema* 264.

69. *Österreichische Film- und Kinozeitung* No. 495 (1956): 1.

70. Both also suffered tragic deaths while abroad. Empress Elisabeth was the victim of a knife-wielding anarchist during an incognito trip to Lake Geneva in 1898.

71. Franz Antel, personal interview, Vienna, June 2002.

72. Wolfgang Gersch, *Film bei Brecht: Bertolt Brechts praktische und theoretische Auseinandersetzung mit dem Film* (Berlin: Henschel, 1975) 295ff.

73. Gottschalk.

74. Fritz, *Im Kino* 243–44.

75. Steiner, *Heimat-Macher* 170.

76. Steiner, *Heimat-Macher* 171.

77. Steiner, *Heimat-Macher* 187.

78. Fritz, *Im Kino* 257.

79. *Funk und Film*, 49 (1958): 16.

80. This Disney film was based on the novel *Das doppelte Lottchen* by German author Erich Kästner, which had first been filmed in West Germany in 1950 by director Josef von Baky.

81. Steiner, *Heimat-Macher* 188–89.

Chapter 5

1. Goswin Dörfler, "Austria," in *International Film Guide 1977*, ed. Peter Cowie (London: Tantivy Press, 1977) 80.

2. For a discussion of the plot and cast of the original, see chapter 4.

3. Steiner, *Heimat-Macher* 246.

4. See chapter 4.

5. See chapter 4.

6. For an analysis of the Wise film as an allegory of the Schuschnigg era, see my article, "An Unclaimed Country: The Austrian Image in American Film and the Sociopolitics of *The Sound of Music*," *Bright Lights Film Journal* 41 July (2003), online.

7. Büttner and Dewald, *Anschluß* 364.

8. Fritz, *Im Kino* 268.

9. Franz Antel, personal interview, Vienna, June 2002.

10. Antel interview.

11. Goswin Dörfler, "Austria," in *International Film Guide 1969*, ed. Peter Cowie (London: Tantivy, 1969) 45.

12. Dörfler, *Guide 1969* 45.

13. Büttner and Dewald, *Anschluß* 163. Translation by Robert von Dassanowsky.

14. Büttner/Dewald, *Anschluß* 320. Translation by Robert von Dassanowsky.

15. Fritz, *Im Kino*, 268–69. Translation by Robert von Dassanowsky.

16. *Österreichische Film- und Kino Zeitung* 815, 3 October 1962: 1.

17. Fritz, *Im Kino* 261. Translation by Robert von Dassanowsky.

18. Hermann Nitsch presented the first Actionist art in his showing at the Galerie Dvorak

in Vienna in March 1963. The bloody carcass of a lamb was hung from the ceiling and then moved through the room in a shaking motion in order to splatter the blood on the viewers. Blood was poured from buckets onto the floor, and an actor flung raw eggs against a wall. The shock value of the Actionists is to be found not only in their provocation of traditional art venues and art audiences but also in the radicalism of their materials and the use of the human body. Blood, animal entrails and carcasses figure strongly in the early performances in what is intended as ritualistic or Dionysian "rapture." Later, the naked human body was directly involved in the action.

19. Thomas Elsaesser and Michael Wedel, eds., *The BFI Companion to German Cinema* (London: BFI, 1999) 29.

20. Büttner and Dewald, *Anschluß* 284.

21. Valie Export, "Expanded Cinema as Expanded Reality," *Senses of Cinema* 28 September–October (2003) online.

22. Export.

23. Export.

24. Elsaesser and Wedel 84.

25. Goswin Dörfler, "Austria," in *International Film Guide 1971*, ed. Peter Cowie (London: Tantivy, 1971) 81.

26. Dörfler, *Guide 1977* 80.

27. Goswin Dörfler, "Austria," in *International Film Guide 1974*, ed. Peter Cowie (London: Tantivy, 1974) 78.

28. Television owners increased from 1,579,000 in 1971 to 1,686,000 in 1972 in a national population of 7,400,000. As of January 1, 1973, there were only 702 cinema theaters in Austria (as compared with the 1,248 in 1964), 103 of which were in Vienna (as compared with 228 in 1953). Dörfler, *Guide 1974* 78.

29. See Michael Omasta, "Eine Frage des Vertrauens," in *Der neue österreichische Film*, ed. Gottfried Schlemmer (Vienna: Wespennest, 1996) 49–62.

Chapter 6

1. Fritz, *Im Kino* 276. See also Goswin Dörfler, "Austria," in *International Film Guide 1982*, ed. Peter Cowie (London: Tantivy, 1982) who reports that "Since then (1978) about 66 films of varying length were subsidized by approximately 100 million Austrian Schillings" 68.

2. Dörfler, *Guide 1982* 68–69.

3. Dörfler, *Guide 1982* 69.

4. Büttner and Dewald, *Anschluß* 207–12.

5. Steiner, *Film Book* 76.

6. Claus Philipp, "An Austrian Picture Show: *Exit ... nur keine Panik* von Franz Novotny — wie der österreichische Kinofilm wieder einmal keine Chance hatte, wie er sich trotzdem nützte, und wie er aus dem Erfolg einige falsche Schlüsse zog," *Der neue Österreichische Film*, ed. Gottfried Schlemmer (Vienna: Wespennest, 1996) 71–83.

7. "Film, Frauen und Fußball," Interview with Franz Antel by Dieter N. Unrath, *Who's Who Magazin* 1, (1998): 8–11. Translation by Robert von Dassanowsky.

8. Franz Antel, personal interview, Vienna, June 2002.

9. Arno Russegger, "Ein Österreicher im *Club der toten Dichter*: Wolfgang Glücks *Der Schüler Gerber*," *Der neue Österreichische Film*, ed. Gottfried Schlemmer (Vienna: Wespennest, 1996) 84–95.

10. Gottfried Schlemmer, "Das alte Vertreiben," in *Der neue Österreichische Film*, ed. Gottfried Schlemmer (Vienna: Wespennest, 1996) 9–14.

11. Elsaesser and Wedel 125.

12. Ulrich, *Österreicher in Hollywood* 601.

13. Fritz, *Im Kino* 279.

14. Isabella Reicher, "Eine Referenz macht noch keine Empfehlung: *Müller's Büro* von Niki List," in *Der neue Österreichische Film*, ed. Gottfried Schlemmer (Vienna: Wespennest, 1996) 221–32.

15. Büttner and Dewald, *Anschluß* 411. Translation by Robert von Dassanowsky.

16. Jack Kindred, "Austria," in *Variety International Film Guide 1991*, ed. Peter Cowie (London: Andre Deutsch, 1991) 77.

17. Steiner, *Film Book* 105.

18. "Films," *Ruth Beckermann*, online.

19. Karen Remmler, "Citing Memory in the Work of Ruth Beckermann and W. G. Sebald," Gender, History, and Memory, MALCA Conference, Rice University, Houston, 25 April 2004.

20. Steiner, *Film Book* 105.

21. Elsaesser and Wedel 44.

22. South Tyrol had been ceded to Italy by the Allies following World War I, despite the majority of its German-speaking Austrian population. Mussolini instigated a culturally destructive Italianization policy by the 1920s, and the 1939 "referendum" that permanently ceded this province to Italy was a Nazi concession to the Italian dictator. The Allies avoided South Tyrol as a territorial issue following World War II. Austria negotiated with Italy for autonomy for the province throughout the 1960s and 1970s, despite acts of sabotage by South Tyrolean freedom fighters. An

Austrian-Italian pact guaranteeing autonomy was agreed to by both Austrian and Italian parliaments and ratified by the Italians in 1992, but most South Tyroleans continue to identify with Austria and the irredentist movement now seeks independent "region" status for the territory in the European Union.

23. See Katherin Bower, "Focal Feminism: Film Technologies, Alienation and Agency in Valie Export's *Invisible Adversaries*," *Women in German Newsletter* Spring (1999) online.

24. Goswin Dörfler, "Austria," in *International Film Guide 1989*, ed. Peter Cowie (London: Tantivy, 1989) 88.

25. Büttner and Dewald, *Anschluß* 47.

26. See Kurt Hickethier, "Bittere Heimkehr: *Welcome in Vienna* von Axel Corti und Georg Stefan Troller," *Der neue Österreichische Film*, ed. Gottfried Schlemmer (Vienna: Wespennest, 1996) 206–20.

27. Thomas Kuchenbuch, "Gesellschaftskritische Dimensionen in melodramatischer Form: *Donauwalzer* von Xaver Schwarzenberger," in *Der neue Österreichische Film*, ed. Gottfried Schlemmer (Vienna: Wespennest, 1996) 169–81.

28. Dörfler, *Guide 1989* 88.

29. Büttner and Dewald, *Anschluß* 405–09.

30. Gustav Ernst in Büttner and Dewald, *Anschluß* 223.

31. Fritz, *Im Kino* 284.

32. Steiner, *Film Book* 84.

33. Büttner and Dewald, *Anschluß* 227.

34. "*Die Fremde*," *Austrian Film News* 3/2000, online.

35. Jack Kindred, "Austria," in *Variety International Film Guide 1991*, ed. Peter Cowie (London: Andre Deutsch, 1991) 76.

36. Susanna Pyrker, "Austria," in *Variety International Film Guide 1994*, ed. Peter Cowie (London: Andre Deutsch, 1994) 86.

37. Steiner, *Film Book* 114.

38. Kindred, *Guide 1991* 77.

39. Pyrker, *Guide 1994* 86.

40. Pyrker, *Guide 1994* 85.

41. Beat Glur, "Austria," in *Variety International Film Guide 1999*, ed. Peter Cowie (London: Faber and Faber, 1999) 93.

42. Glur, *Guide 1999* 93.

43. Stefan Grissemann, "Die aquarellierten Andoiden: Bemerkungen zu *Rote Ohren fetzen durch Asche* von Angela Hans Scheirl, Dietmar Schipek und Ursula Pürrer," in *Der neue Österreichische Film*, ed. Gottfried Schlemmer (Vienna: Wespennest, 1996) 275–85.

44. "Austrian Film Between Festival Success and Market Constraints: Interview with Martin Schweighofer," in *After Postmodernism: Austrian Literature and Film in Transition*, ed. Willy Riemer (Riverside, CA: Ariadne, 2000) 59–60.

45. Rupert Koppold, "*Die Siebtelbauern*: Landleben mit Enrico Caruso," *Stuttgarter Zeitung*, Filmkritik 1999, online.

46. See Robert von Dassanowsky, "Welches Österreich? *The Sound of Music*—Filmbild und Realität," *Filmkunst: Zeitschrift für Filmkultur und Film Wissenschaft*. Special issue of *Austria's Hollywood/Hollywood's Austria* 154 (1997): 5–17.

47. See chapter 2 and endnote 15 of Chapter 2.

48. When Chancellor Dollfuss's directive to disarm the Schutzbund was rejected by the Socialist militia, the artillery was ordered to crush the resistance (in the worker's districts of Vienna) on February 12, 1934. This resulted in more than 300 deaths. Nine Schutzbund leaders were subsequently executed. Dollfuss's new corporate state constitution was instituted in May of that year.

49. The imperial House of Habsburg and its empire has often been referred to as *Casa d'Austria*, in recollection of the dynasty's once-powerful role in Spain.

50. This is nothing like the gentle "grandfather figure" of an Austrian emperor (the image of the old Franz Joseph rather than his young, idealistic and short-lived successor Karl I) in the Habsburg myth that pervaded interwar popular culture, from trivial novels to literary masterworks as Joseph Roth's *Radetzkymarsch* (1932) and *Die Kapuzinergruft* (1938). Claudio Magris' redoubtable if now somewhat surpassed text *Der Habsburgische Mythos in der österreichischen Literatur* (Salzburg: Müller, 1966) still offers a convincing examination of the overriding image of the paternal monarch in Austrian interwar culture.

51. David Schoenbaum's seminal analysis of Hitler's National Socialist "revolution" understands it as a promotion and distortion of traditional petit bourgeois values under the guise of a classless society. See *Hitler's Social Revolution: Class and Status in Nazi Germany 1933–1939* (New York: W. W. Norton, 1980).

52. The record plays Enrico Caruso singing the aria "La donna è mobile" from the 1851 opera *Rigoletto* by Guiseppe Verdi. Ruzowitzky has called his film "an opera" (see "Interviewstatements") and Verdi's violent musical drama on class abuse and the sexual objectification of woman offers the audience an ironic subtext to the story of the new farmers, who unknowingly enjoy music that reflects their own social and sexual conflicts.

53. Koppold. Translation by Robert von Dassanowsky.

54. Robert Acker, "Michael Glawogger's Film *Die Ameisenstraße:* Representing the Modern Malaise," in *After Postmodernism: Austrian Literature and Film in Transition,* ed. Willy Riemer (Riverside, CA: Ariadne, 2000) 127.

55. Acker 128.

56. Acker points out that these were the "same phrases used in the Second Republic after World War II to exculpate the Austrians from any guilt for involvement in the Third Reich, thus leading to the myth of Austria as victim" 136.

57. Elsaesser and Wedel 129.

58. Michael Haneke, "71 Fragments of a Chronology of Chance" in *After Postmodernism* 171–72.

59. Beat Glur, "Austria," in *Variety International Film Guide 1999,* ed. Peter Cowie (London: Faber and Faber, 1999, 92.

60. Michael Haneke, "Gegen den Status Quo," *Austrian Film News* 2/00 (2000): 18–19.

61. Anthony Lane, "Film Notes," *The New Yorker,* 24 and 31 December 2001: 30.

62. Anthony Lane, "The Great Divide: Unsettling Pictures of Parisian Life," *The New Yorker,* 3 December 2001: 106.

63. Matthias Greuling, "Die letzten Zuckungen des Tieres," interview with Michael Haneke, *Celluloid* 2 (2002). Online.

64. Commentary from an audience discussion with Michael Haneke following the screening of *Die Klavierspielerin* at the American Cinematheque/Egyptian Theater, Los Angeles, 23 November 2001.

65. Greuling.

66. Michael Haneke, "Beyond Mainstream Film: An Interview with Michael Haneke" in *After Postmodernism* 170.

67. Roman Scheiber, "Austria," in *Variety International Film Guide 2001,* ed. Peter Cowie (London: Variety, 2002) 85.

68. "Rathaus-und ORF-Gratulation für Michael Haneke," OTS Press Service, 22 May 2001. Translation by Robert von Dassanowsky.

69. "Rathaus."

70. "Anmerkungen zum Überleben: *The Punishment,*" *Austrian Film News* No. 2 June 2000: 6. Translation by Robert von Dassanowsky.

71. Willy Riemer, "*Nordrand* by Barbara Albert," *Modern Austrian Literature* (2000). Online.

72. Karin Schiefer, "A Stormy Winter: Barbara Albert," *Austria Kultur* 10/3 2000: 15.

73. Roman Scheiber, "Austria," in *Variety International Film Guide 2003,* ed. Peter Cowie (London: Button, 2002) 106.

74. Peter Tscherkassky, personal interview, Vienna, June 2002.

75. Peter Tscherkassky, *Peter Tscherkassky Selected Films 1981–1999* (booklet accompanying video), (Vienna: Sixpack Film, 2000) 21.

76. See chapter 5.

77. Tscherkassky, *Films* 25.

78. Scheiber, *Guide 2003* 108.

79. Markus Heltschl, "Am Rande der Arena," in *Austrian Films 2001* (Vienna: Austrian Film Commission, 2001) 12.

80. Karin Schiefer, "Go West: *Ternitz Tennessee,*" *Austrian Film News* 2/2000: 4–5.

81. Martin Schweighofer, "Vorwort," in *Austrian Film Commission—Jahresbericht 2001,* ed. Karin Schiefer (Vienna: Austrian Film Commission, 2002) 3.

Chapter 7

1. Quoted in Martin Schweighofer, introduction, in *Austrian Films 1998* (Vienna: Austrian Film Commission, 1998) 6.

2. City Councilor for the Arts Andreas Mailath-Pokorny greeted this new regime and the popularity of the museum's retrospectives with a half-million Euro increase in funding from the city of Vienna. Michael Omasta, "Hinter verschlossenen Türen: Alexander Horwath Interview," *Falter* 1/2002 online.

3. Scheiber, *Guide 2002* 108.

4. Schweighofer 3.

5. Herbert Muschamp, "Architecture Review: A Gift of Vienna that Skips the Schlag," *The New York Times,* 19 April 2002, online.

6. Jennifer Senior, "Mostly *Not* Mozart," *New York Magazine,* 22 April 2002, online.

7. Carol Strickland, "Austria Makes Soaring Debut on the New York Arts Scene," *The Christian Science Monitor,* 19 April 2002, online.

8. Ed Halter, "Das Experiment," *The Village Voice,* 12–18 November 2003, online.

9. Halter.

10. Valeska Grisebach, "Nicole," in *Austrian Films 2001* 26.

11. "Mein Russland: Ein Filmdebut aus Österreich," *Celluloid* 4 (2002): 10–15.

12. Thomas Draschan, homepage online.

13. Scheiber, *Guide 2002* 85.

14. See: Brigitte Povysil, "Österreichischer Filmstandort als Thema einer Enquete im Parlament," APA-OTS Press Service, 23 May 2002, online; "Parlamentarische Enquete zur Zukunft des Österreichischen Films," APA-OTS Press Service, 23 May 2002, online.

15. "Promotion of the Austrian Film Indus-

try," *News from Austria*, Austrian Federal Press Service, 16 December 2002, online.

16. Clemens Stampf, "Eine neue Hoffnung des österreichischen Films?" *Celluloid* 4 (2003): 30.

17. Titus Leber, personal interview, July 2003.

18. "Amour Fou prolongiert österreichisches Filmwunder," *Celluloid* 2 (2003): 21.

19. Matthias Greuling, "Der Existenzkampf wird härter: Ruth Mader," *Celluloid* 2 (2003): 10–13.

20. Amour Fou, homepage online.

21. Halter.

22. Sandra Wobrazek, "Große Erwartungen: Jessica Hausner," *Celluloid* 1 (2004): 41.

23. Slavoj Žižek, "Passions of the Real, Passions of Semblance," in *Welcome to the Desert of the Real! Five Essays on September 11 and Related Dates* (London and New York: Verso, 2002) 11.

24. Žižek uses the phenomenon of "cutters" who mutilate themselves with razors "in a radical attempt to (re)gain a hold on reality," as an extreme example of "the 'postmodern' passion for the semblance [ending] up in a violent return to the passion of the Real" 10.

25. Scheiber, *Guide 2003* 108.

26. "Treffen des EURIMAGES-Board in Wien," APA-OTS Press Service, 22 April 2004, online. Translated by Robert von Dassanowsky.

Selected Bibliography

Achenbach, Michael, and Karin Moser, eds. *Österreich in Bild und Ton: Die Filmwochenschau des austrofaschistischen Ständestaaates*. Vienna: Filmarchiv Austria, 2002.

Achenbach, Michael, et al., eds. *Projektionen der Sehnsucht. Saturn. Die erotischen Anfänge der österreichischen Kinematographie*. Vienna: Filmarchiv Austria, 1999.

Acker, Robert. "Michael Glawogger's Film *Die Ameisenstrasse*: Representing the Modern Malaise." *After Postmodernism: Austrian Literature and Film in Transition*. Ed. Willy Riemer. Riverside, CA: Ariadne, 2000.

Adorno, Theodor. *Ästhetische Theorie. Gesammelte Schriften*. Vol. 7. Frankfurt: Suhrkamp, 1970.

Albrecht, Gerd. *Nationalsozialistische Filmpolitik: Eine soziologische Untersuchung über die Spielfilme des Dritten Reiches*. Stuttgart: Enke, 1969.

Alles Lei(n)wand. Franz Antel und der österreichische Film. 274. Sonderausstellung des Historisches Museum der Stadt Wien. Vienna: Historisches Museum der Stadt Wien, 2001.

Alton, Juliane, ed. *Handbuch für Filmschaffende*. Vienna: Buchkultur, 1995.

Antel, Franz. "Film, Frauen und Fußball." Interview with Dieter N. Unrath. *Who Is Who Magazin*, 1 (1998).

———. *Verdreht, verliebt, mein Leben*. Vienna: Amalthea, 2001.

Antel, Franz, and Christian F. Winkler. *Hollywood an der Donau. Geschichte der Wien-Film in Sievering*. Vienna: Verlag der Österreichischen Staatsdruckerei, 1991.

Austrian Film Commission. *Austrian Films*. Vienna: PVS, 1981–2003.

Baird, J. W. *The Mythical World of Nazi War Propaganda 1933–1945*. Minneapolis: University of Minnesota Press, 1974.

Balázs, Béla. *Schriften zum Film*, 2 vols., Eds. Helmut H. Diederichs et al. Berlin: Hanser, 1984.

———. *Der sichtbare Mensch, oder die Kultur des Films*. Frankfurt: Suhrkamp, 2001.

Balogh, Gyöngyi. "Die Anfänge zweier internationaler Filmkarrieren: Mihaly Kertez und Sandor Korda." *Elektrische Schatten: Beiträge zur österreichischen Stummfilmgeschischte*. Eds. Francesco Bono et al. Vienna: Filmarchiv Austria, 1999.

Barkhausen, Hans. *Filmpropaganda für Deutschland im Ersten und Zweiten Weltkrieg*. Hildesheim: Olms, 1982.

Bechdolf, Ute. *Wunsch-Bilder? Frauen im nationalsozialistischen Unterhaltungsfilm*. Tübingen: Vereinigung für Volkskunde, 1992.

Becker, Wolfgang. *Film und Herrschaft: Organisationsprinzipien und Organisationsstrukturen der nationalsozialistischen Filmpropaganda*. Berlin: Spiess, 1973.

Beckermann, Ruth, and Christa Blüminger, eds. *Ohne Untertitel. Fragmente einer Geschichte des österreichischen Kinos*. Vienna: Sonderzahl, 1996.

Belach, Helga, ed. *Wir tanzen um die Welt: Deutsche Revuefilme 1933–1945*. Munich: Hanser, 1979.

Belach, Helga, and Wolfgang Jacobsen, eds. *Richard Oswald: Regisseur und Produzent*. Munich: edition text + kritik, 1990.

Berger, Günther. *Bürgermeister Dr. Karl Lueger und seine Beziehungen zur Kunst.* Vienna: Peter Lang, 1998.

Berg-Pan, Renata. *Leni Riefenstahl.* Boston: Twayne, 1980.

Beyer, Friedemann. *Die Ufa-Stars im Dritten Reich. Frauen für Deutschland.* Munich: Heyne, 1991.

Bock, Hans-Michael, ed. *Cine-Graph: Lexikon zum deutschsprachigen Film.* Munich: edition text + kritik, 1984– .

Bondanella, Peter. *Italian Cinema: From Neorealism to the Present.* 3rd ed. New York: Continuum, 2003.

Bower, Katherin. "Focal Feminism: Film Technologies, Alienation and Agency in Valie Export's *Invisible Adversaries.*" *Women in German Newsletter* Spring (1999). Online.

Buchschwenter, Robert and Lukas Maurer, eds. *Halbstark: Georg Tressler zwischen Auftrag und Autor.* Vienna: Filmarchiv Austria, 2002.

Büttner, Elisabeth, and Christian Dewald. *Anschluß an Morgen. Eine Geschichte des österreichischen Films von 1945 bis zur Gegenwart.* Salzburg: Residenz, 1997.

_____. *Das tägliche Brennen. Eine Geschichte des österreichischen Films von den Anfängen bis 1945.* Salzburg: Residenz, 2002.

Courtade, Francis, and Pierre Cadars. *Geschichte des Films im Dritten Reich.* Munich: Hanser, 1975.

Cziffra, Geza von. *Es war eine rauschende Ballnacht. Eine Sittengeschichte des deutschen Films.* Frankfurt: Ullstein, 1987.

_____. *Kauf die einen bunten Luftballon: Erinnerungen an Götter und Halbgötter.* Munich: Herbig, 1975.

_____. *Ungelogen. Erinnerungen an mein Jahrhundert.* Munich: Herbig, 1988.

Dachs, Robert. *Oskar Werner. Ein Nachklang.* Vienna: Kremayr & Scheriau, 1988.

_____. *Willi Forst. Eine Biographie.* Vienna: Kremayr & Scheriau, 1986.

Danielczyk, Julia. "'Unternehmen Eroica'—Entstehungs- und produktionsgeschichtliche Aspekte." *Das Märchen vom Glück. Österreichischer Film in der Besatzungszeit.* Special issue of *Maske und Kothurn* 46.1 (2001).

Dassanowsky, Elfi von. "Märchen vom Glück am Bauernmarkt: Erinnerungen an die Belvedere Filme und das Aufbruchstadium im österreichischen Nachkriegskino." *Wiener Zeitung,* Extra, 10 September 1999.

Dassanowsky, Robert von. "Louise Kolm-Fleck," Great Directors. *Senses of Cinema* (2004). Online.

_____. "Male Sites/Female Visions: Four Female Austrian Film Pioneers." *Modern Austrian Literature* 32.1 (1999).

_____. "*Märchen vom Glück*: Postwar Austrian Cinema's Iconoclastic Missing Link." *Das Märchen vom Glück. Österreichischer Film in der Besatzungszeit.* Special issue of *Maske und Kothurn* 46.1 (2001).

_____. "A Mountain of a Ship: Locating the *Bergfilm* in James Cameron's *Titanic.*" *Cinema Journal* 40.4 Spring/Summer (2001).

_____. *Phantom Empires: The Novels of Alexander Lernet-Holenia and the Question of Postimperial Austrian Identity.* Riverside, CA: Ariadne, 1996.

_____. "An Unclaimed Country: The Austrian Image in American Film and the Sociopolitics of *The Sound of Music.*" *Bright Lights Film Journal* 41 (2003). Online.

_____. "Welches Österreich? *The Sound of Music*—Filmbild und Realität." *Austria's Hollywood/Hollywood's Austria.* Special issue of *Filmkunst: Zeitschrift für Filmkultur und Wissenschaft* 154 (1997).

_____. "'Wherever you may run, you cannot escape him': Leni Riefenstahl's Self-Reflection and Romantic Transcendence of Nazism in *Tiefland.*" *Camera Obscura* 35 (1995).

_____. "Wien-Film, Karl Hartl and Mozart: Aspects of the Failure of Nazi Ideological *Gleichschaltung* in Austrian Film." *Modern Austrian Literature. Special Issue: Austria in Film* 32.3/4 (1999).

Daviau, Donald G. "The Role of Film in the Postwar Revival of Austria." *Das Märchen vom*

Glück. Österreichischer Film in der Besatzungszeit. Special issue of *Maske und Kothurn* 46.1 (2001).

Donner, Wolf. *Propaganda und Film im Dritten Reich.* Berlin: TIP-Verlag, 1995.

Dörfler, Goswin. "Austria." *International Film Guide 1969.* Ed. Peter Cowie. London: Tantivy, 1969.

_____. "Austria." *International Film Guide 1971.* Ed. Peter Cowie. London: Tantivy, 1971.

_____. "Austria." *International Film Guide 1974.* Ed. Peter Cowie. London: Tantivy, 1974.

_____. "Austria." *International Film Guide 1977.* Ed. Peter Cowie. London: Tantivy, 1977.

_____. "Austria." *International Film Guide 1982.* Ed. Peter Cowie. London: Tantivy, 1982.

_____. "Austria." *International Film Guide 1989.* Ed. Peter Cowie. London: Tantivy, 1989.

Drewniak, Boguslaw. *Der deutsche Film 1938–1945.* Düsseldorf: Droste, 1987.

Eicher, Thomas. "*Das gestohlene Jahr* (1950) und *Rausch der Verwandlung* (1988). Transformationen eines Romanstoffes von Stefan Zweig." *Das Märchen vom Glück. Österreichischer Film in der Besatzungszeit.* Special issue of *Maske und Kothurn* 46.1 (2001).

Elsaesser, Thomas. *Early German Cinema: The First Two Decades.* Amsterdam: Amsterdam University Press, 1996.

_____. "Leni Riefenstahl: The Body Beautiful, Art Cinema and Fascist Aesthetics." *Women in Film: A Sight and Sound Reader.* Eds. P. Cook and P. Dodd. Philadelphia: Temple University Press, 1993.

_____. *New German Cinema: A History.* New Brunswick: Rutgers University Press, 1989.

Elsaesser, Thomas, with Michael Wedel. *The BFI Companion to German Cinema.* London: BFI, 1999.

Ernst, Gustav, and Gerhard Schedl, eds. *Nahaufnahmen. Zur Situation des österreichischen Kinofilms.* Vienna: Europa, 1992.

Esser, Michael, ed. *Gleissende Schatten: Kamerapioniere der zwanziger Jahre.* Berlin: Henschel, 1994.

Export, Valie. "Expanded Cinema as Expanded Reality." *Senses of Cinema* 28 September/October (2003). Online.

Femuth-Kronreif, Barbara. "Der 'Österreich-Film.' Die Realisierung einer Idee." *1. April 2000.* Eds. Ernst Kieninger et al. Vienna: Filmarchiv Austria, 2000.

Fibich, Bettina. *Das Projekt "Filmstadt Wien." Die historische Entwicklung der Wiener Rosenhügel-Ateliers (1919–1999).* Diss, U Wien, 2000.

Flippo, Hyde. *The German-Hollywood Connection.* Online.

Fox, Jo. *Filming Women in the Third Reich.* Oxford: Berg, 2000.

Fritz, Raimund, ed. *Oskar Werner: Das Filmbuch.* Vienna: Filmarchiv Austria, 2002.

Fritz, Walter, ed. *Geschichte des österreichischen Films. Aus Anlaß des Jubiläums 75 Jahre Film.* Vienna: Bergland, 1969.

_____. *Im Kino erlebe ich die Welt. 100 Jahre Kino und Film in Österreich.* Vienna: Brandstätter, 1997.

_____. *Kino in Österreich 1896–1930. Der Stummfilm.* Vienna: Österreichischer Bundesverlag, 1981.

_____. *Kino in Österreich 1929–1945. Der Tonfilm.* Vienna: Österreichischer Bundesverlag, 1991.

_____. *Kino in Österreich 1945–1983. Film zwischen Kommerz und Avantgarde.* Vienna: Österreichischer Bundesverlag, 1984.

_____. *Der Wiener Film im Dritten Reich.* Vienna: Österreichische Gesellschaft für Filmwissenschaft, Kommunikations- und Medienforschung, 1988.

Fritz, Walter, and Gerhard Tötschinger. *Maskerade: Kostüme des österreichischen Films. Ein Mythos.* Vienna: Kremayr & Scheriau, 1993.

Gersch, Wolfgang. *Film bei Brecht.* Munich: Hanser, 1975.

Gesek, Ludwig et al., eds. *Kleines Lexikon des österreichischen Films.* Vienna: Filmkunst, 1959.

Geser, Guntram, and Armin Loaker, eds. *Die Stadt ohne Juden.* Vienna: Filmarchiv Austria, 2000.

Glur, Beat. "Austria." *Variety International Film Guide 1999.* Ed. Peter Cowie. London: Faber and Faber, 1999.

Gottlein, Arthur. *Der österreichische Film. Ein Bilderbuch.* Vienna: Selbstverlag, 1977.

Gottschalk, H. J. *100 Years of Cinema in Austria—A Historical Profile*. Fachverband der Licht-spieltheater und Audiovisionsveranstalter Austria, 2000. Online.

Grafe, Frieda. "Wiener Beiträge zu einer wahren Geschichte des Kinos." *Aufbruch ins Ungewisse, Band 1. Österreichische Filmschaffende in der Emigration vor 1945*. Ed. Christian Cargnelli and Michael Omasta. Vienna: Wespennest, 1993.

Grafl, Franz. *Praterbude und Filmpalast. Wiener Kino-Lesebuch*. Vienna: Verlag für Gesellschaft-skritik, 1993.

Griesser-Pecar, Tamara. *Die Mission Sixtus. Österreichs Friedenversuch im Ersten Weltkrieg*. Vienna: Amalthea, 1988.

Grissemann, Stefan. "Die aquarellierten Andoiden: Bemerkungen zu *Rote Ohren fetzen durch Asche* von Angela Hans Scheirl, Dietmar Schipek und Ursula Pürrer." *Der neue Österre-ichische Film*. Ed. Gottfried Schlemmer. Vienna: Wespennest, 1996.

Grob, Norbert, Rolf Aurich, and Wolfgang Jacobsen, eds. *Otto Preminger*. Berlin: Jovis, 1999.

Gunning, Tom. *The Films of Fritz Lang: Modernity, Crime and Desire*. London: BFI, 2000.

Güttinger, Fritz. *Der Stummfilm im Zitat der Zeit*. Frankfurt: Deutsches Filmmuseum, 1984.

Hake, Sabine. *German National Cinema*. London and New York: Routledge, 2002.

_____. *Popular Cinema in the Third Reich*. Austin: University of Texas Press, 2002.

Hall, Murray, G. "Hugo Bettauer." *Elektrische Schatten: Beiträge zur österreichischen Stumm-filmgeschichte*. Eds. Francesco Bono et al. Vienna: Filmarchiv Austria, 1999.

Halter, Ed. "Das Experiment." *The Village Voice*. 12–18 November 2003. Online.

Haneke, Michael. "*71 Fragments of a Chronology of Chance*: Notes to the Film." *After Postmod-ernism: Austrian Literature and Film in Transition*. Ed. Willy Riemer. Riverside, CA: Ari-adne, 2000.

Hansen, Miriam. "Early Silent Cinema, Whose Public Sphere?" *New German Critique* 29 (1983).

Happel, H. G. *Der historische Spielfilm im Nationalsozialismus*. Frankfurt: R. G. Fischer, 1984.

Heer, Fiedrich. *Der Kampf um die österreichische Identität*. Vienna: Böhlaus Nachf., 1981.

Heinzlmeier, Adolf, and Berndt Schulz. *Lexikon der deutschen Film- und TV-Stars*, Berlin: Lexikon-Imprint, 2000.

Heltschel, M. "Am Rande der Arena." *Austrian Films 2001*. Vienna: Austrian Film Commission, 2001.

Hickethier, Kurt. "Bittere Heimkehr: *Welcome in Vienna* von Axel Corti und Georg Stefan Troller." *Der neue Österreichische Film*. Ed. Gottfried Schlemmer. Vienna: Wespennest, 1996.

Hilchenbach, Maria. *Kino im Exil: Die Emigration deutscher Filmkünstler 1933–1945*. Munich: Saur, 1982.

Hochholdinger-Reiterer, Beate. "Das Lied hat Wunder gewirkt..."—Gustav Ucicky's *Singende Engel* (1947) als Österreich-Apotheose." *Das Märchen vom Glück. Österreichischer Film in der Besatzungszeit*. Special issue of *Maske und Kothurn* 46.1 (2001).

_____. "Politik getarnt als Aprilscherz. Zur Rezeption des Österreich-Films *1. April 2000*." *1. April 2000*. Eds. Ernst Kieninger et al. Vienna: Filmarchiv Austria, 2000.

Hoffmann, Hilmar. *The Triumph of Propaganda: Film and National Socialism, 1933–1945*. Trans. John A. Broadwin and V. R. Berghahn. Providence: Berghahn, 1996.

Horak, Jan-Christopher. *Fluchtpunkt Hollywood: Eine Dokumentation zur Filmemigration nach 1933*. Münster: MakS, 1984.

_____. "German Exile Cinema, 1933–1950." *Film History* 8 (1996).

Hörbiger, Paul. *Ich hab für euch gespielt. Erinnerungen*. Munich: Herbig, 1979.

Horwath, Alexander, Lisl Ponger, and Gottfried Schlemmer, eds. *Avantgardefilm Österreich. 1950 bis heute*. Vienna: Wespennest, 1995.

Hübel, Ingrid Maria. *Sascha Kolowrat. Ein Beitrag zur Geschichte der Österreichischen Kinema-tographie*. Dissertation, University of Vienna, 1950.

Hull, David S. *Film in the Third Reich: A Study of the German Cinema 1933–1945*. New York: Simon and Schuster, 1973.

Illetschko, Peter, ed. *Gegenschuß. 16 Regisseure aus Österreich*. Vienna: Wespennest, 1995.

Jacobsen, Wolfgang Anton Kaes, and Hans Helmut Prinzler, eds. *Die Geschichte des deutschen Films*. Stuttgart: Metzler, 1993.

Jacobsen, Wolfgang, and Hans Helmut Prinzler, eds. *Käutner*. Berlin: Spiess, 1992.

Jaray, Hans. *Was ich kaum erträumen konnte. Ein Lebensbericht*. Ed. Michaela Jaray. Vienna: Amalthea, 1990.

Jung, Uli, and Walter Schatzberg. *Beyond Caligari: The Films of Robert Wiene*. New York: Berghan, 1999.

Kaes, Anton. *From Hitler to Heimat: The Return of History as Film*. Cambridge: Harvard University Press, 1989.

_____, ed. *Kino-Debatte: Texte zum Verhältnis von Literatur und Film 1909–1929*. Tübingen: Niemeyer, 1978.

Kanzog, Klaus. *"Staatspolitisch besonders wertvoll." Ein Handbuch zu 30 deutschen Spielfilmen der Jahre 1934 bis 1945*. Munich: Diskurs Film, 1994.

Kessler, Frank et al., eds. *Oskar Messter—Erfinder und Geschäftsmann*. Basel: Stroemfeld, 1994.

Kindred, Jack. *"Austria." Variety International Film Guide 1991*. Ed. Peter Cowie. London: Andre Deutsch, 1991.

Kleinhans, Bernd. *Ein Volk, ein Reich, ein Kino. Lichtspiel in der braunen Provinz*. Köln: Papyrossa, 2003.

Klocker, Hubert. "Gesture and the Object, Liberation as *Aktion*: A European Component of Performance Art." *Out of Actions: Between Performance and the Object, 1949–1979*. Ed. Paul Schimmel. Los Angeles: The Museum of Contemporary Art/Thames and Hudson, 1998.

Koppold, Rupert. "*Die Siebtelbauern*: Landleben mit Enrico Caruso." *Stuttgarter Zeitung*, Filmkritik 1999. Online.

Kracauer, Siegfried. *From Caligari to Hitler: A Psychological History of the German Film*. Princeton: Princeton University Press, 1974.

_____. *The Mass Ornament*. Ed. and Trans. T. Y. Levin. Cambridge: Harvard University Press, 1995.

Kramer, Thomas, ed. *Reclams Lexikon des deutschen Films (Deutschland, Österreich, Schweiz)*. Stuttgart: Reclam, 1995.

Kramer, Thomas, and Martin Prucha. *Film im Lauf der Zeit: 100 Jahre Kino in Deutschland, Österreich und der Schweiz*. Vienna: Ueberreuter, 1994.

Kreimeier, Klaus. *The UFA Story: A History of Germany's Greatest Film Company, 1918–1945*. Trans. Robert and Rita Kimber. New York: Hill and Wang, 1996.

Krenn, Günter. "Der bewegte Mensch—Sascha Kolowrat." *Elektrische Schatten: Beiträge zur österreichischen Stummfilmgeschischte*. Eds. Francesco Bono et al. Vienna: Filmarchiv Austria, 1999.

_____. *Helmut Qualtinger: Die Arbeiten für Film und Fernsehen*. Vienna: Filmarchiv Austria, 2003.

_____. *Die Kulturfilme der Wien-Film 1938–1945*. Vienna: Schriftenreihe des Österreichischen Filmarchivs, 1992.

Krenn, Günter, and Armin Loaker, eds. *Zauber der Boheme. Marta Eggerth, Jan Kiepura und der deutschsprachige Musikfilm*. Vienna: Filmarchiv Austria, 2002.

Kuchenbuch, Thomas. "Gesellschaftskritische Dimensionen in melodramatischer Form: *Donauwalzer* von Xaver Schwarzenberger." *Der neue Österreichische Film*. Ed. Gottfried Schlemmer. Vienna: Wespennest, 1996.

Lane, Anthony. "Film Notes." *The New Yorker*, 24/31 December 2001.

_____. "The Great Divide: Unsettling Pictures of Parisian Life." *The New Yorker*, 3 December 2001.

Leiser, Erwin. *Nazi Cinema*. Trans. G. Mander and D. Wilson. New York: Macmillan, 1974.

Lernet-Holenia, Alexander. "Aristocracy and Society in Austria." Trans. Thomas Ringmayr. *Southern Humanities Review*, Winter 2000.

Liebe, Ulrich. *Verehrt, vervolgt, vergessen. Schauspieler als Naziopfer*. Berlin: Beltz Quadriga, 1992.

Loaker, Armin. *Anschluss im 3/4-Takt: Filmproduktion und Filmpolitik in Österreich 1930–1938*. Trier: WVT Wissenschaftlicher Verlag, 1992.

_____. "Das offizielle Österreich dreht einen Film. Ein Resümee zum Staatsfilm." *1. April 2000*. Eds. Ernst Kieninger et al. Vienna: Filmarchiv Austria, 2000.

_____, ed. *Willi Forst: Ein Filmstil aus Wien*. Vienna: Filmarchiv Austria, 2002.

Loaker, Armin, and Martin Prucha. "Die Unabhängige deutschsprachige Filmproduktion in Österreich, Ungarn und der Tschechoslowakei." *Unerwünschtes Kino: Der deutschsprachige Emigrantenfilm 1934–1937*. Eds. Armin Loacker and Martin Prucha. Vienna: Filmarchiv Austria, 2000.

Loaker, Armin, and Ines Steiner, eds. *Imaginierte Antike: Österreichische Monumentalstummfilme. Historienbilder und Geschichtekonstruktion in* Sodom und Gomorrha, Samson und Delila, Die Sklavenkönigin und Salammbo. Vienna: Filmarchiv Austria, 2002.

Loiperdinger, Martin, ed. *Märtyrerlegenden im NS-Film*. Opladen: Leske + Budrich, 1991.

Lowry, Stephen. *Pathos und Politik: Ideologie in Spielfilmen des Nationalsozialismus*. Tübingen: Niemeyer, 1991.

Luza, Radomir. *Austro-German Relations in the Anschluss Era*. Princeton: Princeton University Press, 1975.

Magris, Claudio. *Der Habsburgische Mythos in der österreichischen Literatur*. Salzburg: Müller, 1966.

Maiwald, K.-J. *Filmzensur im NS-Staat*. Dortmund: Nowotny, 1983.

Marksteiner, Franz."Schubert heiß ich. Bin ich Schubert? Der Komponist ohne Heimat. Zu den Filmen *Leise flehen meine Lieder* (Ö 1933) und *Blossom Time* (GB 1934)." *Aufbruch ins Ungewisse, Band 1. Österreichische Filmschaffende in der Emigration vor 1945*. Eds. Christian Cargnelli and Michael Omasta. Vienna: Wespennest, 1993.

Matejka, Viktor. *Was ist österreichische Kultur*? Vienna: Stadt Wien, 1945.

Moeller, Felix. *Der Filmminister: Goebbels und der Film im Dritten Reich*. Berlin: Henschel, 1998.

Mühl-Benninghaus, Wolfgang. *Das Ringen um den Tonfilm: Strategien der Elektro- und der Filmindustire in den 20er und 30er Jahren*. Düsseldorf: Droste, 1999.

Muschamp, Herbert. "Architecture Review: A Gift of Vienna that Skips the Schlag." *The New York Times*, 19 April 2002.

Nepf, Markus. "Die ersten Filmpioniere in Österreich. Die Aufbauarbeit von Anton Kolm, Luise Veltée/Kolm/Fleck und Jakob Fleck bis zu Beginn des Ersten Weltkriegs." Eds. Francesco Bono et al. *Elektrische Schatten: Beiträge zur österreichischen Stummfilmgeschichte*. Vienna: Filmarchiv Austria, 1999.

Omasta, Michael. "Hinter verschlossenen Türen: Alexander Horwath Interview." *Falter* 1 (2002).

_____. "Stirb langsam. Eine Chronik der Wiener Kinolandschaft 1988 bis 1998." *Österreichisches Kinohandbuch 1998/99*. Ed. Andreas Ungerböck. Vienna: PVS, 1998.

Omasta, Michael, and Christian Cargnelli, eds. *Aufbruch ins Ungewisse. Österreichische Filmschaffende in der Emigration vor 1945*. Vienna: Wespennest, 1993.

Orth, Elisabeth. *Märchen ihres Lebens: Meine Eltern Paula Wessely und Attila Hörbiger*. Munich: Molden, 1982.

Osten, Ulrich von der. *NS-Filme im Kontext sehen! "Staatspolitisch besonders wertvoll." Filme der Jahre 1934–1938*. Munich: Diskurs Film, 1998.

Palm, Michael. "Die Geburt der Nation aus dem Geiste der Operette. Musikalische Rhetorik am 1. April 2000." *1. April 2000*. Eds. Ernst Kieninger et al. Vienna: Filmarchiv Austria, 2000.

Panofsky, Walter. *Die Geburt des Films. Ein Stück Kulturgeschichte. Versuch einer zeitgeschichtlichen Darstellung des Lichtspiels in seinen Anfangsjahren*. Würzburg: Konrad Triltsch, 1944.

Pasternak, Joe. *Easy the Hard Way: The Autobiography of Joe Pasternak as Told to David Chandler*. New York: Putnam's, 1956.

Pertl, Klaus. *Kleine Klagenfurter Kinogeschichte*. Online.

Peter, Birgit. "Der Revuefilm in Österreich 1945–1955. Ein Rückgriff auf die zwanziger und dreißiger Jahre oder eine andere historische Kontinuität?" *Das Märchen vom Glück. Österreichischer Film in der Besatzungszeit*. Special issue of *Maske und Kothurn* 46.1 (2001).

Philipp, Claus. "An Austrian Picture Show: *Exit ... nur keine Panik* von Franz Novotny — wie der österreichische Kinofilm wieder einmal keine Chance hatte, wie er sich trotzdem nützte, und wie er aus dem Erfolg einige falsche Schlüsse zog." *Der neue Österreichische Film*. Ed. Gottfried Schlemmer. Vienna: Wespennest, 1996.

Philipp, Michael. "Selbstbehauptung im Exil. Theater in Shanghai." *Zwischenwelt: Literatur. Wiederstand. Exil*. 18.1 February (2001).

Pinthus, Kurt, ed. *Das Kinobuch*. Frankfurt: Fischer, 1983.

Prinzler, Hans Helmut. *Chronik des deutschen Films 1895–1994*. Stuttgart: Metzler, 1995.

Prommer, Elizabeth. *Kinobesuch im Lebenslauf: Eine historische und medienbiographische Studie*. Konstanz: UKV Medien, 1999.

Pyrker, Susanna. "Austria." *Variety International Film Guide 1994*. Ed. Peter Cowie. London: Andre Deutsch, 1994.

Rathkolb, Oliver, Wolfgang Duchkowitsch, and Fritz Hausjell, eds. *Die veruntreute Wahrheit. Hitlers Propagandisten in Österreich 1938*. Salzburg: Müller, 1988.

Reeves, Nicholas. *The Power of Film Propaganda: Myth or Reality?* London: Cassell, 1999.

Reicher, Isabella. "Eine Referenz macht noch keine Empfehlung: *Müllers Büro* von Niki List." *Der neue Österreichische Film*. Ed. Gottfried Schlemmer. Vienna: Wespennest, 1996.

Reimer, Robert C., ed. *Cultural History Through a National Socialist Lens: Essays on the Cinema of the Third Reich*. Rochester, NY: Camden House, 2000.

Renner, Gerhard. "The Anschluss of the Film Industry after 1934." *Austria in the Thirties: Culture and Politics*. Eds. Kenneth Segar and John Warren. Riverside, CA: Ariadne, 1991.

Rentschler, Eric. *The Films of G. W. Pabst: An Extra Territorial Cinema*. New Brunswick, NJ: Rutgers University Press, 1990.

———. *The Ministry of Illusion: Nazi Cinema and Its Afterlife*. Cambridge: Harvard University Press, 1996.

Riefenstahl, Leni. *Memoiren*. Munich: Knaus, 1987.

Riemer, Willy. "Austrian Film Between Festival Success and Market Constraints: Interview with Martin Schweighofer." *After Postmodernism: Austrian Literature and Film in Transition*. Ed. Willy Riemer. Riverside, CA: Ariadne, 2000.

———. "Beyond Mainstream Film: An Interview with Michael Haneke." *After Postmodernism: Austrian Literature and Film in Transition*. Ed. Willy Riemer. Riverside, CA: Ariadne, 2000.

———. "*Nordrand* by Barbara Albert." *Modern Austrian Literature* (2000). Online.

Roessler, Peter. "Mystifikation und Realismus — Von Hochwälders *Flüchtling* zum österreichischen Nachkriegsfilm *Die Frau am Weg*." *Das Märchen vom Glück. Österreichischer Film in der Besatzungszeit*. Special issue of *Maske und Kothurn* 46.1 (2001).

Romani, Cinzia. *Tainted Goddesses: Female Film Stars of the Third Reich*. Trans. R. Connolly. New York: Sarpedon, 1992.

Rosdy, Paul. "Emigration und Film." *Zwischenwelt: Zeitschrift für Kultur des Exils und des Widerstands*. 18.2 August (2001).

Rosen, Philip. "History, Textuality, Nation: Kracauer, Burch, and Some Problems in the Study of National Cinemas." *Iris* 2.2 (1994).

Rundschrieben und Verordnung an den Filmschaffenden der Wien-Film 1941–1944.

Russeger, Arno. "Ein Österreicher im *Club der toten Dichter*: Wolfgang Glücks *Der Schüler Gerber*." *Der neue Österreichische Film*. Ed. Gottfried Schlemmer. Vienna: Wespennest, 1996.

———. "Kino — Schule der Frauen. Bemerkungen zu *Das Herz einer Frau* (1951) und *Dunja* (1955)." *Das Märchen vom Glück. Österreichischer Film in der Besatzungszeit*. Special issue of *Maske und Kothurn* 46.1 (2001).

Rutz, Gerd-Peter. *Darstellungen von Film in literarischen Fiktionen der zwanziger und dreissiger Jahre*. Münster: LIT, 2000.

Ruzowitzky, Stephan. "Interviewstatements." *Aus dem Presseheft*: Die Siebtelbauern. 1998. Online.

Sakall, S. Z. *The Story of Cuddles: My Life Under the Emperor Francis Joseph, Adolf Hitler and the Warner Brothers*. London: Cassell, 1954.

Sanders-Brahms, Helma. "Tyrannenmord: *Tiefland* von Leni Riefenstahl." *Das Dunkle zwischen den Bildern: Essays, Porträts, Kritiken*. Ed. Norbert Grob. Frankfurt: Verlag der Autoren, 1992.

Saunders, Thomas J. *From Berlin to Hollywood: American Cinema and Weimar Germany*. Berkeley: University of California Press, 1990.

Scheiber, Roman. "Austria." *Variety International Film Guide 2001*. Ed. Peter Cowie. London: Variety, 2001.

———. "Austria." *Variety International Film Guide 2002*. Ed. Peter Cowie. London: Variety, 2002.

_____. "Austria." *Variety International Film Guide 2003*. Ed. Peter Cowie. London: Button, 2003.

Schiefer, Karin. "A Stormy Winter: Barbara Albert." *Austria Kultur* 10.3 (2000).

Schill, Herbert. *Fred Adlmüller—Der Schönheit zu Diensten. Herbert Schill erzählt aus dem Leben des Modeschöpfers*. Vienna: Amalthea, 1990.

Schlemmer, Gottfried. "Das alte Vertreiben." *Der neue Österreichische Film*. Ed. Gottfried Schlemmer. Vienna: Wespennest, 1996.

Schmidt, Jochen. *Die Geschichte des Genie-Gedankens in der deutschen Literatur, Philosophie und Politik 1750–1945*. 2 vols. Darmstadt: Wissenschaftliche Buchgesellschaft, 1985.

Scholar, Nancy. "Leontine Sagan." *Sexual Stratagems*. Trans. P. Erens. New York: Horizon, 1979.

Schönbaum, David. *Hitler's Social Revolution: Class and Status in Nazi Germany 1933–1939*. New York: W. W. Norton, 1980.

Schönemann, Heide. *Fritz Lang. Filmbilder. Vorbilder*. Berlin: Hentrich, 1992.

Schrader, Paul. "Notes on Film Noir." *Film Noir Reader*. Eds. Alain Silver and James Ursini. New York: Limelight, 2003.

Schulte-Sasse, Linda. *Entertaining the Third Reich: Illusions of Wholeness in Nazi Cinema*. Durham, NC: Duke University Press, 1996.

_____. "Leni Riefenstahl's Feature films and the Question of a Fascist Aesthetic." *Framing the Past: The Historiography of German Cinema and Television*. Eds. Bruce A. Murray and Christopher J. Wickham. Carbondale: University of Southern Illinois Press, 1992.

Schwarz, Werner M. *Kino und Kinos in Wien*. Vienna: Turia & Kant, 1992.

Schweighofer, Martin. "Introduction." *Austrian Films 1988*. Vienna: Austrian Film Commission, 1988.

_____. "Vorwort." *Austrian Film Commission—Jahresbericht 2001*. Ed. Karin Schiefer. Online.

Schweinitz, Jörg, ed. *Prolog vor dem Film: Nachdenken über ein neues Medium 1909–1914*. Leipzig: Reclam, 1992.

"Sensationelle Filmaufführung mit Tyrone Power. *Zehn Jahre Später*—Ein großes Erlebnis." *Tiroler Nachrichten*, n.d., 1948.

Smith, David C. *The German Filmography 1895–1949*. Jefferson, NC: McFarland, 2000.

Spieker, Markus. *Hollywood unterm Hakenkreuz: Der amerikanische Spielfilm im Dritten Reich*. Trier: WVT Wissenschaftlicher Verlag, 1999.

Steiner, Gertraud. "'Besides, ich bin Österreicherin.' Elfi von Dassanowsky, eine Wienerin in Hollywood." *Wiener Zeitung*, Extra. 2 August 1996.

_____. "Drehort: Atelier Rosenhügel, Filmographie." *Austria's Hollywood/Hollywood's Austria*. Special issue of *Filmkunst: Zeitschrift für Filmkultur und Wissenschaft* 154 (1997).

_____. *Film Book Austria*. Vienna: Bundespressedienst, 1995.

_____. *Filmbuch Österreich*. Vienna: Bundespressedienst, 1995.

_____. *Die Heimat-Macher: Kino in Österreich 1946–1966*. Vienna: Verlag für Gesellschaftskritik, 1987.

_____. *Traumfabrik Rosenhügel*. Vienna: Compress, 1997.

Steiner, Maria. *Paula Wessely. Die verdrängten Jahre*. Vienna: Verlag für Gesellschaftskritik, 1996.

Steiner-Daviau, Gertraud. "Willi Forst nach 1945—ein Weltregisseur im Schatten. Die verlorenen Jahre: 1945 bis 1950." *Das Märchen vom Glück. Österreichischer Film in der Besatzungszeit*. Special issue of *Maske und Kothurn* 46.1 (2001).

Stourzh, Gerald. *Vom Reich zur Republik. Studien zum Österreichbewußtsein im 20. Jahrhundert*. Vienna: Edition Atelier, 1990.

Strascheck, Günter Peter, dir. *Filmemigration aus Nazideutschland*. WDR broadcast, 1975.

Strasser, Christian, Michael Martischnig, and Kurt Luger. *The Sound of Klein-Hollywood. Filmproduktion in Salzburg—Salzburg im Film*. Vienna: Österreichischer Kunst- und Kulturverlag, 1993.

Strickland, Carol. "Austria Makes Soaring Debut on the New York Arts Scene." *The Christian Science Monitor*, 19 April 2002.

Teng, Guoqiang. "Fluchtpunkt Shanghai. Luise und Jakob Fleck in China 1939–1946." *Filmexil* 4 (1994).

Thomas, Hans Alex. *Die deutsche Tonfilmmusik: Von den Anfängen bis 1956*. Gütersloh: Bertelsmann, 1962.

Thunecke, Jörg. "'Bucina Angelica' oder was für ein Schmarren? Ernst Lothars *Der Engel mit der Posaune* (1948): Roman und Film — ein Vergleich." *Das Märchen vom Glück. Österreichischer Film in der Besatzungszeit*. Special issue of *Maske und Kothurn* 46.1 (2001).

Traudisch, Dora. *Mutterschaft mit Zuckergruss? Frauenfeindliche Propaganda im NS-Spielfilm*. Pfaffenweiler: Centaurus, 1993.

Traumfabrik: Abschied von den Sieveringer Filmateliers. SWF broadcast, 1989.

Trimmel, Gerald. *Heimkehr. Strategien eines nationalsozialistischen Films*. Vienna: Eichbauer, 1998.

Ulrich, Rudolf. *Österreicher in Hollywood*. Vienna: Filmarchiv Austria, 2004.

"Unendliche Geschichte." *Der Spiegel*, 25 October 1993.

Ungerböck, Andreas, *Österreichisches Kinohandbuch 1998/99*. Vienna: PVS, 1998.

Ünlü, Selcuk. "*Das verschwundene Dorf*—die entschwundene Vergangenheit. Ein Film von Andreas Sulzer und Friedrich Ch. Zauner." *Das Märchen vom Glück. Österreichischer Film in der Besatzungszeit*. Special issue of *Maske und Kothurn* 46.1 (2001).

Veigl, Hans. "Hinter den Spiegeln: österreichische Identität. Zwischen Möglichkeits- und Wirklichkeitssinn. Bemerkung zur Konstituierung nationalen Selbstgefühls." *1. April 2000*. Eds. Ernst Kieninger et al. Vienna: Filmarchiv Austria, 2000.

Vogelsang, Konrad. *Filmmusik im Dritten Reich: Eine Dokumentation*. 2nd ed. Pfaffenweiler: Centaurus, 1993.

Walker, John. *Halliwell's Who's Who in the Movies*. 15th ed. New York: HarperCollins, 2003.

Walsh, Michael. "National Cinema, National Imaginary." *Film History* 8.1 (1996).

Welch, David. *Propaganda and The German Cinema 1933–1945*. Oxford: Oxford University Press, 1983.

Wetzel, Kraft, and Peter A. Hagemann. *Zensur — Verbotene deutsche Filme 1933–1945*. Berlin: Spiess, 1982.

"*Wien und 'Der dritte Mann.' Zur Österreich-Premiere von Carol Reeds Film im Wiener Apollo-Kino am 10. März 1950*." Vienna: Bundespressedienst, 2000.

Witte, Karsten. *Lachende Erben, toller Tag: Filmkomödie im Dritten Reich*. Munich: Vorwerk, 1995.

Wuss, Peter, ed. *Kunstwert des Films und Massencharakter des Mediums*. Berlin: Henschel, 1990.

Zuckmayer, Carl. *Geheimreport*. Eds. Gunther Nickel and Johanna Schrön. Göttingen: Wallstein, 2002.

Zglinicki, Friedrich von. *Die Wiege der Traumfabrik: Von Guckkästen, Zauberscheiben, bewegten Bildern bis zur UFA in Berlin*. Berlin: Transit, 1986.

Historical and Current Periodicals on Austrian Cinema

Action

Austrian Film News

Blimp

Celluloid

Film

Filmarchiv

Der Filmbote

Filmdienst

Film-Echo

Filmexil

Film-Kritik

Filmkunst

Filmschau

Film-Spiegel

Die Filmwelt

Die Filmwoche

Der gute Film

Illustrierter Film-Kurier

Kinematographische Rundschau

Kinojournal

Die Kinowoche

Komödie—Wochenrevue für Bühne und Film

Maske und Kothurn

Media Biz

Mein Film

Meteor

Mitteilungen der Österreichisch-Ungarischen Kinoindustrie

Neue Filmwoche   *Paimanns Filmlisten*
Neue Kino-Rundschau   *RAY Kinomagazin*
Neues Film-Programm   *Stadtkino-Programm*
Österreichische Film- und Kino Zeitung   *Wien-Film-Band*
Österreichischer Komet   *Der Wiener Film*

Selected websites

These provide information on various aspects of Austrian film history, the current industry, and the festival scene. Most have links and English-language pages.

Austrian Film Commission: www.afc.at
Austrian Film Institute: www.filminstitut.at
Austrian Film Museum: www.filmmuseum.at
Celluloid Film Magazine: www.celluloid.at
Cineplexx Arthaus: www.cineplexx.at
Cinetirol: www.cinetirol.com
Crossing Europe: www.crossingeurope.at
Diagonale: www.diagonale.at
Film Academy at the University of Music and Performing Arts: www.mdw.ac.at
Film Archive Austria: www.filmarchiv.at
Film Fund Vienna: www.filmfonds.wien.at
Film School Vienna: www.filmschulewien.at
International Film Festival at Innsbruck: www.iffi.at
Media Biz: www.mediabiz.at
Media Desk Austria: www.mediadesk.at
ORF (Austrian Broadcasting Corporation): www.orf.at
Ray Cinema Magazine: www.raykinomagazin.at
Sixpack Film: www.sixpackfilm.com
Skip: www.skip.at
Theater + Filmservice Vienna: www.theaterservice.at
Vienna Film Office: www.filmoffice.wien.at
Viennale: www.viennale.at

Index